# The 700 Most Frequently Used Hindi Verbs: Save Time by Learning the Most Frequently Used Words First

Rajesh Kumar

# Contents

# The 700 Most Frequently Used Hindi Verbs: Save Time by Learning the Most Frequently Used Words First

Rajesh Kumar

# About the Author

Rajesh Kumar is a renowned author who has dedicated his life to teaching Hindi language to people all over the world. Born in a small village in India, Rajesh developed a passion for language at a young age. He spent most of his childhood reading books and learning new words, and soon became fluent in Hindi, English, and several other languages.

After completing his education, Rajesh decided to pursue a career in writing. He started by writing short stories and articles for local newspapers, but soon realized that his true calling was in language education. He began writing language-learning books for Hindi language, and his books quickly became popular among students and teachers alike. Today, Rajesh is considered one of the most influential authors in the field of Hindi language education, and his books have helped countless people around the world learn this beautiful language.

# Other Works by This Author

## Series: Learn Hindi Grammar With Flashcards

Explore Hindi with a unique series focusing on learning through context-rich example sentences. Enhance your understanding with intuitive grammar insights, supplemented by practical flashcards. Ideal for all levels, this approach promises a natural and effective mastery of Hindi.

- Learn Hindi Grammar with Flashcards vol. 1: Understanding the Basic Structure
- Learn Hindi Grammar with Flashcards vol. 2: A Deep Dive into Naming Words - Nouns
- Learn Hindi Grammar with Flashcards vol. 3: Action, State, and Linking Words Unveiled - Verbs
- Learn Hindi Grammar with Flashcards vol. 4: The Art of Description - Adjectives
- Learn Hindi Grammar with Flashcards vol. 5: Amplifying Meaning - Adverbs
- Learn Hindi Grammar with Flashcards vol. 6: Mastering the Stand-ins - Pronouns
- Learn Hindi Grammar with Flashcards vol. 7: Navigating Space, Time, and More - Prepositions
- Learn Hindi Grammar with Flashcards vol. 8: Connecting Thoughts - Conjunctions
- Learn Hindi Grammar with Flashcards vol. 9: Expressing Emotion and Interruption - Interjections
- Learn Hindi Grammar with Flashcards vol. 10: Indicating Quantity and Possession - Determiners

## Series: Most Frequently Used Words

Introducing a unique Hindi language book series, prioritizing the most frequently used words. Covering nouns, verbs and adjectives, it's perfect for enhancing spoken and written skills. Words are sorted by frequency, each with English translations and example sentences for comprehensive learning. Ideal for all levels, it's a great tool to master Hindi vocabulary effectively.

1. The Most Frequently Used Hindi Nouns: Save Time by

Learning the Most Frequently Used Words First
2. The Most Frequently Used Hindi Adjectives: Save Time by Learning the Most Frequently Used Words First
3. The Most Frequently Used Hindi Verbs: Save Time by Learning the Most Frequently Used Words First

# Introduction

Welcome to a vibrant journey through the Hindi language, focusing on its most dynamic elements: verbs. Verbs are the action words that breathe life into sentences, depicting what's happening, whether it's doing, being, or occurring. This book is crafted to guide you through the most frequently used Hindi verbs, essential for anyone looking to communicate effectively and fluently in both spoken and written forms. Whether you are beginning your language learning journey or seeking to refine your mastery of Hindi verbs, our selection is designed to enrich your vocabulary and enhance your ability to express actions and states of being with clarity and confidence.

Verbs are the heart of a sentence, indicating the action that is being performed by the subject or the state of being. For instance, "run," "eat," "think," and "be" are all verbs that show what someone or something is doing or how they exist. "Run" suggests physical movement, "eat" relates to the action of consuming food, "think" denotes the process of considering something, and "be" is used to indicate existence or a state of being. Understanding how to use verbs correctly is crucial for constructing meaningful sentences that accurately convey your intended message. Verbs come in various forms to express time (tenses), including past, present, and future, adding depth and precision to our communication.

In this book, we will explore these essential verbs through practical examples and clear explanations to ensure you grasp their usage and nuances. From action-packed verbs that depict physical activities to stative verbs that describe conditions or perceptions, you'll learn to wield verbs with ease and adaptability. Each chapter is designed to progressively build your understanding and confidence, enabling you to craft sentences that are vibrant and expressive. Join us on this exciting linguistic journey, and let's unlock the power of verbs together, enhancing your Hindi communication skills one verb at a time.

— Rajesh Kumar

# Contents at a Glance

# 1. Full List

Initially, the words will be presented according to their *frequency of use*: starting with the most frequently used words, then slowly going to the least frequently used words. After this, the words will be organized alphabetically.

In the sections containing example sentences, English translations are provided separately, allowing you to concentrate on deciphering the meaning in English before consulting the provided translations for verification.

**1. लेना** — *have, take* — This verb is used to indicate the action of possessing or acquiring something. It can also be used to express the act of taking something from someone or somewhere.

• *1.* मेरा इसके साथ कोई लेना देना नहीं था। *2.* मुझे ये लेना है. *3.* मेरा उससे कोई लेनादेना नहीं था. *4.* उसका इससे कुछ लेना - देना नहीं है। *5.* मेरा इससे कोई लेना-देना नहीं था.' *6.* गहरी साँस लेना। *7.* जो आप लेना चाहते हैं, लें। *8.* मुझे ये लेना है. *9.* मुझे यह लेना होगा. *10.* मुझे पेशाब लेना है. • *1.* I had nothing to do with it. *2.* I have to take this. *3.* I had nothing to do with that. *4.* That has nothing to do with it. *5.* I had nothing to do with this. *6.* Take a deep breath. *7.* Take your pick. *8.* I have to take this. *9.* I gotta take this. *10.* I gotta take a piss.

**2. करना** — *do, make* — 'करना' is a versatile verb used to indicate the action of doing or making something. It is commonly used in various contexts to describe activities, tasks, or creations.

• *1.* क्या करना है? *2.* मुझे क्या करना? *3.* मुझे नहीं पता क्या करना है। *4.* आपको ऐसा क्यों करना होगा? *5.* मुझे क्या करना होगा? *6.* मुझे कबूल करना है। *7.* कॉल करना। *8.* इसे करना ही होगा। *9.* कोई गलती मत करना। *10.* कमरे को सुव्यवस्थित करना। • *1.* Do what? *2.* What do I do? *3.* I don't know what to do. *4.* Why would you do that? *5.* What am I supposed to do? *6.* I have a confession to make. *7.* Make the call. *8.* Make it happen. *9.* Make no mistake. *10.* Make room.

**3. होना** — *be, happen* — The verb 'होना' is used to indicate existence, occurrence, or happening of something. It is commonly used to express the state of being or to describe events or situations.

• *1.* तुम्हें यहां नहीं होना चाहिए. *2.* आपको होना चाहिए। *3.* यह तो होना ही था। *4.* ऐसा नहीं होना चाहिए था. *5.* ये तो होना ही था. *6.* ऐसा क्यों होना पड़ा? • *1.* You shouldn't be here. *2.* You should be. *3.* It was bound to happen. *4.* This wasn't supposed to happen. *5.* It had to happen. *6.* Why did this have to happen?

## 4. जानना — *know* — 'जानना' is used to express knowledge or awareness of something. It can refer to knowing facts, information, or details about a person, place, or thing. It is a versatile verb that is commonly used in everyday conversation.

• *1.* आप क्या जानना चाहते हैं? *2.* मैं जानना नहीं चाहता. *3.* कौन जानना चाहता है? *4.* आप जानना नहीं चाहते. *5.* आप क्यों जानना चाहते हैं? • *1.* What do you want to know? *2.* I don't want to know. *3.* Who wants to know? *4.* You don't want to know. *5.* Why do you want to know?

## 5. आना — *come* — The verb 'आना' is used to indicate the action of moving towards the speaker or a specific location. It is commonly used to express the act of coming or arriving at a particular place.

• *1.* मेरा वापस आना होगा। *2.* मेरा आना हो रहा है। *3.* क्या आप मेरे साथ आना चाहते है? *4.* आप आना चाहोगे? *5.* तुम्हे आना चाहिए। • *1.* I'll come back. *2.* I'm coming in. *3.* Will you come with me? *4.* You wanna come? *5.* You should come.

## 6. सोचना — *think, suppose* — This verb is used to express the act of contemplating or considering something in one's mind, whether it be a thought, idea, or opinion. It can also be used to indicate supposition or assumption.

• *1.* उस बारे में सोचना। *2.* मुझे सोचना होगा। *3.* आप क्या सोचना है कि हमें क्या करना चाहिए? *4.* मैं तुम्हारे बारे में सोचना बंद नहीं कर सकता. *5.* मैं ऐसा सोचना पसंद करता हूं। *6.* मुझे क्या सोचना चाहिए? *7.* खैर, मुझे क्या सोचना चाहिए-? *8.* आख़िर मुझे क्या सोचना चाहिए? • *1.* Think about that. *2.* I need to think. *3.* What do you think we should do? *4.* I can't stop thinking about you. *5.* I like to think so. *6.* What am I supposed to think? *7.* Well, what am I supposed to think? *8.*

What the hell am I supposed to think?

## 7. देखना — *see, look* — This verb is used to describe the action of using one's eyes to perceive something visually. It can refer to both intentional and unintentional acts of seeing or looking at something.

● 1. देखना है कि? 2. आप मुझे देखना चाहते थे? 3. तब आप देखना। 4. आपको देखना बहुत अच्छा लग रहा है। 5. मैं आपको देखना चाहता था। 6. बस देखना। 7. मुझे ऐसे देखना बंद करो। 8. मेरी तरफ देखना बंद करो। ● 1. See that? 2. You wanted to see me? 3. See you then. 4. It's so good to see you. 5. I wanted to see you. 6. Just looking. 7. Stop looking at me like that. 8. Stop looking at me.

## 8. चलो — *let* — 'चलो' is used to express permission or suggestion to do something. It is often used to invite someone to join in an activity or to suggest a course of action.

● 1. चलो मैं तुम्हें दिखाती हूँ। 2. चलो मुझे इसे इस तरह से रखने दें। 3. चलो मैं तुम्हें घर ले चलता हूँ। 4. चलो चलते हैं। ● 1. Let me show you. 2. Let me put it this way. 3. Let me take you home. 4. Come on, lets go.

## 9. चाहेंगे — *would* — 'चाहेंगे' is used to express a desire or wish for something to happen in the future. It is often used to indicate a conditional or hypothetical situation.

● 1. क्या आप नृत्य करना चाहेंगे? 2. क्या आप कुछ पीना चाहेंगे? 3. क्या आप आना चाहेंगे? 4. आप क्या पीना चाहेंगे? 5. आप क्या जानना चाहेंगे? ● 1. Would you like to dance? 2. Would you like something to drink? 3. Would you like to come in? 4. What would you like to drink? 5. What would you like to know?

## 10. कहना — *say, tell* — 'कहना' is used to express the action of speaking or conveying information to someone. It is commonly used to indicate the act of saying or telling something to another person in Hindi language.

● 1. यह कहना। 2. मुझे क्या कहना चाहिए? 3. क्या कहना? 4. फिर से कहना। 5. कहना मुश्किल है। 6. मुझे तुमसे कुछ कहना है। 7. मुझे आपसे कुछ कहना है। 8. मैं आपको कुछ कहना चाहता हूँ। 9. मुझे तुमसे कुछ कहना है. 10. आप मुझसे क्या कहना चाहते हैं?

• 1. Say it. 2. What can I say? 3. Say what? 4. Say it again. 5. It's hard to say. 6. I have to tell you something. 7. I need to tell you something. 8. I want to tell you something. 9. I've got something to tell you. 10. What do you want me to tell you?

## 11. बनाना — make — The verb 'बनाना' is used to indicate the action of creating or producing something. It is commonly used to describe the process of making various items or dishes, as well as constructing or forming objects.

• 1. रास्ता बनाना! 2. यादगार बनाना। 3. यह अच्छा बनाना। 4. मैं एक टोस्ट बनाना चाहूँगा। 5. समय बनाना। • 1. Make way! 2. Make it count. 3. Make it good. 4. I'd like to make a toast. 5. Make time.

## 12. संतुष्ट करना — please, satisfy — This verb is used to express the action of pleasing or satisfying someone. It is often used in requests or commands to indicate a desire for someone to be satisfied or pleased with something.

• 1. क्या आप संतुष्ट हो? 2. क्या आप संतुष्ट हैं? 3. मुझे आशा है कि आप संतुष्ट होंगे। 4. क्या तुम अब संतुष्ट हो? 5. क्या यह आपको संतुष्ट करता है? 6. क्या इससे आप संतुष्ट होंगे? • 1. Are you pleased? 2. Are you satisfied? 3. I hope you're satisfied. 4. Are you satisfied now? 5. Does that satisfy you? 6. Will that satisfy you?

## 13. देना — give — This verb is used to indicate the action of giving or imparting something to someone else. It is commonly used in various contexts to express the act of providing or transferring something to another person.

• 1. छोड़ देना? 2. अपना सर्वश्रेष्ठ देना। 3. मैं तुम्हें यह देना चाहता था। 4. मैं तुम्हें कुछ देना चाहता हूं. • 1. Give up? 2. Give it your best shot. 3. I wanted to give you this. 4. I want to give you something.

## 14. रुकें — stop — The verb 'रुकें' is used to indicate the action of stopping or halting something. It is commonly used to convey the idea of bringing something to a standstill or preventing it from continuing.

• 1. वहाँ रुकें। 2. क्या आप रुकेंगे? 3. चलो रुकें। 4. यहीं रुकें. 5. बस रुकें, ठीक है? • 1. Stop there. 2. Would you stop?

*3.* Let's stop. *4.* Stop right here. *5.* Just stop, okay?

## 15. रखना — *keep, put, maintain, lodge* — This verb is used to indicate the action of keeping or maintaining something in a particular place or condition. It can also be used to express the act of putting something in a specific location.

• *1.* मुझे सूचित रखना। *2.* अभी भी रखना। *3.* संजो कर रखना। *4.* मुझे अद्यतन रखना। *5.* अपनी उंगलियों को पार कर रखना। *6.* मुझे इसे कैसे रखना चाहिए? *7.* मुझे इसे कहां रखना चाहिए? *8.* मैं तुम्हें बाहर नहीं रखना चाहता. *9.* मुझे उन्हें कहाँ रखना चाहिए? *10.* अपनी पवित्रता बनाए रखना महत्वपूर्ण है। • *1.* Keep me informed. *2.* Keep still. *3.* Keep it safe. *4.* Keep me updated. *5.* Keep your fingers crossed. *6.* How shall I put it? *7.* Where should I put it? *8.* I don't wanna put you out. *9.* Where should I put them? *10.* It's important to maintain your sanity.

## 16. मानना — *feel, believe, reckon, presume* — 'Maanna' is used to express one's feelings, beliefs, or opinions about something. It is a versatile verb that can convey a range of emotions and thoughts, from simple acknowledgments to deep convictions.

• *1.* बुरा मत मानना. *2.* मेरा मानना है कि। *3.* हां, मेरा ऐसा मानना है। *4.* मेरा मानना है कि यह है. *5.* मेरा मानना है कि उसने ऐसा किया। *6.* मेरा तो यही मानना है. *7.* हाँ, मेरा मानना है. • *1.* Don't feel bad. *2.* I believe that. *3.* Yes, I believe so. *4.* I believe it is. *5.* I believe he did. *6.* That's what I believe. *7.* Yeah, I reckon.

## 17. समझना — *understand* — This verb is used to convey the act of comprehending or grasping a concept, idea, or situation. It signifies the ability to perceive or make sense of something through mental processing and analysis.

• *1.* आपको समझना होगा। *2.* तुम्हें समझना चाहिए। *3.* मैं समझन-ा चाहता हूँ। *4.* क्या इसे समझना इतना मुश्किल है? *5.* क्या समझना है? • *1.* You have to understand. *2.* You must understand. *3.* I want to understand. *4.* Is that so hard to understand? *5.* What's to understand?

## 18. पूछना — *ask* — 'पूछना' is used to inquire about something or seek information from someone. It is commonly used in conversations to ask questions or clarify doubts. It is a versatile

verb that can be used in various contexts.

• *1.* मैं आपसे एक सवाल पूछना चाहता हूं। *2.* तुमसे मेरा पूछना हो रहा है। *3.* मैं तुमसे कुछ पूछना चाहता हूं। *4.* क्या यह पूछना बहुत बड़ी बात है? *5.* उन्हें पूछना। • *1.* Let me ask you a question. *2.* I'm asking you. *3.* I want to ask you something. *4.* Is that too much to ask? *5.* Ask them.

## 19. दिखाना — *show, demonstrate* — This verb is used to indicate the action of presenting or displaying something to someone, either physically or visually. It is commonly used to convey the act of showing or demonstrating something to others.

• *1.* मैं आपको दिखाता हूँ। *2.* चलो मैं तुम्हें दिखाती हूँ। *3.* चलिए मैं आपको कुछ दिखाता हूँ। *4.* मैं तुम्हें कुछ दिखाना चाहता हूँ. *5.* चलो, मैं तुम्हें दिखाता हूँ. *6.* शेफ ने मैरीनेट करने का तरीका दिखाया। • *1.* I'll show you. *2.* Let me show you. *3.* Let me show you something. *4.* I wanna show you something. *5.* Come on, I'll show you. *6.* The chef demonstrated how to marinate.

## 20. जीना — *live* — 'जीना' is used to describe the act of being alive and experiencing life. It can also refer to surviving or making a living. It is a versatile verb that encompasses various aspects of existence.

• *1.* मैं जीना चाहता हूँ। *2.* क्या आप जीना चाहते हैं? *3.* सपने को जीना। *4.* तुम्हें जीना होगा. *5.* तुम जीना चाहते हो तो मेरे साथ आओ। • *1.* I want to live. *2.* Do you want to live? *3.* Living the dream. *4.* You have to live. *5.* Come with me if you want to live.

## 21. मिलना — *meet, unite* — 'Milna' is used to describe the act of coming together or meeting someone or something. It signifies a union or connection between two or more entities.

• *1.* आपसे मिलना सम्मान की बात है. *2.* मैं उनसे मिलना चाहूँगा. *3.* तुम उसे मिलना था जहां? *4.* वहाँ मुझसे मिलना। *5.* वह आपसे मिलना चाहता है. • *1.* It's an honor to meet you. *2.* I'd like to meet him. *3.* Where did you meet her? *4.* Meet me there. *5.* He wants to meet you.

## 22. चलाना — *run* — The verb 'चलाना' is used to indicate the action of running or operating something, such as a vehicle or a machine. It can also be used to describe the act of managing

or controlling a situation or event.

● *1.* मैं कुछ परीक्षण चलाना चाहूँगा. *2.* मुझे एक व्यवसाय चल-
○ना है. *3.* क्या आप उसे मेरे द्वारा फिर से चलाना चाहते हैं? ●
*1.* I'd like to run some tests. *2.* I have a business to run. *3.* You wanna run that by me again?

## 23. **खेलना** — *play* — The verb 'खेलना' is used to describe the action of engaging in recreational activities, sports, or games. It can also be used to refer to playing a musical instrument or performing in a theatrical production.

● *1.* मैं खेलना चाहता हूँ। *2.* आप खेलना चाहते हैं? *3.* तुम खे-
लना चाहते हो? *4.* इसे फिर से खेलना. *5.* माँ तुम्हारे साथ खेलना
चाहती है. ● *1.* I want to play. *2.* You want to play? *3.* You wanna play? *4.* Play it again. *5.* Mommy wants to play with you.

## 24. **खोलना** — *open, untie* — The verb 'खोलना' is used to de-scribe the action of opening something, such as a door, window, or book. It signifies the act of making something accessible or visible by removing any barriers or obstructions.

● *1.* क्या मुझे इसे खोलना चाहिए? *2.* क्या हमें इसे खोलना
चाहिए? *3.* इसे अभी मत खोलना. *4.* क्या आप इसे खोलना नहीं
चाहते? ● *1.* Should I open it? *2.* Should we open it? *3.* Don't open it now. *4.* Don't you want to open it?

## 25. **भोजन करना** — *eat* — The verb 'भोजन करना' is used to describe the action of consuming food. It is commonly used in conversations and written texts to indicate the act of eating.

● *1.* हमें भोजन करना चाहिए। ● *1.* Let us eat.

## 26. **बैठना** — *sit* — The verb 'बैठना' is used to indicate the action of sitting down or taking a seat. It is commonly used to describe the act of resting one's body on a chair, bench, or any other surface designed for sitting.

● *1.* क्या आप बैठना चाहेंगे? *2.* आप बैठना चाहते हैं? *3.* क्या आप
बैठना चाहते हैं? *4.* मुझे बैठना होगा. *5.* आपको बैठना चाहिए.
● *1.* Would you like to sit down? *2.* You wanna sit down? *3.* Do you want to sit down? *4.* I have to sit down. *5.* You should sit.

## 27. **भूलना** — *forget* — The verb 'भूलना' is used to describe

the action of not being able to remember something or failing to recall a specific piece of information. It signifies the act of forgetting or overlooking something.

● *1.* मत भूलना. *2.* कभी मत भूलना कि। *3.* इसे मत भूलना. *4.* मुझे मत भूलना. *5.* और आप इसे मत भूलना. ● *1.* Don't forget. *2.* Never forget that. *3.* Don't forget it. *4.* Don't forget me. *5.* And don't you forget it.

## 28. पीना — *drink* — The verb 'पीना' is used to describe the action of consuming a liquid by ingesting it through the mouth. It is commonly used to refer to drinking water, tea, coffee, or any other beverage.

● *1.* क्या आप कुछ पीना चाहेंगे? *2.* कुछ पीना के लिए है? *3.* क्या आप कुछ पीना चाहते हैं? *4.* आप क्या पीना चाहेंगे? *5.* आप क्या पीना चाहते हो? ● *1.* Would you like something to drink? *2.* Something to drink? *3.* You want something to drink? *4.* What would you like to drink? *5.* What do you want to drink?

## 29. मारना — *hit* — The verb 'मारना' is used to indicate the action of hitting or striking something or someone. It can be used in various contexts to describe physical force or impact.

● *1.* मुझे मारना बंद करो! *2.* तुम मुझे मारना चाहते हो? *3.* मेरा इरादा तुम्हें मारना नहीं था. *4.* क्या तुम मुझे मारना चाहते हो? *5.* तुम्हें उसे मारना नहीं था. ● *1.* Stop hitting me! *2.* You wanna hit me? *3.* I didn't mean to hit you. *4.* Do you want to hit me? *5.* You didn't have to hit him.

## 30. पढ़ना — *read* — The verb 'पढ़ना' is used to indicate the action of reading. It is used to describe the act of looking at and understanding written or printed material in order to gain knowledge or information.

● *1.* आपको इसे पढ़ना चाहिए. *2.* अख़बार पढ़ना। *3.* मुझे पढ़ना पसंद है। *4.* मैं इसे पढ़ना चाहता हूं. *5.* क्या आप इसे पढ़ना चाहते हैं? ● *1.* You should read it. *2.* Read the paper. *3.* I like to read. *4.* I want to read it. *5.* Do you want to read it?

## 31. तोड़ना — *break, disappoint* — 'तोड़ना' is used to describe the action of breaking or shattering something into pieces. It can be used in various contexts such as breaking objects, relationships, promises, or rules.

● *1.* इसे तोड़ो! *2.* हमने तोड़ दिया। *3.* तुमने मेरा दिल तोड़ दिया। *4.* क्या आप मेरे साथ तोड़ रहे हैं? *5.* तुम मेरा दिल तोड़ रहे हो। ● *1.* Break it up! *2.* We broke up. *3.* You broke my heart. *4.* Are you breaking up with me? *5.* You're breaking my heart.

## 32. चलना — *walk* — 'चलना' is used to describe the action of moving on foot from one place to another. It can also be used to indicate the act of functioning or operating, such as a machine or a system.
● *1.* चलना शुरू करो. *2.* मैं पैदल चलना पसंद करूंगा. *3.* आप चलना चाहते हैं? *4.* आगे चलना। *5.* मैं पैदल चलना पसंद करता हूं. ● *1.* Start walking. *2.* I'd rather walk. *3.* You want to walk? *4.* Walk forward. *5.* I prefer to walk.

## 33. बचाना — *save, defend* — The verb 'बचाना' is used to convey the action of protecting someone or something from harm or danger. It can also be used to describe the act of rescuing or preserving something from a negative situation.
● *1.* हमें उसे बचाना है. *2.* लोगों को बचाना, चीज़ों का शिकार करना। *3.* मुझे उसे बचाना है. *4.* मुझे उन्हें बचाना है! *5.* तुम्हें उसे बचना होगा. *6.* अपने आप को बचाना। ● *1.* We have to save him. *2.* Saving people, hunting things. *3.* I have to save him. *4.* I have to save them! *5.* You have to save him. *6.* Defend yourself.

## 34. बनना — *become* — The verb 'बनना' is used to indicate a transformation or change in state, where someone or something becomes a different form or takes on a new role or identity.
● *1.* ऐसा करने के लिए मुझे कोई और बनना होगा. *2.* मुझे कुछ और बनना होगा. *3.* मुझे कुछ और बनना था. *4.* मुझे कोई और बनना था. *5.* मुझे ग्रीन एरो बनना था। ● *1.* To do this, I must become someone else. *2.* I must become something else. *3.* I had to become something else. *4.* I had to become someone else. *5.* I had to become the Green Arrow.

## 35. चुनना — *pick, choose* — This verb is used to indicate the action of selecting one option from a group of options. It is commonly used when making decisions or choosing between different items or possibilities.
● *1.* उसे चुनना होगा. *2.* लेकिन तुम्हें चुनना होगा. *3.* आपको चुनना होगा। *4.* बुद्धिमानी से चुनना। *5.* तुम्हें चुनना होगा। *6.* मुझे चुनना था. *7.* आपको चुनना होगा. ● *1.* She needs to pick. *2.*

But you gotta pick. *3.* You have to choose. *4.* Choose wisely. *5.* You must choose. *6.* I had to choose. *7.* You'll have to choose.

## 36. खोना — *lose* — 'खोना' is used to describe the action of losing something or someone. It can be used to express the feeling of misplacing an object or the sadness of losing a loved one.

● *1.* मैं तुम्हें खोना नहीं चाहता। *2.* इसे मत खोना। *3.* कुछ खोना? *4.* उसे मत खोना। *5.* मैं उसे खोना नहीं चाहता। ● *1.* I don't want to lose you. *2.* Don't lose it. *3.* Lose something? *4.* Don't lose him. *5.* I don't want to lose her.

## 37. जीतना — *win, overcome, conquer* — 'जीतना' is used to describe the act of achieving victory or conquering something. It is commonly used in contexts related to sports, competitions, battles, and overcoming challenges.

● *1.* मैं जीतना चाहता हूँ। *2.* मुझे जीतना है. *3.* आप जीतना चाहते हैं? *4.* जीतना ही सब कुछ नहीं है। *5.* टीम ने गेम जीतना चाहा. *6.* मैं किसी पर शासन करना या जीतना नहीं चाहता। ● *1.* I want to win. *2.* I need to win. *3.* You want to win? *4.* Winning isn't everything. *5.* The team iked to win the game. *6.* I don't want to rule or conquer anyone.

## 38. अनुसरण करना — *follow* — This verb is used to indicate the action of following someone or something, either physically or in terms of adhering to instructions, rules, or guidelines. It implies a sense of obedience or compliance.

● *1.* मैं अनुसरण नहीं करता. *2.* मेरी बात का अनुसरण करो। *3.* मैं आपका अनुसरण नहीं करता. *4.* तुम अनुसरण करो? *5.* क्या तुमने मेरा अनुसरण किया? ● *1.* I don't follow. *2.* Follow my lead. *3.* I don't follow you. *4.* You follow? *5.* Did you follow me?

## 39. लगता है — *seem* — This verb is used to express an opinion or feeling about something that appears to be true or likely. It is often used to convey a sense of uncertainty or speculation in a statement.

● *1.* तो ऐसा लगता है कि। *2.* वह अच्छा लगता है. *3.* ऐसा लगता है। *4.* लगता है आप समझ नहीं पा रहे हैं. *5.* इसी की तरह लगता है। ● *1.* So it seems. *2.* He seems nice. *3.* Seems so. *4.* You don't seem to understand. *5.* Seems like it.

## 40. लिखना — *write* — The verb 'लिखना' is used to express the action of putting thoughts, ideas, or information onto a surface using a pen, pencil, or keyboard. It is commonly used to communicate through written language.

● *1.* लिखना न भूलें. *2.* कुछ लिखना। *3.* यह लिखना। *4.* मैं लिखना चाहता हूं। *5.* आप क्या लिखना चाहते हैं? ● *1.* Don't forget to write. *2.* Write something. *3.* Write it. *4.* I want to write. *5.* What do you want to write?

## 41. खींचना — *pull, draw* — The verb 'खींचना' is used to describe the action of pulling or drawing something towards oneself. It is commonly used to indicate physically pulling an object or drawing a picture.

● *1.* स्वंय को साथ में खींचना। *2.* ट्रिगर खींचें। *3.* एक कुर्सी खींचो. *4.* बाहर खींचें! *5.* यहाँ खींचो. *6.* अपनी तलवार खींचो. *7.* यहीं पर मैं रेखा खींचता हूं। *8.* मैं उनकी आग खींच लूँगा। *9.* वह किसने खींचा? *10.* क्या आप खींचते हो? ● *1.* Pull yourself together. *2.* Pull the trigger. *3.* Pull up a chair. *4.* Pull out! *5.* Pull over here. *6.* Draw your sword. *7.* That's where I draw the line. *8.* I'll draw their fire. *9.* Who drew that? *10.* Do you draw?

## 42. सीखना — *learn* — The verb 'सीखना' is used to express the action of acquiring knowledge or skills through study, experience, or teaching. It is commonly used to describe the process of gaining new information or abilities.

● *1.* क्या सीखना है? *2.* आपको बहुत कुछ सीखना है. *3.* मैं सीखना चाहता हूँ। *4.* आपको सीखना है। *5.* मैंने सीखना शुरू किया है।
● *1.* Learn what? *2.* You have a lot to learn. *3.* I want to learn. *4.* You have to learn. *5.* I'm just learning.

## 43. समझाना — *explain* — This verb is used to convey information or clarify a concept to someone in a way that they can understand. It is often used to make something clear or comprehensible to another person.

● *1.* मैं बाद में समझाऊंगा. *2.* में समझा सकता हूँ। *3.* मुझे समझाने दो। *4.* मैं इसे समझा नहीं सकता. *5.* मैं समझाता हूँ। ● *1.* I'll explain later. *2.* I can explain. *3.* Let me explain. *4.* I can't explain it. *5.* I'll explain.

## 44. शादी करना — *marry, wed* — This verb is used to describe the act of entering into a legal and social union with another person. It signifies the commitment to a lifelong partnership and the formalization of a romantic relationship.

• *1.* मैं तुमसे शादी करना चाहता हूँ। *2.* शादी करना। *3.* मैं शादी करना चाहता हूँ। *4.* मैं उससे शादी करना चाहता हूं। *5.* मैं शादी नहीं करना चाहता. • *1.* I want to marry you. *2.* Get married. *3.* I want to get married. *4.* I want to marry her. *5.* I don't want to get married.

## 45. जगाना — *wake* — 'जगाना' is used to describe the action of waking someone up from sleep. It is a verb that signifies the act of rousing someone from their slumber.

• *1.* मैं तुम्हें जगाना नहीं चाहता था. *2.* तुम्हें मुझे जगाना चाहिए था. *3.* मैं उसे जगाना नहीं चाहता था. *4.* आप उसे जगाना नहीं चाहते. • *1.* I didn't want to wake you. *2.* You should have woken me. *3.* I didn't want to wake her. *4.* You don't want to wake him.

## 46. बेचना — *sell* — The verb 'बेचना' is used to describe the action of transferring ownership of an item or service in exchange for money or other forms of payment. It is commonly used in transactions involving goods or services.

• *1.* तुम्हें मुझे बेचना नहीं पड़ेगा. *2.* क्या आप इसे बेचना चाहते हैं? *3.* मैं इसे बेचना चाहता हूं. *4.* मुझे यकीन नहीं है कि मैं बेचना चाहता हूं। • *1.* You don't have to sell me. *2.* Do you want to sell it? *3.* I want to sell it. *4.* I'm not sure I want to sell.

## 47. पहनना — *wear* — The verb 'पहनना' is used to describe the action of putting on clothing or accessories. It is used to indicate the act of wearing something on the body, such as clothes, jewelry, or shoes.

• *1.* मुझे क्या पहनना चाहिए? *2.* मुझे यह क्यों पहनना है? *3.* आपको इसे पहनना चाहिए. *4.* उसे आकर्षक पोशाकें पहनना पसंद था। *5.* सुरक्षा गियर पहनना अनिवार्य है. • *1.* What should I wear? *2.* Why do I have to wear this? *3.* You should wear it. *4.* She liked to wear cutesy outfits. *5.* It's mandatory to wear safety gear.

## 48. कल्पना करना — *imagine* — This verb is used to describe the act of creating mental images or scenarios that are

not based on reality. It is often used to express creativity, visualization, or speculation in various contexts.

● *1.* आप कल्पना कर सकते हैं? *2.* मैं कल्पना कर सकता हूँ। *3.* कल्पना करो कि। *4.* मैं कल्पना नहीं कर सकता. *5.* केवल मैं कल्पना कर सकता हूं। ● *1.* Can you imagine? *2.* I can imagine. *3.* Imagine that. *4.* I can't imagine. *5.* I can only imagine.

## 49. अपेक्षा करना — *expect* — This verb is used to convey the act of anticipating or looking forward to something happening in the future. It is often used to express hopes or desires for a specific outcome or result.

● *1.* आपने मुझसे क्या करने की अपेक्षा की थी? *2.* खैर, आपको क्या अपेक्षा है? *3.* आपसे अपेक्षा है. *4.* तुम वह नहीं हो जिसकी मैंने अपेक्षा की थी। *5.* मुझसे यह विश्वास करने की अपेक्षा करें? ● *1.* What did you expect me to do? *2.* Well, what do you expect? *3.* You're expected. *4.* You're not what I expected. *5.* Expect me to believe that?

## 50. संभालना — *handle* — This verb is used to convey the action of managing or taking care of something or someone. It implies the act of being responsible for a situation or individual and ensuring that things are under control.

● *1.* मैं इसे संभाल सकता हूं। *2.* मैं इसे संभाल लूंगा। *3.* मैं इसे संभाल लूंगा. *4.* मुझे इसे संभालने दें। *5.* मैं इसे संभाल सकता हूँ। ● *1.* I can handle it. *2.* I'll handle it. *3.* I'll handle this. *4.* Let me handle this. *5.* I can handle this.

## 51. बिताना — *spend* — The verb 'बिताना' is used to indicate the act of spending time or money. It is commonly used to describe how time or money is used or passed.

● *1.* हमने काफी समय साथ बिताया. *2.* हमने कुछ समय साथ बिताया. *3.* चलो यहीं रात बिताते हैं. *4.* मैंने रात बिताई. *5.* हम यहीं रात बिताएंगे. ● *1.* We spent a lot of time together. *2.* We spent some time together. *3.* Let's spend the night here. *4.* I spent the night. *5.* We'll spend the night here.

## 52. रक्षा करना — *protect, preserve* — This verb is used to describe the action of safeguarding or defending someone or something from harm or danger. It implies taking measures to ensure the safety and well-being of the person or object being

protected.

• *1.* मैं तुम्हारी रक्षा करना चाहता था. *2.* आपकी रक्षा करना मेरा काम है. *3.* सेवा और सुरक्षा करना. *4.* मेरा काम आपकी रक्षा करना है. *5.* मेरा मिशन आपकी रक्षा करना है. • *1.* I wanted to protect you. *2.* It's my job to protect you. *3.* To serve and protect. *4.* My job is to protect you. *5.* My mission is to protect you.

## 53. जुड़ना — *join* — 'जुड़ना' is used to describe the action of connecting or linking two or more things together. It signifies the act of coming together or uniting in a physical, emotional, or abstract sense.

• *1.* हमसे जुड़ें। *2.* क्या मैं आपसे जुड़ सकता हूं? *3.* मुझे जुड़ें। *4.* क्या आपकी हमसे जुड़ने की इच्छा है? *5.* आप हमारे साथ क्यों नहीं जुड़ते? • *1.* Join us. *2.* May I join you? *3.* Join me. *4.* Would you like to join us? *5.* Why don't you join us?

## 54. का आनंद लें — *enjoy* — This verb is used to express the enjoyment or pleasure derived from a particular activity, experience, or situation. It signifies taking delight or finding satisfaction in something.

• *1.* इसका आनंद लें। *2.* अपनी शाम का आनंद लें। *3.* अपनी उड़ान का आनंद लें। *4.* दृश्य का आनंद लें। *5.* अपनी शेष शाम का आनंद लें। • *1.* Enjoy it. *2.* Enjoy your evening. *3.* Enjoy your flight. *4.* Enjoy the view. *5.* Enjoy the rest of your evening.

## 55. छिपाना — *hide* — The verb 'छिपाना' is used to describe the action of concealing or keeping something out of sight. It is commonly used when referring to hiding objects, emotions, or information.

• *1.* आप क्या छिपा रहे हैं? *2.* मेरे पास छिपाने के लिए कुछ भी नहीं है। *3.* मैं कुछ भी नहीं छिपा रहा हूं. *4.* मेरे पास छिपाने के लिए कुछ भी नहीं है. *5.* हमारे पास छिपाने के लिए कुछ भी नहीं है. • *1.* What are you hiding? *2.* I have nothing to hide. *3.* I'm not hiding anything. *4.* I've got nothing to hide. *5.* We have nothing to hide.

## 56. उड़ना — *fly, flit* — The verb 'उड़ना' is used to describe the action of moving through the air with wings or in an aircraft. It can also be used metaphorically to describe a feeling of freedom

or excitement.

● *1.* उड़ना होगा. *2.* मुझे उड़ना होगा. *3.* क्या आप उड़ना चाहते हैं? *4.* मैं उड़ना चाहता था. *5.* मुझे नहीं पता कि कैसे उड़ना है! ● *1.* Gotta fly. *2.* I must fly. *3.* You want to fly? *4.* I wanted to fly. *5.* I don't know how to fly!

## 57. हंसना — *laugh* — The verb 'हंसना' is used to describe the action of laughing. It is used to express joy, amusement, or happiness in response to something funny or enjoyable.

● *1.* हंसना बंद करो! *2.* मुझ पर हंसना बंद करो! ● *1.* Stop laughing! *2.* Stop laughing at me!

## 58. रोना — *cry* — The verb 'रोना' is used to describe the action of shedding tears or expressing sadness or pain through crying. It is commonly used to convey emotions of sorrow, grief, or distress.

● *1.* रोना बंद करो। *2.* मुझे बहुत रोना आ रहा है। *3.* कृपया रोना बंद करें. *4.* मुझे रोना आ रहा था। *5.* कोई रोना नहीं। ● *1.* Stop crying. *2.* I feel like crying. *3.* Please stop crying. *4.* I was crying. *5.* No crying.

## 59. साबित करना — *prove* — The verb 'साबित करना' is used to demonstrate or establish the truth or validity of something. It is used to provide evidence or arguments to support a claim or statement.

● *1.* मुझे कुछ भी साबित नहीं करना है. *2.* जांच का उद्देश्य दोष साबित करना था। ● *1.* I don't have to prove anything. *2.* The investigation aimed to prove culpability.

## 60. ले जाना — *carry* — The verb 'ले जाना' is used to indicate the action of carrying something from one place to another. It implies physically moving an object or person to a different location.

● *1.* क्या ले जाना? ● *1.* Carrying what?

## 61. छोड़ना — *quit, cease* — This verb is used to indicate stopping or giving up an action or habit. It signifies the act of quitting or ceasing something, whether it be a job, a relationship,

a bad habit, or any other activity.

● *1.* मैं छोड़ता हूं। *2.* इसे छोड़ दें! *3.* मैं छोड़ रहा हूं। *4.* आप छोड़-
नहीं सकते. *5.* उसने छोड़ दिया। *6.* आप मुझे आश्चर्यचकित
करना कभी नहीं छोड़ते। ● *1.* I quit. *2.* Quit it! *3.* I'm quitting. *4.*
You can't quit. *5.* She quit. *6.* You never cease to surprise me.

## 62. जारी रखें — *continue* — 'जारी रखें' is used to indicate the
action of continuing or maintaining something without interruption. It is often used to express the idea of persisting or carrying
on with a particular activity or process.

● *1.* हम कल भी जारी रखेंगे. ● *1.* We'll continue tomorrow.

## 63. सराहना — *appreciate* — This verb is used to express
admiration or approval for someone or something. It is used to
show gratitude or acknowledge the value or worth of a person,
action, or object.

● *1.* मैं सराहना करता हूँ। *2.* मैं इसकी सराहना करता हूं। *3.* की
सराहना करे। *4.* यह सराहनीय है। *5.* मैं सचमुच इसकी सराहना
करता हूं। ● *1.* I appreciate that. *2.* I appreciate it. *3.* Appreciate
that. *4.* I'd appreciate it. *5.* I really appreciate this.

## 64. चुनें — *choose* — 'चुनें' is used to indicate the action of
selecting one option from multiple choices. It is commonly used
when making decisions or picking from a variety of options.

● *1.* अपना हथियार चुनें। *2.* तो चुनें. *3.* उनका रास्ता चुनें. *4.*
आप किसे चुनेंगे? *5.* किसी और को चुनें. ● *1.* Choose your
weapon. *2.* So choose. *3.* Choose their path. *4.* Who would
you choose? *5.* Choose someone else.

## 65. निर्णय करना — *decide* — This verb is used to ex-
press the action of making a decision or coming to a conclusion
after considering various options or factors. It signifies the act
of choosing one option among several possibilities.

● *1.* मैंने अभी तक निर्णय नहीं लिया है. *2.* क्या आपने निर्-
णय लिया है? *3.* मैंने निर्णय कर लिया है। *4.* यह निर्णय लेना
आपका काम नहीं है। *5.* मैंने पहले ही निर्णय ले लिया है. ● *1.* I
haven't decided yet. *2.* Have you decided? *3.* I've decided. *4.*
That's not for you to decide. *5.* I've already decided.

## 66. प्रारंभ करना — *begin* — 'प्रारंभ करना' is used to indicate the start or initiation of an action, process, or event. It signifies the beginning of something and is commonly used in various contexts to denote the commencement of an activity.

• *1.* आपने अपना परिवर्तन प्रारंभ कर दिया है. *2.* चरण दो प्रारंभ करें. *3.* प्लेबैक प्रारंभ करें. *4.* डिबग स्कैन प्रारंभ हो रहा है. • *1.* Thou has begun thy transition. *2.* Begin phase two. *3.* Begin playback. *4.* Beginning debug scan.

## 67. अनुमति देना — *allow* — This verb is used to give permission or consent for someone to do something. It indicates that the person has been granted the authority or freedom to proceed with a particular action or activity.

• *1.* मुझे अनुमति दें। *2.* मुझे अपना परिचय देने की अनुमति दें। *3.* क्या इसकी अनुमति है? *4.* मुझे समझाने की अनुमति दें. *5.* कृपया मुझे अनुमति दें. • *1.* Allow me. *2.* Allow me to introduce myself. *3.* Is that allowed? *4.* Allow me to explain. *5.* Please, allow me.

## 68. चुराना — *steal* — The verb 'चुराना' is used to describe the act of taking something without permission or unlawfully. It is used to convey the action of stealing or theft.

• *1.* मैंने इसे चुरा लिया। *2.* मैंने इसे चुराया नहीं. *3.* तुमने इसे चुरा लिया. *4.* क्या तुमने इसे चुराया? *5.* मैंने कुछ भी नहीं चुराया. • *1.* I stole it. *2.* I didn't steal it. *3.* You stole it. *4.* Did you steal it? *5.* I didn't steal anything.

## 69. स्वीकार करना — *admit, accept* — This verb is used to acknowledge or agree to something, whether it be a fact, statement, or responsibility. It signifies accepting or admitting to a situation, idea, or action.

• *1.* यह स्वीकार करते हैं। *2.* इसे स्वीकार करे। *3.* ठीक है, मैं इसे स्वीकार करता हूं। *4.* क्या स्वीकार करें? *5.* आपने जो किया उसे स्वीकार करें. *6.* माफी स्वीकार की जाती है। *7.* मुझे स्वीकार है। *8.* आप स्वीकार करते हैं? *9.* इसे स्वीकार करें। *10.* मैं इसे स्वीकार नहीं करता. • *1.* Admit it. *2.* Just admit it. *3.* Okay, I admit it. *4.* Admit what? *5.* Admit what you did. *6.* Apology accepted. *7.* I accept. *8.* Do you accept? *9.* Accept it. *10.* I don't accept that.

**70. जलना** — *burn* — The verb 'जलना' is used to describe the action of burning or being on fire. It can refer to physical objects or emotions. It is commonly used in contexts related to fire, heat, jealousy, or anger.

● *1.* सूरज की गर्मी, आग की तरह जलना.  *2.* अधिकतम जलना.  *3.* मैं जलना चाहता हूँ.  ● *1.* Heat of the sun, burn like fire. *2.* Maximum burn. *3.* I want to burn.

**71. भीख में मांगना** — *beg* — To ask for something, typically money or food, in a desperate or needy manner.

● *1.* भीख मांगना बंद करें। ● *1.* Stop begging.

**72. अधिकार रखना** — *deserve* — This verb is used to indicate that someone has earned or is entitled to something based on their actions, qualities, or circumstances. It conveys a sense of deserving or being worthy of a particular outcome or treatment.

● *1.* आप इसके अधिकारी हैं। ● *1.* You deserve that.

**73. पकाना** — *cook* — The verb 'पकाना' is used to describe the action of preparing food by heating it. It is commonly used in recipes and cooking instructions to indicate the process of cooking ingredients until they are ready to eat.

● *1.* क्या आपको खाना पकाना अच्छा लगता है?  *2.* उसे घर पर समुद्री भोजन पकाना बहुत पसंद था। ● *1.* Do you like to cook?  *2.* She loved to cook seafood at home.

**74. क्षमा मांगना** — *apologize* — To express regret or remorse for a mistake or wrongdoing, one can use the verb 'क्षमा मांगना'. It is a way to acknowledge fault and seek forgiveness from the person who has been wronged.

● *1.* माफ़ी मांगना बंद करो.  *2.* मैं बस माफ़ी मांगना चाहता था.  *3.* मैं माफ़ी मांगना चाहूँगा.  *4.* मैं फिर से माफ़ी मांगना चाहता था.  *5.* देखिये, मैं माफ़ी मांगना चाहता हूँ। ● *1.* Stop apologizing. *2.* I just wanted to apologize. *3.* I'd like to apologize. *4.* I wanted to apologize again. *5.* Look, I want to apologize.

**75. साँस लेना** — *breathe* — This verb is used to describe the action of inhaling and exhaling air through the nose or mouth. It is a fundamental bodily function necessary for sustaining life.

• *1.* साँस लेना मत भूलना. *2.* साँस लेना कठिन है. *3.* साँस भी मत लेना. • *1.* Don't forget to breathe. *2.* It's hard to breathe. *3.* Don't even breathe.

## 76. संपत्ति होना — *belong* — This verb is used to indicate ownership or possession of something. It is used to express that something is owned by someone or something belongs to a particular person or entity.

• *1.* यह संपत्ति एक धनी परिवार की थी। • *1.* The estate belonged to a wealthy family.

## 77. पहचानना — *recognize* — The verb 'पहचानना' is used to describe the action of identifying or acknowledging someone or something based on previous knowledge or familiarity. It is commonly used in situations where one recognizes a person, object, or situation.

• *1.* क्या तुम मुझे नहीं पहचानते? *2.* क्या आप उसे पहचानते हैं? *3.* क्या तुम मुझे पहचानते हो? *4.* क्या आप इसे पहचानते हैं? *5.* क्या आप इस आदमी को पहचानते हैं? • *1.* Don't you recognize me? *2.* Do you recognize him? *3.* Do you recognize me? *4.* Do you recognize this? *5.* Do you recognize this man?

## 78. प्रार्थना करना — *pray* — The verb 'प्रार्थना करना' is used to express the act of praying or making a request to a higher power. It is commonly used in religious contexts or when asking for help, guidance, or blessings.

• *1.* हमें प्रार्थना करनी चाहिए। *2.* हमारे लिए प्रार्थना करें। *3.* मेरे लिए प्रार्थना करें। *4.* मैं तुम्हारे लिए प्रार्थना करूंगा। *5.* मेरे साथ प्रार्थना करो. • *1.* Let us pray. *2.* Pray for us. *3.* Pray for me. *4.* I'll pray for you. *5.* Pray with me.

## 79. भरना — *fill* — The verb 'भरना' is used to indicate the action of filling something with a substance or material. It can also be used metaphorically to describe filling a space or fulfilling a requirement.

• *1.* क्या तुम मुझे भरना चाहते हो? *2.* क्या आप मुझे भरना चाहते हैं? *3.* मुझे बाद में भरना. *4.* कोई मुझे भरना चाहता है? • *1.* You wanna fill me in? *2.* You want to fill me in? *3.* Fill me in later. *4.* Somebody wanna fill me in?

## 80. धोना — *wash* — The verb 'धोना' is used to describe the action of cleaning or washing something by using water and soap. It is commonly used when referring to washing clothes, dishes, or oneself.

● *1.* बदबूदार मोज़ों को धोना ज़रूरी था। ● *1.* The smelly socks needed to be washed.

## 81. निकालना — *draw, withdraw* — This verb is used to indicate the action of drawing or withdrawing something from a particular place or situation. It can refer to physically removing an object or abstractly taking something out or away.

● *1.* अपने निष्कर्ष स्वयं निकालें. *2.* आप स्वयं निष्कर्ष नि-काल सकते हैं. *3.* हम बहुत कुछ निकालते हैं. *4.* मैनें निकाला। *5.* मैं कुछ नकदी निकालूंगा. ● *1.* Draw your own conclusions. *2.* You can draw your own conclusions. *3.* We draw lots. *4.* I draw. *5.* I will withdraw some cash.

## 82. काटना — *bite, chop* — The verb 'काटना' is used to describe the action of biting or cutting with teeth or a sharp object. It can be used to indicate physical biting as well as metaphorical cutting or hurting someone emotionally.

● *1.* मुझे काटना। *2.* मच्छर का काटना। *3.* मुझे काटना बंद करो! *4.* तुम मुझे काटना चाहते हो? ● *1.* Bite me. *2.* Mosquito bites. *3.* Stop biting me! *4.* You wanna bite me?

## 83. बनाएं — *create* — The verb 'बनाएं' is used to express the action of creating something new or bringing something into existence. It is commonly used to describe the act of making or producing something.

● *1.* अपना भाग्य स्वयं बनाएं. *2.* कुछ सुंदर बनाएं. *3.* कृपया एक उपयोगकर्ता नाम और पासवर्ड बनाएं. *4.* एक डायवर्सन बनाएं. *5.* हम एक नया मनोरंजन बनाएंगे। ● *1.* Create your own destiny. *2.* Create something beautiful. *3.* Please create a username and password. *4.* Create a diversion. *5.* We shall create a new entertainment.

## 84. सुझाना — *suggest* — This verb is used to offer ideas or recommendations to someone in order to help them make a

decision or solve a problem. It implies giving advice or guidance on a particular course of action.

• *1.* आपका क्या सुझाव है? *2.* आप क्या सुझाव दे रहे हैं? *3.* आप क्-
◌्या सुझाव देंगे? *4.* आप क्या सुझाव देते हो कि मैं क्या करूं?
*5.* आपका सुझाव है कि हम क्या करें? • *1.* What do you suggest?
*2.* What are you suggesting? *3.* What would you suggest? *4.*
What do you suggest I do? *5.* What do you suggest we do?

## 85. **बसना** — *settle* — The verb 'बसना' is used to indicate the act of settling down or making a home in a particular place. It can also refer to finding a permanent residence or establishing oneself in a new environment.

• *1.* बसना। • *1.* Settle in.

## 86. **प्रवेश करना** — *enter* — The verb 'प्रवेश करना' is used to describe the action of entering a place or space. It signifies the act of moving from outside to inside, typically through a doorway, gate, or other entrance point.

• *1.* क्या मैं प्रवेश कर सकता हूं? *2.* उसे प्रवेश करने दो. *3.*
प्रवेश करना छोड़ें! *4.* बाड़ जानवरों को प्रवेश करने से रोक-
◌ेगी। *5.* तैयार होने पर आप प्रवेश कर सकते हैं। • *1.* May I enter?
*2.* Let him enter. *3.* Leave to enter! *4.* The fence will prevent animals from entering. *5.* You may enter when ready.

## 87. **जोड़ना** — *add, join, connect* — This verb is used to describe the action of combining two or more things together, whether physically or conceptually. It signifies the act of bringing together separate elements to create a unified whole.

• *1.* क्या आपके पास जोड़ने के लिए कुछ है? *2.* कुछ जोड़ना है? *3.*
इसे सूची में जोड़ें. *4.* कुछ भी आप जोड़ना चाहेंगे? *5.* जोड़ने
के लिए मेरे पास कुछ नहीं है। *6.* उन्हे जोड़ो। *7.* वह बिन्द-
◌ुओं को जोड़ सकती थी। *8.* संयोजक ने दो वाक्यों को जोड़ा।
*9.* ग्रासनली मुंह को पेट से जोड़ती है। *10.* सिनैप्स ने न्यूरॉन्स
को जोड़ा। *11.* पार्कवे कई पड़ोसों को जोड़ता है। • *1.* Do you have anything to add? *2.* Anything to add? *3.* Add it to the list. *4.* Anything you'd like to add? *5.* I have nothing to add. *6.* Join them. *7.* She could connect the dots. *8.* The conjunction connected the two sentences. *9.* The esophagus connects the mouth to stomach. *10.* The synapse connected the neurons. *11.* The parkway connected multiple neighborhoods.

## 88. याद दिलाना — *remind* — This verb is used to prompt someone to remember something or to bring a past event or information back to their attention. It is commonly used in conversations to help someone recall a specific memory or task.

• *1.* मैं तुम्हें याद दिलाना चाहता हूं। • *1.* Let me remind you.

## 89. हिलाना — *shake* — The verb 'हिलाना' is used to describe the action of moving something back and forth or up and down quickly. It is commonly used to indicate shaking an object or body part.

• *1.* चलो इस पर हिलाओ. *2.* मैं उसे हिला नहीं सकता. *3.* मैं इसे हिला नहीं सकता. *4.* अपना सिर मत हिलाओ. *5.* हिलाया गया? • *1.* Let's shake on it. *2.* I can't shake him. *3.* I can't shake it. *4.* Don't shake your head. *5.* Shaken up?

## 90. खोदना — *dig* — The verb 'खोदना' is used to describe the action of digging into the ground or any other surface. It is commonly used when referring to activities such as gardening, construction, or archaeological excavations.

• *1.* खाई खोदना। • *1.* Dig in.

## 91. डराना — *scare* — The verb 'डराना' is used to describe the action of causing fear or fright in someone. It is often used to convey the act of scaring or intimidating someone in various situations.

• *1.* मैं तुम्हें डराना नहीं चाहता था. *2.* मैं बस उसे डराना च-
॰हता था. *3.* मैं उसे डराना नहीं चाहता. *4.* मुझे फिर कभी इस तरह मत डराना. *5.* मैं उसे डराना चाहता था. • *1.* I didn't want to scare you. *2.* I just wanted to scare her. *3.* I don't want to scare her. *4.* Don't ever scare me like that again. *5.* I wanted to scare him.

## 92. दोहराना — *repeat* — The verb 'दोहराना' is used to indicate the action of repeating something. It is commonly used when someone wants to say or do something again, or when they want to emphasize a particular point.

• *1.* मैं दोहराता हूँ। *2.* क्या आप उसे दोहरा सकते हैं? *3.* आप अ-
पने आप को दोहरा रहे हैं. *4.* क्या आप प्रश्न दोहरा सकते हैं?

5. मुझे खुद को दोहराने पर मजबूर मत करो. • *1.* I repeat. *2.* Could you repeat that? *3.* You're repeating yourself. *4.* Could you repeat the question? *5.* Don't make me repeat myself.

## 93. चूसना — *suck* — The verb 'चूसना' is used to describe the action of drawing in or taking in something through the mouth by creating a vacuum. It is commonly used to refer to the act of sucking on a straw, candy, or any other object.

• *1.* यह तो चूसना ही होगा. *2.* दांतों से चूसना! *3.* वह चूसना चाहिए. *4.* वह चूसना नहीं चाहता था. *5.* उसे चूसना ही होगा. • *1.* That's gotta suck. *2.* Sucking with teeth! *3.* That must suck. *4.* He didn't want to suck. *5.* That's got to suck.

## 94. मनाना — *celebrate* — 'Manana' is used to express the act of celebrating or rejoicing in a joyful or festive manner. It is commonly used to describe commemorating special occasions, achievements, or events with happiness and enthusiasm.

• *1.* हमें जश्न मनाना चाहिए। *2.* हमें जश्न मनाना है. *3.* हमें जश्न मनाना चाहिए. *4.* हमें जश्न मनाना होगा. *5.* मैं जश्न मनाना चाहता हूं. • *1.* We should celebrate. *2.* We have to celebrate. *3.* We must celebrate. *4.* We gotta celebrate. *5.* I want to celebrate.

## 95. भुगतना — *suffer* — The verb 'भुगतना' is used to express the act of experiencing pain, hardship, or difficulty. It conveys the idea of enduring suffering or going through a tough situation.

• *1.* वह भुगतता है। *2.* और भुगतो. • *1.* He suffers. *2.* And suffer.

## 96. तैरना — *swim* — The verb 'तैरना' is used to describe the action of moving through water by using one's arms and legs. It is commonly used to talk about recreational activities, exercise, and water safety.

• *1.* मुझे तैरना नहीं आता. *2.* तुम्हें तैरना नहीं आता? *3.* तैरना कैसा रहेगा? *4.* तैरना सीखें! *5.* तैरना पसंद है? • *1.* I can't swim. *2.* You can't swim? *3.* How about a swim? *4.* Learn to swim! *5.* Fancy a swim?

## 97. हटाना — *remove, eliminate* — The verb 'हटाना' is used

to indicate the action of taking something away or eliminating it from a particular place or situation. It conveys the idea of removing or getting rid of something.

• *1.* खून का धब्बा हटाना कठिन था। *2.* नीला दाग हटाना कठिन था। • *1.* The bloodstain was hard to remove. *2.* The bluish stain was difficult to remove.

**98. लूटना** — *rob, ransack* — The verb 'लूटना' is used to describe the act of forcefully taking someone's belongings or valuables without their consent. It can also refer to thoroughly searching a place in order to steal or plunder.

**99. पहुंचना** — *arrive* — This verb is used to indicate the action of reaching a destination or arriving at a particular place. It conveys the idea of physically reaching a location or achieving a goal.

• *1.* आप अपने गंतव्य पर पहुंच गए हैं. *2.* आज सुबह पहुंचे. *3.* मैं पहुंचा। *4.* वह तुरंत सुबह 9 बजे पहुंचे। *5.* पैकेज संदिग्ध रूप से देरी से पहुंचा। • *1.* You have arrived at your destination. *2.* Arrived this morning. *3.* I arrived. *4.* He arrived promptly at 9 am. *5.* The package arrived suspiciously late.

**100. नालिश करना** — *sue* — To 'नालिश करना' means to take legal action against someone in a court of law in order to seek compensation or justice for a wrongdoing or harm that has been done to you.

**101. चेतावनी देना** — *warn* — To give a warning or caution to someone about a potential danger or problem.

• *1.* मैं आपको चेतावनी दे रहा हूं। *2.* मैं आपको चेतावनी दी। *3.* यह मत कहो कि मैंने तुम्हें चेतावनी नहीं दी। *4.* मैंने आपको चेतावनी देने की कोशिश की. *5.* आपको चेतावनी दी गई थी। • *1.* I'm warning you. *2.* I warned you. *3.* Don't say I didn't warn you. *4.* I tried to warn you. *5.* You've been warned.

**102. समाधान करना** — *solve* — This verb is used to describe the action of finding a solution to a problem or resolving a conflict. It signifies the act of addressing and fixing an issue or difficulty.

● *1.* हम इसका समाधान कर सकते हैं. *2.* मैं इसका समाधान करना चाहता हूं. *3.* इसका कभी समाधान नहीं हुआ. *4.* गतिरोध को हल करने के लिए एक समाधान की आवश्यकता थी। *5.* टीम ने समस्य-ा के समाधान के लिए समझदारी से काम लिया। ● *1.* We can solve this. *2.* I want to solve this. *3.* It was never solved. *4.* A solution was needed to solve the gridlock. *5.* The team worked sensibly to solve the problem.

## 103. प्राप्त करना — *receive, achieve* — This verb is used to indicate the action of obtaining something, whether it be a physical object, an award, or a goal. It signifies the act of receiving or achieving something desired or expected.

● *1.* क्या आप मुझे प्राप्त कर रहे हैं? *2.* क्या आप प्राप्त कर रहे हैं? *3.* पूछो और आप प्राप्त करेंगे। *4.* यदि आपको प्राप्त हो रहा है तो कृपया उत्तर दें। *5.* हम एक ट्रांसमिशन प्राप्त कर रहे हैं। *6.* उसने मन की एक उत्कृष्ट स्थिति प्राप्त की। *7.* उन्होंने अमर ख्याति प्राप्त की। *8.* उन्होंने सर्वोच्च पद प्र-ाप्त किया। *9.* उसने अपने लक्ष्य को प्राप्त करने में बहुत दृढ़ संकल्प दिखाया। *10.* समीकरण ने संतुलन प्राप्त कर लिया। ● *1.* Are you receiving me? *2.* Are you receiving? *3.* Ask and you shall receive. *4.* If you are receiving, please respond. *5.* We're receiving a transmission. *6.* She achieved a transcendent state of mind. *7.* He achieved immortal fame. *8.* He achieved the highest rank. *9.* She showed great determination in achieving her goal. *10.* The equation achieved equilibrium.

## 104. समझाने — *convince* — This verb is used to persuade or make someone understand a certain point of view or idea. It is often used in discussions, debates, or arguments to change someone's opinion or belief.

● *1.* मुझे समझाओ। *2.* आप किसे समझाने की कोशिश कर रहे हैं? *3.* उसे समझाओ। *4.* तुम्हें मुझे समझाने की ज़रूरत नहीं है। *5.* मैं तुम्हें समझाने के लिए क्या कर सकता हूँ? ● *1.* Convince me. *2.* Who are you trying to convince? *3.* Convince him. *4.* You don't have to convince me. *5.* What can I do to convince you?

## 105. कमाना — *earn* — 'कमाना' is used to describe the act of receiving money or other forms of compensation in exchange for work or services rendered. It signifies the process of earning a living through employment or business activities.

- *1.* आपको इसे कमाना होगा। *2.* वह और अधिक कमाना चाहती थी।
- *1.* You have to earn it. *2.* She wanted to earn more.

## 106. **मांगना** — *seek* — 'Maangna' is used to express the action of seeking or requesting something. It is commonly used to convey the act of asking for help, information, or a favor from someone.

- *1.* उन्होंने खिलाफत को बहाल करने की मांग की। *2.* उनकी विशेषज्ञता की अत्यधिक मांग थी। *3.* उन्होंने आदरणीय नेताओं से सलाह मांगी। *4.* उन्होंने इस परियोजना के लिए प्राधिकरण की मांग की। *5.* उसने आचार्य से मार्गदर्शन मांगा। • *1.* He sought to restore the caliphate. *2.* His expertise was highly sought after. *3.* He sought the advice of venerable leaders. *4.* He sought authorization for the project. *5.* She sought guidance from the acharya.

## 107. **प्रदान करना** — *provide, impart* — This verb is used to indicate the action of giving or supplying something to someone, whether it be physical objects, information, or assistance. It conveys the idea of providing or imparting something to another person.

- *1.* प्रभु प्रदान करेगा। *2.* तूफान प्रदान करता है। *3.* ब्रह्मांड प्रदान करता है. *4.* भगवान प्रदान करेंगे। *5.* उन्होंने घायलों को सहायता प्रदान की। *6.* उसने अपना ज्ञान प्रदान करने का प्रयास किया। • *1.* The Lord will provide. *2.* The storm provides. *3.* The universe provides. *4.* God will provide. *5.* She provided aid to the injured. *6.* She tried to impart her wisdom.

## 108. **नज़रअंदाज़ करना** — *ignore* — To 'नज़रअंदाज़ करना' means to intentionally disregard or pay no attention to something or someone. It implies ignoring or overlooking a person, situation, or object.

- *1.* मुहे नज़रअंदाज़ करना बंद करो! *2.* पूर्वाग्रह को नज़रअंदाज़ करना असंभव था। *3.* उसने बाहर के शोर को नज़रअंदाज़ करने की कोशिश की। *4.* उसने अपनी कमज़ोरी को नज़रअंदाज़ कर दिया। *5.* वह चेतावनी के संकेतों को नज़रअंदाज़ नहीं कर सका। •
*1.* Stop ignoring me! *2.* The bias was impossible to ignore. *3.* She tried to ignore the noise outside. *4.* He ignored his frailty. *5.* He couldn't ignore the warning signs.

**109. इकट्ठा करना** — *gather, collect* — This verb is used to describe the action of bringing together multiple items or people in one place. It signifies the act of collecting or gathering things or individuals for a specific purpose or reason.

• *1.* तो मैं इकट्ठा होता हूं.  *2.* चारों ओर इकट्ठा करो।  *3.* गोलाई में इकट्ठा।  *4.* मैंने उसे इकट्ठा किया.  *5.* अपनी चीजें इकट्ठा करो.  *6.* मैं उन्हें इकट्ठा करता हूं.  *7.* अपने आप को इकट्ठा करो.  *8.* रीपर आत्माओं को इकट्ठा करता है।  *9.* आप क्या इकट्ठा कर रहे हैं?  *10.* उसने समुद्र तट से एक शंख इकट्ठा किया।  • *1.* So I gather. *2.* Gather around. *3.* Gather round. *4.* I gathered that. *5.* Gather your things. *6.* I collect them. *7.* Collect yourself. *8.* The reaper collects souls. *9.* What are you collecting? *10.* She collected a shell from the beach.

**110. नकारना** — *deny* — The verb 'नकारना' is used to express the action of denying or refusing something. It is commonly used to reject a statement, request, or offer. It conveys a sense of disagreement or disapproval.

• *1.* इससे इनकार मत करो.  *2.* आप इससे इनकार नहीं कर सकते.  *3.* मैं इससे इनकार नहीं करता.  *4.* क्या आप इससे इनकार करते हैं?  *5.* मैं इससे इनकार नहीं कर सकता.  • *1.* Don't deny it. *2.* You can't deny it. *3.* I don't deny it. *4.* Do you deny it? *5.* I can't deny that.

**111. दफनाना** — *bury* — The verb 'दफनाना' is used to describe the action of burying something, typically a deceased person or animal. It is a common practice in many cultures to bury the dead as a way of showing respect and honoring their memory.

• *1.* मैंने इसे दफना दिया.  *2.* उन्हें दफनाओ.  *3.* मैंने उन्हें दफनाया.  *4.* हमने उसे दफनाया.  *5.* हमें उन्हें दफना देना चाहिए.  • *1.* I buried it. *2.* Bury them. *3.* I buried them. *4.* We buried him. *5.* We should bury them.

**112. चिल्लाना** — *shout, yell, exclaim* — The verb 'चिल्लाना' is used to describe the act of raising one's voice loudly in anger, frustration, or excitement. It is often used to convey strong emotions or to get someone's attention.

• *1.* चिल्लाओ मत.  *2.* तुम चिल्ला क्यों रहे हो?  *3.* चिल्लाना बंद करो!  *4.* चिल्लाने की जरूरत नहीं.  *5.* आपको चिल्लाने की जरूरत

नहीं है. 6. तुम क्यों चिल्ला रहे हैं? 7. मुझ पर चिल्लाओ मत. 8. चिल्लाना बंद करें! 9. तुम मुझ पर क्यों चिल्ला रहे हो? 10. मुझ पर चिल्लाना बंद करो! 11. वह चिल्लाए बिना नहीं रह सका। 12. दर्शक चिल्लाने लगे। • 1. Don't shout. 2. Why are you shouting? 3. Stop shouting! 4. No need to shout. 5. You don't have to shout. 6. Why are you yelling? 7. Don't yell at me. 8. Stop yelling! 9. Why are you yelling at me? 10. Stop yelling at me! 11. He couldn't help but exclaim. 12. The audience began to exclaim.

### 113. व्यवस्था करना — *arrange* — This verb is used to describe the action of organizing or setting up something in a systematic or orderly manner. It is commonly used to refer to arranging events, meetings, schedules, or any other kind of plan.

• 1. मैं इसकी व्यवस्था करूंगा. 2. मैं इसकी व्यवस्था कर सकता हूं. 3. मुझे लगता है कि इसकी व्यवस्था की जा सकती है. 4. उसकी व्यवस्था की जा सकती है. 5. खैर, इसकी व्यवस्था की जा सकती है। • 1. I'll arrange it. 2. I can arrange that. 3. I think that can be arranged. 4. That could be arranged. 5. Well, that can be arranged.

### 114. पोंछना — *wipe* — The verb 'पोंछना' is used to describe the action of wiping or cleaning a surface by using a cloth or tissue. It is commonly used in everyday tasks such as wiping a table, cleaning a window, or removing dust.

• 1. अपने पैर पोंछें। 2. अपना चेहरा पोंछो. 3. अपने चेहरे से वह मुस्कान पोंछो। 4. अपने हाथ पोंछो. 5. अपना मुँह पोंछो. • 1. Wipe your feet. 2. Wipe your face. 3. Wipe that smile off your face. 4. Wipe your hands. 5. Wipe your mouth.

### 115. तकलीफ देना — *torture* — This verb is used to describe the act of causing pain, suffering, or distress to someone intentionally. It implies inflicting physical or mental anguish on someone, often in a cruel or sadistic manner.

### 116. उपस्थित होना — *attend* — This verb is used to indicate being present at an event, meeting, or gathering. It conveys the action of attending or being in attendance at a specific place or occasion.

● *1.* यह कार्यक्रम उपस्थित सभी लोगों के लिए यादगार था। *2.* उसे कक्षा में उपस्थित होना होगा। ● *1.* The event was memorable for all who attended. *2.* She must attend the class.

## 117. पुष्टि करना — *confirm, endorse, validate, reaffirm*
— The verb 'पुष्टि करना' is used to express the action of confirming, endorsing, validating, or reaffirming something. It is used to indicate agreement or approval of a statement, decision, or action.
● *1.* इसकी पुष्टि हो गई है। *2.* कृपया पुष्टि करें। *3.* पहचान की पुष्टि. *4.* क्या कोई इसकी पुष्टि कर सकता है? *5.* क्या आप इसकी पुष्टि कर सकते हैं? *6.* डेटा उनके निष्कर्षों की पुष्टि करेगा। *7.* उसे अपनी प्रतिबद्धता की पुष्टि करने की आवश्यकता थी। *8.* अनुभव उनके बंधन की पुनः पुष्टि करेगा। ● *1.* It's confirmed. *2.* Please confirm. *3.* Identity confirmed. *4.* Can anyone confirm that? *5.* Can you confirm that? *6.* The data would reaffirm their findings. *7.* She needed to reaffirm her commitment. *8.* The experience would reaffirm their bond.

## 118. सूचित करना — *inform, imply, signify* — This
verb is used to convey information or knowledge to someone, to make them aware of something. It is used to inform or enlighten others about a particular topic, situation, or event.
● *1.* मुझे अपने परिवार को सूचित करना होगा। ● *1.* I need to inform my family.

## 119. रद्द करना — *cancel, revoke* — To 'रद्द करना' means to
cancel or withdraw something that was previously agreed upon or in effect. It is used to denote the action of revoking a decision, contract, permission, or any other form of agreement.

## 120. पुकारना — *hail* — The verb 'पुकारना' is used to call out
loudly or shout in order to get someone's attention or express a strong emotion. It can also be used to describe the act of hailing or greeting someone.

## 121. छोड़ें — *skip* — 'छोड़ें' is used to indicate the action of
skipping or omitting something. It is commonly used when talking about skipping a meal, skipping a step in a process, or skip-

ping a particular event.
- *1.* इसे छोड़ दें। *2.* चलो इसे छोड़ें. *3.* चलो, छोड़ें. *4.* कभ-ी-कभी यह एक पीढ़ी को छोड़ देता है। *5.* उसे छोड़ें. • *1.* Skip it. *2.* Let's skip it. *3.* Come on, Skip. *4.* Sometimes it skips a generation. *5.* Skip that.

## 122. उधार देना — *lend* — This verb is used when someone gives money or an item to someone else with the expectation that it will be returned in the future. It implies a temporary transfer of ownership from the lender to the borrower.

## 123. की पहचान — *identify* — 'की पहचान' is used to describe the act of recognizing or distinguishing someone or something. It is commonly used in situations where one needs to identify a person, object, or characteristic.
- *1.* मैं इसकी पहचान नहीं कर सकता. • *1.* I can't identify it.

## 124. लपेटना — *wrap* — The verb 'लपेटना' is used to describe the action of wrapping something around an object or person. It signifies the act of enclosing or covering something with a material like cloth, paper, or any other flexible substance.
- *1.* क्या मैं इसे लपेट दूं? *2.* पैकर ने प्रत्येक वस्तु को सावधान-ीपूर्वक लपेटा। *3.* उसने अपने टखने को पट्टी से लपेट लिया। *4.* धुंधली पट्टी कसकर लपेटी गई थी। *5.* उसने गले में गर्म दुपट्टा लपेटा हुआ था। • *1.* Shall I wrap it? *2.* The packer wrapped each item carefully. *3.* She wrapped her ankle with a bandage. *4.* The gauze bandage was wrapped tightly. *5.* She wrapped a warm scarf around her neck.

## 125. रोकना — *prevent, forbid, retain* — This verb is used to describe actions taken to stop something from happening or to restrict someone from doing something. It implies the act of preventing, restraining, or prohibiting a certain action or behavior.
- *1.* कानूनों का उद्देश्य गलत काम को रोकना था। *2.* कानून का उद्देश्य अपराध को रोकना था। • *1.* The laws aimed to prevent wrongdoing. *2.* The law aimed to prevent infliction.

## 126. विरोध — *resist* — 'विरोध' is used to describe the act of

opposing or resisting something. It signifies a strong disagreement or refusal to accept a particular idea, action, or situation.
● *1.* मैं विरोध नहीं कर सका. *2.* विरोध मत करो. *3.* विरोध करना बंद करो! *4.* मैं विरोध नहीं कर सकता. *5.* गिरफ्तारी का विरोध करते हुए। ● *1.* I couldn't resist. *2.* Don't resist. *3.* Stop resisting! *4.* I can't resist. *5.* Resisting arrest.

## 127. शिकायत करना — *complain* — This verb is used to express dissatisfaction or displeasure with a person, situation, or thing. It is used to communicate grievances or concerns in order to seek resolution or address issues.
● *1.* मैं शिकायत नहीं कर रहा हूं। *2.* शिकायत नहीं कर सकते. *3.* शिकायत करना बंद करो। *4.* मैं शिकायत नहीं कर सकता. *5.* ऐसा नहीं है कि मैं शिकायत कर रहा हूं. ● *1.* I'm not complaining. *2.* Can't complain. *3.* Stop complaining. *4.* I can't complain. *5.* Not that I'm complaining.

## 128. प्रोत्साहन देना — *foster* — The verb 'प्रोत्साहन देना' is used to describe the action of encouraging, promoting, or nurturing something or someone in order to help them grow, develop, or succeed. It implies providing support and motivation to foster positive outcomes.

## 129. खोजना — *discover, retrace* — This verb is used to describe the act of finding or uncovering something that was previously unknown or forgotten. It can also be used to describe retracing one's steps or following a trail to find something.
● *1.* यही वह है जिसे हमें खोजना चाहिए। ● *1.* That is what we must discover.

## 130. वू — *woo* — 'वू' is used to describe the act of trying to gain the affection or approval of someone, typically with the intention of forming a romantic relationship. It involves making efforts to impress and attract the person.

## 131. प्रतिनिधित्व करना — *represent* — This verb is used to describe the action of standing in for or acting on behalf of someone or something else. It involves speaking or acting on behalf of a person, group, organization, or idea.

37

- *1.* आप किसका प्रतिनिधित्व करते हैं? *2.* वकील आपका प्रत-
िनिधित्व करेगा. *3.* उन्होंने प्रतियोगिता में गर्व से बामा
का प्रतिनिधित्व किया। *4.* एल्डरमैन ने जिले का प्रतिनिधित-
्व किया। *5.* यह प्रतीक शक्ति का प्रतिनिधित्व करता था। • *1.*
Who do you represent? *2.* The lawyer will represent you. *3.* He
proudly represented Bama in the competition. *4.* The alderman
represented the district. *5.* The emblem represented strength.

## 132. थपथपाना — *pat* — The verb 'थपथपाना' is used to
describe the action of gently tapping or patting something with
the fingers or hand. It is often used to show affection, comfort,
or to create a rhythmic sound.
- *1.* उसने स्कूबी का सिर थपथपाया। *2.* उसने रुमाल से अपना
मुँह थपथपाया। *3.* उसने उसके कंधे को थपथपाया। • *1.* She
patted Scooby's head. *2.* She patted her mouth with the napkin.
*3.* He patted her shoulder.

## 133. सज़ा देना — *punish, chastise* — This verb is used to
describe the action of penalizing someone for their wrongdoing
or bad behavior. It signifies the act of giving consequences or
retribution for an offense committed by an individual.

## 134. जांच करना — *investigate* — The verb 'जांच करना' is
used to describe the action of investigating or examining something in order to gather information or find out the truth about a
particular situation, person, or thing.

## 135. पकड़ना — *capture, seize, tackle, grapple* — The verb
'पकड़ना' is used to describe the action of capturing or seizing
something or someone. It can also mean to grapple or apprehend a person or object.
- *1.* उन्हें पकड़ो। *2.* उसने सार पकड़ लिया. *3.* कला ने उत्कृष्ट-
ता को पकड़ने का प्रयास किया। *4.* रीमेक मूल के जादू को पकड़ने
में विफल रहा। *5.* डाकूओं को पकड़ने के लिए एक दल का गठन किया
गया। *6.* उसे पकड़ो! *7.* उसे पकड़ो! *8.* रक्षकों, उसे पकड़ लो!
- *1.* Capture them. *2.* She captured the essence. *3.* The art
attempted to capture transcendence. *4.* The remake failed to
capture the original's magic. *5.* A posse formed to capture the
outlaws. *6.* Seize him! *7.* Seize her! *8.* Guards, seize him!

# 136. गवाही देना — *testify* — 'गवाही देना' is used to describe the act of giving testimony or bearing witness to something in a legal or formal setting. It signifies the act of providing evidence or speaking about one's knowledge or experience.

# 137. प्रस्ताव करना — *propose* — This verb is used to suggest or put forward an idea, plan, or offer to someone for consideration or acceptance. It is commonly used in the context of proposing marriage or suggesting a solution to a problem.
- *1.* आप क्या प्रस्ताव दे रहे हैं? *2.* मैं एक टोस्ट प्रस्तावित करना चाहूँगा. *3.* मैं एक टोस्ट का प्रस्ताव रखना चाहूँगा. *4.* आप ऐसा करने का प्रस्ताव कैसे रखते हैं? *5.* मैं एक टोस्ट प्रस्तावित करता हूँ. • *1.* What are you proposing? *2.* I'd like to propose a toast. *3.* I would like to propose a toast. *4.* How do you propose to do that? *5.* I propose a toast.

# 138. रगड़ना — *rub* — The verb 'रगड़ना' is used to describe the action of rubbing or scraping something against a surface to create friction. It is commonly used in contexts related to cleaning, polishing, or soothing a sore area on the body.
- *1.* इसे रगड़ें नहीं. *2.* उसमें रगड़ें। *3.* मेरा पेट रगड़ो. *4.* उसने संतुष्ट होकर अपना पेट रगड़ा। *5.* आपको इसे रगड़ने की ज़रूरत नहीं है. • *1.* Don't rub it in. *2.* Rub it in. *3.* Rub my belly. *4.* She rubbed her tummy contentedly. *5.* You don't have to rub it in.

# 139. प्रशंसा करना — *admire* — This verb is used to express a feeling of respect or approval towards someone or something. It is used to show admiration or appreciation for the qualities, actions, or achievements of a person or object.
- *1.* मैं उसकी प्रशंसा करता हूं. *2.* मैं इसकी प्रशंसा करता हूं. *3.* मैं आपके साहस की प्रशंसा करता हूं. *4.* मैं उसकी प्रशंसा करता हूं। *5.* मैं आपके काम की प्रशंसा करता हूं. • *1.* I admire that. *2.* I admire it. *3.* I admire your courage. *4.* I admire him. *5.* I admire your work.

# 140. भनभनाना — *buzz* — The verb 'भनभनाना' is used to describe the sound of buzzing or humming, typically associated with insects or machinery. It conveys a continuous and low-pitched noise that is often heard in nature or in a mechanical

setting.
● *1.* *स्ट्रीटलाइट भनभनाती रही और झपकती रही।* ● *1.* The street-light buzzed and blinked.

## 141. चमकाना — *polish, refine* — The verb 'चमकाना' is used to describe the action of making something shine or sparkle by polishing or refining it. It is often used in the context of cleaning or improving the appearance of an object.

● *1.* *उसने चाँदी को चमकाया। 2. उसने फर्शों को तब तक चमकाया जब तक वे चमकदार न हो गए। 3. ग्रीव्स को चमकाने के लिए पॉलिश किया गया था।* ● *1.* He polished the silver. *2.* He polished the floors until they were shiny. *3.* The greaves were polished to a shine.

## 142. की सिफारिश — *recommend* — 'की सिफारिश' is used to suggest or endorse something to someone. It is a way of expressing approval or support for a particular course of action, product, service, or person.

● *1.* *डॉक्टर ने उदरशूल के उपचार की सिफारिश की। 2. दंत-चिकित्सक ने दंत प्रत्यारोपण की सिफारिश की। 3. उन्होंने स्नेहन का उपयोग करने की सिफारिश की। 4. सलाहकार की रिपोर्ट में बदलाव की सिफारिश की गई। 5. हाड वैद्य ने बेहतर मुद्रा के लिए व्यायाम की सिफारिश की।* ● *1.* The doctor recommended treatments for colic. *2.* The dentist recommended a dental implant. *3.* They recommended using lubrication. *4.* The consultant's report recommended changes. *5.* The chiropractor recommended exercises for better posture.

## 143. प्रभावित करना — *affect* — This verb is used to describe the action of influencing or impacting something or someone in a significant way. It signifies the ability to cause a change or have an effect on a particular situation or individual.

● *1.* *यह मुझे प्रभावित करता है। 2. डिस्लेक्सिया लोगों को अलग-अलग तरह से प्रभावित करता है। 3. नमी सांस लेने को प्रभावित कर सकती है। 4. इस बीमारी ने वेंट्रिकुलर फंक्शन को प्रभावित किया। 5. हवा की गुणवत्ता पार्टिकुलेट मैटर से प्रभावित होती है।* ● *1.* It affects me. *2.* Dyslexia affects people differently. *3.* Humidity can affect breathing. *4.* The disease affected the ventricular function. *5.* The air quality is affected by particulate matter.

## 144. स्वस्थ होना — *recover* — This verb is used to describe the process of returning to a healthy state after an illness or injury. It signifies the act of regaining physical or mental well-being.

- *1.* मैं स्वस्थ हो गया। • *1.* I recovered.

## 145. निगलना — *swallow, merge, ingest* — This verb is used to describe the action of taking something into the mouth and down the throat, typically referring to food or drink. It implies the act of swallowing or ingesting something.

- *1.* इसे निगलें। *2.* मैंने इसे निगल लिया. *3.* इसे निगलो मत. *4.* मैं निगल नहीं सकता. *5.* इसे निगल जाओ. • *1.* Swallow it. *2.* I swallowed it. *3.* Don't swallow it. *4.* I can't swallow. *5.* Swallow this.

## 146. संचालित — *operate* — The verb 'संचालित' is used to describe the action of operating or running something, such as a machine, system, or organization. It signifies the act of controlling or managing a particular entity.

- *1.* मानक संचालन प्रक्रिया। *2.* शासन दण्डमुक्ति के साथ संचालित होता था। *3.* वे संचालन कर रहे हैं. *4.* याकूब छाया में संचालित होता था. *5.* उसने ड्रोन को संचालित करने के लिए नियंत्रक का उपयोग किया। • *1.* Standard operating procedure. *2.* The regime operated with impunity. *3.* They're operating. *4.* The yakuza operated in the shadows. *5.* She used the controller to operate the drone.

## 147. हस्तक्षेप करना — *interfere, intervene, tamper* — This verb is used to describe the act of getting involved in a situation where one is not welcome or needed, often with the intention of changing or disrupting the natural course of events.

- *1.* हस्तक्षेप मत करो. *2.* मैं हस्तक्षेप नहीं करूंगा. *3.* हम हस्तक्षेप नहीं कर सकते. *4.* आपने हस्तक्षेप क्यों किया? *5.* आपको हस्तक्षेप नहीं करना चाहिए था. *6.* हस्तक्षेप करने का कौशल रखने वाला कोई व्यक्ति। *7.* मैंने हस्तक्षेप किया. • *1.* Don't interfere. *2.* I won't interfere. *3.* We can't interfere. *4.* Why did you interfere? *5.* You should not have interfered. *6.* Someone with the skills to intervene. *7.* I intervened.

**148. विस्फोट करना** — *explode* — This verb is used to describe the action of something bursting or shattering violently, often with a loud noise and releasing energy. It is commonly used to refer to the detonation of explosives or fireworks.

● *1.* स्थिति विस्फोटक हो जाएगी. *2.* टकराते ही टॉरपीडो में विस्फोट हो गया। *3.* सबस्टेशन में विस्फोट हो गया. *4.* कृपया विस्फोट न करें. *5.* बारिश के बाद मिज आबादी में विस्फोट हो गया। ● *1.* The situation will explode. *2.* The torpedo exploded on impact. *3.* The substation exploded. *4.* Please don't explode. *5.* The midge population exploded after the rain.

**149. की घोषणा** — *announce* — 'की घोषणा' is used to convey the act of making a formal or public statement to inform others about a decision, event, or important information. It is commonly used in official announcements, news broadcasts, and public declarations.

● *1.* उन्होंने अपने आगमन की घोषणा की. *2.* वे शीघ्र ही विजेता की घोषणा करेंगे। *3.* उन्होंने रीमेक की योजना की घोषणा की। *4.* उन्होंने स्थगन की घोषणा की. *5.* उन्होंने जनता के सामने इसकी घोषणा की। ● *1.* He announced his arrival. *2.* They will announce the winner shortly. *3.* They announced plans for a remake. *4.* He announced the postponement. *5.* They announced it to the public.

**150. क्लिक** — *click* — The verb 'क्लिक' is used to describe the action of pressing a button on a computer mouse or touchscreen device in order to select or activate something on a screen.

● *1.* इसे क्लिक करें। *2.* वहां क्लिक करें. *3.* बस 'विकल्प' पर क्लिक करें! *4.* स्विचब्लेड क्लिक करके खुल गया। ● *1.* Click it. *2.* Click there. *3.* Just click on 'options'! *4.* The switchblade clicked open.

**151. स्कैन** — *scan* — The verb 'स्कैन' is used to describe the action of examining or capturing information from a document or image using a scanner or similar device. It is commonly used in the context of digitizing physical documents for electronic storage or transmission.

● *1.* पूरा स्कैन करें. *2.* हमें स्कैन किया जा रहा है. *3.* पूर-

ण स्कैन। *4.* रेटिनल स्कैन सत्यापित. *5.* वे हमें स्कैन कर रहे हैं. •
*1.* Scan complete. *2.* We're being scanned. *3.* Full scan. *4.*
Retinal scan verified. *5.* They're scanning us.

## 152. विकसित करना — *develop, evolve, cultivate* —
This verb is used to describe the process of growth, progress,
or improvement in something, such as a person, organization,
or idea. It signifies the act of making something better or more
advanced over time.
• *1.* पाठ्यक्रम का उद्देश्य आलोचनात्मक सोच कौशल विकसित
करना है। *2.* नए प्रोजेक्ट से ग्रीनफील्ड विकसित होगी। *3.*
मुझे यह फ़ोटोग्राफ़ विकसित करने की आवश्यकता है. *4.* चि-
कित्सक ने रोगी को सहानुभूति विकसित करने में मदद की। *5.*
कहानी में मेचा तकनीक तेजी से विकसित हुई। *6.* डार्विनवाद
का सिद्धांत समय के साथ विकसित हुआ है। *7.* वह विकसित हो
रहा है. *8.* हम विकसित होते हैं। • *1.* The curriculum aimed to
develop critical thinking skills. *2.* The new project will develop
the greenfield. *3.* I need to develop this photograph. *4.* The
therapist helped the patient develop empathy. *5.* Mecha technology evolved rapidly in the story. *6.* The theory of darwinism
has evolved over time. *7.* He's evolving. *8.* We evolve.

## 153. अनुमोदन करना — *approve* — This verb is used
to express agreement or consent to something, typically in a formal or official context. It signifies giving approval or permission
for a particular action, decision, or request.
• *1.* मुझे आशा है कि आप अनुमोदन करेंगे। *2.* संभागीय बजट का अनु-
मोदन किया गया। • *1.* I hope you approve. *2.* The divisional
budget was approved.

## 154. घूरना — *stare, gloat, ogle* — This verb is used to de-
scribe the action of looking at someone or something intently,
often with a sense of fascination, admiration, or malice. It can
convey a range of emotions from curiosity to hostility.
• *1.* घूरना बंद करें। *2.* मुझे घूरना बंद करो। *3.* घूरना बंद करो.
*4.* मुझे इस तरह घूरना बंद करो. *5.* घूरना शिष्टता नहीं है. *6.*
सार्वजनिक रूप से लोगों को घूरना अशिष्टता है। *7.* घूरना बंद
करो और ध्यान दो। • *1.* Stop staring. *2.* Stop staring at me.
*3.* Quit staring. *4.* Stop staring at me like that. *5.* It's not polite

to stare. *6.* It's rude to ogle people in public. *7.* Stop ogling and pay attention.

**155. धमकाना** — *threaten, intimidate, terrorize* — This verb is used to describe the act of instilling fear or intimidation in someone by making threats or using aggressive behavior. It is often used to describe actions that are meant to coerce or control others.

● *1.* क्या आप मुझे धमका रहे हैं? *2.* मुझे धमकाया जाना पसंद - नहीं है. *3.* अपराधी ने उन्हें पिस्तौल दिखाकर धमकाया. *4.* लुटेरे ने उन्हें हथियार से धमकाया। *5.* तुमने उसे धमकाया. *6.* हुड़दंगियों ने दुकान मालिक को डराया-धमकाया। *7.* क्लान ने ड-राने-धमकाने के लिए हिंसा का इस्तेमाल किया। *8.* ठग ने दुकानदार को डराया-धमकाया। ● *1.* Are you threatening me? *2.* I don't like being threatened. *3.* The criminal threatened them at gunpoint. *4.* The brigand threatened them with a weapon. *5.* You threatened her. *6.* The hoodlum intimidated the shop owner. *7.* The klan used violence to intimidate. *8.* The thug intimidated the shopkeeper.

**156. भरोसा करना** — *rely* — To have trust or confidence in someone or something, to depend on them for support or assistance. It implies a sense of reliability and faith in the person or thing being relied upon.

**157. प्रतिक्रिया करना** — *react* — This verb is used to describe the action of responding or reacting to a stimulus or situation. It signifies the act of giving a response or feedback in response to something that has occurred.

● *1.* उसने कैसी प्रतिक्रिया दी? *2.* उसने कैसी प्रतिक्रिया व्यक्त की? *3.* मुझे नहीं पता था कि आपकी क्या प्रतिक्रिया होगी. *4.* मैंने अभी प्रतिक्रिया व्यक्त की. *5.* उसकी क्या प्रतिक्रिया थी? ● *1.* How did she react? *2.* How did he react? *3.* I didn't know how you'd react. *4.* I just reacted. *5.* How'd she react?

**158. धक्का** — *shove* — The verb 'धक्का' is used to describe the action of forcefully pushing or shoving someone or something. It conveys the idea of using sudden and strong physical force to move an object or person in a particular direction.

• *1.* धक्का देना बंद करो. *2.* मुझे धक्का मत दो. *3.* उसे एक जोर-दार धक्का लगा. *4.* उसने उसे एक धक्का दिया. *5.* मैंने उसे दोस्ताना धक्का दिया। • *1.* Quit shoving. *2.* Don't shove me. *3.* She felt a strong shove. *4.* He gave her a shove. *5.* I gave him a friendly shove.

### 159. मना करना — *forbid, prohibit, dissuade, foreclose*
— This verb is used to indicate the act of prohibiting or dissu-ading someone from doing something, or foreclosing a particular action or behavior. It is used to convey a sense of restriction or prevention.

### 160. तलना — *fry* — The verb 'तलना' is used to describe the action of frying food in hot oil or ghee. It is a common cooking technique in Indian cuisine, where ingredients are cooked in oil until they are crispy and golden brown.

### 161. बदमाशी करना — *hector* — To "hector" means to bully or intimidate someone in a forceful or aggressive man-ner. It involves using threats or coercion to assert dominance over others.

### 162. सुधारना — *improve, modify, improvise, refine* — This verb is used to describe the action of making something better or more refined. It can be used in various contexts to indicate improvement, modification, or refinement of something.
• *1.* आपमें सुधार हो रहा है. *2.* उसमें सुधार हो रहा है. *3.* इस सेमेस्टर में उसके ग्रेड में सुधार हुआ. *4.* नई प्रणाली से कार्यकुशलता में सुधार हुआ. *5.* प्रतिस्थापन से टीम के प्रदर्-शन में सुधार हुआ. *6.* हम सुधार करेंगे. *7.* मैं सुधार करूंगा. *8.* मैंने सुधार किया. *9.* मुझे सुधार करना पड़ा. *10.* मैं सुधार कर रहा हूँ. • *1.* You're improving. *2.* He's improving. *3.* Her grades improved this semester. *4.* The new system improved efficiency. *5.* The substitution improved the team's performance. *6.* We'll improvise. *7.* I'll improvise. *8.* I improvised. *9.* I had to improvise. *10.* I'm improvising.

### 163. मिलकर काम करना — *cooperate* — This verb is used to describe the act of working together with oth-ers towards a common goal or objective. It signifies collabo-

ration, teamwork, and mutual assistance in completing tasks or projects.

## 164. पालन करना — *observe, execute, comply* — The verb 'पालन करना' is used to convey the idea of following rules, guidelines, or traditions. It implies a sense of obedience, adherence, and respect towards the norms or customs that are expected to be observed.

• *1.* आपको नियमों का पालन करना होगा. *2.* आपको अनुपालन करना होगा. • *1.* You need to observe the rules. *2.* You must comply.

## 165. रिटायर हो जाना — *retire* — This verb is used to describe the action of leaving a job or career permanently, typically after reaching a certain age or completing a certain number of years of service.

• *1.* आप रिटायर हो सकते हैं. *2.* मैं रिटायर नहीं हो रहा हूं. *3.* राजसी राशि रिटायर होने के लिए पर्याप्त थी। • *1.* You may retire. *2.* I'm not retiring. *3.* The princely sum was enough to retire on.

## 166. प्रतिस्पर्धा — *compete* — The verb 'प्रतिस्पर्धा' is used to describe the action of striving to outdo or surpass others in a competitive setting. It signifies the act of engaging in a contest or rivalry to demonstrate one's skills or abilities.

• *1.* मैं उससे प्रतिस्पर्धा नहीं कर सकता. *2.* मैं उससे कैसे प्रतिस्पर्धा कर सकता हूँ? *3.* मैं प्रतिस्पर्धा नहीं कर सकता. *4.* टीमें जमकर प्रतिस्पर्धा करती हैं। *5.* मुझे उससे कैसे प्रतिस्पर्धा करनी चाहिए? • *1.* I can't compete with that. *2.* How can I compete with that? *3.* I can't compete. *4.* The teams compete fiercely. *5.* How am I supposed to compete with that?

## 167. रेंगना — *creep, slither* — The verb 'रेंगना' is used to describe the action of moving slowly and quietly in a stealthy or sneaky manner. It is often used to depict someone or something creeping or crawling along the ground.

• *1.* तुम रेंगते कीड़े! • *1.* You creep!

## 168. चाटना — *lick* — The verb 'चाटना' is used to describe the action of using the tongue to touch or move across a surface

in order to taste or consume something.
- *1.* इसे बंद चाटना। • *1.* Lick it off.

**169. चुप रहना** — *hush* — To remain silent or quiet, often in response to a request or command. It is used to indicate a need for silence or to stop talking.

**170. हराना** — *overcome, frustrate, smite, subdue* — The verb 'हराना' is used to describe the act of defeating or overpowering someone or something in a competition, battle, or conflict. It signifies the act of subduing or smiting an opponent or obstacle.

**171. की जांच** — *examine* — 'की जांच' is used to describe the action of examining or investigating something in order to gather information or determine its condition. It is commonly used in medical, academic, and legal contexts.
- *1.* उसने दस्तावेज़ की सावधानीपूर्वक जांच की। *2.* उन्होंने घाव की बारीकी से जांच की. *3.* जौहरी ने हीरे की बारीकी से जांच की। *4.* उन्होंने कॉर्टेक्स की बारीकी से जांच की। *5.* उन्होंने छेद की बारीकी से जांच की। • *1.* She examined the document carefully. *2.* He examined the lesion closely. *3.* The jeweller examined the diamond closely. *4.* They examined the cortex closely. *5.* They examined the perforation closely.

**172. घोषित** — *declare* — 'घोषित' is used to convey the action of officially announcing or proclaiming something. It is commonly used in contexts where a formal declaration or statement is being made to inform or notify others.
- *1.* राष्ट्रपति क्लार्क ने मार्शल लॉ घोषित करने वाले एक डि-क्री पर हस्ताक्षर किए। *2.* क्या आपके पास घोषित करने के लिए कुछ है? *3.* स्वयं घोषित करें. *4.* उन्होंने गर्व से खुद को बेवकूफ घोषित किया। *5.* कार्यक्रम को आधिकारिक तौर पर खुला घोषित किया गया। • *1.* President Clark signed a decree declaring martial law. *2.* Do you have anything to declare? *3.* Declare yourself. *4.* He proudly declared himself a nerd. *5.* The event was officially declared open.

**173. असम्मत होना** — *disagree* — This verb is used to

express a lack of agreement or approval with a statement, idea, or action. It signifies a difference in opinion or a refusal to accept something as true or valid.

## 174. निराश करना — *disappoint* — This verb is used to
describe the feeling of letting someone down or failing to meet their expectations. It conveys a sense of sadness or dissatisfaction in the context of not living up to someone's hopes or desires.

## 175. अभिवादन करना — *greet* — This verb is used
to express the action of greeting someone in a respectful manner, typically by saying hello or offering good wishes. It is a common social custom in Indian culture to greet others with 'अभिवादन करना'.

• *1.* उसने सेनोरिटा का अभिवादन किया। *2.* उसका व्हाट्स-अप अभिवादन मित्रतापूर्ण था। *3.* विक्रेता ने प्रत्येक ग्राहक का अभिवादन किया। *4.* उन्होंने दृढ़ता से हाथ मिलाकर अपने सहकर्मी का अभिवादन किया। *5.* मोनसिग्नूर ने भीड़ का अभिवादन किया। • *1.* She greeted the señorita. *2.* Her whassup greeting was friendly. *3.* The salesperson greeted each customer. *4.* He greeted his colleague with a firm handshake. *5.* Monseigneur greeted the crowd.

## 176. सिकुड़ना — *shrink* — The verb 'सिकुड़ना' is used to
describe the action of something becoming smaller in size or volume. It is often used to indicate a decrease in dimensions or a contraction of a material or substance.

• *1.* मुझे सिकुड़न की जरूरत नहीं है. *2.* आप सिकुड़े हुए हैं. *3.* स्वदेशी आबादी सिकुड़ रही है. *4.* यह एक सेंटीमीटर सिकुड़ गया। *5.* यह सिकुड़ रहा है. • *1.* I don't need a shrink. *2.* You're the shrink. *3.* The indigenous population is shrinking. *4.* It shrank by a centimeter. *5.* It's shrinking.

## 177. सावधान होना — *beware* — This verb is used to
warn someone to be cautious or alert about a potential danger or threat. It is often used to advise someone to be careful and attentive in a particular situation.

• *1.* उससे सावधान रहें. *2.* तांत्रिक के जादू से सावधान रहें। *3.* साँपों से सावधान रहें. *4.* कुत्ते से सावधान। *5.* बिच्छू से सा-

वधान रहें. • *1.* Beware of him. *2.* Beware the necromancer's magic. *3.* Beware of snakes. *4.* Beware of the dog. *5.* Beware of the scorpion.

## 178. चुकाना — *repay, liquidate* — This verb is used to indicate the action of repaying a debt or settling a financial obligation. It can also be used in a broader sense to refer to fulfilling or completing any kind of obligation or duty.

• *1.* मैं तुम्हें कभी कैसे चुका सकता हूँ? *2.* मैं तुम्हें कैसे चुका सकता हूँ? *3.* और इस तरह तुम मुझे बदला चुकाते हो? *4.* और तुम मुझे इसका बदला कैसे चुकाओगे? *5.* हम आपका बदला कैसे चुका सकते हैं? • *1.* How can I ever repay you? *2.* How can I repay you? *3.* And this is how you repay me? *4.* And how do you repay me? *5.* How can we repay you?

## 179. बातचीत करना — *negotiate, converse* — This verb is used to describe the act of engaging in a discussion or conversation with someone in order to reach an agreement or understanding. It involves exchanging ideas, opinions, and information in a formal or informal setting.

• *1.* हम आतंकवादियों से बातचीत नहीं करते. *2.* हम बातचीत कर रहे हैं. *3.* मैं बातचीत नहीं कर रहा हूं. *4.* हम बातचीत नहीं कर रहे हैं. *5.* चलिए बातचीत करते हैं. *6.* मैं जल्द ही उनसे बातचीत करूंगा. *7.* क्या मैं उससे बातचीत कर सकता हूँ? *8.* हमारे पास बातचीत करने का समय था. *9.* मैं उनसे बातचीत करना चाहता हूं. • *1.* We don't negotiate with terrorists. *2.* We're negotiating. *3.* I'm not negotiating. *4.* We're not negotiating. *5.* Let's negotiate. *6.* I shall converse with him soon. *7.* May I converse with her? *8.* We had time to converse. *9.* I want to converse with them.

## 180. स्थापित करना — *establish, install* — This verb is used to describe the action of setting up or creating something in a particular place or position. It is often used in the context of establishing a new system, organization, or structure.

• *1.* हमने इसे स्थापित कर लिया है. *2.* एक परिधि स्थापित करें. *3.* लिंक स्थापित. *4.* वह विश्वास स्थापित करना चाहता है. *5.* हमें पूरा करने के लिए एक समय-सीमा स्थापित करने की आवश्यकता है. *6.* उन्होंने एक जलविद्युत टरबाइन स्थापित किया। *7.* वे एक नया स्विमिंग पूल स्थापित करना चाहते थे। *8.* उन्होंने लकड़ी की छत फर्श स्थापित किया। *9.* उन्होंने एक नई

कैबिनेट स्थापित की। *10.* स्कूल ने एक नया ध्वजस्तंभ स्थापित किया। • *1.* We've established that. *2.* Establish a perimeter. *3.* Link established. *4.* He wants to establish trust. *5.* We need to establish a timeframe for completion. *6.* They installed a hydroelectric turbine. *7.* They wanted to install a new swimming pool. *8.* He installed parquet flooring. *9.* They installed a new cabinet. *10.* The school installed a new flagpole.

## 181. सहारा लेना — *resort* — This verb is used to indicate seeking help or support from someone or something in times of need or difficulty. It conveys the idea of relying on someone or something for assistance or relief.

## 182. सहायता करना — *assist* — This verb is used to describe the action of helping or supporting someone in need. It signifies providing aid or assistance to someone who requires help with a task or problem.
• *1.* सहायता के लिए धन्यवाद. *2.* मेरी सहायता करो। *3.* मैं आपकी किस प्रकार सहायता कर सकता हूँ? *4.* क्या मैं आपकी सह-ायता करूं? *5.* वह मेरी सहायता करता है. • *1.* Thanks for the assist. *2.* Assist me. *3.* How may I assist you? *4.* May I assist you? *5.* He assists me.

## 183. अपहरण करना — *kidnap, abduct* — This verb is used to describe the act of forcefully taking someone away against their will, typically for ransom or other malicious purposes. It implies a criminal and violent action of kidnapping or abduction.

## 184. अन्वेषण करना — *explore* — The verb 'अन्वेषण करना' is used to describe the action of searching or investigating in order to discover or learn more about something. It is often used in the context of exploring new places, ideas, or opportunities.
• *1.* उन्होंने विशाल रेगिस्तान का अन्वेषण किया। *2.* घूमो और अन्वेषण करो। *3.* अन्वेषण करें जहां आपको अन्वेषण करने के लिए कुछ मिले। *4.* मानचित्र ने उन्हें अन्वेषण करने के लिए निर्देशित किया। • *1.* He explored the vast desert. *2.* Rove and explore. *3.* Explore where you find something to explore. *4.* The map guided them to explore.

**185. चबाने** — *chew* — The verb 'चबाने' is used to describe the action of breaking down food with the teeth in order to make it easier to swallow. It is a common activity done during meals to aid in digestion.

• *1.* भोजन के बाद वे पान चबाने का आनंद लेते थे। *2.* उन्होंने कुत्ते को जूते चबाने पर डांटा। • *1.* He enjoyed chewing paan after a meal. *2.* He scolded the dog for chewing the shoes.

**186. सहन करना** — *tolerate* — This verb is used to describe the act of enduring or putting up with something unpleasant or difficult without complaining or showing outward signs of frustration.

**187. नियंत्रित करना** — *contain, restrain* — The verb 'नियंत्रित करना' is used to indicate the action of controlling or limiting something within certain boundaries or limits. It implies the act of keeping something in check or under control.

• *1.* कुछ रोग का प्रकोप नियंत्रित हो गया। *2.* डिप्थीरिया का प्रकोप नियंत्रित हो गया। *3.* उन्होंने प्रकोप को नियंत्रित किया। *4.* उसका क्रोध नियंत्रित नहीं हो सका। • *1.* The leprosy outbreak was contained. *2.* The diphtheria outbreak was contained. *3.* They contained the outbreak. *4.* Her fury could not be contained.

**188. बधाई देना** — *congratulate* — This verb is used to express good wishes or praise someone for their achievements or good fortune. It is commonly used in celebrations, ceremonies, or to acknowledge someone's success or happiness.

• *1.* मैं आपको बधाई देना चाहता था। *2.* मैं बस आपको बधाई देना चाहता था। • *1.* I wanted to congratulate you. *2.* I just wanted to congratulate you.

**189. आगे बढ़ाने** — *pursue* — This verb is used to indicate the act of continuing or advancing towards a goal or target. It implies a sense of determination and persistence in achieving something despite obstacles or challenges.

• *1.* देश ने निरस्त्रीकरण को आगे बढ़ाने का संकल्प लिया। • *1.* The country pledged to pursue disarmament.

**190. को खत्म** — *eliminate* — The verb 'को खत्म' is used to indicate the action of eliminating or getting rid of something or someone. It conveys the idea of removing or eradicating a particular entity or problem.

**191. पिघल** — *melt* — The verb 'पिघल' is used to describe the process of a solid substance turning into a liquid state due to heat. It signifies the transformation of a material from a solid form to a molten form.

● *1.* बर्फ पिघल रही है! *2.* चेडर चीज़ पूरी तरह पिघल गई। *3.* हिममानव सूरज के नीचे पिघल गया। *4.* खट्टा क्रीम का टुकड़ा जल्दी पिघल गया। *5.* गरम पैनकेक पर मक्खन पिघल गया. ● *1.* The ice is melting! *2.* The cheddar cheese melted perfectly. *3.* The snowman melted under the sun. *4.* The dollop of sour cream melted quickly. *5.* The butter melted on the hot pancakes.

**192. समाप्त होना** — *cease, perish, expire* — This verb is used to indicate the end or completion of something, such as a task, event, or period of time. It signifies that something has come to a close or has reached its expiration.

● *1.* प्राणी समाप्त हो गया. *2.* यह समाप्त हो चुका है. *3.* आपका समय समाप्त हो गया है. *4.* लाइसेंस समाप्त हो गया था. *5.* पुस्तक का कॉपीराइट समाप्त हो गया है. *6.* एक माह में अनुबंध समाप्त हो जायेगा. ● *1.* The creature ceased. *2.* It's expired. *3.* Your time has expired. *4.* The licence was expired. *5.* The copyright of the book has expired. *6.* The contract will expire in a month.

**193. पादना** — *fart* — The verb 'पादना' is used to describe the act of releasing gas from the body in an audible and sometimes odorous manner. It is a natural bodily function that can occur at any time.

● *1.* कोन पादना? ● *1.* Who farted?

**194. हिचकिचाना** — *hesitate* — To hesitate or show reluctance in taking action or making a decision. It implies a sense of uncertainty or doubt in one's mind before proceeding with a particular task or course of action.

● *1.* मैं हिचकिचाया। *2.* वह उसका सामना करने से नहीं हिच-किचाती थी। *3.* बॉस कर्मचारियों को डांटने में नहीं हिचकिचाते

थे. ● *1.* I hesitated. *2.* She didn't hesitate to confront him. *3.* The boss did not hesitate to chastise employees.

## 195. फूल का खिलना — *bloom* — This verb is used

to describe the process of a flower opening up and blossoming. It signifies the growth and development of a flower from a bud to a fully bloomed state.

## 196. आरोप — *accuse* — The verb 'आरोप' is used to express

the act of accusing someone of a wrongdoing or crime. It is a strong and direct way to assign blame or responsibility to an individual for a specific action.

● *1.* मैं आप पर कोई आरोप नहीं लगा रहा हूं. *2.* क्या आप मुझ पर कुछ आरोप लगा रहे हैं? *3.* आप मुझ पर क्या आरोप लगा रहे हैं? *4.* क्या आप मुझ पर आरोप लगा रहे हैं? *5.* मैं आप पर आरोप नहीं लगा रहा हूं. ● *1.* I'm not accusing you of anything. *2.* Are you accusing me of something? *3.* What are you accusing me of? *4.* Are you accusing me? *5.* I'm not accusing you.

## 197. आकर्षित — *attract* — This verb is used to describe

the action of drawing someone or something towards oneself, either physically or metaphorically. It signifies the ability to captivate or entice someone's attention or interest.

● *1.* क्या तुम मेरे तरफ आकर्षित हो? *2.* क्या आप उससे आकर्षित हैं? *3.* क्या आप उसकी ओर आकर्षित हैं? *4.* कंपनी की प्रोफ़ाइल ने ध्यान आकर्षित किया. *5.* रैगर ने एक बड़ी भीड़ को आकर्षित किया। ● *1.* Are you attracted to me? *2.* Are you attracted to him? *3.* Are you attracted to her? *4.* The company's profile attracted attention. *5.* The rager attracted a large crowd.

## 198. जब्त — *seize* — The verb 'जब्त' is used to describe the

action of taking possession of something forcefully or legally. It implies the act of seizing or confiscating something, often done by authorities or individuals in power.

● *1.* उन्हें जब्त करें! *2.* वह जब्त कर रहा है. *3.* वह जब्त कर रही है. *4.* को जब्त। *5.* पुलिस ने मारिजुआना की एक खेप जब्त कर ली। ● *1.* Seize them! *2.* He's seizing. *3.* She's seizing. *4.* Seize it. *5.* The police seized a shipment of marijuana.

**199.** *त्यागपत्र देना* — *resign* — This verb is used when someone voluntarily leaves their job or position, typically due to personal reasons or dissatisfaction with their current situation. It signifies the act of formally giving up one's responsibilities and stepping down from a role.

**200.** **प्रोत्साहित करना** — *encourage, stimulate* — This verb is used to inspire or motivate someone to take action or pursue a goal. It is used to boost someone's confidence or enthusiasm in order to help them achieve success or overcome obstacles.

- *1.* उसे प्रोत्साहित मत करो. *2.* उन्हें प्रोत्साहित न करें. *3.* माँ ने अपने बच्चे को दूध पीने के लिए प्रोत्साहित किया। *4.* कक्षा में सक्रिय भागीदारी को प्रोत्साह-ित करें. *5.* उन्होंने इसे प्रोत्साहित किया. *6.* शिक्षक ने चर्चा को प्रोत्साहित करने का प्रयास किया। *7.* पुस्तक का उद्देश्य रचनात्मकता को प्रोत्साहित करना है। •
*1.* Don't encourage him. *2.* Don't encourage them. *3.* The mother encouraged her baby to suckle. *4.* Encourage active participation in the class. *5.* He encouraged it. *6.* The teacher tried to stimulate discussion. *7.* The book aims to stimulate creativity.

**201.** **लौटाना** — *restore* — The verb 'लौटाना' is used to describe the action of bringing something back to its original state or condition. It is commonly used to indicate the act of restoring something to its former state.

**202.** **सहना** — *endure, tolerate* — This verb is used to describe the act of bearing or enduring something difficult or unpleasant without complaining. It implies a sense of patience and resilience in the face of adversity.

- *1.* उसे एक नारकीय अनुभव सहना पड़ा। *2.* उसे दर्द सहना पड़ा. *3.* उसे दर्द सहना पड़ा. • *1.* She endured a hellish experience. *2.* She had to endure the pain. *3.* She had to tolerate the pain.

**203.** **पूजा करना** — *adore* — The verb 'पूजा करना' is used to express deep admiration and reverence towards someone or something. It signifies a strong sense of devotion and respect, often associated with religious or spiritual practices.

**204. अपडेट करें** — *update* — The verb 'अपडेट करें' is used to describe the action of making changes or additions to something in order to bring it up to date or to provide the most recent information.

**205. सामना** — *cope, withstand* — This verb is used to describe the act of dealing with or facing a difficult situation or challenge with strength and resilience. It implies the ability to endure and overcome obstacles or adversity.
- *1.* आप कैसे सामना करते हैं? *2.* मैं सामना कर सकता हूँ. *3.* अविनाशी इमारत ने तूफान का सामना किया। *4.* मस्तूल को भारी तूफानों का सामना करने के लिए बनाया गया था। *5.* टिका-ऊ कपड़ा तूफ़ान का सामना कर गया। • *1.* How do you cope? *2.* I can cope. *3.* The indestructible building withstood the storm. *4.* The mast was built to withstand heavy storms. *5.* The durable fabric withstood the storm.

**206. निवेदन करना** — *plead* — The verb 'निवेदन करना' is used to express the act of pleading or making a request in a formal or earnest manner. It conveys a sense of urgency or desperation in asking for something.
- *1.* आप कैसे निवेदन करते हैं? • *1.* How do you plead?

**207. विभाजित करना** — *divide* — This verb is used to describe the action of separating something into smaller parts or sections. It is commonly used when talking about dividing objects, groups, or tasks into smaller, more manageable portions.
- *1.* क्षेत्र को अलग-अलग क्षेत्रों में विभाजित किया गया था। *2.* सेप्टम ने नाक गुहा को विभाजित किया। *3.* इस विवाद ने जनता की राय को विभाजित कर दिया। *4.* शब्द को शब्दांशों में विभाजित करें। *5.* विवादास्पद मुद्दे ने समूह को विभाजित कर दिया। • *1.* The territory was divided into separate regions. *2.* The septum divided the nasal cavity. *3.* The controversy divided public opinion. *4.* Divide the word into syllables. *5.* The contentious issue divided the group.

**208. तामील करना** — *execute* — 'Taamil karna' is used to describe the action of carrying out a plan, task, or order. It signifies the act of putting something into effect or completing a task as intended.

**209. मिटाना** — *erase* — 'Mitana' is used to describe the action of removing or wiping out something completely. It is often used in the context of erasing pencil marks, deleting digital files, or eliminating memories.
- *1.* संदेश मिटा दिया गया. *2.* इसे मिटाएं। *3.* उसे मिटा दो. *4.* इसे मिटा दिया गया है. *5.* यह सब मिटा दिया गया है. • *1.* Message erased. *2.* Erase it. *3.* Erase that. *4.* It's been erased. *5.* It's all been erased.

**210. मैथुन करना** — *bugger, copulate* — The verb 'मैथुन करना' is used to describe the act of engaging in sexual intercourse. It is a common term used in informal conversations and literature to refer to the physical act of copulation.

**211. विचलित करना** — *distract* — This verb is used to describe the action of diverting someone's attention or focus away from something, causing them to lose concentration or become confused.
- *1.* आप विचलित लग रहे हैं. *2.* मैं विचलित हो गया था। *3.* आप थोड़े विचलित लग रहे हैं. *4.* आप विचलित हैं. *5.* मुझे विचलित मत करो. • *1.* You seem distracted. *2.* I was distracted. *3.* You seem a little distracted. *4.* You're distracted. *5.* Don't distract me.

**212. समायोजन करना** — *adjust, coordinate* — This verb is used to describe the action of making arrangements or coordinating different elements to ensure they work together smoothly and effectively. It involves adjusting and organizing things in a harmonious manner.
- *1.* समायोजन पाठ्यक्रम. • *1.* Adjusting course.

**213. हिस्सा लेना** — *participate* — This verb is used to indicate involvement in an activity, event, or discussion. It sig-

nifies taking part in something or being included in a particular group or situation.
- *1.* उन्होंने सांस्कृतिक महोत्सव में हिस्सा लिया. • *1.* He participated in the cultural festival.

## 214. अपनाना — *adopt, assimilate, siphon* — The verb 'अपनाना' is used to describe the act of taking in or making something one's own, whether it be a new idea, a cultural practice, or a way of thinking. It can also mean to absorb or incorporate something.
- *1.* हम अपनाएंगे. *2.* कंपनी की योजना नई तकनीक अपनाने की है. *3.* उन्होंने उत्सुकता से इस सनक को अपनाया। *4.* उसने आश्रय स्थल से टैलबोट मिश्रण अपनाया। *5.* अपनाएं, अपनाएं और सुधारें।
- *1.* We'll adopt. *2.* The company plans to adopt new technology. *3.* He eagerly adopted the fad. *4.* She adopted a talbot mix from the shelter. *5.* Adopt, adapt and improve.

## 215. चिढ़ाना — *tease, ruffle, rile* — This verb is used to describe the act of playfully provoking or annoying someone in order to get a reaction out of them. It involves teasing or riling someone up in a light-hearted or mischievous manner.
- *1.* क्या तुम मुझे चिढ़ा रहे हो? *2.* मैं सिर्फ तुम्हें चिढ़ा रहा हूं। *3.* मैं सिर्फ चिढ़ा रहा हूँ। *4.* मैं चिढ़ा रहा हूँ। *5.* चिढ़ाओ मत. • *1.* Are you teasing me? *2.* I'm just teasing you. *3.* I'm just teasing. *4.* I'm teasing. *5.* Don't tease.

## 216. बदला लेना — *avenge, retaliate* — This verb is used to describe the act of seeking revenge or retaliation for a perceived wrong or injustice. It implies taking action to settle a score or seek retribution for a past harm.

## 217. मनोरंजन करना — *entertain, amuse* — This verb is used to describe the act of providing enjoyment or amusement to oneself or others through various forms of entertainment such as watching movies, listening to music, playing games, or attending events.
- *1.* मेरा मनोरंजन करें। *2.* मधुर हास्य ने दर्शकों का मनोरंजन किया। *3.* कुकआउट ने मेहमानों का मनोरंजन किया। *4.* बर्लेस्क ने दर्शकों का मनोरंजन किया। *5.* विदूषक ने मूर्खतापूर्ण हरकतों से भीड़ का मनोरंजन किया। *6.* मैं तुम्हारा मनोरंजन करता

हूँ? *7.* इससे आपका मनोरंजन होता है? *8.* यह मेरा मनोरंजन करता है. *9.* क्या मैं आपका मनोरंजन करता हूँ? *10.* मेरा मनोरंजन करो। • *1.* Entertain me. *2.* The cordy humor entertained the audience. *3.* The cookout entertained the guests. *4.* The burlesque entertained the audience. *5.* The buffoon entertained the crowd with silly antics. *6.* I amuse you? *7.* That amuses you? *8.* It amuses me. *9.* Do I amuse you? *10.* Amuse me.

**218. खोल देना** — *untie, unzip, deploy, unleash* — This verb is used to describe the action of releasing or opening something that was previously closed or tied up. It can refer to untying a knot, unzipping a zipper, deploying a mechanism, or unleashing a force.

**219. परामर्श करना** — *consult* — The verb 'परामर्श करना' is used to indicate seeking advice or guidance from someone with expertise or knowledge in a particular subject. It implies a process of discussing and considering different perspectives before making a decision.
• *1.* मुझे परामर्श की आवश्यकता है. *2.* उसने ओयाबुन से परामर्श कि-या। *3.* उसने यात्रा युक्तियों के लिए गाइडबुक से परामर्श लिया। *4.* मार्गदर्शन के लिए कुंडली का परामर्श लिया गया. *5.* मेरे पास एक परामर्श है. • *1.* I need a consult. *2.* She consulted with the oyabun. *3.* She consulted the guidebook for travel tips. *4.* The horoscope was consulted for guidance. *5.* I have a consult.

**220. छोड़कर अन्यत्र जाना** — *evacuate* — This verb is used to describe the action of leaving a place quickly and urgently, typically due to a dangerous or emergency situation. It conveys the idea of evacuating to a safer location.

**221. आरोपित करना** — *transplant* — The verb 'आरोपित करना' is used to describe the action of moving something from one place to another, typically referring to the process of transplanting something, such as organs, plants, or hair.

**222. अनुवाद करना** — *translate* — This verb is used to convey the action of converting text or speech from one language to another, ensuring that the meaning and context remain intact. It involves interpreting and transferring information accurately to facilitate communication between different linguistic groups.

• *1.* क्या आप इसका अनुवाद कर सकते हैं? *2.* क्या तुम अनुवाद कर सकते हो? *3.* मैं अनुवाद करूंगा. *4.* मैं अनुवाद कर सकता हूं। *5.* इसका अनुवाद करें। • *1.* Can you translate it? *2.* Can you translate? *3.* I'll translate. *4.* I can translate. *5.* Translate it.

## 223. सूचित करें — *notify* — This verb is used to inform or alert someone about something. It is used to give a notification or update to someone regarding a particular situation, event, or piece of information.

## 224. प्रकाशित करना — *publish, proclaim* — This verb is used to describe the action of making information or content available to the public through various mediums such as books, newspapers, websites, or social media platforms.

• *1.* अद्वितीय लेखक ने एक नई पुस्तक प्रकाशित की। *2.* सिद्धांतकार ने अभूतपूर्व कार्य प्रकाशित किया। *3.* पत्रिका त्रैमासिक प्रकाशित होती थी। *4.* प्रोफेसर ने अर्थशास्त्र पर एक ग्रंथ प्रकाशित किया। *5.* उन्होंने अपनी आत्मकथा प्रकाशित की। • *1.* The inimitable author published a new book. *2.* The theorist published groundbreaking work. *3.* The magazine was published quarterly. *4.* The professor published a treatise on economics. *5.* He published his autobiography.

## 225. अपमान करना — *offend, desecrate* — The verb 'अपमान करना' is used to describe the act of disrespecting or dishonoring someone or something. It signifies a deliberate action that undermines the dignity or value of a person, belief, or object.

## 226. सेंकना — *bake* — The verb 'सेंकना' is used to describe the action of baking food items in an oven or over an open flame. It involves cooking the ingredients at a high temperature until they are fully cooked and ready to eat.

## 227. यात्रा करना — *hike, hitchhike* — 'यात्रा करना' is used to describe the act of traveling on foot or by hitchhiking. It implies a sense of adventure and exploration, often involving long

distances and unfamiliar places.
- *1.* पदयात्रा के दौरान वह लियान पर फिसल गई। *2.* उन्होंने पदय-
ात्रा के लिए टोपो मानचित्र का उपयोग किया। *3.* उन्होंने
जंगली स्लेड के माध्यम से पदयात्रा की। *4.* उसने सिएरा पर्वत
के माध्यम से पदयात्रा की। *5.* हमने एक मील तक पदयात्रा की।
- *1.* She tripped on a liane while hiking. *2.* She used the topo
map for hiking. *3.* They hiked through the wooded slade. *4.* She
hiked through the Sierra Mountains. *5.* We hiked for a mile.

## 228. अपराधी घोषित करना — *convict* — The
verb 'अपराधी घोषित करना' is used to describe the action of officially
declaring someone guilty of a crime by a court of law. It signifies
the legal process of convicting an individual for their wrongdoing.
- *1.* आप एक सजायाफ्ता अपराधी हैं. *2.* सेनानियों को हिंसक
अपराधी ठहराया जाता है। *3.* वह अपराधी को दोषी ठहराने क-
े लिए कृतसंकल्प है। • *1.* You're a convicted felon. *2.* Fighters
are convicted violent felons. *3.* She's determined to convict the
criminal.

## 229. स्टीयर — *steer* — The verb 'स्टीयर' is used to describe
the action of controlling the direction of a vehicle or vessel by
turning its steering mechanism. It is commonly used in the context of driving cars, boats, and other modes of transportation.
- *1.* स्टीयरिंग व्हील पर हाथ! *2.* उसने स्टीयरिंग व्हील पकड़
लिया। • *1.* Hands on the steering wheel! *2.* He clutched the
steering wheel.

## 230. उच्चारण करना — *pronounce* — To use the verb
'उच्चारण करना', one must articulate words or sounds clearly and accurately. It involves speaking or enunciating words in a specific
manner to ensure proper communication and understanding.
- *1.* क्या मैं इसका सही उच्चारण कर रहा हूँ? *2.* प्रत्येक
अक्षर का स्पष्ट उच्चारण करें। *3.* उसने इसका उच्चारण <span
class="foreignText">'जो' और 'झोउ' की तरह किया। *4.* आप इस
शब्द का उच्चारण कैसे करते हैं? *5.* उन्हें नाम का उच्च-
ारण करने में संघर्ष करना पड़ा। • *1.* Am I pronouncing that right?
*2.* Pronounce every syllable clearly. *3.* She pronounced it like
'Joe' and 'Zhou'. *4.* How do you pronounce this word? *5.* He
struggled to pronounce the name.

**231. एक होना** — *unite* — The verb 'एक होना' is used to convey the idea of coming together or uniting as one. It signifies the act of joining or merging to form a single entity or group.

**232. प्रदर्शन करना** — *demonstrate* — The verb 'प्रदर्शन करना' is used to show or display something in order to explain or prove a point. It is commonly used in educational settings, presentations, and performances to showcase skills or knowledge.

• 1. स्किनर ने शिल्प की तकनीकों का प्रदर्शन किया। 2. उन्होंने कार्य में दक्षता का प्रदर्शन किया। 3. प्रशिक्षक ने तकनीक का प्रदर्शन किया। 4. उन्होंने खेल कौशल का प्रदर्शन किया. 5. उन्होंने बहुमुखी प्रतिभा का प्रदर्शन किया। •
1. The skinner demonstrated the techniques of the craft. 2. He demonstrated competence in the task. 3. The instructor demonstrated the technique. 4. She demonstrated sportsmanship. 5. She demonstrated versatility.

**233. मलना** — *scrub* — The verb 'मलना' is used to describe the action of scrubbing or rubbing something vigorously to clean or remove dirt or stains. It is commonly used when cleaning surfaces, clothes, or utensils.

**234. आविष्कार करना** — *invent* — This verb is used to describe the action of creating or discovering something new that has never existed before. It is often used in the context of scientific or technological advancements.

• 1. इसलिए मैंने एक श्रेष्ठ का आविष्कार किया। 2. मैंने इसका आविष्कार किया. 3. आपने इसका आविष्कार किया. 4. प्रोफेसर, प्रोफेसर, आज आप क्या आविष्कार करेंगे? 5. मैंने इसका आविष्कार नहीं किया. • 1. So I invented a superior. 2. I invented it. 3. You invented it. 4. Professor, Professor, what'll you invent today? 5. I didn't invent it.

**235. बहुत मूल्यवान समझना** — *underestimate* — To 'बहुत मूल्यवान समझना' means to not fully appreciate or recognize the true value or importance of something or someone. It implies a lack of understanding or acknowledgment of the significance of a particular thing.

## 236. प्रतिबिंबित करना — *reflect* — This verb is used
to describe the action of showing an image or likeness of something, typically in a mirror or other reflective surface. It can also
refer to the act of thinking deeply or carefully about something.
● *1.* अरें ने सूर्य के प्रकाश को प्रतिबिंबित किया। *2.* भव्य
उपस्थिति उसके व्यक्तित्व को प्रतिबिंबित नहीं करती। *3.* टि-
नफ़ोइल ने प्रकाश को प्रतिबिंबित किया। *4.* शतरंज की बिसात
ने प्रकाश को प्रतिबिंबित किया। *5.* कांच की सतह सूर्य के प्रका-
श को प्रतिबिंबित करती थी। ● *1.* The arr reflected the sunlight.
*2.* The dowdy appearance did not reflect her personality. *3.* The
tinfoil reflected the light. *4.* The chessboard reflected the light.
*5.* The glassy surface reflected the sunlight.

## 237. तिरस्कार करना — *despise, detest* — This verb
is used to express a strong feeling of dislike or contempt towards
someone or something. It conveys a sense of intense aversion
or disdain towards the object of the verb.
● *1.* तुम मेरा तिरस्कार करते हो। *2.* क्या तुम मेरा तिरस्कार
करते हो? *3.* मैं उसका तिरस्कार करता हूं। *4.* उसने उसकी कायरता
का तिरस्कार किया। *5.* तुम मेरा तिरस्कार क्यों करते हो? ● *1.*
You despise me. *2.* Do you despise me? *3.* I despise her. *4.*
She despised his cowardice. *5.* Why do you despise me?

## 238. वेग से उछालना — *flirt* — The verb 'वेग से उछालना'
is used to describe the act of playfully engaging in romantic or
sexual behavior with someone, often with the intention of showing interest or attraction.

## 239. पुनः प्राप्त — *retrieve* — The verb 'पुनः प्राप्त' is used
to indicate the action of retrieving something that was lost or
misplaced. It conveys the idea of finding and bringing back an
object or information to its original place.
● *1.* इसे पुनः प्राप्त करें। ● *1.* Retrieve it.

## 240. खिलना — *blossom* — The verb 'खिलना' is used to
describe the process of a flower opening up and blooming. It can
also be used metaphorically to describe someone or something
flourishing or reaching their full potential.

**241. जबह् करना** — *lam* — 'जबह् करना' is used to describe the act of coating or covering something with a thin layer of a substance, such as paint or polish. It is a verb that signifies the action of applying a smooth and even layer.

**242. झांसना** — *seduce* — To seduce someone by using charm, flattery, or other tactics to persuade them into engaging in romantic or sexual activities.

**243. सीना** — *sew* — The verb 'सीना' is used to describe the action of joining fabrics together using a needle and thread. It is commonly used in the context of creating or repairing clothing, accessories, or other fabric items.

**244. पुनर्विचार करना** — *reconsider* — This verb is used to describe the action of thinking about something again, especially in order to make a different decision or to take a different course of action.
- *1.* कृपया पुनर्विचार करें. *2.* मैंने पुनर्विचार किया है. *3.* क्या आपने पुनर्विचार किया है? *4.* मुझे लगता है आपको पुनर्विचार करना चाहिए. *5.* क्या आप पुनर्विचार करेंगे? ● *1.* Please reconsider. *2.* I've reconsidered. *3.* Have you reconsidered? *4.* I think you should reconsider. *5.* Will you reconsider?

**245. दान करना** — *donate* — This verb is used to describe the act of giving something, typically money or goods, to a person or organization in need or for a charitable cause. It signifies a voluntary and selfless act of generosity.

**246. अभ्यास करना** — *rehearse* — The verb 'अभ्यास करना' is used to describe the action of practicing or rehearsing something repeatedly in order to improve one's skills or performance. It is commonly used in the context of music, dance, sports, or any other skill-based activity.

**247. फिर से बनाना** — *rebuild, reconstruct, realign* — This verb is used to describe the action of rebuilding or rearranging something that has been previously constructed or organized. It implies the process of restoring or restructuring something to its original form or a new configuration.

## 248. धोखा देना — *deceive, mislead, circumvent* — This verb is used to describe the act of betraying someone's trust, leading them to believe something false, or tricking them into a situation that is not in their best interest.

## 249. हल्का करना — *lighten* — 'Halka karna' is used to describe the action of making something lighter in weight, intensity, or seriousness. It is often used to indicate reducing the burden or impact of something.

## 250. सत्यापित करें — *verify, validate* — This verb is used to confirm the accuracy or truth of something by checking and confirming its validity or authenticity. It is commonly used in various contexts such as verifying information, validating documents, or confirming details.
• *1.* क्या कोई इसे सत्यापित कर सकता है? *2.* मैं इसे सत्यापित कर सकता हूं. *3.* रेटिनल स्कैन सत्यापित. *4.* क्या आप इसे सत्यापित कर सकते हैं? *5.* सत्यापित करने में असमर्थ. • *1.* Can anyone verify that? *2.* I can verify that. *3.* Retinal scan verified. *4.* Can you verify that? *5.* Unable to verify.

## 251. बाहर निकलने देना — *vent* — This verb is used to describe the act of allowing something to escape or be released from a confined space, typically to relieve pressure or emotion. It can also refer to expressing thoughts or feelings openly.

## 252. को बढ़ावा देना — *promote* — This verb is used to indicate the action of advancing someone to a higher position or level, typically in a professional or academic setting. It signifies the act of encouraging growth or progress in someone's career or status.
• *1.* वे ओमेगा-9 फैटी एसिड के लाभों को बढ़ावा देते हैं। *2.* समजवाद समानता को बढ़ावा देता है। *3.* मानवतावाद आंदोलन ने समानता को बढ़ावा दिया। *4.* उन्होंने सभी आवाज़ों के समावेश को बढ़ावा दिया। *5.* महासंघ ने शांति को बढ़ावा देने के लिए काम किया। • *1.* They promote the benefits of omega-9

fatty acids. *2.* Socialism promotes equality. *3.* The humanism movement promoted equality. *4.* She promoted the inclusion of all voices. *5.* The federation worked to promote peace.

**253. फोर्ज** — *forge* — 'फोर्ज' is used to describe the act of creating or shaping something through intense heat and pressure. It is commonly used in the context of metalworking, where metal is heated and hammered into a desired shape.

**254. सूंघना** — *sniff* — The verb 'सूंघना' is used to describe the action of inhaling or smelling something through the nose. It is commonly used to indicate the act of sniffing to detect a scent or odor.

• *1.* सूंघ लो. *2.* तुम इसे सूंघ लो. *3.* इसे सूंघो. • *1.* Take a sniff. *2.* You sniff it. *3.* Sniff this.

**255. संजोना** — *cherish, embellish* — The verb 'संजोना' is used to express the act of cherishing or embellishing something, such as memories, relationships, or possessions. It conveys the idea of valuing and beautifying something with care and affection.

• *1.* प्यार करना और संजोना। *2.* कृतज्ञतापूर्वक प्राप्त उपहार को संजोकर रखा गया। *3.* वह अपनी स्क्रैपबुक को संजो कर रखती थी। *4.* वह अपनी स्वायत्तता को संजोती थी। *5.* उन्होंने स्मृति को संजोया। • *1.* To love and to cherish. *2.* The gratefully received gift was cherished. *3.* She cherished her scrapbook. *4.* She cherished her autonomy. *5.* He cherished the memory.

**256. विनीत करना** — *humiliate* — The verb 'विनीत करना' is used to describe the action of causing someone to feel ashamed or embarrassed by belittling or degrading them in front of others.

**257. अनुकूल बनाना** — *adapt, accommodate* — To make something suitable or adjust to a new situation or environment.

• *1.* हम अनुकूलन करेंगे. *2.* अप्रवासी को अनुकूलन के लिए संघर्ष करना पड़ा. *3.* वे अनुकूलन कर रहे हैं. *4.* मैंने अनुकूलित किया. *5.* उन्होंने अनुकूलन कर लिया है. • *1.* We will adapt.

*2.* The immigrant struggled to adapt. *3.* They're adapting. *4.* I adapted. *5.* They've adapted.

**258. सफ़ाई से बरताना** — *manipulate* — This verb is used to describe the act of handling or managing something in a way that is deceptive or dishonest, often for personal gain or to achieve a specific outcome.

**259. उठना** — *arise* — 'उठना' is used to describe the action of getting up or rising from a sitting or lying position. It can also be used to indicate the beginning or occurrence of something, such as the sun rising in the morning.

**260. पछताना** — *rue, repent* — This verb is used to express regret or remorse for something that has been done in the past. It conveys a sense of feeling sorry or wishing that a different choice had been made.

**261. प्रेरित करना** — *inspire* — This verb is used to describe the action of motivating or encouraging someone to do something positive or creative. It is often used in the context of providing inspiration or encouragement to others.

**262. पेट गिरना** — *abort* — The verb 'पेट गिरना' is used to describe the act of terminating a pregnancy before the fetus can survive outside the uterus. It is a medical procedure that is often a sensitive and controversial topic.

**263. घूमना** — *roam, circulate, revolve* — 'घूमना' is used to describe the action of moving around aimlessly or in a circular motion. It can refer to wandering, roaming, or spinning around.
● *1.* उन्होंने ग्रामीण इलाकों में घूमना चुना। *2.* उसे शहर की सड़कों पर घूमना पसंद था। *3.* कुत्ते को खेतों में घूमना बहुत पसंद था। ● *1.* They chose to roam the countryside. *2.* She liked to roam the city streets. *3.* The dog loved to roam the fields.

**264. उतारना** — *unload, subvert* — 'उतारना' is used to describe the action of removing or taking off something, such as unloading cargo from a truck or subverting a system or authority. It signifies the act of getting rid of a burden or overturning a situation.

• *1.* वह सामान उतारने के लिए उठा नहीं सकती। *2.* कार से किर-
ाने का सामान उतारो। *3.* उसे उतारने के लिए मदद की ज़रूरत
थी। *4.* ट्रक को जल्दी से उतारो! *5.* बक्सों को सावधानी से
उतारें। • *1.* She can't lift to unload. *2.* Unload the groceries
from the car. *3.* He needed help to unload. *4.* Unload the truck
quickly! *5.* Unload the boxes carefully.

## 265. ढालना — *mold, mould* — The verb 'ढालना' is used
to describe the action of shaping or forming something into a
specific shape or structure, typically using a mould or similar
tool. It is commonly used in the context of creating objects out
of clay or other materials.

## 266. स्थगित करना — *postpone* — This verb is used to
describe the action of delaying or rescheduling something to a
later time or date. It is commonly used when referring to events,
meetings, or tasks that have been pushed back or put off.

• *1.* पार्टी अनिश्चित काल के लिए स्थगित कर दी जाएगी। *2.* बैठक
अनिश्चित काल के लिए स्थगित कर दी गई। *3.* संकाय ने बैठक स्थग-
ित करने का निर्णय लिया। *4.* शादी स्थगित करें? • *1.* The party
will be postponed indefinitely. *2.* The meeting was postponed
indefinitely. *3.* The faculty decided to postpone the meeting. *4.*
Postpone the wedding?

## 267. पहुंच जाना — *regain* — The verb 'पहुंच जाना' is
used to indicate the action of regaining something that was lost
or taken away. It signifies the process of recovering or getting
back possession of something that was previously owned.

## 268. अंशदान करना — *contribute* — This verb is used
to describe the action of giving or donating something, typically
money or resources, to support a cause or help someone in
need. It signifies a voluntary act of contributing towards a
greater good.

## 269. नियुक्त करना — *employ, appoint, nominate* —
This verb is used to describe the action of hiring or appointing
someone to a position or role. It signifies the act of selecting

and assigning someone to a specific job or duty.
• *1.* खेत ने एक कुशल चरवाहे को नियुक्त किया। *2.* राजा न-
े उसे शाही बैनरमैन के रूप में नियुक्त किया। *3.* वे एक नया ने-
ता नियुक्त करते हैं। *4.* मैं तुम्हें मैनेजर नियुक्त कर दूंगा।
*5.* उन्हें प्रोवोस्ट नियुक्त किया गया था. *6.* उन्ह-
े एतद्द्वारा प्रबंधक नियुक्त किया गया है। • *1.* The ranch
employed a skilled cowgirl. *2.* The king appointed him as the
royal bannerman. *3.* They appoint a new leader. *4.* I'll appoint
you as manager. *5.* She was appointed provost. *6.* He is hereby
appointed manager.

### 270. आक्रमण करना — *invade* — This verb is used
to describe the act of forcefully entering and taking control of
a place or territory. It implies aggression and often involves at-
tacking or overpowering the existing inhabitants or defenses.
• *1.* बर्बर भीड़ ने आक्रमण किया। • *1.* Barbarian hordes
invaded.

### 271. अलसाना — *slug* — To 'slug' means to move slowly
and lazily, lacking energy or motivation. It can also refer to being
sluggish or inactive.

### 272. एकत्र करना — *assemble* — This verb is used to
describe the action of bringing together or gathering people or
things in one place. It signifies the act of assembling or collecting
items or individuals in a specific location or group.

### 273. मिथ्या जानना — *misunderstand* — 'Mithya janna'
is used to describe when someone has a false or incorrect understanding of something. It signifies a misunderstanding or misin-
terpretation of information or a situation.

### 274. नष्ट हो जाना — *perish* — This verb is used to
describe something being destroyed or lost completely, often in
a sudden or irreversible manner. It conveys a sense of finality
and irreparable damage.

### 275. मुंहतोड़ प्रहार मारना — *swat* — This verb
is used to describe the action of hitting or striking something or
someone with force using one's hand or an object. It is often

used to describe a quick and forceful action to get rid of pests or insects.

## 276. तराशना — *trim, pare* — 'Tarashna' is used to describe the action of cutting or trimming something to make it smaller or more refined. It is often used in the context of grooming, shaping, or refining objects or materials.

## 277. विश्लेषण — *analyze, analyse* — This verb is used to describe the process of examining something in detail in order to understand its components, structure, and function. It involves breaking down information and drawing conclusions based on the analysis.

- *1.* वैज्ञानिक ने नमूने का विश्लेषण किया। *2.* समाजशास्त्री ने सामाजिक प्रवृत्तियों का विश्लेषण किया। *3.* उन्होंने स्थितिि की जटिलता का विश्लेषण किया। *4.* उन्होंने प्रक्षेपण डेटा का विश्लेषण किया। *5.* वीर्य के नमूने का विश्लेषण किया गया।
- *1.* The scientist analyzed the specimen. *2.* The sociologist analyzed social trends. *3.* They analyzed the complexity of the situation. *4.* They analyzed the projection data. *5.* The semen sample was analyzed.

## 278. डांटना — *scold, chide* — The verb 'डांटना' is used to express the act of scolding or chiding someone for their actions or behavior. It conveys a sense of reprimand or admonishment towards the person being addressed.

- *1.* उसने ब्लैकगार्ड को डांटा। *2.* उसने गलती के लिए खुद को डांटा। *3.* डांटने के बाद बच्चा नाराज हो गया था. *4.* उनकी बचकानी शरारत के लिए उन्हें डांट पड़ी थी. *5.* वह अपनी सहेली को डांटना नहीं चाहती थी. • *1.* She scolded the blackguard. *2.* He scolded himself for the mistake. *3.* The child had a sulk after being scolded. *4.* He was scolded for his childish prank. *5.* She didn't want to scold her friend.

## 279. खड़ा होना — *oppose* — This verb is used to express resistance or disagreement with something or someone. It signifies standing against a particular idea, action, or person. It conveys a sense of defiance or opposition.

**280. मिलाना** — *combine, wed, unite, harmonize* — 'Milana' is used to describe the act of bringing together or joining different entities to create unity, harmony, or affiliation. It signifies the process of uniting or connecting things or people in a cohesive manner.

**281. शोक करना** — *mourn, grieve* — This verb is used to express deep sadness and sorrow over the loss of someone or something. It is commonly used to describe the act of grieving or mourning for a loved one or a tragic event.

**282. झुंझुला देना** — *annoy* — This verb is used to describe the action of causing irritation or frustration to someone. It signifies the act of bothering or pestering someone to the point of annoyance.

**283. पांव रखना** — *tread* — This verb is used to describe the action of stepping or walking on something, typically with the feet. It conveys the idea of placing one's foot down in a deliberate manner.

**284. शोषण करना** — *exploit* — The verb 'शोषण करना' is used to describe the act of taking advantage of someone or something for personal gain. It implies using someone or something unfairly or selfishly for one's own benefit.

**285. अवहेलना करना** — *defy* — To go against or refuse to obey a rule, authority, or expectation.
• *1.* यह समझ की अवहेलना करता है। 2. हम शुभ संकेत की - अवहेलना करते हैं। 3. मैं आपकी अवहेलना करता हूँ! 4. तुम्हारी हिम्मत कैसे हुई मेरी अवहेलना करने की! 5. मेरी अवहेलना मत करो! • *1.* It defies understanding. *2.* We defy augury. *3.* I defy you! *4.* How dare you defy me! *5.* Do not defy me!

**286. सुनाना** — *recite, pronounce* — The verb 'सुनाना' is used to convey the action of reciting or narrating something aloud. It is commonly used when someone is sharing a story, poem, or information with others by speaking it out loud.

• 1. उन्होंने समारोह में एक हाइकु सुनाया। 2. उन्होंने एक श्लोक सुनाया। 3. उसने पाई को 50 दशमलव स्थानों तक सुनाया। 4. उन्होंने एक लिमरिक सुनाया जिसने सभी को हंसने पर मजबूर कर दिया। 5. उन्होंने ढेर सारी शिकायतें सुनाईं. • 1. They recited a haiku at the ceremony. 2. She recited a verse. 3. She recited pi to 50 decimal places. 4. He recited a limerick that made everyone laugh. 5. She recited a litany of complaints.

## 287. ध्यान केन्द्रित करना — *dwell* — This verb is used to describe the act of focusing or concentrating on something, often for an extended period of time. It implies a deep level of attention and mindfulness towards a particular subject or task.

## 288. कब्ज़ा — *occupy* — 'कब्ज़ा' is used to describe the action of taking control or possession of something. It signifies the act of occupying a space, territory, or property.

• 1. इस पर कब्ज़ा है। 2. उसने ऊपरी बेर पर कब्ज़ा कर लिय- ा। 3. सैनिक शहर पर कब्ज़ा कर लेंगे। 4. उसने कब्ज़ा कर लिया है. 5. प्रदर्शनकारी सरकारी इमारत पर कब्ज़ा कर लेंगे. • 1. It's occupied. 2. She occupied the upper ber. 3. The soldiers will occupy the city. 4. He's occupied. 5. The protesters will occupy the government building.

## 289. अतिरंजना करना — *exaggerate* — This verb is used to describe the act of making something seem larger, more important, or more extreme than it actually is. It involves overstating or embellishing the truth for dramatic effect.

## 290. समर्पित करना — *dedicate* — This verb is used to convey the act of giving something, such as time, effort, or resources, to a cause, person, or deity with a sense of commitment and devotion.

• 1. मैं समर्पित हूं. 2. उन्होंने यह गाना मरे को समर्पित किया। 3. वह खुद को इस परियोजना के लिए समर्पित कर देंगे।' 4. उन्होंने घंटों रियाज को समर्पित किया। 5. उन्होंने अपना जीवन वंचितों की मदद के लिए समर्पित कर दिया • 1. I'm dedicated. 2. He dedicated the song to Murray. 3. He will dedicate himself to the project. 4. He dedicated hours to riyaz. 5. He dedicated his life to helping the underprivileged.

**291. चुप बनाना** — *shush* — To make someone quiet or silent by telling them to stop talking or making noise.

**292. काम करना** — *retard* — The verb 'काम करना' is used to describe the action of slowing down or hindering progress. It can be used to indicate a delay or obstruction in a process or activity.

**293. चोंच मारना** — *peck* — This verb is used to describe the action of a bird using its beak to quickly and lightly strike something, such as when a bird pecks at food or pecks at another bird in a playful or aggressive manner.

**294. आरंभ करना** — *initiate, undertake* — This verb is used to describe the action of starting or beginning something, such as a project, task, or process. It signifies taking the first step towards a goal or objective.

**295. कड़ी आलोचना करना** — *slash* — This verb is used to describe the act of harshly criticizing or condemning someone or something. It implies a strong and severe judgment or disapproval towards a particular person, idea, or action.

**296. भिगोना** — *soak, dabble* — The verb 'भिगोना' is used to describe the action of soaking something in a liquid or dabbling in water. It implies the process of making something wet or partially submerged in a liquid.
• *1.* गीला भिगोना। *2.* बहती हुई चटनी पास्ता में भिगो दी गई। *3.* चिकन को रात भर मैरिनेड में भिगो दें। *4.* उसने जैतून को नमकीन पानी में भिगोया। • *1.* Soaking wet. *2.* The runny sauce soaked into the pasta. *3.* The chicken soaked in marinade overnight. *4.* He soaked the olives in brine.

**297. पैदा करना** — *generate, pique, procreate* — This verb is used to describe the action of creating, producing, or giving rise to something. It can also refer to the act of sparking interest or curiosity in someone, as well as the biological process of reproduction.

**298. थोपना** — *impose, inflict* — The verb 'थोपना' is used to describe the action of forcing something onto someone or something, often in a deceitful or unfair manner. It implies the act of imposing something without consent or approval.

• *1.* मैं थोपना नहीं चाहता. *2.* मैं थोपना नहीं चाहूँगा. • *1.* I don't want to impose. *2.* I wouldn't want to impose.

**299. घुसना** — *penetrate* — 'घुसना' is used to describe the action of entering or piercing through something. It conveys the idea of penetrating or going through a surface or barrier.

**300. निहारना** — *pry, behold* — 'निहारना' is used to describe the act of observing something closely or prying into a situation. It conveys the idea of beholding or scrutinizing something with curiosity or interest.

**301. स्पष्ट करना** — *clarify* — The verb 'स्पष्ट करना' is used to make something clear or understandable by providing more information or details. It is used to remove any confusion or ambiguity in a situation or communication.

• *1.* बस स्पष्ट करने के लिए। *2.* स्पष्टीकरण देने के लिए धन्यवाद। *3.* उसने स्पष्ट करने के लिए एक ईएफ शामिल किया। *4.* स्पष्ट करने के लिए आपको धन्यवाद। *5.* स्पष्टीकरण से सब कुछ स्पष्ट हो गया। • *1.* Just to clarify. *2.* Thanks for clarifying. *3.* She included an ef to clarify. *4.* Thank you for clarifying. *5.* The explanation clarified everything.

**302. लगाना** — *paste* — The verb 'लगाना' is used to describe the action of attaching or sticking something onto a surface. It is commonly used when referring to pasting paper, stickers, or any other material onto a wall, book, or object.

**303. चिल्लाई** — *holler* — 'चिल्लाई' is used to describe the act of shouting loudly or calling out in a high-pitched voice. It conveys a sense of urgency, excitement, or frustration depending on the context in which it is used.

• *1.* उसने खुशी से चिल्लाकर कहा. *2.* अगर मुझे तुम्हारी जरूरत होगी तो मैं चिल्लाऊंगा। • *1.* She gave a holler of joy. *2.* If I need you, I'll holler.

**304. टिंग** — *ting* — The verb 'टिंग' is used to describe a high-pitched ringing or tinkling sound. It is often used to depict the sound of a small bell, chime, or similar object.

**305. लिस** — *indulge* — The verb 'लिस' is used to describe the act of indulging in something, typically in a pleasurable or excessive manner. It conveys the idea of immersing oneself in an activity or experience.

**306. मेल कराना** — *wed* — The verb 'मेल कराना' is used to describe the act of getting married or joining two individuals in a marital relationship. It signifies the union of two people in a formal ceremony.

**307. अलग कर देना** — *isolate* — This verb is used to describe the action of separating or setting something apart from others. It implies creating a sense of isolation or detachment from a group or larger entity.

**308. वितरित करना** — *distribute, administer* — This verb is used to describe the action of giving out or spreading something among a group of people. It is often used in the context of distributing resources, responsibilities, or tasks among individuals.
• *1.* हमें कार्यभार वितरित करने की आवश्यकता है। *2.* कार्यक्रम में प्रचार सामग्री वितरित की गई। *3.* वजन असमान रूप से वितरित किया गया था। *4.* क्वार्टरमास्टर ने आपूर्ति वितरित की। *5.* उन्होंने कार्डों को असमान रूप से वितरित किया। • *1.* We need to distribute the workload. *2.* The promotional material was distributed at the event. *3.* The weight was distributed unevenly. *4.* The quartermaster distributed supplies. *5.* He distributed the cards unevenly.

**309. संलग्न करें** — *attach* — This verb is used to indicate the action of connecting or joining something to another object or surface. It is commonly used to describe the act of physically attaching or linking two things together.
• *1.* कोई सेटिंग संलग्न नहीं है। *2.* संलग्न मत होइए। *3.* मैं बहुत

अधिक संलग्न नहीं होऊंगा. *4.* मुझे यह बटन संलग्न करना होगा. *5.* समझौता इसके साथ संलग्न है। • *1.* No strings attached. *2.* Don't get attached. *3.* I wouldn't get too attached. *4.* I need to attach this button. *5.* The agreement is hereto attached.

## 310. धब्बे लगाना — *sully* — To 'sully' means to tarnish or damage someone's reputation or image by spreading false or damaging information about them. It is used to describe the act of ruining someone's good name or character.

## 311. ज़मानत करना — *vouch* — To vouch is to give assurance or guarantee for someone or something. It is a verb that signifies taking responsibility for the truth or accuracy of a statement or action.

## 312. अभियुक्त करना — *prosecute* — This verb is used to describe the legal action taken against someone for committing a crime. It signifies the process of bringing a criminal case against an individual in a court of law.

## 313. लुभाना — *tempt, seduce, entice* — This verb is used to describe the act of enticing or seducing someone into doing something, often by appealing to their desires or weaknesses. It implies a sense of temptation or allure towards a particular action or outcome.

• *1.* केवल हमारे दिलों को लुभाने का प्रयास करता है। *2.* विदेशी इत्र उसे लुभाएगा। *3.* ख़ज़ाने का नक़्शा उन्हें लुभाएगा। *4.* उसने उसे लुभाने के लिए अपने आकर्षण का इस्तेमाल किया। *5.* बेकरी का ह्यांग लुभावना था। *6.* स्ट्रूडल की मीठी गंध ने उसे लुभाया। *7.* उन्होंने नए ग्राहकों को लुभाने के लिए एक अभियान चलाया। *8.* वित्तीय प्रलोभन बहुत लुभावना था। • *1.* Seeks only to seduce our hearts. *2.* The exotic perfume will seduce him. *3.* The treasure map will seduce them. *4.* He used his charm to entice her. *5.* The hyang from the bakery was enticing. *6.* The sweet smell of the strudel enticed her. *7.* They launched a campaign to entice new customers. *8.* The financial inducement was too enticing.

## 314. डरपोक समझा — *wimp* — To describe someone

as 'डरपोक समझा' is to imply that they are seen as cowardly or lacking courage in a particular situation. It is a term used to criticize or belittle someone for their perceived lack of bravery.

**315. डालना** — *insert, infuse* — The verb 'डालना' is used to describe the action of putting something into something else, typically in a forceful or deliberate manner. It can also be used to convey the idea of infusing or injecting something into a substance.

**316. शराब बनाना** — *brew* — The verb 'शराब बनाना' is used to describe the process of making alcoholic beverages through fermentation or distillation. It refers to the act of brewing or creating alcohol, typically from ingredients like grains, fruits, or vegetables.

**317. आनन्द करे** — *rejoice* — This verb is used to express the feeling of joy, happiness, or delight. It is often used to describe the act of celebrating or enjoying something pleasant or fulfilling.

**318. खटखटाना** — *clatter* — The verb 'खटखटाना' is used to describe the sound of objects hitting each other repeatedly, creating a loud and sharp noise. It is often used to depict the sound of metal, glass, or other hard materials clattering against each other.

**319. अवशोषित करना** — *absorb* — This verb is used to describe the action of absorbing or soaking up something, such as liquid being absorbed by a sponge or information being absorbed by the mind.
• *1.* बृहदान्त्र पानी को अवशोषित करने का कार्य करता है। • *1.* The colon functions to absorb water.

**320. ग़लती होना** — *err* — 'ग़लती होना' is used to express making a mistake or error. It signifies the act of unintentionally doing something wrong or incorrect. It is a common verb used in everyday conversations to acknowledge faults.

**321. क्षति से बचाना** — *salvage* — The verb 'क्षति से

बचाना' is used to describe the act of rescuing or saving something from harm or damage. It implies protecting or preserving something that is at risk of being lost or destroyed.

**322. शोक मानना** — *grieve* — This verb is used to express the feeling of deep sadness or sorrow, typically in response to a loss or tragedy. It conveys the act of mourning and reflecting on the pain and emotional distress caused by the event.

**323. झेलना** — *withstand* — 'झेलना' is used to describe the act of enduring or tolerating something difficult or unpleasant. It implies the ability to withstand challenges or hardships without giving up.

**324. फक-फक करना** — *chug* — 'फक-फक करना' is used to describe the action of drinking something quickly and in large gulps. It implies a sense of urgency or eagerness in consuming the liquid.

**325. दबाना** — *clamp, stifle, strangle, pacify* — The verb 'दबाना' is used to describe the action of applying pressure or force to restrict movement or expression. It can also mean to calm or suppress emotions or reactions.

**326. शरमाना** — *blush* — The verb 'शरमाना' is used to describe the act of blushing or feeling embarrassed. It is often used to convey a sense of shyness or modesty in response to a compliment or embarrassing situation.
• *1.* तुम शरमा रहे हो। *2.* क्या तुम शरमा रहे हो? *3.* क्या मैं शरमा रहा हूँ? *4.* तुम क्यों शरमा रहे हैं? *5.* मुझे शरमाओ मत. •
*1.* You're blushing. *2.* Are you blushing? *3.* Am I blushing? *4.* Why are you blushing? *5.* Don't make me blush.

**327. टिन से मढ़ना** — *tinker* — To 'tinker' means to attempt to repair or improve something in a casual or experimental way, often without the proper tools or expertise. It involves making small adjustments or modifications to something in order to fix or enhance it.

**328. मन बहलाना** — *amuse* — The verb 'मन बहलाना' is used to describe the action of entertaining or amusing someone. It refers to the act of providing enjoyment or pleasure to someone through various means such as jokes, stories, or activities.

**329. छाती से लगाना** — *cuddle* — This verb is used to describe the act of embracing someone closely in a loving or affectionate manner. It conveys a sense of warmth and intimacy between individuals.

**330. लीन होना** — *merge* — 'लीन होना' is used to describe the action of two or more things coming together to form a single entity. It signifies the process of merging or blending different elements into one cohesive unit.

**331. आलोचना करना** — *criticize, maul* — This verb is used to express the act of pointing out faults or shortcomings in someone or something, often in a harsh or negative manner. It conveys the idea of offering critical feedback or disapproval.
- *1.* मैं आलोचना नहीं कर रहा हूं. *2.* उन्होंने उनके व्यवहार की तीखी आलोचना की. *3.* उन्होंने उनकी कड़ी आलोचना की. *4.* उन्होंने फासीवाद की जमकर आलोचना की. *5.* उन्होंने मूर्तिपूजा को पाप बताकर उसकी आलोचना की। ● *1.* I'm not criticizing. *2.* She sharply criticized his behavior. *3.* She criticized him harshly. *4.* He criticized fascism fiercely. *5.* He criticized idolatry as a sin.

**332. कहलवाना** — *transmit* — 'कहलवाना' is used to convey the action of transmitting or passing on information, messages, or signals from one person or place to another. It signifies the act of sending or relaying something to someone else.

**333. मार डालना** — *slay* — The verb 'मार डालना' is used to describe the act of killing someone or something in a violent or brutal manner. It is often used in a figurative sense to indicate defeating or overpowering someone or something.

**334. छमकना** — *clink* — The verb 'छमकना' is used to describe the sound or action of two hard objects hitting each other, typically producing a clear, ringing sound. It can also be used metaphorically to describe something shining or sparkling.

## 335. ताज़गी लाना — *freshen* — The verb 'ताज़गी लाना' is used to describe the action of making something fresh or bringing freshness to something. It is often used in reference to food, air, or a person's appearance.

## 336. प्रभुत्व रखना — *dominate* — This verb is used to describe the act of having control or power over a situation, person, or group. It signifies a sense of authority and influence in a particular context.
- *1.* बाज़ार पर निगम का प्रभुत्व था। • *1.* The corporation dominated the market.

## 337. ट्रैश किए गए — *trashed* — The verb 'ट्रैश किए गए' is used to describe the action of discarding or disposing of something as trash or garbage. It signifies getting rid of something in a careless or haphazard manner.

## 338. फिर से लिखना — *rewrite* — The verb 'फिर से लिखना' is used when you want to write something again in a different way or with corrections. It implies the action of rewriting or rephrasing a piece of text.

## 339. सजाना — *decorate, adorn* — The verb 'सजाना' is used to describe the action of decorating or embellishing something, such as a room, house, or object, to make it more attractive or visually appealing.
- *1.* वह घर को सजाना चाहती थी. *2.* वह अपने अपार्टमेंट को सजाना चाहती थी। • *1.* She wanted to decorate the house. *2.* She wanted to decorate her apartment.

## 340. पालन करना — *comply, abide, adhere* — This verb is used to convey the idea of following rules, regulations, or guidelines. It implies a sense of obedience and adherence to a set standard or code of conduct.

## 341. धरण करना — *retain* — This verb is used to describe the action of keeping or holding onto something, whether

it be physical or abstract. It implies the act of preserving or maintaining something in its current state.

**342. हिलना** — *budge* — The verb 'हिलना' is used to describe the action of moving slightly or shifting position. It is often used to indicate a small movement or change in position, without necessarily moving a significant distance.

**343. प्रसारित कर देना** — *deploy* — The verb 'प्रसारित कर देना' is used to describe the action of deploying or spreading something out, such as resources, troops, or information, in a strategic manner. It implies a deliberate and organized distribution or placement.

**344. खुलना** — *uncover* — This verb is used to describe the action of revealing or exposing something that was previously hidden or covered. It signifies the act of uncovering or opening up something to reveal what is underneath.

**345. राँभना** — *moo* — The verb 'राँभना' is used to describe the sound made by cows. It is a common verb used in Hindi to represent the vocalization of cows.

**346. ठगना** — *fudge* — The verb 'ठगना' is used to describe the act of manipulating or deceiving someone in a cunning or dishonest way. It is often used to refer to trickery or fraud in various situations.
● *1.* ओह, ठगना। *2.* वह स्वादिष्ट ठगना बेचता था। ● *1.* Oh, fudge. *2.* He sold gourmet fudge.

**347. जकड़ना** — *fasten* — 'जकड़ना' is used to describe the action of securing or attaching something firmly in place. It implies the act of fastening or tightening something to ensure it stays in position.
● *1.* अपनी सीट बेल्ट जकड़ना। ● *1.* Fasten your seat belt.

**348. मज़बूत बनाना** — *strengthen* — This verb is used to describe the action of making something stronger or more resilient. It is often used in the context of building physical strength, improving relationships, or enhancing skills and abilities.

## 349. सौंपना — *assign, entrust, commend* — This verb is used to indicate giving someone a task, responsibility, or duty to carry out. It implies trust and confidence in the person being assigned the task. It can also mean handing over something to someone for safekeeping or care.

- *1.* उसने भूमिकाएँ सौंपीं। *2.* वे जिम्मेदारियां सौंपेंगे। *3.* उन्होंने डिब अधिकार सौंपे। *4.* वह कार्य सौंप देगा। *5.* शिक्षक ने होमवर्क सौंपा। *6.* वह सम्मानित महसूस कर रहा था कि उसने उसे यह जिम्मेदारी सौंपी। *7.* वह उसे अपने रहस्य सौंप सकती थी। *8.* नेता उसे सौंपना नहीं चाहता था. *9.* मैं तुम्हें अपने रहस्य सौंपता हूं। *10.* टीम ने परियोजना सौंपने का निर्णय लिया। • *1.* She assigned the roles. *2.* They will assign the duties. *3.* They assigned dib rights. *4.* He will assign the task. *5.* The teacher assigned homework. *6.* He was honored she entrust him. *7.* She could entrust him with her secrets. *8.* The leader didn't want to entrust her. *9.* I entrust thine with my secrets. *10.* The team decided to entrust the project.

## 350. निलंबित — *suspend* — The verb 'निलंबित' is used to indicate the action of suspending or halting something temporarily. It is commonly used in contexts where an activity, process, or decision is put on hold for a period of time.

- *1.* आप निलंबित हैं. *2.* मुझे लगा कि आपको निलंबित कर दिया गया है. *3.* मैं निलंबित हूं. *4.* उसने परियोजना को अस्थायी रूप से निलंबित करने का निर्णय लिया। *5.* सज़ा निलंबित. • *1.* You're suspended. *2.* I thought you were suspended. *3.* I'm suspended. *4.* She chose to suspend the project temporarily. *5.* Sentence suspended.

## 351. पूरा करना — *suffice, offset, finalize* — This verb is used to indicate completing a task or fulfilling a requirement. It can also mean to offset or make up for something. It signifies finalizing or finishing a job or duty.

## 352. शिकस्त देना — *spank* — This verb is used to describe the action of striking someone on the buttocks as a form of punishment or discipline. It is typically used in a parental

or authoritative context to correct behavior.
- *1.* मुझे शिकस्त दिया। • *1.* Spank me.

## 353. प्रचलित होना — *prevail* — The verb 'प्रचलित होना'
is used to indicate that something is prevailing or widespread in a particular situation or context. It is often used to describe a common practice, belief, or trend.
- *1.* प्रचलित भावना आशा की थी। • *1.* The prevailing sentiment was one of hope.

## 354. धारा निकलना — *squirt* — This verb is used to describe the action of liquid forcefully coming out in a thin stream or jet. It is often used in reference to liquids being squirted out of a container or object.

## 355. संपादन करना — *edit, procure* — This verb is used to make changes or corrections to a written document, video, or any other form of media in order to improve its quality or accuracy. It can also refer to obtaining or acquiring something through negotiation or effort.
- *1.* उन्होंने विकिपीडिया पृष्ठ का संपादन किया। • *1.* He edited the wikipedia page.

## 356. फिर से भरना — *refill, replenish* — To fill something up again after it has been used or emptied.

## 357. उतार देना — *upgrade* — The verb 'उतार देना' is used to indicate the action of upgrading or improving something to a higher or better version. It signifies the process of enhancing the quality or performance of something.

## 358. समाविष्ट करना — *implant* — This verb is used to describe the action of inserting or embedding something into a particular place or object. It signifies the act of incorporating or integrating something into a larger system or structure.

## 359. कुचलना — *throttle* — 'कुचलना' is used to describe the action of forcefully restricting or controlling something, typically

by applying pressure or force. It conveys the idea of suppressing or limiting something's movement or function.

**360. घुस पड़ना** — *intrude* — 'घुस पड़ना' is used to describe the act of entering a place or situation without permission or welcome. It implies intrusion or trespassing into someone else's space or affairs.

**361. हुक्म चलाना** — *dictate* — The verb 'हुक्म चलाना' is used to convey the action of giving orders or commands in a authoritative manner. It implies a sense of authority and control over others.

**362. पवित्र करना** — *cleanse, purify, consecrate, sanctify* — This verb is used to describe the act of removing impurities or negative energies from a person, object, or place in order to make it spiritually pure and sacred. It is often used in religious rituals and ceremonies.

• *1.* पुजारी पवित्र स्थान को शुद्ध करेगा. *2.* वे पवित्र भूमि को - पवित्र करेंगे. *3.* चर्च को पिछले साल पवित्र किया गया था। *4.* उन्होंने अपने विचारों को पवित्र करने का प्रयास किया। *5.* पानी का उपयोग क्षेत्र को पवित्र करने के लिए किया जाता था। *6.* पुजारी ने पवित्र करने के लिए पवित्र जल छिड़का। *7.* धार्मिक अनुष्ठान का उद्देश्य पवित्र करना था। *8.* उन्होंने मंदिर को पवित्र करने के लिए एक समारोह आयोजित किया। • *1.* The priest will purify the sacred space. *2.* They will consecrate the holy ground. *3.* The church was consecrated last year. *4.* He tried to sanctify his thoughts. *5.* The water was used to sanctify the area. *6.* The priest sprinkled holy water to sanctify. *7.* The religious ritual was meant to sanctify. *8.* They held a ceremony to sanctify the temple.

**363. भिन्न होना** — *differ* — This verb is used to indicate a contrast or disagreement between two or more things. It is used to express differences in opinions, beliefs, characteristics, or qualities.

**364. कायम रखना** — *uphold* — 'कायम रखना' is used to convey the idea of maintaining or preserving something in its current state or position. It implies a sense of stability and

continuity in upholding a particular belief, value, or tradition.
- *1.* अनुबंध को कायम रखना महत्वपूर्ण है. • *1.* It's important to uphold the covenant.

**365. फड़फड़ाना** — *flop, snicker* — 'फड़फड़ाना' is used to describe the action of making a quick, light, and often nervous or excited movement. It can also be used to describe a quiet, suppressed laugh or snicker.

**366. कामयाब होना** — *thrive* — The verb 'कामयाब होना' is used to describe the state of being successful, prosperous, or flourishing. It signifies achieving desired goals, reaching a high level of accomplishment, and experiencing growth and progress in various aspects of life.

**367. ओवरलुक** — *overlook* — To 'overlook' means to fail to notice or consider something, typically because it is not seen as important or relevant. It can also refer to intentionally ignoring or disregarding something.
- *1.* ओवरलुक ने एक मनमोहक दृश्य प्रस्तुत किया। • *1.* The overlook offered a breathtaking view.

**368. धड़ाका करना** — *detonate* — This verb is used to describe the action of causing an explosion or setting off a bomb. It is often used in the context of a sudden and powerful release of energy, resulting in a loud noise and destruction.

**369. अवज्ञा करना** — *disobey* — This verb is used to describe the act of deliberately not following rules, orders, or instructions. It signifies a refusal to comply with authority or to adhere to established norms or regulations.
- *1.* मैंने आपकी अवज्ञा की. *2.* कानून की अवज्ञा करने के दुष्परिणाम हुए। *3.* बच्चों को चेतावनी दी गई कि वे अवज्ञा न करें। • *1.* I disobeyed you. *2.* Disobeying the law had consequences. *3.* The children were warned not to disobey.

**370. अंतर करना** — *distinguish, differ* — This verb is used to highlight the differences between two or more things, ideas, or concepts. It is used to separate or distinguish one from another based on specific characteristics or qualities.

## 371. निर्माण करना — *construct* — The verb 'निर्माण करना' is used to describe the action of building or creating something, such as a house, bridge, or road. It signifies the process of constructing or assembling something from various materials or components.
• 1. उन्होंने एक मजबूत बीम का निर्माण किया। 2. इमारत का निर्माण मोटे तौर पर किया गया था। • 1. They constructed a sturdy beam. 2. The building was roughly constructed.

## 372. सूचना देना — *herald, publicize* — This verb is used to convey information or news to the public, to announce or promote something. It is often used in the context of spreading awareness or making an official announcement.

## 373. मोड़ना — *divert, deflect* — The verb 'मोड़ना' is used to describe the action of changing the direction of something, typically to divert it from its original path or course. It implies a deliberate act of redirection or avoidance.

## 374. पागल होना — *rave* — This verb is used to describe someone becoming extremely excited, enthusiastic, or passionate about something. It can also convey a sense of losing control or behaving in a wild or irrational manner.

## 375. गाली मार देना — *zap* — 'गाली मार देना' is used to describe the act of quickly and effortlessly defeating or overpowering someone or something. It implies a sense of sudden and decisive action, often resulting in a swift victory or success.

## 376. निहुरना — *stoop* — 'निहुरना' is used to describe the action of bending down or lowering oneself, typically in a submissive or humble manner. It can also convey the idea of showing respect or deference to someone or something.

## 377. प्रस्तुत करना — *render, submit* — This verb is used to convey the action of presenting or submitting something,

such as a report, assignment, or proposal. It implies the act of offering or providing something for consideration or approval.

• *1.* वह वीडियो प्रस्तुत कर सकती है. *2.* मुझे एनीमेशन प्रस्तुत करने की आवश्यकता है। *3.* कलाकार चित्र प्रस्तुत करेगा. *4.* उसे प्राधिकार के समक्ष प्रस्तुत होना पड़ा। *5.* ठेकेदार ने एक विस्तृत प्रस्ताव प्रस्तुत किया। *6.* उन्होंने साक्ष्यात्मक रिपोर्ट प्रस्तुत की। *7.* कृपया अपना कार्य शीघ्र प्रस्तुत करें। *8.* ग्राहक ने उत्पाद के बारे में पूछताछ प्रस्तुत की। •
*1.* She can render the video. *2.* I need to render the animation. *3.* The artist will render the portrait. *4.* She had to submit to authority. *5.* The contractor submitted a detailed proposal. *6.* They submitted the evidentiary report. *7.* Please submit your work promptly. *8.* The customer submitted an enquiry about the product.

## 378. प्रबुद्ध करना — *enlighten* — The verb 'प्रबुद्ध करना'
is used to describe the action of enlightening or providing knowledge and understanding to someone or a group of people. It signifies the act of bringing clarity and awareness to a particular subject or situation.

• *1.* अनुभव आपको प्रबुद्ध करेगा. *2.* उसने दूसरों को प्रबुद्ध करने का प्रयास किया। *3.* कक्षा का उद्देश्य छात्रों को प्रबुद्ध करना है। *4.* तो फिर मुझे प्रबुद्ध करो. *5.* हमें प्रबुद्ध करें. •
*1.* The experience will enlighten you. *2.* She sought to enlighten others. *3.* The class aims to enlighten students. *4.* Enlighten me, then. *5.* Enlighten us.

## 379. शुरू करना — *unleash* — This verb is used to describe the action of starting or initiating something, often with a sense of releasing or unleashing energy or potential. It signifies the beginning of a process or activity.

## 380. झगड़ा तय करना — *accommodate* — This verb is used to describe the act of making arrangements or adjustments to fit someone or something in a particular place or situation. It implies the willingness to make space or adjustments for others.

## 381. डुबो देना — *dunk* — The verb 'डुबो देना' is used to describe the action of submerging something completely in a

liquid. It implies forcefully pushing or plunging an object into a liquid until it is fully covered or soaked.

## 382. विनाश करना — *exterminate, destruct* — This verb is used to describe the act of completely destroying or eliminating something, often with the intention of causing harm or damage. It signifies the process of extermination or destruction.

## 383. घुलाना — *dissolve* — The verb 'घुलाना' is used to describe the action of causing a solid substance to mix with a liquid until it becomes a homogeneous solution. It is commonly used in cooking and chemistry.
- *1.* सीवन ठीक से नहीं घुला। • *1.* The suture didn't dissolve properly.

## 384. फ़रार होना — *elope* — The verb 'फ़रार होना' is used to describe the act of running away secretly to get married, typically without the consent of family or society. It implies a sense of rebellion and defiance against traditional norms.

## 385. डिस्कनेक्ट — *disconnect* — To disconnect means to separate or break the connection between two or more things. It is used when referring to cutting off communication, power, or physical links between devices or people.
- *1.* हम डिस्कनेक्ट हो गए थे। *2.* डिस्कनेक्ट ने प्रभावी संचार में बाधा डाली। • *1.* We were disconnected. *2.* The disconnect hindered effective communication.

## 386. गुणा करना — *multiply* — The verb 'गुणा करना' is used to indicate the action of multiplying one number by another. It is commonly used in mathematical contexts to describe the process of increasing a quantity by a certain factor.

## 387. आपस में मिलना — *mingle* — This verb is used to describe the act of socializing or interacting with others in a casual or friendly manner. It implies coming together and mixing with people in a social setting.

## 388. प्रयास करते हैं — *strive* — This verb is used to con-

vey the idea of making a strong effort or attempting to achieve something, often in the face of challenges or obstacles. It implies determination and perseverance in pursuing a goal.

● 1. न्यायालय न्यायसंगत होने का प्रयास करता है। 2. वे कार्य-स्थल में समानता के लिए प्रयास करते हैं। ● 1. The court strives to be equitable. 2. They strive for equality in the workplace.

### 389. मजबूर करना — *oblige, coerce* — The verb 'मजबूर करना' is used to describe the act of forcing or compelling someone to do something against their will. It implies using pressure or manipulation to make someone act in a certain way.

### 390. आगे बढ़ना — *outrun, slog* — This verb is used to describe moving forward or progressing faster than others, surpassing them in a race or competition. It can also mean working hard or putting in extra effort to achieve a goal.

### 391. कपटवध करना — *assassinate* — The verb 'कपटवध करना' is used to describe the act of intentionally killing someone, usually for political or malicious reasons. It implies a premeditated and secretive nature to the killing.

### 392. ध्यान में लाना — *conceive* — This verb is used to describe the act of bringing something into one's mind or imagination, often in a creative or abstract way. It implies the process of conceiving an idea or concept.

### 393. ताज़ा करना — *refresh, freshen* — This verb is used to describe the action of making something fresh or new again. It is often used in the context of revitalizing something that has become stale or outdated.

### 394. आपत्ति में डालना — *jeopardize* — To put in jeopardy or endanger something.

### 395. जासूसी करना — *snoop* — The verb 'जासूसी करना' is used to describe the act of secretly investigating or prying into someone else's private affairs or personal information without their knowledge or consent.

**396. भागना** — *scoot, shirk, skedaddle* — The verb 'भागना' is used to describe the action of quickly moving away or avoiding a situation or responsibility. It implies a sense of urgency or haste in escaping or avoiding something.
- *1.* उसे तेजी से भागना पड़ा। • *1.* She had to scoot over.

**397. नष्ट करना** — *devour, dissipate, extinguish* — The verb 'नष्ट करना' is used to describe the action of consuming or destroying something completely. It can also be used to convey the idea of dissipating or extinguishing something entirely.

**398. दस्तंदाज़ी करना** — *meddle* — This verb is used to describe the act of interfering or getting involved in someone else's business or affairs without being asked to do so. It implies meddling in a situation where one is not welcome.

**399. फिर से सोचना** — *rethink* — To 'rethink' means to consider something again, usually with the intention of changing one's previous thoughts or decisions. It involves reflecting on a situation or idea in order to come up with a new perspective or solution.

**400. कृतार्थ होना** — *prosper* — This verb is used to express the state of being fulfilled or satisfied, typically in relation to achieving a goal or desire. It conveys a sense of prosperity, contentment, and accomplishment.

**401. नेविगेट** — *navigate* — To 'नेविगेट' means to plan and follow a route to reach a destination, whether physically or metaphorically. It involves making decisions and finding the best way to move forward towards a goal or objective.
- *1.* वह नेविगेट करने के लिए ब्रेल पर निर्भर थे। *2.* नाविक ने नेविगेट करने के लिए मानचित्र का उपयोग किया। *3.* दलदली क्षेत्र में नेविगेट करना मुश्किल था। *4.* उनका काम नौकरशाही को नेविगेट करना है। *5.* आप नेविगेट करें. • *1.* He relied on braille to navigate. *2.* The navigator used a map to navigate. *3.* The swampy area was difficult to navigate. *4.* His job is to navigate the bureaucracy. *5.* You navigate.

**402. सीधे खड़े हो** — *shun* — This verb is used to describe the act of avoiding or ignoring someone or something intentionally. It implies a deliberate decision to distance oneself from a person or situation.

**403. परिचालित करना** — *govern* — This verb is used to describe the act of governing or ruling over a group of people or an organization. It implies the exercise of authority and control in a systematic and organized manner.

**404. निष्कासित करना** — *expel* — This verb is used to describe the action of forcing someone to leave a place or organization, typically as a punishment or as a result of their behavior.
• 1. मुझे निष्कासित कर दिया गया। 2. तुम्हें निष्कासित कर दिया गया है! 3. शिक्षक ने उपद्रवी छात्र को निष्कासित करने की धमकी दी। 4. स्कूल ने उपद्रवियों को निष्कासित करने का फैसला किया। 5. उसके व्यवहार के कारण उसे निष्कासित कर दिया गया। • 1. I was expelled. 2. You're expelled! 3. The teacher threatened to expel the disruptive student. 4. The school decided to expel the troublemakers. 5. He was expelled for his behavior.

**405. फिर से खोलना** — *reopen* — The verb 'फिर से खोलना' is used to describe the action of opening something again after it has been closed or shut. It signifies the act of reopening a closed object or establishment.

**406. संकेत करना** — *imply, insinuate* — This verb is used to subtly suggest or hint at something without explicitly stating it. It is often used to convey a message indirectly or to imply something without directly saying it.

**407. दुर्बल करना** — *undermine* — The verb 'दुर्बल करना' is used to describe the action of weakening or diminishing something, often in a subtle or indirect way. It implies a gradual erosion of strength or effectiveness.

### 408. टुकड़े टुकड़े करना — *crumble* — This verb is used to describe the action of breaking something into small pieces or fragments. It signifies the process of disintegrating or breaking apart into smaller parts.

• *1.* कुकी के ऐसे ही टुकड़े होते हैं। • *1.* That's the way the cookie crumbles.

### 409. कृषि योग्य बनाना — *reclaim* — The verb 'कृषि योग्य बनाना' means to make land suitable for agriculture again. It is used to describe the process of restoring land that has been previously used for other purposes back to a condition where it can be used for farming.

### 410. हार्न बजाना — *toot* — The verb 'हार्न बजाना' is used to describe the action of breaking or shattering something into pieces. It signifies the act of something being fractured or destroyed, resulting in a broken or shattered state.

### 411. बिखेरना — *disperse* — The verb 'बिखेरना' is used to describe the action of scattering or spreading something out in different directions. It is often used to convey the idea of dispersing or distributing something widely.

### 412. टूटने — *shatter* — The verb 'टूटने' is used to describe the action of breaking or shattering into pieces. It is often used to convey the idea of something being destroyed or damaged beyond repair.

• *1.* उसका आत्मविश्वास टूटने लगा. • *1.* His confidence began to shatter.

### 413. बुझाना — *suffocate, extinguish, quench* — The verb 'बुझाना' is used to describe the action of extinguishing or quenching something, such as a fire, a light, or a desire. It signifies the act of putting an end to something by removing its source of fuel or energy.

• *1.* उसने पानी से आग बुझाई। *2.* उसने अपनी प्यास बुझाने की कोशिश की. *3.* उन्होंने गर्मी बुझाने का प्रयास किया। • *1.* He quench the fire with water. *2.* She tried to quench her thirst. *3.* They sought to quench the heat.

## 414. संचालन करना — *supervise* — The verb 'संचालन करना' is used to describe the act of overseeing or managing a task, project, or group of people. It involves directing and monitoring activities to ensure they are carried out effectively and efficiently.

## 415. विज्ञापन करना — *advertise* — This verb is used to describe the action of promoting a product, service, or event through various mediums such as television, radio, print, or online platforms in order to attract potential customers or participants.

• *1.* फ़्लायर ने आगामी कार्यक्रम का विज्ञापन किया। *2.* कंपनी ने फेसबुक पर विज्ञापन दिया। *3.* फ़्लायर ने एक बिक्री का विज्ञापन दिया। *4.* बिलबोर्ड ने नवीनतम उत्पाद का विज्ञापन किया। *5.* इन्फोमेरियल ने रसोई उत्पादों का विज्ञापन किया। • *1.* The flyer advertised the upcoming event. *2.* The company advertised on Facebook. *3.* The flier advertised a sale. *4.* The billboard advertised the latest product. *5.* The infomercial advertised kitchen products.

## 416. लागू करना — *enforce* — This verb is used to describe the action of making a rule, law, or system be obeyed or followed strictly. It is used to indicate the implementation or enforcement of a particular regulation or policy.

## 417. अनुकरण करना — *imitate, simulate, emulate* — This verb is used to describe the act of copying or mimicking someone or something in order to replicate their actions, behavior, or style. It is often used to show admiration or to learn from someone else's example.

• *1.* कृपया मॉडल का अनुकरण करें. *2.* बच्चे उसका मज़ाक उड़ाते हुए अनुकरण करते थे। *3.* उसका लक्ष्य सफलता का अनुकरण करना है। *4.* परीक्षण का उद्देश्य वास्तविक जीवन की स्थितियों का अनुकरण करना था। *5.* सिम्युलेटर ड्राइविंग स्थितियों का सटीक अनुकरण कर सकता है। *6.* मॉडल हवाई जहाज़ उड़ान का अनुकरण कर सकता है। *7.* सॉफ़्टवेयर को वास्तविक दुनिया की स्थितियों का अनुकरण करने के लिए डिज़ाइन किया गया था। *8.* कलाकार ने महान उस्तादों का अनुकरण करने का प्रयास

किया। 9. उन्हें अपने पिता की उपलब्धियों का अनुकरण क-
रने की आशा थी। 10. नृत्य समूह ने अपने प्रशिक्षक का अनुकरण
करने का प्रयास किया। • 1. Please imitate the model. 2. The
children imitated her mockingly. 3. His goal is to imitate success. 4. The test aimed to simulate real-life conditions. 5. The
simulator could accurately simulate driving conditions. 6. The
model airplane could simulate flight. 7. The software was designed to emulate real-world conditions. 8. The artist sought to
emulate the great masters. 9. He hoped to emulate his father's
achievements. 10. The dance group attempted to emulate their
instructor.

## 418. प्रतिलिपि प्रस्तुत करना — *reproduce* — The
verb 'प्रतिलिपि प्रस्तुत करना' is used to describe the action of creating a copy or duplicate of something, whether it be a document,
artwork, or any other form of media.
• 1. प्रिंटर दस्तावेज़ को पुन: प्रस्तुत कर सकता है। 2. कल-
ाकार ने मूल पेंटिंग को पुन: प्रस्तुत करने का प्रयास किया। •
1. The printer can reproduce the document. 2. The artist tried
to reproduce the original painting.

## 419. पनपने — *flourish* — 'पनपने' is used to describe the
growth, development, and flourishing of something, such as a
plant, business, or relationship. It signifies progress and success in various aspects of life.

## 420. भंग करना — *disrupt* — This verb is used to describe
the action of causing disturbance or interruption to a process,
event, or situation. It implies breaking the continuity or smooth
functioning of something.

## 421. घुमाएँ — *rotate* — This verb is used to describe the
action of turning or spinning something around a central axis.
It can refer to physical objects rotating or to people or animals
moving in a circular motion.
• 1. उसे फसलों को घुमाने की जरूरत थी। 2. उसने उससे टायर
घुमाने के लिए कहा। • 1. He needed to rotate the crops. 2.
She asked him to rotate the tires.

**422. शुद्ध करना** — *purge, purify, rectify* — This verb is used to describe the action of removing impurities, correcting mistakes, or purifying something. It signifies the process of making something clean, pure, or free from errors.
● *1.* अनुष्ठान का उद्देश्य आत्मा को शुद्ध करना है। ● *1.* The ritual aims to purify the soul.

**423. सोते सोते चूकना** — *snore* — This verb is used to describe the action of making loud breathing noises while sleeping. It is often associated with deep sleep and can be disruptive to others nearby.

**424. स्थिर बनाना** — *stabilize* — The verb 'स्थिर बनाना' is used to describe the action of making something stable or steady. It is used to indicate the process of establishing a firm or secure position for an object or situation.

**425. हस्त-मैथुन करना** — *masturbate* — This verb refers to the act of self-stimulation for sexual pleasure. It is a common practice among individuals of all genders and ages, and is considered a normal and healthy part of human sexuality.

**426. शपथ दिलाना** — *administer* — To 'शपथ दिलाना' means to officially give someone a pledge or oath, typically in a formal or ceremonial setting. It is often used in contexts such as government ceremonies, religious rituals, or legal proceedings.

**427. लिखें** — *compose* — The verb 'लिखें' is used to indicate the action of composing or writing something, such as a letter, essay, or poem. It is commonly used to express the act of putting thoughts or ideas into written form.
● *1.* एक हार्दिक पत्र लिखें. *2.* उत्तम शॉट लिखें. ● *1.* Compose a heartfelt letter. *2.* Compose the perfect shot.

**428. घास काटना** — *mow* — 'घास काटना' is used to describe the action of cutting grass or mowing a lawn. It is a common verb used in gardening and landscaping activities to maintain the appearance of outdoor spaces.

**429. डींग मारना** — *boast, rant* — This verb is used to describe the act of speaking loudly and angrily about something, often in a repetitive or long-winded manner. It conveys a sense of frustration or annoyance towards a particular topic or situation.

**430. मूल्यांकन करना** — *evaluate* — 'मूल्यांकन करना' is used to assess or determine the value, worth, or importance of something. It involves carefully examining and analyzing various factors to make a judgment or decision.

- 1. उन्होंने संभावित निवेश अवसरों का मूल्यांकन किया। 2. अध्ययन ने प्रभावकारिता का मूल्यांकन किया। 3. ग्रैंडमास्टर ने अपने छात्रों का मूल्यांकन किया। 4. उन्होंने प्रदर्शन का मूल्यांकन करने के लिए बेंचमार्क का उपयोग किया।
- 1. She evaluated the prospective investment opportunities. 2. The study evaluated the efficacy. 3. The grandmaster evaluated his students. 4. They used the benchmark to evaluate performance.

**431. संदूषित करना** — *infect* — This verb is used to describe the act of spreading a disease or illness from one person to another. It signifies the transmission of a pathogen or virus that causes the recipient to become sick or unwell.

**432. विस्मित करना** — *amaze* — This verb is used to describe the feeling of being surprised or amazed by something. It conveys a sense of wonder or astonishment towards a person, event, or situation.

**433. जोखिम में डालना** — *endanger* — This verb is used to describe the action of putting someone or something at risk or in danger. It signifies the act of exposing someone or something to potential harm or peril.

**434. पहरे में डालना** — *nab* — This verb is used to describe the act of catching or seizing someone or something, typically in a sudden or unexpected manner. It implies a quick and decisive action to capture or apprehend.

95

**435.** **दूषित करना** — *mar, sully* — This verb is used to describe the action of tarnishing or damaging something, often in a figurative sense. It implies causing harm or bringing disgrace to something or someone.

**436.** **ऊंची उड़ान भरना** — *soar* — 'ऊंची उड़ान भरना' is used to describe the action of flying high in the sky with great speed and grace. It signifies a sense of freedom, achievement, and success in overcoming obstacles.

**437.** **अधिकार देना** — *authorize* — To give someone the power or permission to do something; to grant authority or permission for a specific action or decision.

**438.** **जोर से मारना** — *lash, bash* — This verb is used to describe hitting or striking something or someone with force. It implies a strong and forceful action, often resulting in physical harm or damage.

**439.** **समझने** — *decipher* — The verb 'समझने' is used to convey the action of deciphering or understanding something that may be complex or difficult to comprehend. It implies the process of making sense of information or situations.
• *1.* कोडब्रेकर ने सिफर को समझने का काम किया। • *1.* The code-breaker worked to decipher the cipher.

**440.** **गति बढ़ाना** — *accelerate* — This verb is used to describe the action of increasing speed or rate of movement. It signifies a quickening or intensifying of motion or progress.

**441.** **उत्तेजित करना** — *excite, irritate, agitate, stimulate* — This verb is used to describe the action of causing excitement, agitation, stimulation, or aggravation in someone or something. It is used to convey the idea of stirring up emotions or reactions.
• *1.* उत्तेजित मत होइए. *2.* मै बहुत उत्तेजित हूँ। *3.* मैं - उत्तेजित हो गया। *4.* यह मुझे उत्तेजित करता है। *5.* अब,

उत्तेजित मत होइए. 6. आप उत्तेजित लग रहे हैं. 7. तुम इतने उत्तेजि-त क्यों हो? 8. मैं उत्तेजित नहीं हूं. 9. आप शर्त लगा सकते हैं कि मैं उत्तेजित हूँ! 10. मालिश से रक्त प्रवाह उत्तेजित होगा। 11. रंग इंद्रियों को उत्तेजित करते हैं। 12. कॉफ़ी आपके मस्तिष्क को उत्तेजित करेगी। • 1. Don't get excited. 2. I'm very excited. 3. I got excited. 4. It excites me. 5. Now, don't get excited. 6. You seem agitated. 7. Why are you so agitated? 8. I'm not agitated. 9. You bet I'm agitated! 10. The massage will stimulate blood flow. 11. The colors stimulate the senses. 12. The coffee will stimulate your brain.

## 442. कमज़ोर करना — *weaken* — The verb 'कमज़ोर करना' is used to describe the action of making something weaker or less strong. It is often used to indicate a decrease in physical, mental, or emotional strength or power.
• 1. तूफ़ान कमज़ोर हो जाएगा. • 1. The storm will weaken.

## 443. ज़ोर से मारना — *swipe* — This verb is used to describe the action of forcefully moving one's hand or fingers across a surface, typically a touchscreen, in order to navigate or interact with a digital device or application.

## 444. उभाड़ना — *hoist* — 'उभाड़ना' is used to describe the action of lifting or raising something, typically using a pulley or other mechanical device. It signifies the act of hoisting an object or material to a higher position.

## 445. वंचित करना — *deprive* — The verb 'वंचित करना' is used to describe the action of taking away or denying someone of something that they need or desire. It signifies the act of depriving someone of a particular thing or opportunity.

## 446. नापसन्द करना — *loathe* — This verb is used to express a strong feeling of dislike or disgust towards something or someone. It conveys a sense of intense aversion or repulsion.

## 447. सहानुभूति रखना — *sympathize* — This verb is used to express understanding and compassion towards someone who is going through a difficult situation. It conveys the idea

97

of sharing in someone's feelings and offering support in times of need.

• *1.* मुझे सहानुभूति है। *2.* ऐसा प्रतीत नहीं होता था कि उसे उससे कोई सहानुभूति है। *3.* उसे उसकी स्थिति से कोई सहानुभूति नहीं थी। *4.* मुझे इस त्रासदी के पीड़ितों के प्रति सहानुभूति है। *5.* आप जिस दौर से गुजर रहे हैं, उससे मुझे सहानुभूति है। • *1.* I sympathize. *2.* She didn't seem to sympathize with him. *3.* He didn't seem to sympathize with her situation. *4.* I sympathize with the victims of the tragedy. *5.* I sympathize with what you're going through.

**448. प्रगट करना** — *proclaim* — The verb 'प्रगट करना' is used to express the action of making something known or declaring it publicly. It is often used to announce or reveal information, beliefs, or intentions to others.

**449. आग लगना** — *ignite* — This verb is used to describe the action of setting something on fire or causing it to start burning. It can also be used metaphorically to describe a situation or emotion becoming intense or heated.

**450. खंडन करना** — *contradict, deflate, refute, disprove* — This verb is used to express the action of contradicting, deflating, refuting, or disproving a statement or argument. It is commonly used in debates, discussions, or disagreements to challenge or invalidate a claim.

**451. ज़ब्त करना** — *confiscate, impound* — This verb is used to describe the action of taking possession of something, typically by a legal authority. It implies that the item is being seized or held by force, often due to a violation of rules or laws.

**452. बेअसर करना** — *neutralize* — The verb 'बेअसर करना' is used to describe the action of neutralizing or counteracting the effects of something, making it ineffective or having no impact. It is often used in situations where one wants to nullify the influence of something.

**453. छिड़कना** — *sprinkle, dredge* — 'छिड़कना' is used to describe the action of sprinkling or dredging something, typically

a dry substance like flour or sugar, over a surface. It is commonly used in cooking to evenly distribute ingredients over food.
• *1.* उसने बगीचे में तारों की धूल छिड़क दी। *2.* उसने सलाद पर गोर-ोगोन्ज़ोला छिड़का। *3.* ऊपर से जड़ी-बूटियाँ छिड़कें। *4.* उसने अनाज पर किशमिश छिड़क दी। *5.* कुकीज़ में चीनी का छिड़काव किया गया था। • *1.* She sprinkled stardust over the garden. *2.* She sprinkled gorgonzola on the salad. *3.* Sprinkle the herbs on top. *4.* She sprinkled raisin on the cereal. *5.* The cookies had a sprinkle of sugar.

**454. क्रूस पर** — *crucify* — The verb 'क्रूस पर' is used to describe the act of crucifying someone, typically in a religious or historical context. It signifies the act of nailing or tying someone to a cross as a form of punishment.
• *1.* उसे क्रूस पर चढ़ाओ! • *1.* Crucify him!

**455. टकराना** — *collide* — The verb 'टकराना' is used to describe the action of two objects coming into contact with each other forcefully. It signifies a collision or impact between the two entities.
• *1.* न्यूट्रॉन अन्य कणों से टकराया। *2.* प्रायोगिक क्वार्क तेज़ गति से टकराया। *3.* उनके रास्ते टकराने के लिए नियत थे। *4.* गाड़िय-ोँ टकराने वाली थीं। *5.* यदि जहाज़ों को दूर नहीं हटाया गया तो वे टकरा जायेंगे। • *1.* The neutron collided with other particles. *2.* The experimental quark collided at high speeds. *3.* Their paths were destined to collide. *4.* The cars were about to collide. *5.* The ships would collide if not steered away.

**456. झुंझलाना** — *madden* — 'झुंझलाना' is used to describe the act of making someone extremely angry or frustrated. It signifies the feeling of being driven to madness or losing control due to intense emotions.

**457. सड़ना** — *fester, decompose* — This verb is used to describe the process of something rotting or decaying, typically referring to organic matter. It signifies the gradual breakdown and deterioration of a substance over time, resulting in a foul smell and appearance.

**458. दण्ड देना** — *inflict* — This verb is used to describe the action of causing harm or punishment to someone as a form of retribution or discipline. It signifies the act of inflicting consequences or penalties on an individual for their actions.

**459. लगना** — *embark* — This verb is used to indicate the beginning or initiation of an action or activity. It can also convey the sense of setting out on a journey or starting a new project.

**460. गहरा बनाना** — *sharpen, escalate* — To 'गहरा बनाना' means to intensify or increase something, typically a situation or a problem. It signifies a rise in intensity or severity, often leading to a more serious or complicated state.

**461. अंडे रखना** — *spawn* — This verb is used to describe the action of laying eggs or giving birth to offspring, typically used in reference to animals or insects. It signifies the process of reproduction and the continuation of a species.

**462. पीछे पीछे फिरना** — *lug* — The verb 'पीछे पीछे फिरना' is used to describe the action of dragging or pulling something heavy or cumbersome behind oneself. It implies a sense of effort or struggle in moving the object.

**463. आरोप लगा देना** — *denounce* — This verb is used to accuse or blame someone for a wrongdoing or crime, often publicly or formally. It implies a strong disapproval or condemnation of the actions or behavior of the person being denounced.

**464. दैनिक काम करना** — *char* — This verb is used to describe the act of performing daily tasks or routine work. It implies engaging in regular activities or responsibilities on a consistent basis.

**465. विवश करना** — *compel, coerce* — This verb is used to describe the act of forcing someone to do something against their will or desire. It implies using pressure or threats to make someone comply with a certain action.

**466. दिखाऊ बनाना** — *visualize* — This verb is used to describe the act of creating a mental image or representation of something in one's mind. It is often used in contexts where one is trying to imagine or picture something that is not physically present.

**467. बाहर रखना** — *exclude* — To keep something outside or apart from a group or category.

**468. सुलझाना** — *unravel* — The verb 'सुलझाना' is used to describe the action of untangling or solving a complex or confusing situation. It implies the process of unraveling or clarifying something that is difficult to understand or untangle.
• *1.* उसने समस्या को सुलझाने के लिए काम किया। • *1.* She worked to unravel the problem.

**469. मंडराना** — *hover* — The verb 'मंडराना' is used to describe the action of hovering or moving around in a particular place without any specific direction. It implies a sense of floating or lingering in one spot.
• *1.* हमिंगबर्ड फीडर के पास मंडराने लगा। *2.* हेलीकॉप्टर इमारत के ऊपर मंडराता रहा। • *1.* The hummingbird hovered near the feeder. *2.* The helicopter hovered above the building.

**470. खरोंचना** — *scrabble* — The verb 'खरोंचना' is used to describe the action of scratching or scraping something with a sharp object. It can also refer to the act of scrambling or struggling to move or climb over something.

**471. उत्तर में कहना** — *replicate* — To 'उत्तर में कहना' means to replicate or repeat something exactly as it was said or done before. It is used to describe the act of copying or reproducing something in the same manner.

**472. बम बरसाना** — *blitz* — To 'बम बरसाना' means to attack or strike with great force and speed. It is often used to describe a sudden and intense military or verbal assault.

**473. आशंका करना** — *apprehend* — The verb 'आशंका करना' is used to express the action of apprehending or suspecting something. It is commonly used to convey a sense of doubt or uncertainty about a situation or person.

**474. बढ़ती करना** — *exceed* — The verb 'बढ़ती करना' is used to indicate surpassing a certain limit or expectation. It signifies going beyond what is considered normal or standard, often in a positive or negative context.

**475. विशेषज्ञ बनना** — *specialize* — To 'specialize' means to focus on a specific area of expertise or knowledge, becoming highly skilled and knowledgeable in that particular field. It involves gaining in-depth understanding and proficiency in a particular subject or profession.
● *1.* उन्होंने बाल मनोचिकित्सा में विशेषज्ञता हासिल की। *2.* किताबों की दुकान साउथलैंड साहित्य में विशेषज्ञता रखती है। *3.* हस्तनिर्मित आभूषणों में विशेषज्ञता वाला बूटीक। *4.* डॉक्टर प्रसवोत्तर में विशेषज्ञ हैं। *5.* उन्होंने प्रतिलेखन में विशेषज्ञता हासिल की। ● *1.* He specialized in child psychiatry. *2.* The bookstore specializes in Southland literature. *3.* The boutique specialized in handmade jewelry. *4.* The doctor specializes in postpartum. *5.* He specialized in transcription.

**476. खिन्न होना** — *yearn* — 'खिन्न होना' is used to express a deep longing or desire for something or someone. It conveys a sense of intense yearning or craving, often accompanied by feelings of sadness or nostalgia.

**477. पीछे रह जाना** — *lag* — This verb is used to describe falling behind or being left behind in a race, competition, or any other situation where someone is not able to keep up with others.

**478. खड़ा करना** — *erect* — This verb is used to describe the action of making something stand upright or straight. It is often used to refer to the act of erecting a structure or object, or to describe the physical state of something being upright.

**479. रटना** — *cram* — The verb 'रटना' is used to describe the act of memorizing information quickly and without fully understanding it. It is often used by students who are preparing for exams or tests.

**480. वचन देना** — *undertake* — 'वचन देना' is used to express the action of taking on a responsibility or commitment. It signifies the act of agreeing to do something or promising to fulfill a task.

**481. काटकर अलग करना** — *sever* — The verb 'काटकर अलग करना' is used to describe the action of cutting or separating something into two or more parts. It signifies a complete division or separation of an object or entity.

**482. छलकाना** — *slop* — 'छलकाना' is used to describe the action of spilling or overflowing a liquid, typically in a messy or uncontrolled manner. It conveys the idea of something flowing out or leaking from a container.

**483. कुम्हलाना** — *wither* — The verb 'कुम्हलाना' is used to describe the process of something losing its vitality and becoming dry or shriveled. It is often used to depict plants, flowers, or other living things that are wilting or decaying.

**484. होड़ करना** — *vie* — To 'होड़ करना' means to compete or strive for something, especially in a competitive or ambitious manner. It implies a desire to outdo others and achieve success or recognition in a particular field.

**485. ठहराना** — *nominate, mete, allocate* — This verb is used to assign or designate someone or something for a specific purpose or role. It is also used to allocate resources or distribute tasks among individuals or groups.

**486. फिर से जोड़ना** — *rejoin* — The verb 'फिर से जोड़ना' is used to describe the action of reconnecting or reuniting something that was previously separated or disconnected. It signifies the act of joining together again after a period of separation.

**487. आगे निकल** — *overtake* — This verb is used to describe the action of passing someone or something in a race or competition. It signifies moving ahead or surpassing others in terms of speed, progress, or achievement.

**488. उछालना** — *hurl* — The verb 'उछालना' is used to describe the action of forcefully throwing or launching something with great strength or energy. It conveys the idea of propelling an object through the air with a sudden and powerful motion.

• *1.* पानी ने उसे उछालने पर मजबूर कर दिया। *2.* उन्होंने गेंद उछालने की कोशिश की. *3.* मुझे लगता है मैं उछाल दूँगा. • *1.* The water made her want to hurl. *2.* He tried to hurl the ball. *3.* I think I'm gonna hurl.

**489. फिराना** — *wield* — 'फिराना' is used to describe the action of wielding or handling something, typically a weapon or tool. It implies a sense of control and power over the object being wielded.

**490. पहले से देखना** — *foresee* — This verb is used to describe the act of predicting or anticipating an event or outcome before it actually happens. It implies having the ability to foresee or anticipate something in advance.

**491. संचित करना** — *garner* — The verb 'संचित करना' is used to describe the action of collecting or accumulating something over time. It implies the process of gathering or amassing resources, information, or wealth for future use.

**492. शांत करना** — *soothe, quell, placate, assuage* — This verb is used to describe the action of calming or soothing someone or a situation, typically by reducing anger, tension, or anxiety. It implies bringing peace or tranquility to a person or a situation.

**493. झनकना** — *clank* — The verb 'झनकना' is used to describe the sound of metal objects hitting each other, creating a loud and sharp noise. It is often used to depict the clanking of chains, keys, or other metallic objects.

**494. रद्द करें** — *discard* — This verb is used to indicate the action of getting rid of something that is no longer needed or wanted. It is commonly used in various contexts to express the act of discarding or disposing of something.

**495. पुनर्मिलन करना** — *reunite* — This verb is used to describe the action of coming together again after being separated, often used in the context of reuniting with family members, friends, or loved ones.

**496. डाका मारना** — *hijack* — This verb is used to describe the act of forcefully taking control of a vehicle, especially a plane or a train, by threatening violence or using weapons in order to steal goods or demand ransom.

**497. दृढ़ रहना** — *persist, persevere* — To 'दृढ़ रहना' means to continue with determination and persistence despite challenges or obstacles. It signifies a strong resolve to achieve a goal or overcome difficulties through unwavering perseverance.

**498. पुनर्निर्माण करना** — *rearrange, reorganize* — This verb is used to describe the action of restructuring or rearranging something in order to improve its organization or efficiency. It involves making changes to the existing structure or system to make it more effective.

**499. अति घृणा करना** — *detest* — This verb is used to express a strong feeling of dislike or hatred towards someone or something. It conveys a sense of extreme aversion or repulsion towards the object of detestation.

**500. रूपांतरित करना** — *modify* — This verb is used to describe the action of making changes or alterations to something in order to improve or adjust its appearance, structure, or function.

**501. सुड़कना** — *sup* — The verb 'सुड़कना' is used to describe the action of sipping or drinking something slowly and quietly. It is often used to indicate the gentle and controlled manner in which a liquid is consumed.

**502. कुढ़ाना** — *irritate* — 'कुढ़ाना' is used to describe the feeling of annoyance or frustration caused by someone or something. It signifies a sense of irritation or agitation towards a person or situation.

**503. मलामत करना** — *disapprove* — 'Malamat karna' is used to express disapproval or criticism towards someone or something. It conveys a sense of disapproval or dissatisfaction with a particular action, behavior, or decision.

**504. बदनाम करना** — *discredit* — This verb is used to describe the action of causing someone or something to lose their good reputation or credibility by spreading negative information or rumors about them.

**505. नंगा करना** — *dismantle, disrobe* — This verb is used to describe the action of taking apart or removing clothing or other items. It can also be used metaphorically to describe breaking down or destroying something.

**506. पुनप्र्रारंभ करें** — *restart* — This verb is used to indicate the action of starting something again after it has been stopped or paused. It is commonly used in the context of technology, work projects, or any other situation where something needs to be restarted.

**507. फिर से खेलना** — *replay* — The verb 'फिर से खेलना' is used to describe the action of playing something again or replaying it. It signifies the act of repeating a game, sport, or any other activity that involves playing.

**508. पृष्टांकन करना** — *endorse* — To endorse means to officially approve, support, or recommend something or someone. It is often used in the context of signing a document or statement to show agreement or approval.

**509. कुतरना** — *nibble* — 'कुतरना' is used to describe the action of taking small bites or nibbles of food. It implies eating in a delicate or dainty manner, often used to describe how someone is eating something slowly and carefully.

**510. इठलाना** — *strut, flaunt, dally* — The verb 'इठलाना' is used to describe the action of showing off or flaunting something in a playful or teasing manner. It can also mean to dally or linger over something in a leisurely or carefree way.

**511. वापस लेना** — *retract, revoke* — This verb is used to describe the action of taking something back or canceling a previous decision or statement. It implies the act of retracting or revoking something that was previously given or done.

**512. मिटा देना** — *annihilate, quash, annul* — 'Mita dena' is used to describe the act of completely destroying or eliminating something, whether it be physical objects, ideas, or relationships. It signifies the complete annihilation or cancellation of something.

**513. संरक्षण करना** — *patronize* — This verb is used to describe the act of supporting or protecting someone or something, often in a condescending or overprotective manner. It implies a sense of superiority or control over the person or thing being patronized.
- *1.* मुझे संरक्षण मत दो. *2.* मैं तुम्हें संरक्षण नहीं दे रहा हूं. *3.* वे स्थानीय व्यवसायों को संरक्षण देते हैं। *4.* मैं आपके स्टोर का संरक्षण करूंगा. *5.* मैं ऐसे प्रतिष्ठानों को संरक्षण नहीं देता. • *1.* Don't patronize me. *2.* I'm not patronizing you. *3.* They patronize local businesses. *4.* I will patronize your store. *5.* I don't patronize such establishments.

**514. ध्वस्त करना** — *demolish* — The verb 'ध्वस्त करना' is used to describe the action of completely destroying or tearing down something, such as a building, structure, or object. It signifies the act of demolishing or ruining something completely.
- *1.* सेना ने दुश्मन के गढ़ को ध्वस्त करने की योजना बनाई. *2.* तूफान जल्द ही तटीय शहर को ध्वस्त कर देगा। *3.* विस्फोट अपने र-

ास्ते में आने वाली हर चीज को ध्वस्त कर देगा। *4.* पुरानी इमारत के अवशेषों को ध्वस्त कर दिया गया। • *1.* The army planned to demolish the enemy's stronghold. *2.* The hurricane would soon demolish the coastal town. *3.* The explosion would demolish everything in its path. *4.* The remnants of the old building were demolished.

### 515. उबाल आना — *perk* — 'उबाल आना' is used to describe the action of something coming to a boil or reaching a high point of excitement or activity. It signifies a sudden increase in intensity or energy.

### 516. भौंकना — *yap* — The verb 'भौंकना' is used to describe the action of a dog making a sharp, high-pitched bark. It is often used to convey the sound of a dog barking loudly and repeatedly.

### 517. चढ़ना — *ascend* — The verb 'चढ़ना' is used to describe the action of moving upwards or climbing. It is commonly used to indicate ascending stairs, mountains, or any other elevated surface.

### 518. मंडित कतना — *corroborate* — 'मंडित कतना' is used to indicate the act of confirming or verifying the truth or accuracy of something. It is often used in formal or legal contexts to establish the validity of a statement or claim.

### 519. अपनी बात दोहराना — *recycle* — To repeat or reuse something, especially for a different purpose or in a different form.

### 520. छाँटना — *prune, pare* — 'छाँटना' is used to describe the action of trimming or cutting away excess or unwanted parts of something, such as branches from a tree or skin from a fruit. It is a verb that signifies the act of pruning or paring.

### 521. चरमराना — *creak* — The verb 'चरमराना' is used to describe the sound made by a door, floorboard, or other object when it makes a high-pitched, squeaking noise as it moves or is stepped on.

● *1.* फ़्लोरबोर्ड चरमराने लगे। *2.* उसकी कुर्सी से ज़ोर क-
ी चरमराहट की आवाज आई। *3.* लिमोज़ीन का दरवाज़ा चरमराहट
के साथ खुला। ● *1.* The floorboards began to creak. *2.* His
chair emitted a loud creak. *3.* The limousine door opened with
a creak.

## 522. हिम्मत तोड़ना — *discourage* — This verb is used
to describe the act of causing someone to lose confidence or
determination in pursuing a goal or course of action. It implies
the act of dissuading or demoralizing someone.

## 523. बाहर फैंकना — *eject* — The verb 'बाहर फैंकना' is
used to describe the action of forcefully removing something or
someone from a particular place or situation. It implies a sudden
and forceful expulsion or rejection.

## 524. चमकीला — *bling* — The verb 'चमकीला' is used to de-
scribe something that is shiny, sparkly, or flashy. It is often used
to refer to jewelry, clothing, or accessories that are adorned with
glittering embellishments.

## 525. बपतिस्मा देना — *baptize* — This verb is used to
describe the act of performing a religious ritual involving water
to symbolize purification or initiation into a particular faith. It is
commonly practiced in Christian and Sikh traditions.
● *1.* क्या आपने बपतिस्मा लिया था? ● *1.* Were you baptized?

## 526. निष्क्रिय करें — *deactivate* — The verb 'निष्क्रिय करें'
is used to describe the action of deactivating or disabling something, such as an account, device, or service. It signifies the act
of rendering something inactive or non-functional.
● *1.* कंप्यूटर, बल क्षेत्र को निष्क्रिय करें। *2.* इसे निष्क्रिय कर-
ें. *3.* अलार्म सिस्टम स्वचालित रूप से निष्क्रिय हो सकता
है। *4.* सिस्टम निष्क्रिय. *5.* उपयोग के बाद मशीन निष्क्रिय हो
जाएगी। ● *1.* Computer, deactivate force field. *2.* Deactivate it.
*3.* The alarm system can deactivate automatically. *4.* System
deactivated. *5.* The machine will deactivate after use.

## 527. कूजना — *coo* — The verb 'कूजना' is used to describe

the soft, murmuring sound made by doves, pigeons, or other birds. It is a gentle and soothing sound that is often associated with peace and tranquility.

528. **झुकाना** — *flex, incline* — The verb 'झुकाना' is used to describe the action of bending or leaning forward or downward. It is often used to indicate a physical movement or gesture of inclining or bowing in a respectful manner.

529. **पुनः कनेक्ट** — *reconnect* — The verb 'पुनः कनेक्ट' is used to describe the action of establishing a connection or re-establishing a connection between two or more things, such as devices, people, or ideas, that were previously linked or in communication with each other.

530. **उत्साहित करना** — *motivate* — This verb is used to describe the action of inspiring or encouraging someone to take action or achieve a goal. It is often used in the context of providing support, encouragement, or positive reinforcement to boost someone's morale or determination.

531. **प्रतिकार करना** — *retaliate* — This verb is used to describe the act of responding to an attack or insult with a similar action in return. It signifies a form of retaliation or revenge in response to a perceived wrongdoing.

532. **चरना** — *graze* — The verb 'चरना' is used to describe the action of animals feeding on grass or plants by grazing. It signifies the act of moving around and eating small amounts of vegetation from a pasture or field.

533. **सुरक्षित रखना** — *conserve, safekeeping* — This verb is used to describe the act of protecting something or someone from harm or damage, ensuring their safety and well-being. It implies the action of preserving or maintaining something in a secure and protected state.
• *1. अपना बारूद सुरक्षित रखें.* • *1. Conserve your ammo.*

534. **ठहरना** — *snuggle* — This verb is used to describe

the act of getting close to someone or something in a cozy and comfortable manner, often for warmth or affection. It implies a sense of intimacy and closeness.

**535. ठनकाना** — *tinkle* — The verb 'ठनकाना' is used to describe the sound of a small bell or metal object making a light, high-pitched ringing noise. It is often used to depict the sound of small objects hitting each other.

**536. विजय प्राप्त करना** — *vanquish* — The verb 'विजय प्राप्त करना' is used to describe the act of defeating or conquering someone or something in a battle, competition, or conflict. It signifies achieving victory or success over an opponent.

**537. गला घोंटना** — *smother, throttle* — This verb is used to describe the action of forcefully restricting someone's breathing by covering their mouth and nose, usually with the intention of causing harm or death. It implies a violent and aggressive act of suffocation.
- *1.* वापस गला घोंटना. • *1.* Throttle back.

**538. मिलाप करना** — *condone, pacify* — This verb is used to describe the act of forgiving or making peace with someone after a disagreement or conflict. It implies a sense of understanding and acceptance towards the other person's actions or behavior.

**539. प्रतिबंधित करना** — *confine* — This verb is used to describe the action of restricting someone or something within certain boundaries or limits. It implies the act of confining or limiting movement, freedom, or access.

**540. बल देना** — *emphasize* — This verb is used to highlight or stress a particular point or idea in a conversation or discussion. It is used to draw attention to something important or significant.

**541. स्थानांतरित करना** — *relocate* — This verb is used to describe the action of moving from one place to another, typically referring to a person or group of people relocating to a new residence or office space.

542. **सुदृढ बनाना** — *reinforce* — This verb is used to describe the action of making something stronger or more secure. It is often used in the context of adding support or stability to something that is weak or vulnerable.

543. **मचलना** — *sulk, pester* — 'मचलना' is used to describe someone who is sulking or pestering someone else. It conveys a sense of annoyance or irritation, often in a passive-aggressive manner.

544. **कांपना** — *vibrate* — The verb 'कांपना' is used to describe the action of vibrating or shaking. It is often used to convey a sense of movement or trembling in objects or individuals.
• *1.* उसकी आवाज़ कांपती हुई सी लग रही थी. *2.* कुत्ता जोर से भौंका, उसकी श्वास नली कांप रही थी। • *1.* Her voice seemed to vibrate. *2.* The dog barked loudly, his windpipe vibrating.

545. **महत्त्वाकांक्षा करना** — *aspire* — This verb is used to express a strong desire or ambition to achieve something significant or important. It conveys the idea of aiming for a goal or dream with determination and motivation.

546. **प्रकट अपनी** — *divulge* — The verb 'प्रकट अपनी' is used to describe the action of revealing or disclosing information that was previously unknown or secret. It is often used in contexts where someone is sharing personal or confidential details.

547. **जड़ से उखाड़ना** — *eradicate, uproot* — This verb is used to describe the action of completely removing or destroying something, typically a problem or obstacle, from its roots or source. It signifies a thorough and complete elimination of the issue.
• *1.* उसे अपना जीवन उखाड़ना पड़ा। • *1.* She had to uproot her life.

548. **माफ** — *waive* — The verb 'माफ' is used to indicate the

act of waiving or forgiving something, such as a fee, penalty, or debt. It is commonly used in formal and informal settings to show leniency or generosity.

**549. सुन पाना** — *overhear* — This verb is used to describe the act of unintentionally hearing something that was not meant for you to hear. It implies that the information was heard without the speaker's knowledge or consent.

**550. वश में करना** — *subdue, quell* — This verb is used to describe the act of bringing something under control or suppressing it. It implies the use of power or authority to calm or pacify a situation or individual.

**551. संघर्ष करना** — *contend* — This verb is used to describe the act of struggling or fighting against something, whether it be a physical opponent, a difficult situation, or one's own inner conflicts. It conveys a sense of resistance and determination.
• *1.* उसे एक कठिन बॉस से संघर्ष करना पड़ा। • *1.* She had to contend with a difficult boss.

**552. भेष बदलना** — *simulate* — The verb 'भेष बदलना' is used to describe the act of imitating or pretending to be someone or something else. It is often used in the context of acting or role-playing to simulate a different persona.

**553. छोटा करना** — *shorten, minimize* — This verb is used to describe the action of making something shorter or reducing its size or duration. It is often used when referring to tasks, time, or physical objects that need to be minimized or shortened.

**554. डालती** — *exert* — The verb 'डालती' is used to convey the action of exerting physical or mental effort. It signifies putting in energy or force to achieve a particular goal or outcome.

**555. सेवा करना** — *cater* — The verb 'सेवा करना' is used to describe the act of providing food or services at a social gathering or event. It implies the act of serving or catering to the needs of others.

**556. चोट पहुंचाना** — *injure* — This verb is used to describe the action of causing harm or injury to someone or something. It signifies the act of physically or emotionally hurting someone, resulting in pain or damage.

**557. रौंदे** — *trample* — The verb 'रौंदे' is used to describe the action of stepping heavily or forcefully on something, typically causing damage or destruction. It conveys the idea of crushing or flattening something underfoot.

**558. बुझाने** — *extinguish* — The verb 'बुझाने' is used to describe the action of extinguishing or putting out a fire, light, or any other source of flame or heat. It signifies the act of making something stop burning.

**559. एक्सेल** — *excel* — To perform exceptionally well or surpass others in a particular task or skill.

**560. उतरना** — *dismount, alight* — 'उतरना' is used to describe the action of getting off a vehicle or descending from a higher place. It can also be used to indicate the act of coming down from a particular position or status.

**561. हर्क जमाना** — *assert* — To 'हर्क जमाना' means to confidently state or declare something with conviction. It is used to assert one's opinion, belief, or authority on a particular matter.

**562. बेदखल करना** — *evict* — To 'evict' means to force someone to leave a property, typically because they have not paid rent or have violated the terms of their lease. It involves legally removing someone from a place they are occupying.

**563. कुड़कुड़ाना** — *cluck, cackle* — This verb is used to describe the sound made by chickens or other birds. It is often used to depict the noise made by a group of birds, typically in a lively or excited manner.

**564. विनियमित** — *regulate* — The verb 'विनियमित' is used to describe the action of controlling or managing something according to a set of rules or guidelines. It is often used in the context of regulating behavior, activities, or processes.
● *1.* उन्होंने व्यापार को विनियमित करने के लिए कानून बनाए। *2.* सरकार ने उद्योग को विनियमित करने की मांग की। *3.* फार्मास्युटिकल उद्योग अत्यधिक विनियमित है। ● *1.* They enacted laws to regulate trade. *2.* The government sought to regulate the industry. *3.* The pharmaceutical industry is highly regulated.

**565. फिर से आना** — *revisit* — The verb 'फिर से आना' is used to describe the action of revisiting a place, situation, or topic. It implies returning to something that has been previously experienced or discussed.

**566. मर जाना** — *succumb* — The verb 'मर जाना' is used to indicate when someone succumbs to a situation or condition, often resulting in death. It can also be used metaphorically to describe giving in to pressure or defeat.

**567. फंसाना** — *implicate* — 'फंसाना' is used to describe the act of implicating someone in a situation or crime. It signifies the act of involving someone in a difficult or problematic situation, often leading to consequences for that person.

**568. ठीक कर लेना** — *insure* — To 'ठीक कर लेना' means to ensure or make sure of something. It implies taking necessary actions to guarantee a certain outcome or result.

**569. हथकंडा करना** — *juggle* — To perform the action of 'हथकंडा करना' means to skillfully manipulate multiple objects in the air using hands. It requires coordination, dexterity, and focus to successfully juggle.

**570. संगठित करना** — *mobilize* — This verb is used to describe the action of organizing and bringing together resources, people, or forces for a specific purpose or goal. It involves coordinating efforts and rallying support towards a common objective.

**571. गरदानना** — *circulate* — 'गरदानना' is used to describe the action of circulating or spreading something, such as information, news, or rumors, among a group of people or within a community.

**572. तलाशी करना** — *prowl* — 'Talashi karna' is used to describe the action of moving around quietly and stealthily in search of something or someone. It implies a sense of caution and secrecy in the pursuit of a target.

**573. अंत होना** — *expire* — This verb is used to indicate the end or expiration of something, such as a contract, subscription, or warranty. It signifies the completion or termination of a specific period or duration.

**574. फूटना** — *erupt* — The verb 'फूटना' is used to describe sudden and violent outbursts or eruptions, such as a volcano erupting or a person bursting into anger. It signifies a rapid and intense release of energy or emotion.

**575. ऊपर उठाना** — *elevate* — This verb is used to describe the action of lifting something up or raising it to a higher position. It signifies the act of increasing the height or level of an object or person.

**576. ईंधन झोंकना** — *stoke* — This verb is used to describe the action of adding fuel or stirring a fire to increase its intensity or keep it burning. It is commonly used in the context of cooking or heating.

**577. सामूहीकरण करना** — *socialize* — This verb is used to describe the act of interacting and engaging with others in a social setting. It involves forming connections, building relationships, and participating in group activities to foster a sense of community and belonging.

**578. निवास करना** — *inhabit, reside* — This verb is used to describe the action of living or staying in a particular place for an extended period of time. It implies a sense of permanence or regularity in one's residence or dwelling.

**579. जल्दी करना** — *hasten* — The verb 'जल्दी करना' is used to convey the idea of speeding up or doing something quickly. It is often used to urge someone to hurry or to emphasize the need for prompt action.

**580. बन्दी बनाना** — *imprison* — This verb is used to describe the action of confining someone in a prison or jail as a form of punishment or to prevent them from causing harm or escaping.

**581. टुकड़े करना** — *dissect* — This verb is used to describe the action of cutting or dividing something into smaller pieces or parts, typically for the purpose of analysis, study, or examination.

**582. टालना** — *avert, postpone, defer* — The verb 'टालना' is used to indicate the act of postponing or deferring something, or to describe someone avoiding or skulking a responsibility or task.

**583. नाचना** — *frisk* — The verb 'नाचना' is used to describe the action of frisking or searching someone for hidden items. It is commonly used in situations where security personnel or law enforcement officers need to conduct a thorough search.

**584. मित्र बनाना** — *befriend* — 'Mitri banana' is used to describe the action of forming a friendship with someone. It signifies the act of establishing a bond or connection with another person based on mutual trust, respect, and understanding.

**585. अभिनय करना** — *portray, enact, impersonate* — This verb is used to describe the action of portraying a character or acting out a role, often in a theatrical or dramatic context. It involves embodying the emotions, gestures, and mannerisms of the character being portrayed.

**586. ठमकना** — *flinch* — 'ठमकना' is used to describe the action of flinching or reacting suddenly to a sudden noise, movement, or sensation. It conveys the idea of a quick, involuntary movement in response to a stimulus.

**587. पढ़ने में भूलना** — *misread* — The verb 'पढ़ने में भूलना' is used to describe the act of misreading something, such as misinterpreting words or sentences while reading. It signifies a mistake made while trying to understand written text.

**588. तैयार करना** — *constitute* — 'तैयार करना' is used to describe the act of forming or creating something, typically a group, organization, or system. It signifies the process of putting together various elements to establish a particular entity or structure.

**589. उताने पड़ जाना** — *grovel* — 'उताने पड़ जाना' is used to describe the act of behaving in a submissive or overly obedient manner in order to gain favor or forgiveness from someone in a position of power or authority.

**590. नाम लिखना** — *enroll, subscribe* — The verb 'नाम लिखना' is used to indicate the action of enrolling or subscribing to something, such as a course, membership, or service. It signifies the act of officially registering or signing up for a particular program or offering.

**591. सरसराना** — *swish* — This verb is used to describe the sound or movement of something moving quickly through the air, typically with a smooth and continuous motion.

**592. फिर से लेना** — *retake* — The verb 'फिर से लेना' is used when someone wants to take something again, especially in the context of a photograph, test, or video recording. It implies a repetition or a second attempt at acquiring something.

**593. बंद कर देना** — *desist* — This verb is used to indicate stopping or ceasing an action or behavior. It implies putting an end to something that was previously happening or being done.

**594. अभियोग लगाना** — *indict, impeach* — This verb is used to formally accuse someone of a crime or wrongdoing, typically in a legal or official setting. It implies a serious allegation and initiates a legal process against the accused individual.
• *1.* ग्रांड जूरी ने अभियोग लगाने का निर्णय लिया। *2.* अभिय-ोजक ने अभियोग लगाने की मांग की। • *1.* The grand jury decided to indict. *2.* The prosecutor sought to indict.

**595. सम्मोहित** — *hypnotize* — The verb 'सम्मोहित' is used to describe the act of putting someone into a trance-like state through the power of suggestion or concentration. It is often used in the context of hypnotism or mind control.

**596. लुभाने** — *entice* — The verb 'लुभाने' is used to describe the action of enticing or luring someone into doing something by using persuasion or temptation. It is often used in contexts where someone is trying to manipulate or influence another person's actions.
• *1.* उसने उसे लुभाने के लिए अपने आकर्षण का इस्तेमाल किया। *2.* बेकरी का ह्यांग लुभावना था। *3.* स्टूडल की मीठी गंध ने उसे लुभाया। *4.* उन्होंने नए ग्राहकों को लुभाने के लिए एक अभियान चलाया। *5.* वित्तीय प्रलोभन बहुत लुभावना था। • *1.* He used his charm to entice her. *2.* The hyang from the bakery was enticing. *3.* The sweet smell of the strudel enticed her. *4.* They launched a campaign to entice new customers. *5.* The financial inducement was too enticing.

**597. मीठा करना** — *sweeten* — The verb 'मीठा करना' is used to describe the action of adding sugar or sweetening agents to food or drinks in order to make them taste sweeter.

**598. जोड़ देना** — *weld* — 'जोड़ देना' is used to describe the action of joining two or more pieces of metal together by using heat or pressure. It is a process commonly used in metalworking to create strong and durable connections between materials.

**599. सरल करना** — *simplify* — This verb is used to describe the action of making something easier to understand or do by removing complexities or difficulties. It is used to streamline processes or explanations for better comprehension.

**600. छिपकर बातें सुनना** — *eavesdrop* — To listen secretly to someone else's conversation without their knowledge or permission.

**601. शान दिखाना** — *flaunt* — To 'शान दिखाना' means to show off or display something in a boastful or proud manner. It is used to describe someone flaunting their possessions, achievements, or status in order to impress others.

**602. जमा करना** — *accumulate, constitute* — This verb is used to describe the action of gathering or collecting items or resources over time to build up a larger quantity or amount. It can also refer to forming a part of a whole or making up a certain percentage.

**603. पेश आना** — *deport* — The verb 'पेश आना' is used to describe the action of forcibly removing someone from a country, typically due to a violation of immigration laws or for security reasons.

**604. तंग करना** — *pester, peddle, vex, molest* — 'Tang karna' is used to describe the act of annoying, bothering, or harassing someone. It can also refer to persistently trying to sell something or causing discomfort or distress to someone.

**605. दिक करना** — *molest* — This verb is used to describe unwanted and inappropriate physical or sexual advances towards someone, typically in a forceful or aggressive manner. It conveys a sense of violation and disrespect towards the victim.

**606. सही करना** — *rectify, proofread* — This verb is used

120

to correct errors or mistakes in a written document or any other form of communication. It is used to ensure accuracy and improve the quality of the content.

**607. कांव-कांव करना** — *caw* — This verb is used to describe the sound made by a crow. It is an onomatopoeic word that mimics the sound of a crow's call.

**608. वापस जाना** — *retrace* — The verb 'वापस जाना' is used to describe the action of retracing one's steps or going back to a previous location or situation. It implies a return to a previous state or position.

**609. मेल खाना** — *coincide, tally* — This verb is used to describe when two or more things align or match up perfectly in terms of timing, location, or characteristics. It signifies a harmonious agreement or correspondence between different elements.

**610. बना होना** — *consist* — This verb is used to describe the composition or makeup of something, indicating what it consists of or is made up of. It is used to convey the idea of something being comprised of certain elements or components.

**611. हस्ताक्षर करना** — *subscribe* — To 'हस्ताक्षर करना' means to officially agree to receive or support something, such as a publication or service, by signing one's name.

**612. अंग-विच्छेद करना** — *amputate* — This verb is used to describe the surgical removal of a body part, typically a limb or digit, due to injury, disease, or medical necessity. It involves separating the affected body part from the rest of the body.

**613. टुकड़े में करना** — *sunder* — The verb 'टुकड़े में करना' is used to describe the action of breaking or separating something into smaller pieces or parts. It signifies the act of dividing or splitting something into fragments.

**614. नली लगाना** — *intubate* — The verb 'नली लगाना' is used in medical contexts to describe the process of inserting a tube into a person's airway to assist with breathing. This procedure is typically done by trained medical professionals in emergency situations.

**615. लडखडाना** — *wobble* — The verb 'लडखडाना' is used to describe the action of moving unsteadily from side to side, as if about to fall. It conveys the idea of instability or lack of balance.

**616. घटित होना** — *befall* — 'घटित होना' is used to describe an event or situation that happens unexpectedly or suddenly. It is often used to convey a sense of something unfortunate or negative occurring.

**617. अयुक्त आचरण करना** — *misbehave* — This verb is used to describe actions or behaviors that are inappropriate, disrespectful, or unacceptable. It refers to behaving in a manner that goes against social norms or expectations.

**618. कम होना** — *lessen* — This verb is used to indicate a decrease in quantity, intensity, or degree of something. It is used to express the action of reducing or diminishing something in amount or size.

**619. सिर काट लेना** — *behead* — The verb 'सिर काट लेना' is used to describe the act of cutting off someone's head. It is a violent and extreme action often associated with punishment or execution.

**620. हिम्मत करना** — *daresay* — This verb is used to express a sense of daring or courage in making a statement or assumption. It implies taking a risk in expressing an opinion or belief, often in a situation where there is uncertainty or doubt.
• 1. मैं हिम्मत करके कहता हूं कि आज बारिश होगी. 2. उन्होंने हिम्मत करके कहा कि यह एक गलती थी। • 1. I daresay it will rain today. 2. He daresay it was a mistake.

**621. लौट आना** — *revert* — The verb 'लौट आना' is used to describe the action of returning to a previous state or condition. It signifies going back to a previous position, situation, or behavior.

**622. ऐंठना** — *squirm* — The verb 'ऐंठना' is used to describe the action of twisting or wriggling in discomfort or unease. It conveys the idea of moving in a contorted or awkward manner, often due to physical or emotional discomfort.

**623. बजना** — *jiggle, clang, clank* — The verb 'बजना' is used to describe the sound produced by hitting two objects together, creating a loud and metallic noise. It is often used to convey the idea of something striking or hitting another object.

**624. संशोधन करना** — *amend, rectify* — This verb is used to describe the action of making changes or corrections to something in order to improve or correct it. It is often used in legal, academic, or administrative contexts.

**625. दाँत निपोड़ना** — *smirk* — This verb is used to describe the act of smiling in a smug or self-satisfied manner, often in response to someone else's misfortune or mistake. It conveys a sense of superiority or amusement.

**626. मैला करना** — *contaminate, sully* — This verb is used to describe the action of making something dirty or impure. It is often used to convey the idea of tarnishing or polluting something that was previously clean or pure.

**627. स्मरण करना** — *recollect* — This verb is used to describe the act of recalling or remembering something from the past. It is often used to bring back memories or thoughts that have been forgotten or overlooked.

**628. जिंदा रहना** — *liven* — The verb 'जिंदा रहना' is used to convey the idea of staying alive, vibrant, and full of energy. It is often used to describe someone or something that is lively, active, and thriving.

**629. व्यापक बनाने** — *broaden* — The verb 'व्यापक बनाने' is used to describe the action of expanding or extending something in order to make it more comprehensive or inclusive. It is often used to indicate the process of broadening one's perspective or understanding.

**630. आतंकित करना** — *terrorize* — This verb is used to describe the act of instilling fear or terror in someone or a group of people through violent or threatening actions. It conveys the idea of causing extreme fear and anxiety.
● *1.* उस पागल ने शहर को आतंकित कर दिया। *2.* उन्होंने आबादी को आतंकित कर दिया। *3.* उन्होंने शहर को बेधड़क आतंकित कर दिया। *4.* एक लड़ाई ने शहर को आतंकित कर दिया। ● *1.* The maniac terrorized the town. *2.* They terrorized the population. *3.* They terrorized the town with impunity. *4.* A wight terrorized the town.

**631. पहचान करना** — *discriminate* — This verb is used to describe the act of distinguishing or recognizing differences between people, things, or situations based on specific characteristics or qualities. It involves making judgments or decisions based on these distinctions.

**632. आस्थगित करें** — *defer* — To defer means to postpone or delay an action or decision to a later time. It is used when one chooses to put off something that was originally planned or scheduled to happen sooner.

**633. कैंची से काटना** — *scissor* — The verb 'कैंची से काटना' is used to describe the action of cutting something with scissors. It specifically refers to using a pair of scissors to separate or trim something.

**634. फोड़ना** — *cleave* — The verb 'फोड़ना' is used to describe the action of splitting or breaking something into two or more parts. It signifies a forceful and decisive action that results in a clean separation.

124

**635. कठोर बनाना** — *harden* — The verb 'कठोर बनाना' is used to describe the action of making something rigid or firm. It is often used to indicate the process of toughening or strengthening something.

**636. मंज़ूर करना** — *validate, condescend* — 'Manzoor karna' is used to indicate the act of approving, accepting, or agreeing to something. It can also be used to show a sense of condescension or patronizing behavior towards someone or something.

**637. उलझाना** — *confound* — 'उलझाना' is used to describe the act of causing confusion or perplexity. It signifies the state of being tangled or entangled in a complex or difficult situation, leading to a sense of bewilderment or uncertainty.
- *1.* इसे उलझाओ! • *1.* Confound it!

**638. नीचे गिर पड़ना** — *topple* — The verb 'नीचे गिर पड़ना' is used to describe the action of something falling or toppling downwards suddenly or unexpectedly. It signifies a loss of balance or stability resulting in a sudden descent.

**639. धमकी देकर मांगना** — *extort* — This verb is used to describe the act of obtaining something, typically money, through threats or intimidation. It implies coercing someone into giving up something of value by instilling fear or using force.

**640. पीछे हटाना** — *recapture* — The verb 'पीछे हटाना' is used to describe the action of recapturing something that was lost or taken away. It signifies the act of regaining possession or control over something that was previously held.

**641. भेद जान लेना** — *differentiate* — This verb is used to describe the action of distinguishing or recognizing the differences between two or more things. It is commonly used when discussing the process of identifying unique characteristics or qualities in order to make distinctions.

**642. कोड़े लगाना** — *flog* — The verb 'कोड़े लगाना' is used to describe the act of beating or whipping someone as a form of punishment or discipline. It signifies inflicting physical pain on someone as a means of correction or retribution.

**643. प्रतिपूर्ति करना** — *reimburse* — To 'प्रतिपूर्ति करना' means to repay or compensate someone for expenses or losses incurred. It involves giving back money or resources that were spent or lost in a particular situation.
- *1.* मैं तुम्हें प्रतिपूर्ति करूंगा. • *1.* I'll reimburse you.

**644. प्रवृत्त करना** — *incite* — This verb is used to describe the action of encouraging or provoking someone to engage in a particular behavior or activity. It implies influencing someone to take action or behave in a certain way.

**645. चीरना** — *disintegrate* — The verb 'चीरना' is used to describe the process of breaking or tearing something into small pieces or fragments. It signifies the act of disintegrating or falling apart, often resulting in the destruction or deterioration of the object.

**646. वश में रखना** — *enslave* — This verb is used to describe the act of controlling or dominating someone or something completely, often in a negative or oppressive manner. It implies a sense of power and control over the person or object.

**647. जा बसना** — *migrate* — 'जा बसना' is used to describe the act of permanently moving from one place to another, typically for better opportunities or living conditions. It signifies a significant change in residence and lifestyle.

**648. गंवाना** — *squander* — The verb 'गंवाना' is used to describe the act of wasting or losing something valuable, such as money, time, or resources. It implies a careless or reckless behavior that leads to the depletion or loss of something.

**649. डराकर रोकना** — *deter* — To deter means to

prevent or discourage someone from doing something by instilling fear or doubt in their mind. It is used to stop or hinder a particular action or behavior from occurring.

**650. लुप्त हो जाना** — *evaporate* — The verb 'लुप्त हो जाना' is used to describe the process of something disappearing or vanishing into thin air. It signifies the act of evaporating or dissipating completely, leaving no trace behind.

**651. बहाल करना** — *reinstate* — The verb 'बहाल करना' is used to describe the action of restoring someone or something to a previous position, status, or condition. It signifies the act of reinstating or bringing back something that was lost or removed.

**652. उथल-पुथल होना** — *overturn* — 'उथल-पुथल होना' is used to describe a situation where something is turned upside down or overturned. It signifies chaos, confusion, or disorder. It is often used to depict a state of disarray or upheaval.

**653. परिसमाप्त करना** — *liquidate* — The verb 'परिसमाप्त करना' is used to describe the action of settling or closing out a financial account or business, typically by selling off assets to pay off debts or distribute remaining funds to stakeholders.

**654. परिणाम निकालना** — *deduce, infer* — This verb is used to draw conclusions or make educated guesses based on available information or evidence. It involves using reasoning and logic to come to a specific outcome or understanding.

**655. खीझाना** — *vex* — 'खीझाना' is used to describe the feeling of annoyance or frustration caused by someone or something. It signifies a sense of irritation or vexation towards a particular situation or individual.

**656. प्रकट करना** — *signify, disclose, divulge* — This verb is used to express the action of revealing or making something known that was previously hidden or secret. It is often used in contexts where information or truth is being shared openly.

**657. फुलाना** — *inflate* — The verb 'फुलाना' is used to describe the action of filling something with air or gas to make it expand or become larger in size. It is commonly used when talking about inflating balloons, tires, or balls.
• *1.* उन्होंने गुब्बारे फुलाने के लिए एक पंप का इस्तेमाल किया। • *1.* They used a pump to inflate the balloons.

**658. दाह-संस्कार करना** — *cremate* — This verb is used to describe the act of burning a deceased person's body as part of funeral rites. It is a traditional practice in Hindu culture to perform this ritual to honor the deceased and release their soul.

**659. संख्या से बढ़ना** — *outnumber* — This verb is used to describe a situation where one group or thing has a greater quantity or number than another group or thing. It signifies a comparison in terms of numerical superiority.
• *1.* हमारी संख्या अधिक है. *2.* आपकी संख्या अधिक है. *3.* हमारी संख्या अधिक थी. *4.* मेरी संख्या अधिक है. *5.* उनकी संख्या अधिक नहीं की जा सकी. • *1.* We're outnumbered. *2.* You're outnumbered. *3.* We were outnumbered. *4.* I'm outnumbered. *5.* They could not be outnumbered.

**660. संपुष्टि करना** — *attest* — The verb 'संपुष्टि करना' is used to confirm or verify the truth or accuracy of something. It is often used in legal or official contexts to provide evidence or support for a claim or statement.

**661. धोना और प्रेस** — *launder* — The verb 'धोना और प्रेस' is used to describe the act of washing and pressing clothes to make them clean and neat. It is a common household chore that involves cleaning and ironing garments.

**662. खाल उतारना** — *flay* — The verb 'खाल उतारना' is used to describe the action of removing the skin or outer covering of something, typically an animal. It is often used in the context of preparing meat or hides for various purposes.

**663. न पहिचानना** — *disown* — This verb is used to

describe the act of refusing to acknowledge or accept someone or something as one's own. It signifies a deliberate decision to distance oneself from a person or thing.

**664. तरफ़ चलना** — *sidle* — 'तरफ़ चलना' means to move sideways in a cautious or sneaky manner. It implies a subtle or sly movement, often used to describe someone trying to avoid attention or sneak past someone else.

**665. खाद डालना** — *nourish, fertilize* — This verb is used to describe the action of providing nutrients to plants or soil in order to promote growth and health. It is commonly used in agriculture and gardening contexts to describe the process of fertilizing.

**666. उढ़ाना** — *clothe* — 'उढ़ाना' is used to describe the action of putting clothes on someone or oneself. It signifies the act of dressing or covering oneself with garments.

**667. अलग करना** — *detach, disassemble, insulate* — This verb is used to describe the action of separating or breaking apart something into its individual parts, isolating or insulating something from its surroundings, distinguishing or differentiating between two or more things, or dividing or splitting something into separate parts.

**668. मार्ग बनाना** — *pave* — This verb is used to describe the action of creating a path or road, typically by clearing obstacles or making way for others to follow. It signifies the act of paving the way for something or someone.

**669. ऊंचा उठना** — *transcend* — The verb 'ऊंचा उठना' is used to describe the action of surpassing or rising above something, often in a metaphorical sense. It signifies going beyond limitations or boundaries to achieve a higher level of success or understanding.

**670. वसीयत में देना** — *bequeath* — This verb is used to describe the act of leaving property or assets to someone in a will or testament. It signifies the process of passing on one's belongings to another person after one's death.

**671. हटना** — *deviate* — The verb 'हटना' is used to describe the action of deviating or moving away from a particular path, direction, or course of action. It signifies a change in direction or movement away from a specified point.

**672. टटोलना** — *grope* — The verb 'टटोलना' is used to describe the action of feeling or searching for something with one's hands, especially in a clumsy or fumbling manner. It can also refer to groping in a sexual context.

**673. नीचा दिखाना** — *degrade, downplay, demean, disparage* — This verb is used to describe the act of belittling or diminishing someone or something, often by making them seem less important, valuable, or worthy than they actually are.
• *1.* वह खुद को नीचा नहीं दिखाना चाहता था. *2.* उम्मीदवार ने अपने प्रतिद्वंद्वी को नीचा दिखाना चुना। • *1.* He didn't want to degrade himself. *2.* The candidate chose to disparage his opponent.

**674. टिमटिमाना** — *shimmer* — This verb is used to describe something that shines or glimmers with a soft, flickering light. It is often used to depict something sparkling or twinkling, creating a beautiful and radiant effect.

**675. गड़बड़ कर देना** — *fumble* — To 'गड़बड़ कर देना' means to make a mistake or error while doing something, resulting in confusion or clumsiness. It implies a lack of coordination or skill in performing a task.
• *1.* वह ऑक्स कनेक्शन में गड़बड़ी कर रही थी। • *1.* She fumbled with the aux connection.

**676. ठीक गोली चलाना** — *snipe* — This verb is used to describe the action of shooting accurately and precisely at a target from a hidden or distant position. It implies a sense of skill and precision in aiming and hitting the target.

**677. दुबकना** — *lurk* — The verb 'दुबकना' is used to describe the action of lurking or hiding in a secretive or sneaky manner. It implies staying out of sight or remaining unnoticed while observing or waiting for something.

**678. छिपकर जाना** — *tiptoe, prowl, slink, skulk* — This verb is used to describe the action of moving stealthily or furtively, often with the intention of avoiding detection or observation. It implies a sense of secrecy or sneakiness in one's movements.

**679. लड़खड़ाना** — *falter* — The verb 'लड़खड़ाना' is used to describe a situation where someone is unsteady or unsure in their actions or speech. It conveys the idea of stumbling or hesitating in a task or conversation.

**680. जानवर खिलाना** — *browse* — This verb is used to describe the action of allowing animals to graze or feed on plants in a specific area. It can also refer to the act of browsing or scrolling through content on the internet or a digital device.

**681. मिलने** — *trickle* — The verb 'मिलने' is used to describe the action of something flowing or moving in a slow, steady stream. It is often used to describe the movement of liquids or small particles.

**682. नाम देना** — *christen* — This verb is used to give a name to someone or something, typically in a formal or ceremonial manner. It is often used in the context of naming a child or giving a title to a new creation.

**683. देख लेना** — *discern* — 'Dekh lena' is used to convey the act of discerning or perceiving something with clarity or understanding. It implies the ability to see or understand something clearly or to notice subtle details.

**684. है प्रदान** — *impart* — The verb 'है प्रदान' is used to convey the action of imparting knowledge, skills, or information to someone. It signifies the act of sharing or giving something valuable to another person for their benefit or growth.

● *1.* उसने अपना ज्ञान प्रदान करने का प्रयास किया। ● *1.* She tried to impart her wisdom.

**685. भटकना** — *swerve, rove* — The verb 'भटकना' is used to describe the action of wandering aimlessly or roaming around without a specific destination. It implies a sense of being lost or disoriented while moving from place to place.

**686. झंझट करना** — *haggle* — This verb is used to describe the act of negotiating or arguing over a price or terms of a deal in order to reach a mutually agreeable outcome. It is commonly used in marketplaces and during business transactions.

**687. श्रेणीबद्ध करना** — *classify* — To organize or arrange items into specific categories based on their similarities or differences. This verb is used when grouping things together based on certain criteria to make it easier to understand or manage them.

**688. कम हो जाना** — *belittle* — This verb is used to describe the act of making someone or something seem less important, impressive, or valuable. It is often used to diminish someone's achievements, abilities, or worth.

**689. भुनभुनाना** — *grumble* — This verb is used to describe the act of complaining or expressing dissatisfaction in a low, muttering voice. It conveys a sense of discontent or annoyance with a situation or person.

**690. रूप देना** — *sculpt* — This verb is used to describe the action of shaping or forming something, typically in a creative or artistic manner. It implies the act of creating a physical representation of an idea or concept through careful manipulation of materials.

**691. आनंद लेना** — *revel* — To 'revel' is to take great pleasure or delight in something. It is used to describe the act of enjoying oneself immensely, often in a celebratory or joyful manner.

**692. भरपाई** — *replenish* — The verb 'भरपाई' is used to describe the action of filling or refilling something that has been depleted or emptied. It signifies the act of replenishing or restoring something to its original state.

**693. अपवित्र करना** — *defile, desecrate* — This verb is used to describe the action of making something impure or unholy. It is often used in religious contexts to refer to the act of defiling a sacred place or object.
• *1.* युद्ध ने ऐतिहासिक स्थल को अपवित्र कर दिया। *2.* उसने अपने सिद्धांतों को अपवित्र करने से इनकार कर दिया। *3.* शहर प्रदूषण से अपवित्र हो गया था। • *1.* The battle defiled the historic site. *2.* She refused to defile her principles. *3.* The town was defiled by pollution.

**694. गरमाना** — *bask* — This verb is used to describe the action of exposing oneself to warmth or sunlight in order to feel comfortable or relaxed. It conveys the idea of enjoying the warmth and feeling content.

**695. हीत्च हैक करना** — *hitchhike* — To hitchhike is to travel by getting free rides from passing vehicles, typically by standing on the side of the road and signaling for a ride.

**696. समृद्ध बनाना** — *enrich* — This verb is used to describe the action of making something or someone richer, more prosperous, or more abundant. It signifies the process of enhancing or improving the quality or quantity of something.
• *1.* यह पाठ्यक्रम आपके कौशल को समृद्ध करने के लिए डिज़ाइन किया गया है। *2.* संगीत अनुभव को समृद्ध करेगा। *3.* पुस्तक आपके ज्ञान को समृद्ध करेगी। *4.* उर्वरक मिट्टी को समृद्ध करेगा। *5.* हमें अपने जीवन को समृद्ध बनाने की जरूरत है। • *1.* The course is designed to enrich your skills. *2.* The music will enrich the experience. *3.* The book will enrich your knowledge. *4.* The fertilizer will enrich the soil. *5.* We need to enrich our lives.

**697. शांति लाना** — *pacify* — This verb is used to describe the action of calming or soothing someone or a situation in order to bring peace and tranquility. It is often used in contexts where conflicts or tensions need to be resolved.

**698. मथना** — *churn* — The verb 'मथना' is used to describe the action of churning or mixing ingredients together in a circular motion. It is commonly used in cooking to blend ingredients or in religious rituals to symbolize transformation or purification.

**699. अधिक प्रार्थना करना** — *peddle* — To 'अधिक प्रार्थना करना' means to sell goods or services by going from place to place or door to door. It involves persuading people to buy what you are offering through direct interaction.

**700. अलग धकेलना** — *shunt* — To 'shunt' means to move or transfer something to a different position or place, typically in a forceful or abrupt manner. It is often used in the context of trains being redirected onto a different track.

# 2. Index of Words

| | |
|---|---|
| अंग-विच्छेद करना (612) | amputate |
| अंडे रखना (461) | spawn |
| अंत होना (573) | expire |
| अंतर करना (370) | distinguish, differ |
| अंशदान करना (268) | contribute |
| अति घृणा करना (499) | detest |
| अतिरंजना करना (289) | exaggerate |
| अधिक प्रार्थना करना (699) | peddle |
| अधिकार देना (437) | authorize |
| अधिकार रखना (72) | deserve |
| अनुकरण करना (417) | imitate, simulate, emulate |
| अनुकूल बनाना (257) | adapt, accommodate |
| अनुमति देना (67) | allow |
| अनुमोदन करना (153) | approve |
| अनुवाद करना (222) | translate |
| अनुसरण करना (38) | follow |
| अन्वेषण करना (184) | explore |
| अपडेट करें (204) | update |
| अपनाना (214) | adopt, assimilate, siphon |
| अपनी बात दोहराना (519) | recycle |
| अपमान करना (225) | offend, desecrate |
| अपराधी घोषित करना (228) | convict |
| अपवित्र करना (693) | defile, desecrate |
| अपहरण करना (183) | kidnap, abduct |

| | |
|---|---|
| अपेक्षा करना (49) | expect |
| अभिनय करना (585) | portray, enact, impersonate |
| अभियुक्त करना (312) | prosecute |
| अभियोग लगाना (594) | indict, impeach |
| अभिवादन करना (175) | greet |
| अभ्यास करना (246) | rehearse |
| अयुक्त आचरण करना (617) | misbehave |
| अलग कर देना (307) | isolate |
| अलग करना (667) | detach, disassemble, insulate |
| अलग धकेलना (700) | shunt |
| अलसाना (271) | slug |
| अवज्ञा करना (369) | disobey |
| अवशोषित करना (319) | absorb |
| अवहेलना करना (285) | defy |
| असम्मत होना (173) | disagree |
| आकर्षित (197) | attract |
| आक्रमण करना (270) | invade |
| आग लगना (449) | ignite |
| आगे निकल (487) | overtake |
| आगे बढ़ना (390) | outrun, slog |
| आगे बढ़ाने (189) | pursue |
| आतंकित करना (630) | terrorize |
| आनंद लेना (691) | revel |
| आनन्द करे (317) | rejoice |
| आना (5) | come |

| | |
|---|---|
| आपत्ति में डालना (394) | jeopardize |
| आपस में मिलना (387) | mingle |
| आरंभ करना (294) | initiate, undertake |
| आरोप (196) | accuse |
| आरोप लगा देना (463) | denounce |
| आरोपित करना (221) | transplant |
| आलोचना करना (331) | criticize, maul |
| आविष्कार करना (234) | invent |
| आशंका करना (473) | apprehend |
| आस्थगित करें (632) | defer |
| इकट्ठा करना (109) | gather, collect |
| इठलाना (510) | strut, flaunt, dally |
| ईंधन झोंकना (576) | stoke |
| उच्चारण करना (230) | pronounce |
| उछालना (488) | hurl |
| उठना (259) | arise |
| उड़ना (56) | fly, flit |
| उढ़ाना (666) | clothe |
| उतरना (560) | dismount, alight |
| उताने पड़ जाना (589) | grovel |
| उतार देना (357) | upgrade |
| उतारना (264) | unload, subvert |
| उत्तर में कहना (471) | replicate |
| उत्तेजित करना (441) | excite, irritate, agitate, stimulate |

| | |
|---|---|
| उत्साहित करना (530) | motivate |
| उथल-पुथल होना (652) | overturn |
| उधार देना (122) | lend |
| उपस्थित होना (116) | attend |
| उबाल आना (515) | perk |
| उभाड़ना (444) | hoist |
| उलझाना (637) | confound |
| ऊंचा उठना (669) | transcend |
| ऊंची उड़ान भरना (436) | soar |
| ऊपर उठाना (575) | elevate |
| एक होना (231) | unite |
| एकत्र करना (272) | assemble |
| एक्सेल (559) | excel |
| ऐंठना (622) | squirm |
| ओवरलुक (367) | overlook |
| कठोर बनाना (635) | harden |
| कड़ी आलोचना करना (295) | slash |
| कपटवध करना (391) | assassinate |
| कब्ज़ा (288) | occupy |
| कम हो जाना (688) | belittle |
| कम होना (618) | lessen |
| कमज़ोर करना (442) | weaken |
| कमाना (105) | earn |
| करना (2) | do, make |
| कल्पना करना (48) | imagine |

| | |
|---|---|
| कहना (10) | say, tell |
| कहलवाना (332) | transmit |
| का आनंद लें (54) | enjoy |
| कांपना (544) | vibrate |
| कांव-कांव करना (607) | caw |
| काटकर अलग करना (481) | sever |
| काटना (82) | bite, chop |
| काम करना (292) | retard |
| कामयाब होना (366) | thrive |
| कायम रखना (364) | uphold |
| की घोषणा (149) | announce |
| की जांच (171) | examine |
| की पहचान (123) | identify |
| की सिफारिश (142) | recommend |
| कुचलना (359) | throttle |
| कुड़कुड़ाना (563) | cluck, cackle |
| कुढ़ाना (502) | irritate |
| कुतरना (509) | nibble |
| कुम्हलाना (483) | wither |
| कूजना (527) | coo |
| कृतार्थ होना (400) | prosper |
| कृषि योग्य बनाना (409) | reclaim |
| कैंची से काटना (633) | scissor |
| को खत्म (190) | eliminate |
| को बढ़ावा देना (252) | promote |

| | |
|---|---|
| कोड़े लगाना (642) | flog |
| क्रूस पर (454) | crucify |
| क्लिक (150) | click |
| क्षति से बचाना (321) | salvage |
| क्षमा मांगना (74) | apologize |
| खंडन करना (450) | contradict, deflate, refute, disprove |
| खटखटाना (318) | clatter |
| खड़ा करना (478) | erect |
| खड़ा होना (279) | oppose |
| खरोंचना (470) | scrabble |
| खाद डालना (665) | nourish, fertilize |
| खाल उतारना (662) | flay |
| खिन्न होना (476) | yearn |
| खिलना (240) | blossom |
| खींचना (41) | pull, draw |
| खीझाना (655) | vex |
| खुलना (344) | uncover |
| खेलना (23) | play |
| खोजना (129) | discover, retrace |
| खोदना (90) | dig |
| खोना (36) | lose |
| खोल देना (218) | untie, unzip, deploy, unleash |
| खोलना (24) | open, untie |
| गंवाना (648) | squander |

| | |
|---|---|
| गड़बड़ कर देना (675) | fumble |
| गति बढ़ाना (440) | accelerate |
| गरदानना (571) | circulate |
| गरमाना (694) | bask |
| गला घोंटना (537) | smother, throttle |
| गवाही देना (136) | testify |
| गहरा बनाना (460) | sharpen, escalate |
| ग़लती होना (320) | err |
| गाली मार देना (375) | zap |
| गुणा करना (386) | multiply |
| घटित होना (616) | befall |
| घास काटना (428) | mow |
| घुमाएँ (421) | rotate |
| घुलाना (383) | dissolve |
| घुस पड़ना (360) | intrude |
| घुसना (299) | penetrate |
| घूमना (263) | roam, circulate, revolve |
| घूरना (154) | stare, gloat, ogle |
| घोषित (172) | declare |
| चढ़ना (517) | ascend |
| चबाने (185) | chew |
| चमकाना (141) | polish, refine |
| चमकीला (524) | bling |
| चरना (532) | graze |
| चरमराना (521) | creak |

| | |
|---|---|
| चलना (32) | walk |
| चलाना (22) | run |
| चलो (8) | let |
| चाटना (168) | lick |
| चाहेंगे (9) | would |
| चिढ़ाना (215) | tease, ruffle, rile |
| चिल्लाई (303) | holler |
| चिल्लाना (112) | shout, yell, exclaim |
| चीरना (645) | disintegrate |
| चुकाना (178) | repay, liquidate |
| चुनना (35) | pick, choose |
| चुनें (64) | choose |
| चुप बनाना (291) | shush |
| चुप रहना (169) | hush |
| चुराना (68) | steal |
| चूसना (93) | suck |
| चेतावनी देना (101) | warn |
| चोंच मारना (293) | peck |
| चोट पहुंचाना (556) | injure |
| छमकना (334) | clink |
| छलकाना (482) | slop |
| छाँटना (520) | prune, pare |
| छाती से लगाना (329) | cuddle |
| छिड़कना (453) | sprinkle, dredge |
| छिपकर जाना (678) | tiptoe, prowl, slink, skulk |

| | |
|---|---|
| छिपकर बातें सुनना (600) | eavesdrop |
| छिपाना (55) | hide |
| छोटा करना (553) | shorten, minimize |
| छोड़कर अन्यत्र जाना (220) | evacuate |
| छोड़ना (61) | quit, cease |
| छोड़ें (121) | skip |
| जकड़ना (347) | fasten |
| जगाना (45) | wake |
| जड़ से उखाड़ना (547) | eradicate, uproot |
| जबह करना (241) | lam |
| जब्त (198) | seize |
| जमा करना (602) | accumulate, constitute |
| जलना (70) | burn |
| जल्दी करना (579) | hasten |
| ज़ब्त करना (451) | confiscate, impound |
| ज़मानत करना (311) | vouch |
| ज़ोर से मारना (443) | swipe |
| जा बसना (647) | migrate |
| जांच करना (134) | investigate |
| जानना (4) | know |
| जानवर खिलाना (680) | browse |
| जारी रखें (62) | continue |
| जासूसी करना (395) | snoop |
| जिंदा रहना (628) | liven |
| जीतना (37) | win, overcome, conquer |

| | |
|---|---|
| जीना (20) | live |
| जुड़ना (53) | join |
| जोखिम में डालना (433) | endanger |
| जोड़ देना (598) | weld |
| जोड़ना (87) | add, join, connect |
| जोर से मारना (438) | lash, bash |
| झंझट करना (686) | haggle |
| झगड़ा तय करना (380) | accommodate |
| झनकना (493) | clank |
| झांसना (242) | seduce |
| झुंझलाना (456) | madden |
| झुंझुला देना (282) | annoy |
| झुकाना (528) | flex, incline |
| झेलना (323) | withstand |
| टकराना (455) | collide |
| टटोलना (672) | grope |
| टालना (582) | avert, postpone, defer |
| टिंग (304) | ting |
| टिन से मढ़ना (327) | tinker |
| टिमटिमाना (674) | shimmer |
| टुकड़े करना (581) | dissect |
| टुकड़े टुकड़े करना (408) | crumble |
| टुकड़े में करना (613) | sunder |
| टूटने (412) | shatter |
| ट्रैश किए गए (337) | trashed |

| | |
|---|---|
| ठगना (346) | fudge |
| ठनकाना (535) | tinkle |
| ठमकना (586) | flinch |
| ठहरना (534) | snuggle |
| ठहराना (485) | nominate, mete, allocate |
| ठीक कर लेना (568) | insure |
| ठीक गोली चलाना (676) | snipe |
| डरपोक समझा (314) | wimp |
| डराकर रोकना (649) | deter |
| डराना (91) | scare |
| डांटना (278) | scold, chide |
| डाका मारना (496) | hijack |
| डालती (554) | exert |
| डालना (315) | insert, infuse |
| डिस्कनेक्ट (385) | disconnect |
| डींग मारना (429) | boast, rant |
| डुबो देना (381) | dunk |
| ढालना (265) | mold, mould |
| तंग करना (604) | pester, peddle, vex, molest |
| तकलीफ देना (115) | torture |
| तरफ़ चलना (664) | sidle |
| तराशना (276) | trim, pare |
| तलना (160) | fry |
| तलाशी करना (572) | prowl |
| ताज़गी लाना (335) | freshen |

| | |
|---|---|
| ताज़ा करना (393) | refresh, freshen |
| तामील करना (208) | execute |
| तिरस्कार करना (237) | despise, detest |
| तैयार करना (588) | constitute |
| तैरना (96) | swim |
| तोड़ना (31) | break, disappoint |
| त्यागपत्र देना (199) | resign |
| थपथपाना (132) | pat |
| थोपना (298) | impose, inflict |
| दण्ड देना (458) | inflict |
| दफनाना (111) | bury |
| दबाना (325) | clamp, stifle, strangle, pacify |
| दस्तंदाज़ी करना (398) | meddle |
| दाँत निपोड़ना (625) | smirk |
| दान करना (245) | donate |
| दाह-संस्कार करना (658) | cremate |
| दिक करना (605) | molest |
| दिखाऊ बनाना (466) | visualize |
| दिखाना (19) | show, demonstrate |
| दुबकना (677) | lurk |
| दुर्बल करना (407) | undermine |
| दूषित करना (435) | mar, sully |
| दृढ़ रहना (497) | persist, persevere |
| देख लेना (683) | discern |
| देखना (7) | see, look |

| | |
|---|---|
| देना (13) | give |
| दैनिक काम करना (464) | char |
| दोहराना (92) | repeat |

| | |
|---|---|
| धक्का (158) | shove |
| धड़ाका करना (368) | detonate |
| धब्बे लगाना (310) | sully |
| धमकाना (155) | threaten, intimidate, terrorize |
| धमकी देकर मांगना (639) | extort |
| धरण करना (341) | retain |
| धारा निकलना (354) | squirt |
| धोखा देना (248) | deceive, mislead, circumvent |
| धोना (80) | wash |
| धोना और प्रेस (661) | launder |
| ध्यान केन्द्रित करना (287) | dwell |
| ध्यान में लाना (392) | conceive |
| ध्वस्त करना (514) | demolish |
| न पहिचानना (663) | disown |
| नंगा करना (505) | dismantle, disrobe |
| नकारना (110) | deny |
| नज़रअंदाज़ करना (108) | ignore |
| नली लगाना (614) | intubate |
| नष्ट करना (397) | devour, dissipate, extinguish |
| नष्ट हो जाना (274) | perish |

| | |
|---|---|
| नाचना (583) | frisk |
| नापसन्द करना (446) | loathe |
| नाम देना (682) | christen |
| नाम लिखना (590) | enroll, subscribe |
| नालिश करना (100) | sue |
| निकालना (81) | draw, withdraw |
| निगलना (145) | swallow, merge, ingest |
| नियंत्रित करना (187) | contain, restrain |
| नियुक्त करना (269) | employ, appoint, nominate |
| निराश करना (174) | disappoint |
| निर्णय करना (65) | decide |
| निर्माण करना (371) | construct |
| निलंबित (350) | suspend |
| निवास करना (578) | inhabit, reside |
| निवेदन करना (206) | plead |
| निष्कासित करना (404) | expel |
| निष्क्रिय करें (526) | deactivate |
| निहारना (300) | pry, behold |
| निहुरना (376) | stoop |
| नीचा दिखाना (673) | degrade, downplay, demean, disparage |
| नीचे गिर पड़ना (638) | topple |
| नेविगेट (401) | navigate |
| पकड़ना (135) | capture, seize, tackle, grapple |
| पकाना (73) | cook |

| | |
|---|---|
| पछताना (260) | rue, repent |
| पढ़ना (30) | read |
| पढ़ने में भूलना (587) | misread |
| पनपने (419) | flourish |
| परामर्श करना (219) | consult |
| परिचालित करना (403) | govern |
| परिणाम निकालना (654) | deduce, infer |
| परिसमाप्त करना (653) | liquidate |
| पवित्र करना (362) | cleanse, purify, consecrate, sanctify |
| पहचान करना (631) | discriminate |
| पहचानना (77) | recognize |
| पहनना (47) | wear |
| पहरे में डालना (434) | nab |
| पहले से देखना (490) | foresee |
| पहुंच जाना (267) | regain |
| पहुंचना (99) | arrive |
| पांव रखना (283) | tread |
| पागल होना (374) | rave |
| पादना (193) | fart |
| पालन करना (164) | observe, execute, comply |
| पालन करना (340) | comply, abide, adhere |
| पिघल (191) | melt |
| पीछे पीछे फिरना (462) | lug |
| पीछे रह जाना (477) | lag |

| | |
|---|---|
| पीछे हटाना (640) | recapture |
| पीना (28) | drink |
| पुकारना (120) | hail |
| पुनः कनेक्ट (529) | reconnect |
| पुनः प्राप्त (239) | retrieve |
| पुनर्निर्माण करना (498) | rearrange, reorganize |
| पुनर्प्रारंभ करें (506) | restart |
| पुनर्मिलन करना (495) | reunite |
| पुनर्विचार करना (244) | reconsider |
| पुष्टि करना (117) | confirm, endorse, validate, reaffirm |
| पूछना (18) | ask |
| पूजा करना (203) | adore |
| पूरा करना (351) | suffice, offset, finalize |
| पृष्ठांकन करना (508) | endorse |
| पेट गिरना (262) | abort |
| पेश आना (603) | deport |
| पैदा करना (297) | generate, pique, procreate |
| पोंछना (114) | wipe |
| प्रकट अपनी (546) | divulge |
| प्रकट करना (656) | signify, disclose, divulge |
| प्रकाशित करना (224) | publish, proclaim |
| प्रगट करना (448) | proclaim |
| प्रचलित होना (353) | prevail |
| प्रतिकार करना (531) | retaliate |

| | |
|---|---|
| प्रतिक्रिया करना (157) | react |
| प्रतिनिधित्व करना (131) | represent |
| प्रतिपूर्ति करना (643) | reimburse |
| प्रतिबंधित करना (539) | confine |
| प्रतिबिंबित करना (236) | reflect |
| प्रतिलिपि प्रस्तुत करना (418) | reproduce |
| प्रतिस्पर्धा (166) | compete |
| प्रदर्शन करना (232) | demonstrate |
| प्रदान करना (107) | provide, impart |
| प्रबुद्ध करना (378) | enlighten |
| प्रभावित करना (143) | affect |
| प्रभुत्व रखना (336) | dominate |
| प्रयास करते हैं (388) | strive |
| प्रेरित करना (261) | inspire |
| प्रवृत्त करना (644) | incite |
| प्रवेश करना (86) | enter |
| प्रशंसा करना (139) | admire |
| प्रसारित कर देना (343) | deploy |
| प्रस्ताव करना (137) | propose |
| प्रस्तुत करना (377) | render, submit |
| प्राप्त करना (103) | receive, achieve |
| प्रारंभ करना (66) | begin |
| प्रार्थना करना (78) | pray |
| प्रोत्साहन देना (128) | foster |
| प्रोत्साहित करना (200) | encourage, stimulate |

| | |
|---|---|
| फंसाना (567) | implicate |
| फक-फक करना (324) | chug |
| फड़फड़ाना (365) | flop, snicker |
| फ़रार होना (384) | elope |
| फिर से आना (565) | revisit |
| फिर से खेलना (507) | replay |
| फिर से खोलना (405) | reopen |
| फिर से जोड़ना (486) | rejoin |
| फिर से बनाना (247) | rebuild, reconstruct, realign |
| फिर से भरना (356) | refill, replenish |
| फिर से लिखना (338) | rewrite |
| फिर से लेना (592) | retake |
| फिर से सोचना (399) | rethink |
| फिराना (489) | wield |
| फुलाना (657) | inflate |
| फूटना (574) | erupt |
| फूल का खिलना (195) | bloom |
| फोड़ना (634) | cleave |
| फोर्ज (253) | forge |
| बंद कर देना (593) | desist |
| बचाना (33) | save, defend |
| बजना (623) | jiggle, clang, clank |
| बढ़ती करना (474) | exceed |
| बण्दी बनाना (580) | imprison |
| बदनाम करना (504) | discredit |

| | |
|---|---|
| बदमाशी करना (161) | hector |
| बदला लेना (216) | avenge, retaliate |
| बधाई देना (188) | congratulate |
| बनना (34) | become |
| बना होना (610) | consist |
| बनाएं (83) | create |
| बनाना (11) | make |
| बपतिस्मा देना (525) | baptize |
| बम बरसाना (472) | blitz |
| बल देना (540) | emphasize |
| बसना (85) | settle |
| बहाल करना (651) | reinstate |
| बहुत मूल्यवान समझना (235) | underestimate |
| बातचीत करना (179) | negotiate, converse |
| बाहर निकलने देना (251) | vent |
| बाहर फैंकना (523) | eject |
| बाहर रखना (467) | exclude |
| बिखेरना (411) | disperse |
| बिताना (51) | spend |
| बुझाना (413) | suffocate, extinguish, quench |
| बुझाने (558) | extinguish |
| बेअसर करना (452) | neutralize |
| बेचना (46) | sell |
| बेदख़ल करना (562) | evict |
| बैठना (26) | sit |

| | |
|---|---|
| भंग करना (420) | disrupt |
| भटकना (685) | swerve, rove |
| भनभनाना (140) | buzz |
| भरना (79) | fill |
| भरपाई (692) | replenish |
| भरोसा करना (156) | rely |
| भागना (396) | scoot, shirk, skedaddle |
| भिगोना (296) | soak, dabble |
| भिन्न होना (363) | differ |
| भीख में मांगना (71) | beg |
| भुगतना (95) | suffer |
| भुनभुनाना (689) | grumble |
| भूलना (27) | forget |
| भेद जान लेना (641) | differentiate |
| भेष बदलना (552) | simulate |
| भोजन करना (25) | eat |
| भौंकना (516) | yap |
| मंज़ूर करना (636) | validate, condescend |
| मंडराना (469) | hover |
| मंडित कतना (518) | corroborate |
| मचलना (543) | sulk, pester |
| मजबूर करना (389) | oblige, coerce |
| मज़बूत बनाना (348) | strengthen |
| मथना (698) | churn |
| मन बहलाना (328) | amuse |

| | |
|---|---|
| मना करना (159) | forbid, prohibit, dissuade, foreclose |
| मनाना (94) | celebrate |
| मनोरंजन करना (217) | entertain, amuse |
| मर जाना (566) | succumb |
| मलना (233) | scrub |
| मलामत करना (503) | disapprove |
| महत्त्वाकांक्षा करना (545) | aspire |
| मांगना (106) | seek |
| मानना (16) | feel, believe, reckon, presume |
| माफ़ (548) | waive |
| मार डालना (333) | slay |
| मारना (29) | hit |
| मार्ग बनाना (668) | pave |
| मिटा देना (512) | annihilate, quash, annul |
| मिटाना (209) | erase |
| मित्र बनाना (584) | befriend |
| मिथ्या जानना (273) | misunderstand |
| मिलकर काम करना (163) | cooperate |
| मिलना (21) | meet, unite |
| मिलने (681) | trickle |
| मिलाना (280) | combine, wed, unite, harmonize |
| मिलाप करना (538) | condone, pacify |
| मीठा करना (597) | sweeten |
| मुंहतोड़ प्रहार मारना (275) | swat |

| | |
|---|---|
| मूल्यांकन करना (430) | evaluate |
| मेल कराना (306) | wed |
| मेल खाना (609) | coincide, tally |
| मैथुन करना (210) | bugger, copulate |
| मैला करना (626) | contaminate, sully |
| मोड़ना (373) | divert, deflect |
| यात्रा करना (227) | hike, hitchhike |
| याद दिलाना (88) | remind |
| रक्षा करना (52) | protect, preserve |
| रखना (15) | keep, put, maintain, lodge |
| रगड़ना (138) | rub |
| रटना (479) | cram |
| रद्द करना (119) | cancel, revoke |
| रद्द करें (494) | discard |
| राँभना (345) | moo |
| रिटायर हो जाना (165) | retire |
| रुकें (14) | stop |
| रूप देना (690) | sculpt |
| रूपांतरित करना (500) | modify |
| रेंगना (167) | creep, slither |
| रोकना (125) | prevent, forbid, retain |
| रोना (58) | cry |
| रौंदे (557) | trample |
| लगता है (39) | seem |
| लगना (459) | embark |

| | |
|---|---|
| लगाना (302) | paste |
| लडखडाना (615) | wobble |
| लड़खड़ाना (679) | falter |
| लपेटना (124) | wrap |
| लागू करना (416) | enforce |
| लिखना (40) | write |
| लिखें (427) | compose |
| लिप्त (305) | indulge |
| लीन होना (330) | merge |
| लुप्त हो जाना (650) | evaporate |
| लुभाना (313) | tempt, seduce, entice |
| लुभाने (596) | entice |
| लूटना (98) | rob, ransack |
| ले जाना (60) | carry |
| लेना (1) | have, take |
| लौट आना (621) | revert |
| लौटाना (201) | restore |
| वंचित करना (445) | deprive |
| वचन देना (480) | undertake |
| वश में करना (550) | subdue, quell |
| वश में रखना (646) | enslave |
| वसीयत में देना (670) | bequeath |
| वापस जाना (608) | retrace |
| वापस लेना (511) | retract, revoke |
| विकसित करना (152) | develop, evolve, cultivate |

| | |
|---|---|
| विचलित करना (211) | distract |
| विजय प्राप्त करना (536) | vanquish |
| विज्ञापन करना (415) | advertise |
| वितरित करना (308) | distribute, administer |
| विनाश करना (382) | exterminate, destruct |
| विनियमित (564) | regulate |
| विनीत करना (256) | humiliate |
| विभाजित करना (207) | divide |
| विरोध (126) | resist |
| विवश करना (465) | compel, coerce |
| विशेषज्ञ बनना (475) | specialize |
| विश्लेषण (277) | analyze, analyse |
| विस्फोट करना (148) | explode |
| विस्मित करना (432) | amaze |
| वू (130) | woo |
| वेग से उछालना (238) | flirt |
| व्यवस्था करना (113) | arrange |
| व्यापक बनाने (629) | broaden |
| शपथ दिलाना (426) | administer |
| शरमाना (326) | blush |
| शराब बनाना (316) | brew |
| शांत करना (492) | soothe, quell, placate, assuage |
| शांति लाना (697) | pacify |
| शादी करना (44) | marry, wed |

| | |
|---|---|
| शान दिखाना (601) | flaunt |
| शिकस्त देना (352) | spank |
| शिकायत करना (127) | complain |
| शुद्ध करना (422) | purge, purify, rectify |
| शुरू करना (379) | unleash |
| शोक करना (281) | mourn, grieve |
| शोक मानना (322) | grieve |
| शोषण करना (284) | exploit |
| श्रेणीबद्ध करना (687) | classify |
| संकेत करना (406) | imply, insinuate |

| | |
|---|---|
| संख्या से बढ़ना (659) | outnumber |
| संगठित करना (570) | mobilize |
| संघर्ष करना (551) | contend |
| संचालन करना (414) | supervise |
| संचालित (146) | operate |
| संचित करना (491) | garner |
| संजोना (255) | cherish, embellish |
| संतुष्ट करना (12) | please, satisfy |
| संदूषित करना (431) | infect |
| संपत्ति होना (76) | belong |
| संपादन करना (355) | edit, procure |
| संपुष्टि करना (660) | attest |
| संभालना (50) | handle |

| | |
|---|---|
| संरक्षण करना (513) | patronize |
| संलग्र करें (309) | attach |
| संशोधन करना (624) | amend, rectify |
| सज़ा देना (133) | punish, chastise |
| सजाना (339) | decorate, adorn |
| सड़ना (457) | fester, decompose |
| सत्यापित करें (250) | verify, validate |
| सफ़ाई से बरतना (258) | manipulate |
| समझना (17) | understand |
| समझने (439) | decipher |
| समझाना (43) | explain |
| समझाने (104) | convince |
| समर्पित करना (290) | dedicate |
| समाधान करना (102) | solve |
| समाप्त होना (192) | cease, perish, expire |
| समायोजन करना (212) | adjust, coordinate |
| समाविष्ट करना (358) | implant |
| समृद्ध बनाना (696) | enrich |
| सम्मोहित (595) | hypnotize |
| सरल करना (599) | simplify |
| सरसराना (591) | swish |
| सराहना (63) | appreciate |
| सहन करना (186) | tolerate |
| सहना (202) | endure, tolerate |
| सहानुभूति रखना (447) | sympathize |

| | |
|---|---|
| सहायता करना (182) | assist |
| सहारा लेना (181) | resort |
| सही करना (606) | rectify, proofread |
| साँस लेना (75) | breathe |
| साबित करना (59) | prove |
| सामना (205) | cope, withstand |
| सामूहीकरण करना (577) | socialize |
| सावधान होना (177) | beware |
| सिकुड़ना (176) | shrink |
| सिर काट लेना (619) | behead |
| सीखना (42) | learn |
| सीधे खड़े हो (402) | shun |
| सीना (243) | sew |
| सुझाना (84) | suggest |
| सुड़कना (501) | sup |
| सुदृढ़ बनाना (542) | reinforce |
| सुधारना (162) | improve, modify, improvise, refine |
| सुन पाना (549) | overhear |
| सुनाना (286) | recite, pronounce |
| सुरक्षित रखना (533) | conserve, safekeeping |
| सुलझाना (468) | unravel |
| सूंघना (254) | sniff |
| सूचना देना (372) | herald, publicize |
| सूचित करना (118) | inform, imply, signify |

| सूचित करें (223) | notify |
|---|---|
| सेंकना (226) | bake |
| सेवा करना (555) | cater |
| सोचना (6) | think, suppose |
| सोते सोते चूकना (423) | snore |
| सौंपना (349) | assign, entrust, commend |
| स्कैन (151) | scan |
| स्टीयर (229) | steer |
| स्थगित करना (266) | postpone |
| स्थानांतरित करना (541) | relocate |
| स्थापित करना (180) | establish, install |
| स्थिर बनाना (424) | stabilize |
| स्पष्ट करना (301) | clarify |
| स्मरण करना (627) | recollect |
| स्वस्थ होना (144) | recover |
| स्वीकार करना (69) | admit, accept |
| हंसना (57) | laugh |
| हटना (671) | deviate |
| हटाना (97) | remove, eliminate |
| हथकंडा करना (569) | juggle |
| हराना (170) | overcome, frustrate, smite, subdue |
| हर्क जमाना (561) | assert |
| हल्का करना (249) | lighten |
| हस्त-मैथुन करना (425) | masturbate |

| | |
|---|---|
| हस्तक्षेप करना (147) | interfere, intervene, tamper |
| हस्ताक्षर करना (611) | subscribe |
| हार्न बजाना (410) | toot |
| हिचकिचाना (194) | hesitate |
| हिम्मत करना (620) | daresay |
| हिम्मत तोड़ना (522) | discourage |
| हिलना (342) | budge |
| हिलाना (89) | shake |
| हिस्सा लेना (213) | participate |
| हीत्च हैक करना (695) | hitchhike |
| हुक्म चलाना (361) | dictate |
| है प्रदान (684) | impart |
| होड़ करना (484) | vie |
| होना (3) | be, happen |

# 3. Index of Words (English)

| | |
|---|---|
| abduct | 183. अपहरण करना |
| abide | 340. पालन करना |
| abort | 262. पेट गिरना |
| absorb | 319. अवशोषित करना |
| accelerate | 440. गति बढ़ाना |
| accept | 69. स्वीकार करना |
| accommodate | 257. अनुकूल बनाना, 380. झगड़ा तय करना |
| accumulate | 602. जमा करना |
| accuse | 196. आरोप |
| achieve | 103. प्राप्त करना |
| adapt | 257. अनुकूल बनाना |
| add | 87. जोड़ना |
| adhere | 340. पालन करना |
| adjust | 212. समायोजन करना |
| administer | 308. वितरित करना, 426. शपथ दिलाना |
| admire | 139. प्रशंसा करना |
| admit | 69. स्वीकार करना |
| adopt | 214. अपनाना |
| adore | 203. पूजा करना |
| adorn | 339. सजाना |
| advertise | 415. विज्ञापन करना |
| affect | 143. प्रभावित करना |
| agitate | 441. उत्तेजित करना |

| alight | 560. उतरना |
| allocate | 485. ठहराना |
| allow | 67. अनुमति देना |
| amaze | 432. विस्मित करना |
| amend | 624. संशोधन करना |
| amputate | 612. अंग-विच्छेद करना |
| amuse | 328. मन बहलाना, 217. मनोरंजन करना |
| analyse | 277. विश्लेषण |
| analyze | 277. विश्लेषण |
| annihilate | 512. मिटा देना |
| announce | 149. की घोषणा |
| annoy | 282. झुंझला देना |
| annul | 512. मिटा देना |
| apologize | 74. क्षमा मांगना |
| appoint | 269. नियुक्त करना |
| appreciate | 63. सराहना |
| apprehend | 473. आशंका करना |
| approve | 153. अनुमोदन करना |
| arise | 259. उठना |
| arrange | 113. व्यवस्था करना |
| arrive | 99. पहुंचना |
| ascend | 517. चढ़ना |
| ask | 18. पूछना |
| aspire | 545. महत्त्वाकांक्षा करना |

| | |
|---|---|
| assassinate | 391. कपटवध करना |
| assemble | 272. एकत्र करना |
| assert | 561. हक़ जमाना |
| assign | 349. सौंपना |
| assimilate | 214. अपनाना |
| assist | 182. सहायता करना |
| assuage | 492. शांत करना |
| attach | 309. संलग्न करें |
| attend | 116. उपस्थित होना |
| attest | 660. संपुष्टि करना |
| attract | 197. आकर्षित |
| authorize | 437. अधिकार देना |
| avenge | 216. बदला लेना |
| avert | 582. टालना |
| bake | 226. सेंकना |
| baptize | 525. बपतिस्मा देना |
| bash | 438. जोर से मारना |
| bask | 694. गरमाना |
| be | 3. होना |
| become | 34. बनना |
| befall | 616. घटित होना |
| befriend | 584. मित्र बनाना |
| beg | 71. भीख में मांगना |
| begin | 66. प्रारंभ करना |
| behead | 619. सिर काट लेना |

| | |
|---|---|
| behold | 300. निहारना |
| believe | 16. मानना |
| belittle | 688. कम हो जाना |
| belong | 76. संपत्ति होना |
| bequeath | 670. वसीयत में देना |
| beware | 177. सावधान होना |
| bite | 82. काटना |
| bling | 524. चमकीला |
| blitz | 472. बम बरसाना |
| bloom | 195. फूल का खिलना |
| blossom | 240. खिलना |
| blush | 326. शरमाना |
| boast | 429. डींग मारना |
| break | 31. तोड़ना |
| breathe | 75. साँस लेना |
| brew | 316. शराब बनाना |
| broaden | 629. व्यापक बनाने |
| browse | 680. जानवर खिलाना |
| budge | 342. हिलना |
| bugger | 210. मैथुन करना |
| burn | 70. जलना |
| bury | 111. दफनाना |
| buzz | 140. भनभनाना |
| cackle | 563. कुड़कुड़ाना |
| cancel | 119. रद्द करना |

| | |
|---|---|
| capture | 135. पकड़ना |
| carry | 60. ले जाना |
| cater | 555. सेवा करना |
| caw | 607. कांव-कांव करना |
| cease | 61. छोड़ना, 192. समाप्त होना |
| celebrate | 94. मनाना |
| char | 464. दैनिक काम करना |
| chastise | 133. सज़ा देना |
| cherish | 255. संजोना |
| chew | 185. चबाने |
| chide | 278. डांटना |
| choose | 35. चुनना, 64. चुनें |
| chop | 82. काटना |
| christen | 682. नाम देना |
| chug | 324. फक-फक करना |
| churn | 698. मथना |
| circulate | 571. गरदानना, 263. घूमना |
| circumvent | 248. धोखा देना |
| clamp | 325. दबाना |
| clang | 623. बजना |
| clank | 493. झनकना, 623. बजना |
| clarify | 301. स्पष्ट करना |
| classify | 687. श्रेणीबद्ध करना |
| clatter | 318. खटखटाना |
| cleanse | 362. पवित्र करना |

| | |
|---|---|
| cleave | 634. फोड़ना |
| click | 150. क्लिक |
| clink | 334. छमकना |
| clothe | 666. उढ़ाना |
| cluck | 563. कुड़कुड़ाना |
| coerce | 389. मजबूर करना, 465. विवश करना |
| coincide | 609. मेल खाना |
| collect | 109. इकट्ठा करना |
| collide | 455. टकराना |
| combine | 280. मिलाना |
| come | 5. आना |
| commend | 349. सौंपना |
| compel | 465. विवश करना |
| compete | 166. प्रतिस्पर्धा |
| complain | 127. शिकायत करना |
| comply | 164. पालन करना, 340. पालन करना |
| compose | 427. लिखें |
| conceive | 392. ध्यान में लाना |
| condescend | 636. मंज़ूर करना |
| condone | 538. मिलाप करना |
| confine | 539. प्रतिबंधित करना |
| confirm | 117. पुष्टि करना |
| confiscate | 451. ज़ब्त करना |
| confound | 637. उलझाना |

| | |
|---|---|
| congratulate | 188. बधाई देना |
| connect | 87. जोड़ना |
| conquer | 37. जीतना |
| consecrate | 362. पवित्र करना |
| conserve | 533. सुरक्षित रखना |
| consist | 610. बना होना |
| constitute | 602. जमा करना, 588. तैयार करना |
| construct | 371. निर्माण करना |
| consult | 219. परामर्श करना |
| contain | 187. नियंत्रित करना |
| contaminate | 626. मैला करना |
| contend | 551. संघर्ष करना |
| continue | 62. जारी रखें |
| contradict | 450. खंडन करना |
| contribute | 268. अंशदान करना |
| converse | 179. बातचीत करना |
| convict | 228. अपराधी घोषित करना |
| convince | 104. समझाने |
| coo | 527. कूजना |
| cook | 73. पकाना |
| cooperate | 163. मिलकर काम करना |
| coordinate | 212. समायोजन करना |
| cope | 205. सामना |
| copulate | 210. मैथुन करना |

| | |
|---|---|
| corroborate | 518. मंडित कतना |
| cram | 479. रटना |
| creak | 521. चरमराना |
| create | 83. बनाएं |
| creep | 167. रेंगना |
| cremate | 658. दाह-संस्कार करना |
| criticize | 331. आलोचना करना |
| crucify | 454. क्रूस पर |
| crumble | 408. टुकड़े टुकड़े करना |
| cry | 58. रोना |
| cuddle | 329. छाती से लगाना |
| cultivate | 152. विकसित करना |
| dabble | 296. भिगोना |
| dally | 510. इठलाना |
| daresay | 620. हिम्मत करना |
| deactivate | 526. निष्क्रिय करें |
| deceive | 248. धोखा देना |
| decide | 65. निर्णय करना |
| decipher | 439. समझने |
| declare | 172. घोषित |
| decompose | 457. सड़ना |
| decorate | 339. सजाना |
| dedicate | 290. समर्पित करना |
| deduce | 654. परिणाम निकालना |
| defend | 33. बचाना |

| | |
|---|---|
| defer | 632. आस्थगित करें, 582. टालना |
| defile | 693. अपवित्र करना |
| deflate | 450. खंडन करना |
| deflect | 373. मोड़ना |
| defy | 285. अवहेलना करना |
| degrade | 673. नीचा दिखाना |
| demean | 673. नीचा दिखाना |
| demolish | 514. ध्वस्त करना |
| demonstrate | 19. दिखाना, 232. प्रदर्शन करना |
| denounce | 463. आरोप लगा देना |
| deny | 110. नकारना |
| deploy | 218. खोल देना, 343. प्रसारित कर देना |
| deport | 603. पेश आना |
| deprive | 445. वंचित करना |
| desecrate | 225. अपमान करना, 693. अपवित्र करना |
| deserve | 72. अधिकार रखना |
| desist | 593. बंद कर देना |
| despise | 237. तिरस्कार करना |
| destruct | 382. विनाश करना |
| detach | 667. अलग करना |
| deter | 649. डराकर रोकना |
| detest | 499. अति घृणा करना, 237. तिरस्कार करना |
| detonate | 368. धड़ाका करना |

| | |
|---|---|
| develop | 152. विकसित करना |
| deviate | 671. हटना |
| devour | 397. नष्ट करना |
| dictate | 361. हुक्म चलाना |
| differ | 370. अंतर करना, 363. भिन्न होना |
| differentiate | 641. भेद जान लेना |
| dig | 90. खोदना |
| disagree | 173. असम्मत होना |
| disappoint | 31. तोड़ना, 174. निराश करना |
| disapprove | 503. मलामत करना |
| disassemble | 667. अलग करना |
| discard | 494. रद्द करें |
| discern | 683. देख लेना |
| disclose | 656. प्रकट करना |
| disconnect | 385. डिस्कनेक्ट |
| discourage | 522. हिम्मत तोड़ना |
| discover | 129. खोजना |
| discredit | 504. बदनाम करना |
| discriminate | 631. पहचान करना |
| disintegrate | 645. चीरना |
| dismantle | 505. नंगा करना |
| dismount | 560. उतरना |
| disobey | 369. अवज्ञा करना |
| disown | 663. न पहिचानना |
| disparage | 673. नीचा दिखाना |

| disperse | 411. बिखेरना |
| disprove | 450. खंडन करना |
| disrobe | 505. नंगा करना |
| disrupt | 420. भंग करना |
| dissect | 581. टुकड़े करना |
| dissipate | 397. नष्ट करना |
| dissolve | 383. घुलाना |
| dissuade | 159. मना करना |
| distinguish | 370. अंतर करना |
| distract | 211. विचलित करना |
| distribute | 308. वितरित करना |
| divert | 373. मोड़ना |
| divide | 207. विभाजित करना |
| divulge | 546. प्रकट अपनी, 656. प्रकट करना |
| do | 2. करना |
| dominate | 336. प्रभुत्व रखना |
| donate | 245. दान करना |
| downplay | 673. नीचा दिखाना |
| draw | 41. खींचना, 81. निकालना |
| dredge | 453. छिड़कना |
| drink | 28. पीना |
| dunk | 381. डुबो देना |
| dwell | 287. ध्यान केन्द्रित करना |
| earn | 105. कमाना |

| | |
|---|---|
| eat | 25. भोजन करना |
| eavesdrop | 600. छिपकर बातें सुनना |
| edit | 355. संपादन करना |
| eject | 523. बाहर फैंकना |
| elevate | 575. ऊपर उठाना |
| eliminate | 190. को खत्म, 97. हटाना |
| elope | 384. फ़रार होना |
| embark | 459. लगना |
| embellish | 255. संजोना |
| emphasize | 540. बल देना |
| employ | 269. नियुक्त करना |
| emulate | 417. अनुकरण करना |
| enact | 585. अभिनय करना |
| encourage | 200. प्रोत्साहित करना |
| endanger | 433. जोखिम में डालना |
| endorse | 117. पुष्टि करना, 508. पृष्ठांकन करना |
| endure | 202. सहना |
| enforce | 416. लागू करना |
| enjoy | 54. का आनंद लें |
| enlighten | 378. प्रबुद्ध करना |
| enrich | 696. समृद्ध बनाना |
| enroll | 590. नाम लिखना |
| enslave | 646. वश में रखना |
| enter | 86. प्रवेश करना |

| | |
|---|---|
| entertain | 217. मनोरंजन करना |
| entice | 313. लुभाना, 596. लुभाने |
| entrust | 349. सौंपना |
| eradicate | 547. जड़ से उखाड़ना |
| erase | 209. मिटाना |
| erect | 478. खड़ा करना |
| err | 320. ग़लती होना |
| erupt | 574. फूटना |
| escalate | 460. गहरा बनाना |

| | |
|---|---|
| establish | 180. स्थापित करना |
| evacuate | 220. छोड़कर अन्यत्र जाना |
| evaluate | 430. मूल्यांकन करना |
| evaporate | 650. लुप्त हो जाना |
| evict | 562. बेदख़ल करना |
| evolve | 152. विकसित करना |
| exaggerate | 289. अतिरंजना करना |
| examine | 171. की जांच |
| exceed | 474. बढ़ती करना |
| excel | 559. एक्सेल |
| excite | 441. उत्तेजित करना |
| exclaim | 112. चिल्लाना |
| exclude | 467. बाहर रखना |
| execute | 208. तामील करना, 164. पालन करना |

| | |
|---|---|
| exert | 554. डालती |
| expect | 49. अपेक्षा करना |
| expel | 404. निष्कासित करना |
| expire | 573. अंत होना, 192. समाप्त होना |
| explain | 43. समझाना |
| explode | 148. विस्फोट करना |
| exploit | 284. शोषण करना |
| explore | 184. अन्वेषण करना |
| exterminate | 382. विनाश करना |
| extinguish | 397. नष्ट करना, 413. बुझाना, 558. बुझाने |
| extort | 639. धमकी देकर मांगना |
| falter | 679. लड़खड़ाना |
| fart | 193. पादना |
| fasten | 347. जकड़ना |
| feel | 16. मानना |
| fertilize | 665. खाद डालना |
| fester | 457. सड़ना |
| fill | 79. भरना |
| finalize | 351. पूरा करना |
| flaunt | 510. इठलाना, 601. शान दिखाना |
| flay | 662. खाल उतारना |
| flex | 528. झुकाना |
| flinch | 586. ठमकना |
| flirt | 238. वेग से उछालना |

| | |
|---|---|
| flit | 56. उड़ना |
| flog | 642. कोड़े लगाना |
| flop | 365. फड़फड़ाना |
| flourish | 419. पनपने |
| fly | 56. उड़ना |
| follow | 38. अनुसरण करना |
| forbid | 159. मना करना, 125. रोकना |
| foreclose | 159. मना करना |
| foresee | 490. पहले से देखना |
| forge | 253. फोर्ज |
| forget | 27. भूलना |
| foster | 128. प्रोत्साहन देना |
| freshen | 335. ताज़गी लाना, 393. ताज़ा करना |
| frisk | 583. नाचना |
| frustrate | 170. हराना |
| fry | 160. तलना |
| fudge | 346. ठगना |
| fumble | 675. गड़बड़ कर देना |
| garner | 491. संचित करना |
| gather | 109. इकट्ठा करना |
| generate | 297. पैदा करना |
| give | 13. देना |
| gloat | 154. घूरना |
| govern | 403. परिचालित करना |

| grapple | 135. पकड़ना |
|---------|-----------|
| graze | 532. चरना |
| greet | 175. अभिवादन करना |
| grieve | 281. शोक करना, 322. शोक मानना |
| grope | 672. टटोलना |
| grovel | 589. उताने पड़ जाना |
| grumble | 689. भुनभुनाना |
| haggle | 686. झंझट करना |
| hail | 120. पुकारना |
| handle | 50. संभालना |
| happen | 3. होना |
| harden | 635. कठोर बनाना |
| harmonize | 280. मिलाना |
| hasten | 579. जल्दी करना |
| have | 1. लेना |
| hector | 161. बदमाशी करना |
| herald | 372. सूचना देना |
| hesitate | 194. हिचकिचाना |
| hide | 55. छिपाना |
| hijack | 496. डाका मारना |
| hike | 227. यात्रा करना |
| hit | 29. मारना |
| hitchhike | 227. यात्रा करना, 695. हीत्च हैक करना |
| hoist | 444. उभाड़ना |

| | |
|---|---|
| holler | 303. चिल्लाई |
| hover | 469. मंडराना |
| humiliate | 256. विनीत करना |
| hurl | 488. उछालना |
| hush | 169. चुप रहना |
| hypnotize | 595. सम्मोहित |
| identify | 123. की पहचान |
| ignite | 449. आग लगना |
| ignore | 108. नज़रअंदाज़ करना |
| imagine | 48. कल्पना करना |
| imitate | 417. अनुकरण करना |
| impart | 107. प्रदान करना, 684. है प्रदान |
| impeach | 594. अभियोग लगाना |
| impersonate | 585. अभिनय करना |
| implant | 358. समाविष्ट करना |
| implicate | 567. फंसाना |
| imply | 406. संकेत करना, 118. सूचित करना |
| impose | 298. थोपना |
| impound | 451. ज़ब्त करना |
| imprison | 580. बण्दी बनाना |
| improve | 162. सुधारना |
| improvise | 162. सुधारना |
| incite | 644. प्रवृत्त करना |
| incline | 528. झुकाना |

| | |
|---|---|
| indict | 594. अभियोग लगाना |
| indulge | 305. लिप्त |
| infect | 431. संदूषित करना |
| infer | 654. परिणाम निकालना |
| inflate | 657. फुलाना |
| inflict | 298. थोपना, 458. दण्ड देना |
| inform | 118. सूचित करना |
| infuse | 315. डालना |
| ingest | 145. निगलना |
| inhabit | 578. निवास करना |
| initiate | 294. आरंभ करना |
| injure | 556. चोट पहुंचाना |
| insert | 315. डालना |
| insinuate | 406. संकेत करना |
| inspire | 261. प्रेरित करना |
| install | 180. स्थापित करना |
| insulate | 667. अलग करना |
| insure | 568. ठीक कर लेना |
| interfere | 147. हस्तक्षेप करना |
| intervene | 147. हस्तक्षेप करना |
| intimidate | 155. धमकाना |
| intrude | 360. घुस पड़ना |
| intubate | 614. नली लगाना |
| invade | 270. आक्रमण करना |
| invent | 234. आविष्कार करना |

| | |
|---|---|
| investigate | 134. जांच करना |
| irritate | 441. उत्तेजित करना, 502. कुढ़ाना |
| isolate | 307. अलग कर देना |
| jeopardize | 394. आपत्ति में डालना |
| jiggle | 623. बजना |
| join | 53. जुड़ना, 87. जोड़ना |
| juggle | 569. हथकंडा करना |
| keep | 15. रखना |
| kidnap | 183. अपहरण करना |
| know | 4. जानना |
| lag | 477. पीछे रह जाना |
| lam | 241. जबह करना |
| lash | 438. जोर से मारना |
| laugh | 57. हंसना |
| launder | 661. धोना और प्रेस |
| learn | 42. सीखना |
| lend | 122. उधार देना |
| lessen | 618. कम होना |
| let | 8. चलो |
| lick | 168. चाटना |
| lighten | 249. हल्का करना |
| liquidate | 178. चुकाना, 653. परिसमाप्त करना |
| live | 20. जीना |
| liven | 628. जिंदा रहना |

| | |
|---|---|
| loathe | 446. नापसन्द करना |
| lodge | 15. रखना |
| look | 7. देखना |
| lose | 36. खोना |
| lug | 462. पीछे पीछे फिरना |
| lurk | 677. दुबकना |
| madden | 456. झुंझलाना |
| maintain | 15. रखना |
| make | 2. करना, 11. बनाना |
| manipulate | 258. सफ़ाई से बरताना |
| mar | 435. दूषित करना |
| marry | 44. शादी करना |
| masturbate | 425. हस्त-मैथुन करना |
| maul | 331. आलोचना करना |
| meddle | 398. दस्तंदाज़ी करना |
| meet | 21. मिलना |
| melt | 191. पिघल |
| merge | 145. निगलना, 330. लीन होना |
| mete | 485. ठहराना |
| migrate | 647. जा बसना |
| mingle | 387. आपस में मिलना |
| minimize | 553. छोटा करना |
| misbehave | 617. अयुक्त आचरण करना |
| mislead | 248. धोखा देना |
| misread | 587. पढ़ने में भूलना |

| | |
|---|---|
| misunderstand | 273. मिथ्या जानना |
| mobilize | 570. संगठित करना |
| modify | 500. रूपांतरित करना, 162. सुधारना |
| mold | 265. ढालना |
| molest | 604. तंग करना, 605. दिक करना |
| moo | 345. राँभना |
| motivate | 530. उत्साहित करना |
| mould | 265. ढालना |
| mourn | 281. शोक करना |
| mow | 428. घास काटना |
| multiply | 386. गुणा करना |
| nab | 434. पहरे में डालना |
| navigate | 401. नेविगेट |
| negotiate | 179. बातचीत करना |
| neutralize | 452. बेअसर करना |
| nibble | 509. कुतरना |
| nominate | 485. ठहराना, 269. नियुक्त करना |
| notify | 223. सूचित करें |
| nourish | 665. खाद डालना |
| oblige | 389. मजबूर करना |
| observe | 164. पालन करना |
| occupy | 288. कब्ज़ा |
| offend | 225. अपमान करना |
| offset | 351. पूरा करना |

| | |
|---|---|
| ogle | 154. घूरना |
| open | 24. खोलना |
| operate | 146. संचालित |
| oppose | 279. खड़ा होना |
| outnumber | 659. संख्या से बढ़ना |
| outrun | 390. आगे बढ़ना |
| overcome | 37. जीतना, 170. हराना |
| overhear | 549. सुन पाना |
| overlook | 367. ओवरलुक |
| overtake | 487. आगे निकल |
| overturn | 652. उथल-पुथल होना |
| pacify | 325. दबाना, 538. मिलाप करना, 697. शांति लाना |
| pare | 520. छाँटना, 276. तराशना |
| participate | 213. हिस्सा लेना |
| paste | 302. लगाना |
| pat | 132. थपथपाना |
| patronize | 513. संरक्षण करना |
| pave | 668. मार्ग बनाना |
| peck | 293. चोंच मारना |
| peddle | 699. अधिक प्रार्थना करना, 604. तंग करना |
| penetrate | 299. घुसना |
| perish | 274. नष्ट हो जाना, 192. समाप्त होना |
| perk | 515. उबाल आना |

| | |
|---|---|
| persevere | 497. दृढ़ रहना |
| persist | 497. दृढ़ रहना |
| pester | 604. तंग करना, 543. मचलना |
| pick | 35. चुनना |
| pique | 297. पैदा करना |
| placate | 492. शांत करना |
| play | 23. खेलना |
| plead | 206. निवेदन करना |
| please | 12. संतुष्ट करना |
| polish | 141. चमकाना |
| portray | 585. अभिनय करना |
| postpone | 582. टालना, 266. स्थगित करना |
| pray | 78. प्रार्थना करना |
| preserve | 52. रक्षा करना |
| presume | 16. मानना |
| prevail | 353. प्रचलित होना |
| prevent | 125. रोकना |
| proclaim | 224. प्रकाशित करना, 448. प्रगट करना |
| procreate | 297. पैदा करना |
| procure | 355. संपादन करना |
| prohibit | 159. मना करना |
| promote | 252. को बढ़ावा देना |
| pronounce | 230. उच्चारण करना, 286. सुनाना |
| proofread | 606. सही करना |

| | |
|---|---|
| propose | 137. प्रस्ताव करना |
| prosecute | 312. अभियुक्त करना |
| prosper | 400. कृतार्थ होना |
| protect | 52. रक्षा करना |
| prove | 59. साबित करना |
| provide | 107. प्रदान करना |
| prowl | 678. छिपकर जाना, 572. तलाशी करना |
| prune | 520. छाँटना |
| pry | 300. निहारना |
| publicize | 372. सूचना देना |
| publish | 224. प्रकाशित करना |
| pull | 41. खींचना |
| punish | 133. सज़ा देना |
| purge | 422. शुद्ध करना |
| purify | 362. पवित्र करना, 422. शुद्ध करना |
| pursue | 189. आगे बढ़ाने |
| put | 15. रखना |
| quash | 512. मिटा देना |
| quell | 550. वश में करना, 492. शांत करना |
| quench | 413. बुझाना |
| quit | 61. छोड़ना |
| ransack | 98. लूटना |
| rant | 429. डींग मारना |

| | |
|---|---|
| rave | 374. पागल होना |
| react | 157. प्रतिक्रिया करना |
| read | 30. पढ़ना |
| reaffirm | 117. पुष्टि करना |
| realign | 247. फिर से बनाना |
| rearrange | 498. पुनर्निर्माण करना |
| rebuild | 247. फिर से बनाना |
| recapture | 640. पीछे हटाना |
| receive | 103. प्राप्त करना |
| recite | 286. सुनाना |
| reckon | 16. मानना |
| reclaim | 409. कृषि योग्य बनाना |
| recognize | 77. पहचानना |
| recollect | 627. स्मरण करना |
| recommend | 142. की सिफारिश |
| reconnect | 529. पुनः कनेक्ट |
| reconsider | 244. पुनर्विचार करना |
| reconstruct | 247. फिर से बनाना |
| recover | 144. स्वस्थ होना |
| rectify | 422. शुद्ध करना, 624. संशोधन करना, 606. सही करना |
| recycle | 519. अपनी बात दोहराना |
| refill | 356. फिर से भरना |

| | |
|---|---|
| refine | 141. चमकाना, 162. सुधारना |
| reflect | 236. प्रतिबिंबित करना |
| refresh | 393. ताज़ा करना |
| refute | 450. खंडन करना |
| regain | 267. पहुंच जाना |
| regulate | 564. विनियमित |
| rehearse | 246. अभ्यास करना |
| reimburse | 643. प्रतिपूर्ति करना |
| reinforce | 542. सुदृढ़ बनाना |
| reinstate | 651. बहाल करना |
| rejoice | 317. आनन्द करे |
| rejoin | 486. फिर से जोड़ना |
| relocate | 541. स्थानांतरित करना |
| rely | 156. भरोसा करना |
| remind | 88. याद दिलाना |
| remove | 97. हटाना |
| render | 377. प्रस्तुत करना |
| reopen | 405. फिर से खोलना |
| reorganize | 498. पुनर्निर्माण करना |
| repay | 178. चुकाना |
| repeat | 92. दोहराना |
| repent | 260. पछताना |
| replay | 507. फिर से खेलना |
| replenish | 356. फिर से भरना, 692. भरपाई |
| replicate | 471. उत्तर में कहना |

| | |
|---|---|
| represent | 131. प्रतिनिधित्व करना |
| reproduce | 418. प्रतिलिपि प्रस्तुत करना |
| reside | 578. निवास करना |
| resign | 199. त्यागपत्र देना |
| resist | 126. विरोध |
| resort | 181. सहारा लेना |
| restart | 506. पुनर्प्रारंभ करें |
| restore | 201. लौटाना |
| restrain | 187. नियंत्रित करना |
| retain | 341. धरण करना, 125. रोकना |
| retake | 592. फिर से लेना |
| retaliate | 531. प्रतिकार करना, 216. बदला लेना |
| retard | 292. काम करना |
| rethink | 399. फिर से सोचना |
| retire | 165. रिटायर हो जाना |
| retrace | 129. खोजना, 608. वापस जाना |
| retract | 511. वापस लेना |
| retrieve | 239. पुनः प्राप्त |
| reunite | 495. पुनर्मिलन करना |
| revel | 691. आनंद लेना |
| revert | 621. लौट आना |
| revisit | 565. फिर से आना |
| revoke | 119. रद्द करना, 511. वापस लेना |
| revolve | 263. घूमना |

| | |
|---|---|
| rewrite | 338. फिर से लिखना |
| rile | 215. चिढ़ाना |
| roam | 263. घूमना |
| rob | 98. लूटना |
| rotate | 421. घुमाएँ |
| rove | 685. भटकना |
| rub | 138. रगड़ना |
| rue | 260. पछताना |
| ruffle | 215. चिढ़ाना |
| run | 22. चलाना |
| safekeeping | 533. सुरक्षित रखना |
| salvage | 321. क्षति से बचाना |
| sanctify | 362. पवित्र करना |
| satisfy | 12. संतुष्ट करना |
| save | 33. बचाना |
| say | 10. कहना |
| scan | 151. स्कैन |
| scare | 91. डराना |
| scissor | 633. कैंची से काटना |
| scold | 278. डांटना |
| scoot | 396. भागना |
| scrabble | 470. खरोंचना |
| scrub | 233. मलना |
| sculpt | 690. रूप देना |
| seduce | 242. झांसना, 313. लुभाना |

| | |
|---|---|
| see | 7. देखना |
| seek | 106. मांगना |
| seem | 39. लगता है |
| seize | 198. जब्त, 135. पकड़ना |
| sell | 46. बेचना |
| settle | 85. बसना |
| sever | 481. काटकर अलग करना |
| sew | 243. सीना |
| shake | 89. हिलाना |
| sharpen | 460. गहरा बनाना |
| shatter | 412. टूटने |
| shimmer | 674. टिमटिमाना |
| shirk | 396. भागना |
| shorten | 553. छोटा करना |
| shout | 112. चिल्लाना |
| shove | 158. धक्का |
| show | 19. दिखाना |
| shrink | 176. सिकुड़ना |
| shun | 402. सीधे खड़े हो |
| shunt | 700. अलग धकेलना |
| shush | 291. चुप बनाना |
| sidle | 664. तरफ़ चलना |
| signify | 656. प्रकट करना, 118. सूचित करना |
| simplify | 599. सरल करना |

| | |
|---|---|
| simulate | 417. अनुकरण करना, 552. भेष बदलना |
| siphon | 214. अपनाना |
| sit | 26. बैठना |
| skedaddle | 396. भागना |
| skip | 121. छोड़ें |
| skulk | 678. छिपकर जाना |
| slash | 295. कड़ी आलोचना करना |
| slay | 333. मार डालना |
| slink | 678. छिपकर जाना |
| slither | 167. रेंगना |
| slog | 390. आगे बढ़ना |
| slop | 482. छलकाना |
| slug | 271. अलसाना |
| smirk | 625. दाँत निपोड़ना |
| smite | 170. हराना |
| smother | 537. गला घोंटना |
| snicker | 365. फड़फड़ाना |
| sniff | 254. सूंघना |
| snipe | 676. ठीक गोली चलाना |
| snoop | 395. जासूसी करना |
| snore | 423. सोते सोते चूकना |
| snuggle | 534. ठहरना |
| soak | 296. भिगोना |
| soar | 436. ऊंची उड़ान भरना |

| | |
|---|---|
| socialize | 577. सामूहीकरण करना |
| solve | 102. समाधान करना |
| soothe | 492. शांत करना |
| spank | 352. शिकस्त देना |
| spawn | 461. अंडे रखना |
| specialize | 475. विशेषज्ञ बनना |
| spend | 51. बिताना |
| sprinkle | 453. छिड़कना |
| squander | 648. गंवाना |
| squirm | 622. ऐंठना |
| squirt | 354. धारा निकलना |
| stabilize | 424. स्थिर बनाना |
| stare | 154. घूरना |
| steal | 68. चुराना |
| steer | 229. स्टीयर |
| stifle | 325. दबाना |
| stimulate | 441. उत्तेजित करना, 200. प्रोत्साहित करना |
| stoke | 576. ईंधन झोंकना |
| stoop | 376. निहुरना |
| stop | 14. रुकें |
| strangle | 325. दबाना |
| strengthen | 348. मज़बूत बनाना |
| strive | 388. प्रयास करते हैं |
| strut | 510. इठलाना |

| | |
|---|---|
| subdue | 550. वश में करना, 170. हराना |
| submit | 377. प्रस्तुत करना |
| subscribe | 590. नाम लिखना, 611. हस्ताक्षर करना |
| subvert | 264. उतारना |
| succumb | 566. मर जाना |
| suck | 93. चूसना |
| sue | 100. नालिश करना |
| suffer | 95. भुगतना |
| suffice | 351. पूरा करना |
| suffocate | 413. बुझाना |
| suggest | 84. सुझाना |
| sulk | 543. मचलना |
| sully | 435. दूषित करना, 310. धब्बे लगाना, 626. मैला करना |
| sunder | 613. टुकड़े में करना |
| sup | 501. सुड़कना |
| supervise | 414. संचालन करना |
| suppose | 6. सोचना |
| suspend | 350. निलंबित |
| swallow | 145. निगलना |
| swat | 275. मुंहतोड़ प्रहार मारना |
| sweeten | 597. मीठा करना |
| swerve | 685. भटकना |
| swim | 96. तैरना |
| swipe | 443. ज़ोर से मारना |

| | |
|---|---|
| swish | 591. सरसराना |
| sympathize | 447. सहानुभूति रखना |
| tackle | 135. पकड़ना |
| take | 1. लेना |
| tally | 609. मेल खाना |
| tamper | 147. हस्तक्षेप करना |
| tease | 215. चिढ़ाना |
| tell | 10. कहना |
| tempt | 313. लुभाना |
| terrorize | 630. आतंकित करना, 155. धमकाना |
| testify | 136. गवाही देना |
| think | 6. सोचना |
| threaten | 155. धमकाना |
| thrive | 366. कामयाब होना |
| throttle | 359. कुचलना, 537. गला घोंटना |
| ting | 304. टिंग |
| tinker | 327. टिन से मढ़ना |
| tinkle | 535. ठनकाना |
| tiptoe | 678. छिपकर जाना |
| tolerate | 186. सहन करना, 202. सहना |
| toot | 410. हार्न बजाना |
| topple | 638. नीचे गिर पड़ना |
| torture | 115. तकलीफ देना |
| trample | 557. रौंदे |

| | |
|---|---|
| transcend | 669. ऊंचा उठना |
| translate | 222. अनुवाद करना |
| transmit | 332. कहलवाना |
| transplant | 221. आरोपित करना |
| trashed | 337. ट्रैश किए गए |
| tread | 283. पांव रखना |
| trickle | 681. मिलने |
| trim | 276. तराशना |
| uncover | 344. खुलना |
| underestimate | 235. बहुत मूल्यवान समझना |
| undermine | 407. दुर्बल करना |
| understand | 17. समझना |
| undertake | 294. आरंभ करना, 480. वचन देना |
| unite | 231. एक होना, 21. मिलना, 280. मिलाना |
| unleash | 218. खोल देना, 379. शुरू करना |
| unload | 264. उतारना |
| unravel | 468. सुलझाना |
| untie | 218. खोल देना, 24. खोलना |
| unzip | 218. खोल देना |
| update | 204. अपडेट करें |
| upgrade | 357. उतार देना |
| uphold | 364. कायम रखना |
| uproot | 547. जड़ से उखाड़ना |
| validate | 117. पुष्टि करना, 636. मंज़ूर करना, 250. सत्यापित करें |

| | |
|---|---|
| vanquish | 536. विजय प्राप्त करना |
| vent | 251. बाहर निकलने देना |
| verify | 250. सत्यापित करें |
| vex | 655. खीझाना, 604. तंग करना |
| vibrate | 544. कांपना |
| vie | 484. होड़ करना |
| visualize | 466. दिखाऊ बनाना |
| vouch | 311. ज़मानत करना |
| waive | 548. माफ |
| wake | 45. जगाना |
| walk | 32. चलना |
| warn | 101. चेतावनी देना |
| wash | 80. धोना |
| weaken | 442. कमज़ोर करना |
| wear | 47. पहनना |
| wed | 280. मिलाना, 306. मेल कराना, 44. शादी करना |
| weld | 598. जोड़ देना |
| wield | 489. फिराना |
| wimp | 314. डरपोक समझा |
| win | 37. जीतना |
| wipe | 114. पोंछना |
| withdraw | 81. निकालना |
| wither | 483. कुम्हलाना |
| withstand | 323. झेलना, 205. सामना |

| | |
|---|---|
| wobble | 615. लडखडाना |
| woo | 130. वू |
| would | 9. चाहेंगे |
| wrap | 124. लपेटना |
| write | 40. लिखना |
| yap | 516. भौंकना |
| yearn | 476. खिन्न होना |
| yell | 112. चिल्लाना |
| zap | 375. गाली मार देना |

# Appendix: Phrase Practice Drills

This appendix contains phrases for practice. Each phrase includes at least one **verb**.

You can use this appendix for practice in two ways:

- **Read practice:** Read the original phrases, try to guess the English translation, and then check your guess against the provided translation.
- **Speak practice:** Read the English translations, and try to recall and say the original phrases.

To facilitate this, the English translations are provided separately from the original phrases.

The phrases are organized into several groups. They start with the easiest and shortest phrases, gradually increasing in complexity as you progress through the groups.

In the initial groups, the phrases are deliberately repetitive to reinforce beginner vocabulary.

We hope you enjoy this appendix and find it helpful in your language learning journey.

## Difficulty Level: 1

[1] *1.* मैं। *2.* मैं नहीं। *3.* नहीं। *4.* क्या है? *5.* क्या मैं? *6.* क्या नहीं? *7.* यह है। *8.* क्या यह? *9.* यह। *10.* क्या आप? *11.* आप क्या? *12.* आप हैं।
- *1.* I might. *2.* I don't. *3.* Scratch that. *4.* What is? *5.* Do I? *6.* Don't what? *7.* It is. *8.* Does it? *9.* It's not? *10.* Do you? *11.* What are you? *12.* You're on.

[2] *1.* आप। *2.* वह है। *3.* क्या वह? *4.* वह। *5.* मुझे। *6.* एक है। *7.* मैं था। *8.* वह था। *9.* क्या था? *10.* यह था। *11.* नहीं था। *12.* आप कर? *13.* तुम हो। *14.* क्या तुम? *15.* तुम नहीं!
- *1.* You will be. *2.* He is. *3.* Did he? *4.* She was. *5.* Let me. *6.* There's one. *7.* I was. *8.* It was. *9.* What was? *10.* This was it. *11.* Was not. *12.* You do? *13.* You are. *14.* Could you? *15.* You don't!

[3] *1.* यह रहा। *2.* रहा है। *3.* क्या किया? *4.* नहीं किया। *5.* मैं हूँ। *6.* क्या हम? *7.* हम हैं? *8.* हम नहीं? *9.* हो गया। *10.* उसने किया। *11.* मैंने किया।

200

*12.* क्या मैंने?

• *1.* Here it is. *2.* Used to be. *3.* Did what? *4.* Did not. *5.* I am. *6.* Shall we? *7.* We are? *8.* We don't? *9.* You're done. *10.* He did. *11.* I did. *12.* Did I?

[4] *1.* मैंने नहीं! *2.* मैंने। *3.* और क्या? *4.* ठीक है। *5.* ठीक था। *6.* क्या ऐसा? *7.* ऐसा है। *8.* मैं भी। *9.* भी किया। *10.* वे हैं। *11.* क्या वे? *12.* किया वे?

• *1.* I did not! *2.* I left. *3.* And guess what? *4.* It's alright. *5.* It was OK. *6.* Would it? *7.* That is so. *8.* So am I. *9.* Did too. *10.* They are. *11.* Do they? *12.* Did they?

[5] *1.* वह मेरे। *2.* पास है? *3.* आपको चाहिए। *4.* तुम्हें चाहिए? *5.* वे चाहिए। *6.* क्या दिया? *7.* बहुत अच्छा। *8.* अच्छा अच्छा। *9.* अच्छा होगा। *10.* क्या होगा? *11.* यह होगा? *12.* ऐसा होगा.

• *1.* He is mine. *2.* Has it? *3.* You must. *4.* You want? *5.* They should. *6.* What gives? *7.* Well done. *8.* I see, I see. *9.* Be nice. *10.* What's it gonna be? *11.* Will it? *12.* It'll happen.

[6] *1.* वह होगा। *2.* नहीं थे। *3.* तुम थे? *4.* हम थे? *5.* वह थे। *6.* में थे! *7.* वे थे? *8.* पता नहीं। *9.* कुछ करो! *10.* करो? *11.* इसे करें। *12.* क्या करें?

• *1.* She would. *2.* We're not. *3.* You were? *4.* We were. *5.* They were. *6.* We're in! *7.* Were they? *8.* Don't know. *9.* Do something! *10.* Do ya? *11.* Do it. *12.* What to do?

[7] *1.* और बस। *2.* बस एक। *3.* आपके पास? *4.* जा रहा। *5.* क्या करता? *6.* हमें चाहिए। *7.* क्या हमें? *8.* चलो भी। *9.* अब चलो। *10.* नहीं, चलो। *11.* बस चलो। *12.* चलो, क्या?

• *1.* And that's it. *2.* One, please. *3.* Have you? *4.* Keep it going. *5.* What could I do? *6.* We should. *7.* Should we? *8.* Come on. *9.* Come on now. *10.* No, come on. *11.* Just come on. *12.* Come on, what?

[8] *1.* उसे दो। *2.* काम किया? *3.* हाँ हम। *4.* हाँ, मैं। *5.* हाँ करो। *6.* क्या हुआ? *7.* कुछ हुआ। *8.* उन्हें चाहिए। *9.* बस जाओ। *10.* जाओ, जाओ! *11.* तुम जाओ। *12.* अब जाओ।

• *1.* Let him. *2.* Did it work? *3.* Yes, we are. *4.* Yeah, I will. *5.* Yes, do. *6.* What happened? *7.* Something happened. *8.* He would. *9.* Just go. *10.* Go, go! *11.* You go. *12.* Now go.

[9] *1.* यहाँ जाओ। *2.* तो जाओ। *3.* चलो जाओ! *4.* हाँ, जाओ। *5.* और जाओ! *6.* ऐसा क्यों? *7.* यह क्यों? *8.* उसे ले। *9.* इसे ले! *10.* कृपया नहीं। *11.* कृपया कृपया। *12.* हाँ, कृपया।

• *1.* Get in here. *2.* Then go. *3.* Come on, go! *4.* Yeah, go. *5.*

And go! *6.* Why is that? *7.* Why do this? *8.* Take him. *9.* Take it up! *10.* No, please. *11.* Please, please. *12.* Yeah, please.

[10] *1.* कृपया दो। *2.* कृपया क्या? *3.* कृपया कोई! *4.* कृपया आप? *5.* ऐसा कैसे? *6.* तुम कैसे? *7.* कैसे करें? *8.* आ जा! *9.* आ जाओ। *10.* उसने आ। *11.* उसके पास। *12.* मैंने लिया।
• *1.* Two, please. *2.* Please what? *3.* Somebody, please! *4.* Would you, please? *5.* How come? *6.* How can you? *7.* How do? *8.* Come on, man! *9.* Come on up. *10.* He came. *11.* She has. *12.* I had it.

[11] *1.* अभी करो! *2.* कृपया अभी। *3.* अभी है। *4.* ओह, कृपया। *5.* कहाँ है? *6.* कहाँ थे? *7.* कहाँ गया? *8.* कभी नहीं। *9.* आपने कहा। *10.* वापस जाओ। *11.* आपकी बात? *12.* कौन था?
• *1.* Do it now! *2.* Now, please. *3.* Still is. *4.* Oh, please. *5.* Where is it? *6.* Where were you? *7.* Where did he go? *8.* Never have. *9.* You said. *10.* Go back. *11.* Your point being? *12.* Who was it?

[12] *1.* कौन है? *2.* आपकी मदद? *3.* मदद! *4.* की मदद। *5.* फिर जाओ। *6.* धन्यवाद। *7.* नहीं धन्यवाद। *8.* ओह धन्यवाद। *9.* हाँ धन्यवाद। *10.* धन्यवाद धन्यवाद। *11.* ठीक धन्यवाद। *12.* लेकिन धन्यवाद।
• *1.* Who is? *2.* Help you? *3.* Help! *4.* To help. *5.* Go then. *6.* Thank you. *7.* No, thank you. *8.* Oh, thank you. *9.* Yes, thank you. *10.* Thank you, thank you. *11.* Fine, thank you. *12.* But thank you.

[13] *1.* और धन्यवाद। *2.* क्यों धन्यवाद। *3.* धन्यवाद, नहीं. *4.* आपको धन्यवाद। *5.* कृपया धन्यवाद। *6.* अच्छा धन्यवाद। *7.* धन्यवाद, हाँ. *8.* तुमने किया? *9.* क्या तुमने?
• *1.* And thank you. *2.* Why, thank you. *3.* Thank you, no. *4.* Thank you, man. *5.* Thank you kindly. *6.* Good, thank you. *7.* Thank you, yes. *8.* You did? *9.* Did you?

[14] *1.* ये रहा। *2.* जो हैं? *3.* यही है। *4.* यही तो। *5.* यहाँ आओ। *6.* वापस आओ! *7.* साथ आओ। *8.* आओ आओ। *9.* कृपया आओ। *10.* आप आओ'? *11.* तुम आओ। *12.* मैंने देखा।
• *1.* Here we go. *2.* Which are? *3.* That's the one. *4.* That's what. *5.* Come here. *6.* Come back! *7.* Come along. *8.* Come, come. *9.* Please come. *10.* You comin'? *11.* You come. *12.* I saw that.

[15] *1.* क्या देखा? *2.* हाँ, देखा? *3.* आपने देखा? *4.* यह देखा। *5.* बाहर

आओ! *6.* बाहर जाओ। *7.* मुझे लगा। *8.* अच्छा लगा? *9.* यह देखो। *10.* बाहर देखो! *11.* उसे देखो। *12.* इसे देखो।
• *1.* Saw what? *2.* Yeah, see? *3.* Have you noticed? *4.* Seen it. *5.* Come out! *6.* Go outside. *7.* I figured. *8.* Does that feel good? *9.* Look at this. *10.* Look out! *11.* Look at him. *12.* Look at it.

**[16]** *1.* यहाँ देखो। *2.* देखो क्या? *3.* मुझे देखो। *4.* हमें देखो। *5.* देखो देखो। *6.* अभी देखो। *7.* फिर देखो। *8.* आप देखो। *9.* आओ देखो। *10.* उन्हें देखो? *11.* तुम देखो। *12.* ओह, देखो?
• *1.* Look here. *2.* See what? *3.* Watch me. *4.* Look at us. *5.* Look, look. *6.* Just watch. *7.* Look again. *8.* You watch. *9.* Come see. *10.* See them? *11.* You look. *12.* Oh, see?

**[17]** *1.* जाओ देखो। *2.* वापस जाना! *3.* में जाना। *4.* जाना होगा। *5.* जाना है? *6.* बाहर जाना? *7.* जाना! *8.* यहां थे! *9.* कृपया यहां। *10.* घर जाओ। *11.* घर चलो. *12.* चलो घर।
• *1.* Go see. *2.* Move back! *3.* Go in. *4.* Gotta run. *5.* Wanna go? *6.* Going out? *7.* Go! *8.* We're here! *9.* Here, please. *10.* Go home. *11.* Go on home. *12.* Come on home.

**[18]** *1.* मुझसे होगा। *2.* वहाँ है। *3.* वहाँ देखो। *4.* वहाँ गया। *5.* वहाँ था। *6.* वहाँ हैं। *7.* वहां जाओ। *8.* वहां थे। *9.* वहां। *10.* आप करेंगे। *11.* हम करेंगे? *12.* सही जाना।
• *1.* I will, I will. *2.* There it is. *3.* Look there. *4.* Been there. *5.* There was. *6.* There are. *7.* Get in there. *8.* We're there. *9.* There will be. *10.* You will. *11.* Will we? *12.* Go right.

**[19]** *1.* सही बात? *2.* क्या उस? *3.* कहाँ गए? *4.* क्या मिला? *5.* कुछ मिला। *6.* मुझे मिला। *7.* उन्हें मिला। *8.* है ना? *9.* अंदर जाओ। *10.* चलो अंदर. *11.* अंदर आओ। *12.* हमारे पास?
• *1.* Make sense? *2.* Does he? *3.* Gone where? *4.* Get what? *5.* Got something. *6.* Got me. *7.* Found them. *8.* Doesn't it? *9.* Go inside. *10.* Come on inside. *11.* Step inside. *12.* Have we?

**[20]** *1.* बंद करो। *2.* बंद था। *3.* आगे है। *4.* करूंगा। *5.* मैं करूंगा। *6.* अभी करूंगा। *7.* अरे देखो! *8.* अरे, चलो. *9.* अरे, धन्यवाद. *10.* उसे याद? *11.* होना चाहिए। *12.* वहाँ होना।
• *1.* Stop that. *2.* We're close. *3.* Let's continue. *4.* Will do. *5.* I shall. *6.* I'll do it now. *7.* Oh, look! *8.* Aw, come on. *9.* Hey, thank you. *10.* Remember him? *11.* Must be. *12.* Be there.

**[21]** *1.* दे। *2.* जाने दो! *3.* नहीं जाने। *4.* कोशिश करो। *5.* क्या विश्वास? *6.*

बेहतर था। 7. बेहतर होगा। 8. इतना ही। 9. हाँ बिल्कुल। 10. हमने किया।
11. क्या हमने? 12. रुको!

• 1. Give it. 2. Let go! 3. Let's not. 4. Have at it. 5. Believe
what? 6. Been better. 7. Better be. 8. That's it. 9. Of course I
would. 10. We did. 11. Did we? 12. Wait, wait!

[22] 1. रुको रुको। 2. अरे, रुको! 3. रुको मत! 4. अब, रुको। 5. पर रुको।
6. बस रुको! 7. ओह, रुको. 8. नहीं, रुको. 9. हाँ, रुको. 10. रुको, देखो।
11. रुको, क्यों? 12. अभी रुको।

• 1. Hold on, hold on. 2. Hey, wait! 3. Don't stop! 4. Now, hold
on. 5. But wait. 6. Just wait! 7. Oh, hold on. 8. No, hold on.
9. Yeah, hold on. 10. Wait, look. 11. Wait, why? 12. Hold on
now.

[23] 1. यहीं रुको. 2. रुको, सचमुच? 3. अच्छी है? 4. नीचे आओ! 5. नीचे
जाना। 6. नीचे रहो। 7. यहीं रहो। 8. फिर रहो. 9. आदमी जाओ! 10. सब
तैयार। 11. तैयार रहो। 12. तैयार करें!

• 1. Wait right here. 2. Wait, really? 3. Is it good? 4. Come
down! 5. Going down. 6. Stand down. 7. Stay put. 8. Then
stay. 9. Go, man! 10. All set. 11. Be ready. 12. Make ready!

[24] 1. हमेशा करो. 2. चलो, दोस्त. 3. धन्यवाद दोस्त। 4. चलो, माँ. 5.
माँ, कृपया. 6. माँ, चलो. 7. माँ, देखो! 8. धन्यवाद माँ। 9. माँ, रुको! 10. मैं
चला। 11. इसे लो। 12. नाम लो।

• 1. Always do. 2. Come on, mate. 3. Thank you, buddy. 4.
Come on, Mom. 5. Mother, please. 6. Mom, come on. 7. Mom,
look! 8. Thank you, Mommy. 9. Mom, stop! 10. I walked. 11.
Take this. 12. Name it.

[25] 1. उसे लो। 2. ये लो। 3. एक लो। 4. यह लो। 5. कहां गई? 6. दूर
जाओ। 7. दूर जाना। 8. दूर रहो! 9. दूर देखो। 10. आप शायद। 11. वे शायद।
12. शायद हम।

• 1. Take that! 2. There you have it. 3. Take one. 4. Take this
one. 5. Where did it go? 6. Go away. 7. Walk away. 8. Keep
away! 9. Look away. 10. You might. 11. They might. 12. We
might.

[26] 1. शायद मुझे। 2. अंदर आइए। 3. समझ गया। 4. समझ आया? 5.
समझ गए। 6. कैसा है? 7. कैसा गया? 8. सच में। 9. तुमने सुना? 10. क्या
सुना? 11. हमने सुना। 12. मैंने सुना।

• 1. Maybe I should. 2. Do come in. 3. Got it. 4. Does that
make sense? 5. That's clear. 6. How is it? 7. How does it go?
8. I mean, really. 9. Did you hear? 10. Heard what? 11. We

heard. *12.* I hear.

**[27]** *1.* मुझे बताओ। *2.* उसे बताओ। *3.* उन्हें बताओ। *4.* हमें बताओ। *5.* सच बताओ। *6.* बताओ कौन? *7.* वह होगी। *8.* जल्दी करो! *9.* जल्दी करना! *10.* जल्दी आ! *11.* चलो, जल्दी। *12.* धन्यवाद भगवान।
● *1.* Tell me. *2.* Tell him. *3.* Tell them. *4.* Tell us. *5.* Tell the truth. *6.* Tell who? *7.* She will. *8.* Hurry up! *9.* Step on it! *10.* Come quick! *11.* Come on, quick. *12.* Thank you, Lord.

**[28]** *1.* चलो, बच्चे। *2.* देखो, बच्चे। *3.* सुनो। *4.* अरे सुनो। *5.* बस सुनो। *6.* उसे सुनो। *7.* नहीं, सुनो। *8.* सुनो सुनो। *9.* तुम सुनो? *10.* वह सुनो। *11.* मत सुनो। *12.* अच्छा, सुनो।
● *1.* Come on, kid. *2.* Look, kid. *3.* Listen up. *4.* Hey, listen. *5.* Just listen. *6.* Listen to him. *7.* No, listen. *8.* Listen, listen. *9.* You listening? *10.* Listen to that. *11.* Don't listen. *12.* Well, listen.

**[29]** *1.* यहाँ सुनो। *2.* सुनो, बच्चे। *3.* लेकिन सुनो। *4.* ओह, सुनो। *5.* अब, सुनो। *6.* इसे सुनो। *7.* सुनो, लोग. *8.* ध्यान से। *9.* चलो यार! *10.* आओ यार। *11.* देखो यार. *12.* सुनो यार।
● *1.* Listen here. *2.* Listen, kid. *3.* But listen. *4.* Oh, listen. *5.* Now, listen up. *6.* Listen to this one. *7.* Listen up, people. *8.* Be careful. *9.* Come on, guys! *10.* Come on, you. *11.* Look, man. *12.* Listen, man.

**[30]** *1.* रुको यार. *2.* यार, चलो. *3.* बताया तो। *4.* कार ले। *5.* ऊपर देखो। *6.* ऊपर जाओ। *7.* ऊपर जाना! *8.* कहाँ गये? *9.* कॉल करना। *10.* करेंगे सर. *11.* रुको सर. *12.* सुंदर है।
● *1.* Hold on, man. *2.* Dude, come on. *3.* I told you. *4.* Take the car. *5.* Look up. *6.* Go upstairs. *7.* Go up! *8.* Where have they gone? *9.* Make the call. *10.* Will do, sir. *11.* Hold on, sir. *12.* It's sweet.

**[31]** *1.* काफी था? *2.* यकीन है। *3.* सिर्फ मैं। *4.* सिर्फ देखो। *5.* सिर्फ बात। *6.* आराम से। *7.* आराम करो। *8.* तक आराम। *9.* वह करेगा। *10.* करेगा क्या *11.* ये करेगा? *12.* कौन करेगा?
● *1.* Had enough? *2.* Sure is. *3.* It's just me. *4.* Just look. *5.* Just talk. *6.* Easy does it. *7.* Take a rest. *8.* Rest up. *9.* He will. *10.* Will you do it? *11.* Will this do? *12.* Who will?

**[32]** *1.* करना पड़ा। *2.* कृपया शांत। *3.* शांत रहो। *4.* बस देखना। *5.* वहाँ देखना? *6.* देखना! *7.* इसे रखें। *8.* पीछे जाओ। *9.* यह कहना। *10.* क्या कहना? *11.* धन्यवाद कहना। *12.* मुझे दें!

• *1.* Had to. *2.* Quiet, please. *3.* Be calm. *4.* Just looking. *5.* There, see? *6.* Look! *7.* Keep it. *8.* Get in the back. *9.* Say it. *10.* Say what? *11.* Say thank you. *12.* Give me!

[33] *1.* चले जाओ! *2.* चले चलो। *3.* चले आओ। *4.* जाता रहना। *5.* शांत रहना। *6.* डॉक्टर, कृपया. *7.* खुश रहो। *8.* खुश थे। *9.* वहीं है। *10.* वहीं रुको. *11.* आपका इंतजार। *12.* अलग थे।
• *1.* Be gone! *2.* Walk on. *3.* Come away. *4.* Keep going. *5.* Remain calm. *6.* Doctor, please. *7.* Be happy. *8.* We're happy. *9.* It's right there. *10.* Wait right there. *11.* Waiting for you. *12.* We're different.

[34] *1.* ध्यान रहें! *2.* शांत रहें। *3.* ठीक रहें। *4.* तैयार रहें। *5.* वो करें। *6.* क्या वो? *7.* उसने फोन। *8.* धन्यवाद पिताजी। *9.* चलो, पिताजी. *10.* पिताजी, कृपया. *11.* पिताजी, आइए. *12.* पिताजी, रुको!
• *1.* Watch out! *2.* Keep calm. *3.* Be well. *4.* Be prepared. *5.* Do that. *6.* Was she? *7.* He called. *8.* Thank you, Father. *9.* Come on, Dad. *10.* Dad, please. *11.* Dad, come on. *12.* Dad, stop!

[35] *1.* देखो पिताजी. *2.* पिताजी, चलो! *3.* आशा करो। *4.* क्या गलत? *5.* चलो, प्रिये. *6.* प्रिये, चलो। *7.* आओ, प्रिये. *8.* देखो प्रिये. *9.* जाने देना। *10.* ध्यान देना। *11.* छोड़ देना। *12.* चल देना।
• *1.* Look, Dad. *2.* Dad, come on! *3.* Let's hope. *4.* What's wrong? *5.* Come on, sweetheart. *6.* Honey, come on. *7.* Come, darling. *8.* Look, honey. *9.* Let it go. *10.* Pay attention. *11.* Give up. *12.* To go.

[36] *1.* सुन सुन। *2.* आप आये। *3.* दोबारा कहना। *4.* आने दो। *5.* तुम मूर्ख। *6.* वह मूर्ख! *7.* बहुत बढ़िया। *8.* या था. *9.* बदल जाओ। *10.* आनंद लेना? *11.* चलो चलें। *12.* अब चलें।
• *1.* Hear, hear. *2.* You came. *3.* Say that again. *4.* Keep it coming. *5.* You moron. *6.* That idiot! *7.* Well played. *8.* Or was. *9.* Get changed. *10.* Enjoying yourself? *11.* Let's move. *12.* Let us go.

[37] *1.* आओ चलें। *2.* सिर्फ चलें। *3.* कृपया चलें। *4.* चलते रहो। *5.* बस सोच। *6.* पकड़ लो! *7.* चलो भाई। *8.* शादी करना। *9.* तुमसे शादी? *10.* शादी होना। *11.* वे होंगे। *12.* हम होंगे।
• *1.* Let's go now. *2.* Just walk. *3.* Let's go, please. *4.* Keep moving. *5.* Just thinking. *6.* Catch it! *7.* Come on, men. *8.* Get married. *9.* Marry you? *10.* Getting married. *11.* They will. *12.* We will be.

**[38]** *1.* अंदर आना। *2.* वापस आना। *3.* घर आना। *4.* आगे आना। *5.* पास आना। *6.* ऊपर आना। *7.* नीचे आना। *8.* चुप रहो! *9.* चुप रहें। *10.* चुप हो! *11.* आप रह। *12.* मिली।

• *1.* Get in. *2.* Get back. *3.* Come home. *4.* Come forward. *5.* Get closer. *6.* Come upstairs. *7.* Coming down. *8.* Shut up! *9.* Be quiet. *10.* Be silent! *11.* You stay. *12.* Found her.

**[39]** *1.* इसे लें। *2.* आनंद लें। *3.* पकड़ लें। *4.* मदद लें! *5.* मुझे लें! *6.* उसे लें। *7.* इंतज़ार करो। *8.* इंतज़ार! *9.* कितने हैं? *10.* मजाक नहीं। *11.* कुछ कहो। *12.* कहो कब।

• *1.* Take it. *2.* Enjoy yourself. *3.* Get a grip. *4.* Get help! *5.* Pick me! *6.* Pick her up. *7.* You wait. *8.* Wait! *9.* How many are there? *10.* No pun intended. *11.* Say something. *12.* Say when.

**[40]** *1.* लड़का हुआ। *2.* भुगतान करें। *3.* आगे बढ़ो। *4.* लोगों बढ़ो। *5.* किसने किया? *6.* किसने कहा? *7.* मैं करूँगा। *8.* भर दें। *9.* दोस्तों, चलो। *10.* आओ दोस्तों। *11.* दोस्तों, आओ! *12.* दोस्तों, कृपया।

• *1.* It's a boy. *2.* Pay up. *3.* Go ahead. *4.* Come on, people. *5.* Who did? *6.* Who said? *7.* I will. *8.* Fill it up. *9.* Guys, come on. *10.* Come on, lads. *11.* Guys, come on! *12.* Guys, please.

**[41]** *1.* रुको दोस्तों। *2.* दोस्तों, रुको। *3.* देखते रहो। *4.* देखते रहें। *5.* गंभीर रहो। *6.* वे मिले। *7.* दर्द हुआ। *8.* हे देखो! *9.* खुशी हुई। *10.* तुम्हें देखकर। *11.* आप देखें? *12.* उन्हें देखें।

• *1.* Wait, guys. *2.* Guys, stop. *3.* Keep looking. *4.* Keep watching. *5.* Be serious. *6.* Got them. *7.* It hurt. *8.* Hey, look! *9.* I am glad. *10.* Be seeing you. *11.* You see? *12.* Look at them.

**[42]** *1.* उसे देखें। *2.* इसे देखें? *3.* देखें कौन? *4.* यहाँ देखें। *5.* इसमें देखें। *6.* इसे पकड़ो। *7.* उसे पकड़ो! *8.* कृपया पकड़ो। *9.* अरे, पकड़ो! *10.* पकड़ो। *11.* अच्छा बनो। *12.* बहुत शानदार।

• *1.* Watch him. *2.* See it? *3.* See who? *4.* See here. *5.* Look into it. *6.* Hold it. *7.* Grab him! *8.* Hold, please. *9.* Hey, hold it! *10.* Catch up. *11.* Be good. *12.* This is incredible.

**[43]** *1.* अरे हां? *2.* हां, वे। *3.* हां धन्यवाद। *4.* हां वह। *5.* सो है। *6.* सो जाओ! *7.* कर लेंगे? *8.* अकेले आओ। *9.* आओ लड़के। *10.* मिलते हैं। *11.* चलो बेटा। *12.* धन्यवाद बेटा।

• *1.* Oh yeah? *2.* Yes, they are. *3.* Yeah, thank you. *4.* Yes, she will. *5.* So it is. *6.* Go to sleep! *7.* Will that do? *8.* Come alone. *9.* Come on, boy. *10.* I see you. *11.* Come on, son. *12.*

Thank you, son.

**[44]** *1.* सावधान रहना। *2.* अरे, सावधान! *3.* सावधान, सावधान! *4.* तेज़ चलो! *5.* जल्द जल्दा *6.* मैं लगभग। *7.* चलो, महिला। *8.* पूछ लेना। *9.* ऐसे मैं। *10.* खड़े होना। *11.* आपका वादा? *12.* सिर नीचे।
● *1.* Just be careful. *2.* Hey, watch out! *3.* Watch out, watch out! *4.* Go faster! *5.* Chop, chop. *6.* I'll be around. *7.* Come on, lady. *8.* Ask away. *9.* So will I. *10.* Standing by. *11.* You promise? *12.* Head down.

**[45]** *1.* दरवाज़ा देखो। *2.* वह आएगा। *3.* यह आएगा। *4.* व्यस्त थे। *5.* बैठो, बैठो। *6.* कृपया बैठो। *7.* आओ बैठो। *8.* अरे, बैठो। *9.* चलो, बैठो। *10.* यहाँ, बैठो। *11.* आओ बच्चों। *12.* मज़बूत बनो।
● *1.* Watch the door. *2.* He'll come. *3.* It'll come. *4.* We're busy. *5.* Sit, sit. *6.* Sit, please. *7.* Come sit. *8.* Hey, sit down. *9.* Come on, have a seat. *10.* Here, sit. *11.* Come on, kids. *12.* Be strong.

**[46]** *1.* जान कृपया। *2.* मैं ज़ोर। *3.* हम जायेंगे। *4.* बहुत प्यारा। *5.* खून है। *6.* बातचीत करना। *7.* खोलो इसे। *8.* इसे खोलो। *9.* पूरा खोलो। *10.* उसे खोलो। *11.* दरवाज़ा खोलो! *12.* चलो, खोलो।
● *1.* Baby, please. *2.* I insist. *3.* We'll go. *4.* That's sweet. *5.* There's blood. *6.* To talk. *7.* Open it. *8.* Open it up. *9.* Open wide. *10.* Untie him. *11.* Open the damn door! *12.* Come on, open up.

**[47]** *1.* कृपया खोलो। *2.* मुझे खोलो! *3.* हम सहमत। *4.* दिल रखो। *5.* उह, धन्यवाद. *6.* उह, कृपया। *7.* यह पाया। *8.* उन्हें पाया। *9.* आपको पाया। *10.* जारी रखें। *11.* जारी रखो। *12.* उसे मारो!
● *1.* Open up, please. *2.* Unhand me! *3.* We agree. *4.* Have a heart. *5.* Uh, thank you. *6.* Uh, please. *7.* Found it. *8.* Found him. *9.* Found you. *10.* Go on. *11.* Carry on. *12.* Shoot him!

**[48]** *1.* मारो उसे! *2.* ओह, मारो! *3.* आदेश दो। *4.* आदेश दीजिए. *5.* इसे रोक! *6.* बताएं। *7.* उससे मिलना? *8.* नौकरी मिलना। *9.* मुझे मिलना? *10.* कहां जाओगे? *11.* तुम करोगे। *12.* महान धन्यवाद।
● *1.* Hit him! *2.* Oh, shoot! *3.* Say the word. *4.* Give the order. *5.* Stop it! *6.* Explain that. *7.* See him? *8.* Get a job. *9.* Get me? *10.* Where are you going to go? *11.* You'll do. *12.* Great, thank you.

**[49]** *1.* महान थे। *2.* मैं उठा। *3.* तुमने बुलाया? *4.* उन्होंने बुलाया। *5.* बिलकुल। *6.* उसे बुलाओ। *7.* डॉक्टर बुलाओ! *8.* स्थान लें। *9.* स्थान, कृपया.

*10.* कॉफ़ी चाहिए? *11.* कृपया रुकें. *12.* वहाँ रुकें।

• *1.* We're great. *2.* I woke up. *3.* You called? *4.* They called. *5.* You bet. *6.* Call her. *7.* Get a doctor! *8.* Hold position. *9.* Places, please. *10.* Want a coffee? *11.* Stop, please. *12.* Stop there.

**[50]** *1.* चलो रुकें। *2.* यहीं रुकें. *3.* आते रहना। *4.* सोचो मत. *5.* वापस सोचो। *6.* चलो, सोचो. *7.* हाँ सोचो? *8.* तोड़ दो। *9.* धन्यवाद बेबी। *10.* आप रहेंगे। *11.* तब आना। *12.* इसलिए।

• *1.* Let's stop. *2.* Stop right here. *3.* Keep coming. *4.* Don't think. *5.* Think back. *6.* Come on, think. *7.* Ya think? *8.* Break it down. *9.* Thank you, baby. *10.* You're in. *11.* Then come. *12.* This is why.

**[51]** *1.* मामला बंद। *2.* मैं जाऊँगा। *3.* बैठ जाएं। *4.* घर जाएं। *5.* कृपया जाएं। *6.* उसका पीछा। *7.* मिलने आना। *8.* सुन्दर है। *9.* किसके पास? *10.* अंदर मिलता। *11.* ऐसा सोचता? *12.* उसे रोको!

• *1.* Case closed. *2.* I'll go. *3.* Take a seat. *4.* Just go home. *5.* Go, please. *6.* Follow him. *7.* Come over. *8.* That's pretty. *9.* Who has? *10.* Get inside. *11.* Think so? *12.* Stop him!

**[52]** *1.* कार रोको! *2.* अभी रोको। *3.* इसे रोको! *4.* बस रोको! *5.* मुझे रोको। *6.* सड़क देखो! *7.* बेशक मैं। *8.* आप समाप्त? *9.* लगभग समाप्त। *10.* उचित बनो। *11.* बाहर कदम। *12.* नहीं चलेगा।

• *1.* Stop the car! *2.* Just stop. *3.* Stop this! *4.* Stop the bus! *5.* Stop me. *6.* Watch the road! *7.* Of course I do. *8.* You finished? *9.* Almost finished. *10.* Be reasonable. *11.* Step outside. *12.* Nothing doing.

**[53]** *1.* यह चलेगा. *2.* ये चलेगा. *3.* मैं देखूंगा। *4.* हमेशा रहेगा। *5.* आगे बढ़ें। *6.* मैंने मारा! *7.* इसे लाओ। *8.* उन्हें लाओ। *9.* क्या मैं? *10.* उन्हें पूछना। *11.* सिर्फ पूछना। *12.* आपने खरीदा?

• *1.* It'll do. *2.* This'll do. *3.* I'll be watching. *4.* Always will be. *5.* Move forward. *6.* I'm hit! *7.* Bring it. *8.* Bring them. *9.* If I may? *10.* Ask them. *11.* Just ask. *12.* You bought it?

**[54]** *1.* रोशनी मिली? *2.* रोशनी मारा। *3.* धन्यवाद प्रिय। *4.* आओ प्रिय। *5.* आपने दिखाया. *6.* प्रतीक्षा करना! *7.* हम देखेंगे। *8.* आप देखेंगे। *9.* सुरक्षित हों। *10.* शांत हों। *11.* उसे लगाओ। *12.* उन्हें लगाओ।

• *1.* Got a light? *2.* Hit the lights. *3.* Thank you, dear. *4.* Come, dear. *5.* You showed up. *6.* Wait up! *7.* We'll see. *8.* You'll see. *9.* Be safe. *10.* Be cool. *11.* Put him on. *12.* Put 'em on.

**[55]** *1.* अनुमान लगाओ। *2.* लगे रहो। *3.* वाकई। *4.* वाह धन्यवाद। *5.* वाह, रुको. *6.* बस खत्म। *7.* आवश्यक। *8.* ओह समझा। *9.* मैं समझा। *10.* इसीलिए।
*11.* इसीलिए नहीं. *12.* क्या इसीलिए?
• *1.* Take a wild guess. *2.* Keep up. *3.* I mean it. *4.* Wow, thank you. *5.* Whoa, hold on. *6.* That's over. *7.* It should. *8.* Ah, I see. *9.* I understood. *10.* That's why. *11.* That's not why. *12.* Is that why?

**[56]** *1.* फोन उठाओ। *2.* मुझे उठाओ। *3.* उन्हें उठाओ! *4.* उसे उठाओ. *5.* इसे उठाओ। *6.* सोने जाओ। *7.* सांस लें। *8.* यहाँ उठो. *9.* अब उठो. *10.* फिर मिलेंगे। *11.* जल्द मिलेंगे। *12.* इसे छोड़ो।
• *1.* Pick up the phone. *2.* Let me up. *3.* Get 'em up! *4.* Pick that up. *5.* Flip it. *6.* Go to bed. *7.* Take a breath. *8.* Get up here. *9.* Now get up. *10.* See ya. *11.* I'll see you soon. *12.* Leave it.

**[57]** *1.* इससे छोड़ो। *2.* उसे छोड़ो। *3.* मुझे बनाओ। *4.* क्या रोकें? *5.* उसे रोकें। *6.* मैं रहूंगा। *7.* अंदाज़ा लगाओ? *8.* मैंने पढ़ा। *9.* आह, चलो। *10.* नज़र रखना। *11.* नज़र रखो। *12.* कसम से।
• *1.* Leave that. *2.* Screw him. *3.* Make me. *4.* Stop what? *5.* Stop her. *6.* I'll stay. *7.* Guess what? *8.* I read that. *9.* Ah, come on. *10.* Take a look. *11.* Keep watch. *12.* I swear it.

**[58]** *1.* एक बेवकूफ। *2.* बेकार इंसान। *3.* धन्यवाद मित्र। *4.* कृपया जाए। *5.* ईमानदार हो। *6.* कहना मुश्किल। *7.* धन्यवाद, जासूस. *8.* धन्यवाद मालिक। *9.* परीक्षण, परीक्षण.
• *1.* An idiot. *2.* You suck. *3.* Thank you, friend. *4.* Please leave. *5.* Be honest. *6.* Hard to say. *7.* Thank you, Detective. *8.* Thank you, boss. *9.* Testing, testing.

**[59]** *1.* अवश्य करें. *2.* अवश्य है. *3.* अवश्य होगा। *4.* हाँ मिस? *5.* अलविदा कहो। *6.* इसे स्थापित। *7.* नियम हैं. *8.* कवर ले! *9.* अगले कृपया। *10.* यह इतिहास। *11.* धन्यवाद, लड़कों. *12.* ओह तस्वीर।
• *1.* Sure do. *2.* Certainly is. *3.* Sure will. *4.* Yes, miss? *5.* Say goodbye. *6.* Set it up. *7.* There are rules. *8.* Take cover! *9.* Next, please. *10.* It's history. *11.* Thank you, boys. *12.* Oh, snap.

**[60]** *1.* प्रार्थना करो। *2.* उससे पूछो। *3.* आसपास पूछो। *4.* समर्थन करना। *5.* केंद्रित रहो। *6.* नीचे आए। *7.* आए? *8.* वे आए। *9.* चलो, आओगे? *10.* कृपया कहें। *11.* अंदर आएं। *12.* करीब आएं।
• *1.* Say your prayers. *2.* Ask him. *3.* Ask around. *4.* Stand by. *5.* Stay focused. *6.* Come on down. *7.* Did you come? *8.* They

came. *9.* Come on, will you? *10.* Say please. *11.* Come in. *12.* Come closer.

**[61]** *1.* आएं। *2.* कृपया आएं। *3.* खाओ। *4.* कुछ खाओ। *5.* कसम खाओ। *6.* चलो, खाओ। *7.* खाओ खाओ। *8.* गर्मी है। *9.* मां कृपया। *10.* धन्यवाद मां। *11.* उत्कृष्ट है। *12.* सीधे ऊपर।
● *1.* Come up. *2.* Come, please. *3.* Eat up. *4.* Eat something. *5.* Swear it. *6.* Come on, eat. *7.* Eat, eat. *8.* It's hot. *9.* Mom, please. *10.* Thank you, Mama. *11.* It's excellent. *12.* Straight up.

**[62]** *1.* सीधे बैठो। *2.* फेंक दो! *3.* सुनिश्चित होना। *4.* सुनिश्चित करें। *5.* उसे उतारो! *6.* उन्हें उतारो। *7.* आगे बोलो। *8.* रास्ता बनाना! *9.* यह सुनकर? *10.* बताना ज़रूर। *11.* ज़रूर है। *12.* ज़रूर था।
● *1.* Sit up straight. *2.* Throw it! *3.* To be sure. *4.* Make sure. *5.* Get him off! *6.* Take 'em off. *7.* Keep talking. *8.* Make way! *9.* Hear it? *10.* Do tell. *11.* Sure there is. *12.* Sure was.

**[63]** *1.* ज़रूर, चलो। *2.* ज़रूर हैं। *3.* किए गए? *4.* धन्यवाद पापा। *5.* आओ पापा. *6.* पीछे हटो। *7.* चलो, हटो! *8.* दूर हटो। *9.* अब, हटो! *10.* कड़ी मेहनत? *11.* आप चाहें। *12.* इसे डालें।
● *1.* Sure, come on. *2.* Sure are. *3.* We're done? *4.* Thank you, Daddy. *5.* Come on, Father. *6.* Stand back. *7.* Come on, move! *8.* Stand clear. *9.* Now, move! *10.* Working hard? *11.* You wish. *12.* Put this on.

**[64]** *1.* जाग जाओ! *2.* उसे पकड़ने! *3.* धन्यवाद कैप्टन. *4.* माफ़ करें। *5.* उसे देखिए? *6.* मज़ा करना? *7.* मज़ा आएगा। *8.* खिड़की खोलो। *9.* मैं जाऊं? *10.* किसका है? *11.* वे आएंगे। *12.* ब्रेक मारो!
● *1.* Come on, wake up! *2.* Catch him! *3.* Thank you, Captain. *4.* Excuse me. *5.* See her? *6.* Having fun? *7.* This is going to be fun. *8.* Open the window. *9.* Shall I go? *10.* Whose is it? *11.* They will come. *12.* Hit the brakes!

**[65]** *1.* उधर देखो। *2.* साँस छोड़ना। *3.* छोड़ना। *4.* मैंने बदला। *5.* पता लगाना। *6.* धन्यवाद, अधिकारी. *7.* बने रहें। *8.* उन्हें हटाओ! *9.* शुभ रात्रि। *10.* कृपया जाएँ। *11.* वहाँ जाएँ। *12.* प्रस्तुत करें!
● *1.* Look over there. *2.* Breathe out. *3.* Pack up. *4.* I changed. *5.* Find out. *6.* Thank you, officer. *7.* Stay tuned. *8.* Get them off! *9.* Have a nice night. *10.* Please go. *11.* Go there. *12.* Put them up!

**[66]** *1.* शॉट लें! *2.* बेच दो। *3.* मैं कहूंगा। *4.* धक्का धक्का। *5.* जी हाँ। *6.*

बियर चाहिए? *7.* गहरी साँस। *8.* तुमने बजाया? *9.* इसे लाने। *10.* किसकी प्रतीक्षा? *11.* भागो मत। *12.* बहादुर बनो।

● *1.* Take the shot! *2.* Sell it. *3.* I'll say. *4.* Push, push. *5.* Oh, yes, please. *6.* Want a beer? *7.* Breathe deeply. *8.* You rang? *9.* Bring it up. *10.* Wait, what? *11.* Don't run. *12.* Be brave.

**[67]** *1.* बहुत बहादुर। *2.* वह आएगी. *3.* ट्रक रोको! *4.* किसलिए तैयार? *5.* मुझे जरूर। *6.* यहाँ उतरो! *7.* उतरो, उतरो. *8.* नीचे उतरो। *9.* धैर्य रखें। *10.* कृपया समझे। *11.* इन्हें लें। *12.* इन्हें लगाओ।

● *1.* Very brave. *2.* She'll come. *3.* Stop the truck! *4.* Prepared for what? *5.* I must. *6.* Get down here! *7.* Get down, get down. *8.* Go downstairs. *9.* Be patient. *10.* Please understand. *11.* Take these. *12.* Put these on.

**[68]** *1.* इन्हें देखें? *2.* मुझे छुओ। *3.* ट्रेन रोको! *4.* क्या फायदा? *5.* प्यार मे। *6.* धन्यवाद, प्रमुख. *7.* सीधा। *8.* मैं जीता। *9.* कौन जीता? *10.* वह जीता। *11.* सिगरेट मिली? *12.* सिगरेट ले।

● *1.* See these? *2.* Touch me. *3.* Stop the train! *4.* What's the use? *5.* Look at the time. *6.* Thank you, Chief. *7.* Straighten up. *8.* I win. *9.* Who won? *10.* He won. *11.* Got a cigarette? *12.* Have a cigarette.

**[69]** *1.* सिगरेट चाहिए? *2.* इसे पढ़ें। *3.* इस पढ़ें। *4.* अंधेरा था। *5.* अंग्रेजी बोलो। *6.* कृपया अंग्रेजी। *7.* पांच लो। *8.* इसे खेलने। *9.* खेलने जाना। *10.* उसे ढूंढो। *11.* दया करना। *12.* सकारात्मक सोचो।

● *1.* Want a cigarette? *2.* Read it. *3.* Read this. *4.* It was dark. *5.* Speak English. *6.* English, please. *7.* Take five. *8.* Play it. *9.* Go play. *10.* Go get him. *11.* Have mercy. *12.* Think positive.

**[70]** *1.* नही यह। *2.* इसे खोजें। *3.* कौन खोजें? *4.* विनम्र रहो। *5.* विनम्र रहें। *6.* यह वर्णन। *7.* पर चलाना। *8.* उच्च थे। *9.* उसने खोया। *10.* रुकना! *11.* रुकना छोड़ो। *12.* उन्हें सुनें।

● *1.* No, it is. *2.* Find it. *3.* Find who? *4.* Go easy. *5.* Be polite. *6.* Describe it. *7.* Drive on. *8.* We're up. *9.* He missed. *10.* Stop! *11.* Quit stalling. *12.* Listen to them.

**[71]** *1.* विशिष्ट रहो। *2.* बैठे रहो. *3.* चलो, जिम. *4.* धन्यवाद, जिम. *5.* दरवाजा पकड़ो! *6.* महोदया, कृपया. *7.* शाबाश, सर. *8.* शाबाश, शाबाश. *9.* शाबाश बेटा. *10.* धन्यवाद, कर्नल. *11.* लिफ्ट चाहिए? *12.* लिफ्ट पकड़ो।

● *1.* Be specific. *2.* Stay seated. *3.* Come on, Jim. *4.* Thank you, Jim. *5.* Hold the door! *6.* Ma'am, please. *7.* Well done, sir. *8.* Well done, well done. *9.* Well done, son. *10.* Thank you, Colonel. *11.* Want a lift? *12.* Hold the elevator.

**[72]** *1.* इसे जला। *2.* मुझे समझो? *3.* धन्यवाद, माननीय. *4.* उससे मिलो! *5.* तेज़ दिखा। *6.* वापसी! *7.* मुझे खोलें। *8.* दरवाजा खोलें। *9.* सुखद सपने। *10.* सज्जनो, कृपया. *11.* आज़ाद थे! *12.* स्मार्ट हों।

● *1.* Burn it. *2.* Understand me? *3.* Thanks, hon. *4.* Get him! *5.* Look sharp. *6.* Turn back! *7.* Untie me. *8.* Unlock the door. *9.* Pleasant dreams. *10.* Gentlemen, please. *11.* We're free! *12.* Be smart.

**[73]** *1.* पकड़े रहो। *2.* जल्दी सोचें। *3.* चुंबन चुंबन। *4.* मत भूलना. *5.* धन्यवाद, लेफ्टिनेंट. *6.* धन्यवाद स्वर्ग। *7.* क्या कहूँ? *8.* उम्म, धन्यवाद. *9.* उतर जाओ!

● *1.* Hold it up. *2.* Think fast. *3.* Kiss, kiss. *4.* Don't forget. *5.* Thank you, Lieutenant. *6.* Thank heaven. *7.* What should I say? *8.* Um, thank you. *9.* Step off!

**[74]** *1.* सोना हे। *2.* कुछ खेलो. *3.* मुझसे पूछें। *4.* क्या पूछें? *5.* जा मर। *6.* कुछ खोना? *7.* उसे पहचाना? *8.* इसे तोड़ो! *9.* लापता है। *10.* शुक्रिया डॉक्टर। *11.* शुक्रिया अलविदा। *12.* धन्यवाद सज्जनों.

● *1.* It's gold. *2.* Play something. *3.* Ask me. *4.* Ask what? *5.* Screw you. *6.* Lose something? *7.* Recognize him? *8.* Break it up! *9.* It's missing. *10.* Thank you, Doctor. *11.* Thank you, goodbye. *12.* Thank you, gentlemen.

**[75]** *1.* सज्जनों, कृपया! *2.* पनीर कहो. *3.* उपस्थिति! *4.* चल दर। *5.* सदैव है. *6.* मुकदमा करना। *7.* मुकदमा खारिज। *8.* हल्का होना। *9.* चलो, विल. *10.* जागो! *11.* जागो, यार. *12.* धन्यवाद प्रोफेसर।

● *1.* Gentlemen, please! *2.* Say cheese. *3.* Roll call! *4.* Let's go. *5.* Always is. *6.* Suit up. *7.* Case dismissed. *8.* Lighten up. *9.* Come on, Will. *10.* Wake up! *11.* Wake up, man. *12.* Thank you, Professor.

**[76]** *1.* कमीने! *2.* तुम, कमीने! *3.* खुली आग! *4.* कहाँ जाएंगे? *5.* पलट देना. *6.* पलटा। *7.* कसकर पकड़ें। *8.* उसे पकड़ें! *9.* उन्हें पकड़ें! *10.* धन्यवाद, नर्स. *11.* नमस्ते कहें। *12.* अरे, कोच.

● *1.* You bastard! *2.* You fucker! *3.* Open fire! *4.* Where will we go? *5.* Turn over. *6.* Turn it around. *7.* Hold on tight. *8.* Seize him! *9.* Catch them! *10.* Thank you, nurse. *11.* Say hi. *12.* Hey, Coach.

**[77]** *1.* त्याग देना। *2.* जरा सोचो। *3.* उससे लड़ो। *4.* लड़ो मत. *5.* देवियों, कृपया। *6.* द्वार खोलो! *7.* और काटो! *8.* एक चुनें। *9.* मस्ती करो। *10.* मैं बुद्धिमान। *11.* डरो नहीं। *12.* पकड़ना।

● *1.* Step aside. *2.* Just imagine. *3.* Fight it. *4.* Don't fight. *5.*

Ladies, please. *6.* Open the gates! *7.* And cut! *8.* Pick one. *9.* Have fun. *10.* I'm smart. *11.* Do not be afraid. *12.* Hold on.

**[78]** *1.* फोन पकड़ना। *2.* हमसे जुड़ें। *3.* मुझे जुड़ें। *4.* बैठक कक्ष। *5.* धन्यवाद, शेरिफ. *6.* इसे गाओ। *7.* घोषित करना। *8.* धन्यवाद, कमांडर. *9.* बचाओ। *10.* मुझे बचाओ! *11.* बचाओ बचाओ! *12.* उसे बचाओ।

● *1.* Hold the phone. *2.* Join us. *3.* Join me. *4.* Living room. *5.* Thank you, Sheriff. *6.* Sing it. *7.* Speak up. *8.* Thank you, Commander. *9.* Save it. *10.* Save me! *11.* Help, help! *12.* Save her.

**[79]** *1.* हमें बचाओ! *2.* ढीला करो। *3.* और बढ़ाओ। *4.* आगे बढ़ाओ। *5.* चाकू गिराओ। *6.* क्लास समाप्त। *7.* उन्हें खोलने। *8.* अकेली हो? *9.* दस्तक दस्तक। *10.* धन्यवाद, बॉब. *11.* बहुत चिकना। *12.* भीतर देखो।

● *1.* Save us! *2.* Loosen up. *3.* Turn it up. *4.* Pass it on. *5.* Drop the knife. *6.* Class dismissed. *7.* Open them. *8.* Are you alone? *9.* Knock, knock. *10.* Thank you, Bob. *11.* Very smooth. *12.* Look inside.

**[80]** *1.* धन्यवाद, महामहिम. *2.* में स्थानांतरित। *3.* आप सोचेंगे। *4.* आप जीते। *5.* धन्यवाद, जनरल. *6.* आओ देखें। *7.* किसके विपरीत? *8.* सशस्त्र पुलिस! *9.* अत्यावश्यक है?

● *1.* Thank you, Your Honor. *2.* Move in. *3.* You'd think. *4.* You won. *5.* Thank you, General. *6.* Let's look. *7.* As opposed to what? *8.* Armed police! *9.* Is it urgent?

**[81]** *1.* चलो, दादाजी. *2.* धन्यवाद, दादाजी. *3.* विभाजित करना। *4.* लूटा। *5.* सबक सीखा। *6.* चूसो इसे! *7.* इसे चूसो। *8.* इधर मुड़ें। *9.* गणित करें। *10.* गेट खोलने! *11.* गेंद खेलें! *12.* अरे डार्लिंग।

● *1.* Come on, Grandpa. *2.* Thank you, Grandpa. *3.* Split up. *4.* Hold up. *5.* Lesson learned. *6.* Suck it! *7.* Suck it up. *8.* Turn here. *9.* Do the math. *10.* Open the gate! *11.* Play ball! *12.* Come on, darling.

**[82]** *1.* मैं भागा. *2.* दरवाज़े खोलो! *3.* बाहर निकलो। *4.* कोमल हो। *5.* मैं चलूंगा. *6.* कपड़े पहनो। *7.* इसे पहनो। *8.* उनको रोको! *9.* आगे मार्च! *10.* त्वरित मार्च! *11.* घटित हुआ। *12.* सशस्त्र डकैती।

● *1.* I ran. *2.* Open the doors! *3.* Come on out. *4.* Be gentle. *5.* I'll walk. *6.* Get dressed. *7.* Wear it. *8.* Stop them! *9.* Forward march! *10.* Quick march! *11.* It happened. *12.* Armed robbery.

**[83]** *1.* तिरस्कार करना। *2.* उठना। *3.* पवित्र धुआं! *4.* उसे चूमो! *5.* धन्यवाद जानेमन। *6.* कृपया घूमो। *7.* समझदार बनना। *8.* बैठिए। *9.* कृपया बैठिए। *10.*

214

चिल्लाओ मत! *11.* कहाँ जाऊँ? *12.* ज़रा सोचो।
• *1.* Look down. *2.* Get up. *3.* Holy smokes! *4.* Kiss her! *5.* Thank you, sweetheart. *6.* Turn around, please. *7.* Be sensible. *8.* Have a seat. *9.* Please, sit. *10.* Don't shout! *11.* Where do I go? *12.* Think of it.

**[84]** *1.* उबर पाना! *2.* आओ, देवियो. *3.* यथार्थवादी बनें। *4.* धन्यवाद, टिम. *5.* धन्यवाद, सार्जेंट. *6.* सचेत। *7.* उठाना। *8.* मैं चलाऊंगा। *9.* घबराओ मत. *10.* तिजोरी खोलो। *11.* संभालो क्या? *12.* धन्यवाद, डौग।
• *1.* Get over! *2.* Come on, ladies. *3.* Be realistic. *4.* Thank you, Tim. *5.* Thank you, Sergeant. *6.* Heads up. *7.* Pick up. *8.* I'll drive. *9.* Don't be nervous. *10.* Open the safe. *11.* Handle what? *12.* Thank you, Doug.

**[85]** *1.* मुझे समझाओ। *2.* जवाबी हमला। *3.* गाड़ी संभालना। *4.* हैलो कहें। *5.* दुर्भाग्य से। *6.* अच्छा लगना? *7.* चलने लगना! *8.* इसे उठाएं। *9.* आप उठाएं। *10.* घंटी बजाना? *11.* तुम हारे। *12.* मई जा।
• *1.* Convince me. *2.* Fight back. *3.* Take the wheel. *4.* Say hello. *5.* That's bad luck. *6.* Feeling better? *7.* Get a move on! *8.* Pick it up. *9.* You pick. *10.* Ring a bell? *11.* You lose. *12.* I go.

**[86]** *1.* मई हु। *2.* सच्ची में? *3.* मैं सुनूंगा। *4.* मुझे काटना। *5.* अभिभूत हूँ। *6.* उसे बुलाएं। *7.* उनको बुलाएं। *8.* इसको खोलो। *9.* उसे जगाओ। *10.* यह आकृति। *11.* धन्यवाद, शुल्त्स। *12.* शॉवर लें।
• *1.* It is me. *2.* Is it really? *3.* I'll listen. *4.* Bite me. *5.* I'm overwhelmed. *6.* Call him. *7.* Call them. *8.* Open this. *9.* Wake her up. *10.* It figures. *11.* Thank you, Schultz. *12.* Take a shower.

**[87]** *1.* शनिवार है। *2.* निश्चिंत रहना। *3.* निश्चिंत रहें। *4.* हा बोलना। *5.* यहाँ उतरें। *6.* उन्हे लाओ! *7.* उन्हे देखे। *8.* आप उन्हे? *9.* हम लड़े। *10.* ट्रिगर खींचें। *11.* बाहर खींचें! *12.* इसे खींचें!
• *1.* It's Saturday. *2.* Hanging in there. *3.* Rest assured. *4.* Say yes. *5.* Come down here. *6.* Get them! *7.* Watch them. *8.* How do you like them apples? *9.* We fought. *10.* Pull the trigger. *11.* Pull out! *12.* Pull it up!

**[88]** *1.* बायां मोड़! *2.* वादे, वादे. *3.* आप पहल। *4.* धन्यवाद, सीनेटर। *5.* वह पढ़ो। *6.* उसे संभालें। *7.* इसे संभालें। *8.* पलटो मत. *9.* अब पलटो. *10.* सोमवार है। *11.* चलो, बालक. *12.* जागते रहना।
• *1.* Right turn! *2.* Promises, promises. *3.* You start. *4.* Thank you, Senator. *5.* Read that. *6.* Hold her. *7.* Handle it. *8.* Don't

turn around. *9.* Now turn around. *10.* It's Monday. *11.* Come on, lad. *12.* Sit up.

**[89]** *1.* टेक टू। *2.* हालात बदलना। *3.* त्रासदी है। *4.* धन्यवाद महोदय। *5.* बढ़िया बचत। *6.* मुड़ो। *7.* साला बकवास। *8.* साला! *9.* इसे तोड़ना। *10.* गति बढ़ाना! *11.* बढ़ाना! *12.* हम जीतेंगे।

● *1.* Take two. *2.* Things change. *3.* It's a tragedy. *4.* Thank you, sir. *5.* Nice save. *6.* Turn around. *7.* Fuckin' hell. *8.* Fuckin' hell! *9.* Break it. *10.* Speed up! *11.* Move up! *12.* We win.

**[90]** *1.* ट्रंक खोलो। *2.* यकीनन मैं। *3.* यादगार बनाना। *4.* पासपोर्ट, कृपया। *5.* सेट, झोपड़ी! *6.* मुझे पहचानें? *7.* कूदो मत! *8.* रुपये लो। *9.* धन्यवाद, एडमिरल. *10.* तुम खोदो? *11.* प्रचार कीजिये। *12.* कृपया शहद।

● *1.* Open the trunk. *2.* Sure I am. *3.* Make it count. *4.* Passport, please. *5.* Set, hut! *6.* Recognize me? *7.* Don't jump! *8.* Take the money. *9.* Thank you, Admiral. *10.* You dig? *11.* Spread the word. *12.* Honey, please.

**[91]** *1.* भागते रहें! *2.* शान्त होना! *3.* जी कहिये। *4.* धन्यवाद, महाशय. *5.* अभी सुने। *6.* मैं जाउंगा। *7.* उड़ान भरना। *8.* क्या ढूंढें? *9.* उसे लाएं। *10.* चढ़ना। *11.* पर चढ़ना। *12.* मुझे मारें।

● *1.* Keep running! *2.* Settle down! *3.* Yes, please. *4.* Thank you, monsieur. *5.* Now listen. *6.* I will go. *7.* Take off. *8.* Find what? *9.* Bring her. *10.* Hop on. *11.* Climb aboard. *12.* Hit me.

**[92]** *1.* आपकी मर्जी। *2.* तुम्हारे सहित। *3.* मेरे सहित। *4.* मत भूलो! *5.* नहाना। *6.* बने रहिए। *7.* शुभरात्रि कहें! *8.* ओ शुक्रिया। *9.* इसे खाएं। *10.* पर्याप्त कथन। *11.* टीवी चलाएं। *12.* धन्यवाद, इंस्पेक्टर.

● *1.* Have it your way. *2.* Including you. *3.* Including me. *4.* Don't forget! *5.* Take a bath. *6.* Keep at it. *7.* Say good night. *8.* Aw, thank you. *9.* Eat it. *10.* Enough said. *11.* Turn on the TV. *12.* Thank you, Inspector.

**[93]** *1.* चलिये। *2.* शैम्पेन, कृपया। *3.* शुक्रिया अंकल। *4.* जलता हे! *5.* शरमाओ मत। *6.* मुझसे लड़ें! *7.* दौड़ो दौड़ो! *8.* जाओ दौड़ो! *9.* तुम दौड़ो। *10.* जीतो क्या? *11.* बिना हिले। *12.* उसे खोजो।

● *1.* Go on, then. *2.* Champagne, please. *3.* Thank you, Uncle. *4.* It burns! *5.* Don't be shy. *6.* Fight me! *7.* Run, run! *8.* Go, run! *9.* You run. *10.* Win what? *11.* Hold still. *12.* Search him.

**[94]** *1.* कब्जा। *2.* ढाल उठाएँ. *3.* हम जाएँगे। *4.* धन्यवाद, आदरणीय. *5.* मुझे खिलाओ! *6.* जूम इन। *7.* घंटी बजाएं। *8.* इसे खाये। *9.* मैं प्रतिलिपि। *10.*

इसे छूओ। 11. धन्यवाद, राज्यपाल. 12. चलो, मुस्कुराओ.

• 1. Take over. 2. Raise shields. 3. We're gonna go. 4. Thank you, Reverend. 5. Feed me! 6. Zoom in. 7. Ring the bell. 8. Eat this. 9. I copy. 10. Touch it. 11. Thank you, Governor. 12. Come on, smile.

**[95]** 1. मुस्कुराओ मत. 2. अभ्यस्त। 3. आओ नाचें। 4. आपनें पूछा। 5. पहनकर देखो। 6. सेंध। 7. खिसको खिसको! 8. उतारना। 9. टहलें। 10. चलो टहलें। 11. नहीं युवती। 12. विन्यास करें।

• 1. Don't smile. 2. Used to. 3. Let's dance. 4. You asked. 5. Try it on. 6. Breaking and entering. 7. Move, move! 8. Take that off. 9. Take a walk. 10. Let's walk. 11. No, miss. 12. Spell it.

**[96]** 1. अच्छा है। 2. उन्होनें किया। 3. रेडी चलो! 4. कसी पकड़। 5. धन्यवाद, बर्नार्ड। 6. सिर्फ दौड़ें! 7. धन्यवाद, नवयुवक. 8. क्या समझाएं? 9. खुद समझाएं। 10. इसे समझाएं। 11. बाएँ दांए। 12. उसे ढूँढो।

• 1. It is good. 2. They did. 3. Ready, go! 4. Hold tight. 5. Thank you, Bernard. 6. Just run! 7. Thank you, young man. 8. Explain what? 9. Explain yourself. 10. Explain this. 11. Left, right. 12. Find her.

**[97]** 1. इसे सूंघो। 2. उन्हें जलाये! 3. अबे साले! 4. साले! 5. धन्यवाद हनी। 6. बैठो, बैठोगे? 7. धन्यवाद मोहतरमा। 8. खाई खोदना। 9. दांए मुड़िए। 10. पुल ओवर। 11. आगे झुको। 12. इसे हटाएं!

• 1. Smell it. 2. Burn them! 3. You idiot! 4. You fuckers! 5. Thank you, honey. 6. Sit down, will you? 7. Thank you, ma'am. 8. Dig in. 9. Turn right. 10. Pull over. 11. Lean forward. 12. Move it!

**[98]** 1. तो सुनिए। 2. आमने - सामने। 3. क्या उन्होने? 4. यह जाँचें। 5. मैं फिसला। 6. नकाब उतारो. 7. हलो रुको! 8. उसे खोजों। 9. धुआँ मिला? 10. आओ उड़ें। 11. वह दिखाएगा. 12. मेरा लेलो।

• 1. So listen. 2. Face to face. 3. Has she? 4. Check it. 5. I slipped. 6. Take off the mask. 7. Hey, stop! 8. Find him. 9. Got a smoke? 10. Let's fly. 11. He'll show. 12. Take mine.

**[99]** 1. खींचो! 2. ऐम्बुलेंस बुलाएं! 3. मैं खेलेंगे। 4. इसे पीयो। 5. वह टुटा। 6. अब अ◦अ◦ो। 7. ज़रा ठहरिये। 8. कुछ तलाशें? 9. इसे आज़माइए। 10. इसे उछालें। 11. वे क्रोव्स। 12. खुलना!

• 1. Pull it! 2. Call an ambulance! 3. I'll play. 4. Drink it. 5. It broke. 6. Now come. 7. Wait a minute. 8. Find something? 9. Give it a try. 10. Toss it. 11. They know. 12. Open up!

**[100]** *1.* तुम्हारा यहे। *2.* इसे गिनो। *3.* पेंच कसना। *4.* नृत्य चाहना? *5.* चाहना? *6.* इसे दबाएं। *7.* इसे पहचानो? *8.* हड़पना! *9.* हलका करना। *10.* इसे अजमाएं। *11.* धन्यवाद कुमारी। *12.* चेष्टा करना।

● *1.* This is yours. *2.* Count it. *3.* Screw it. *4.* Wanna dance? *5.* Want to? *6.* Push it. *7.* Recognize this? *8.* Grab on! *9.* Ease up. *10.* Try it. *11.* Thank you, miss. *12.* Make an effort.

**[101]** *1.* जय भगवन! *2.* सिर बचाके। *3.* मैंने जाँचा। *4.* विराजना। *5.* तुम रंडी! *6.* टलना। *7.* इसे निगलें। *8.* आद पकड़ना! *9.* छंटनी। *10.* बांए मुड़िए। *11.* कृपया खाइए। *12.* इसे आजमाएं।

● *1.* Praise God! *2.* Mind your head. *3.* I checked. *4.* Be seated. *5.* You whore! *6.* Move away. *7.* Swallow it. *8.* Hold fire! *9.* Lay off. *10.* Turn left. *11.* Please eat. *12.* Try this one.

**[102]** *1.* गोल घूमिए। *2.* वहाँ पहुचें। *3.* उसे हथियाएं! *4.* संकोचशील। *5.* त्यागपत्र देना। *6.* इसे फूँको। *7.* सुस्वागतम्। *8.* बढ़िया है। *9.* इन्कलाब जिंदाबाद! *10.* खेलत रहो। *11.* कृपया समझाएँ। *12.* बैटर अप!

● *1.* Turn round. *2.* Get over there. *3.* Grab her! *4.* It's embarrassing. *5.* Step down. *6.* Blow it. *7.* Welcome home. *8.* Is good. *9.* Long live the revolution! *10.* Keep playing. *11.* Please explain. *12.* Batter up!

**[103]** *1.* उसे चूमों। *2.* उसे भरदो। *3.* गोलिया चलाना। *4.* अंदर आजाओ। *5.* ठहराना! *6.* मुझे ढूँढें। *7.* घबड़ाएं नहीं। *8.* देअर सी? *9.* जबान संभालो। *10.* असलम अलैकुम। *11.* छितराया हुआ! *12.* दरवाजा खोलें!

● *1.* Kiss her. *2.* Fill her up. *3.* Shots fired. *4.* Come on in. *5.* Pull back! *6.* Find me. *7.* Do not panic. *8.* See there? *9.* Watch your mouth. *10.* Peace be upon you. *11.* Spread out! *12.* Open the door!

**[104]** *1.* घुण्डी दबाना। *2.* उड़ाना! *3.* सोखना। *4.* मुझे पकड़ो! *5.* धन्यवाद, लिनस। *6.* वह लौटेगा। *7.* आप झिझके। *8.* कृपया मुस्कुराएं। *9.* नजदीकी था। *10.* सुखी भव। *11.* बैठ जाईये। *12.* बिदा देना।

● *1.* Push the button. *2.* Go around! *3.* Drink up. *4.* Catch me! *5.* Thank you, Linus. *6.* He'll be back. *7.* You hesitated. *8.* Smile, please. *9.* It was close. *10.* Blessed be. *11.* Just sit. *12.* Signing off.

**[105]** *1.* काय करते? *2.* आप खेलिए? *3.* कृपया कॉफी। *4.* खिसकना! *5.* मैं जीऊँगा। *6.* निशाना साधो! *7.* क्या सुनौ? *8.* गो फ़िश। *9.* वें करेंगे? *10.* घुटने टेकना। *11.* होय आ। *12.* उसे भगाएं!

● *1.* What should we do? *2.* You play? *3.* Coffee, please. *4.* Move over! *5.* I'll live. *6.* Take aim! *7.* Hear what? *8.* Go fish.

9. Will they? *10.* Kneel down. *11.* Yes, come. *12.* Kick him!

## Difficulty Level: 2

**[1]** *1.* नहीं, मैं नहीं! *2.* क्या क्या है? *3.* क्या नहीं है? *4.* क्या नहीं हैं? *5.* यह क्या है? *6.* नहीं यह नहीं। *7.* यह क्या हैं? *8.* यह नहीं है. *9.* यह आप है।
• *1.* No, I don't! *2.* What's what? *3.* What isn't? *4.* What's missing? *5.* What is it? *6.* No, it's not. *7.* What are these? *8.* It ain't. *9.* It's you.

**[2]** *1.* यह आप हैं। *2.* आप क्या हैं? *3.* नहीं आप नहीं। *4.* वह क्या है? *5.* क्या वह है? *6.* यह वह है। *7.* वह नहीं है. *8.* नहीं वह है। *9.* वह मैं है। *10.* वह वह है. *11.* वह एक है। *12.* वह क्या था?
• *1.* That's you. *2.* You're what? *3.* No, you do not. *4.* What's that? *5.* Is he? *6.* This is she. *7.* She isn't. *8.* No, he is. *9.* She is me. *10.* That she is. *11.* He's the one. *12.* What was that?

**[3]** *1.* यह क्या था? *2.* मैं नहीं था. *3.* यह नहीं था. *4.* वह मैं था। *5.* वह में था। *6.* यह मैं हूं। *7.* वह मैं हूं। *8.* क्या मैं हूं? *9.* मैं मैं हूं. *10.* मैं नहीं हूं. *11.* तुम वह हो. *12.* मैं तुम हूं।
• *1.* What was it? *2.* I wasn't. *3.* It wasn't. *4.* That was me. *5.* It was me. *6.* It's me. *7.* That's me. *8.* Am I? *9.* I'm me. *10.* I ain't. *11.* You're him. *12.* I'm you.

**[4]** *1.* तुम तुम हो *2.* नहीं हो रहा। *3.* आप को क्या? *4.* मैं नहीं हूँ? *5.* नहीं, मैं हूँ। *6.* मैं क्या हूँ? *7.* मैं यह हूँ। *8.* मैं रहा हूँ। *9.* यह है कि। *10.* कि मैं हूँ। *11.* हम नहीं हैं? *12.* हम क्या हैं?
• *1.* You're you. *2.* Not happening. *3.* What is it to you? *4.* I'm not? *5.* No, I am. *6.* I'm what? *7.* This is who I am. *8.* I have been. *9.* That it is. *10.* That I am. *11.* Aren't we? *12.* What are we?

**[5]** *1.* हम एक हैं। *2.* नहीं, हम नहीं! *3.* क्या रहे हैं? *4.* यह हो गया? *5.* हो गया है. *6.* यह कुछ है। *7.* वह कुछ था. *8.* उसने क्या किया? *9.* उसने यह किया। *10.* उसने नहीं किया। *11.* नहीं उसने नहीं। *12.* बहुत हो गया।
• *1.* We are one. *2.* No, we're not! *3.* What are they? *4.* Is it done? *5.* That's done. *6.* That's something. *7.* That was something. *8.* What did he do? *9.* She did it. *10.* He did not. *11.* No, he did not. *12.* It's enough.

**[6]** *1.* वह बहुत है। *2.* यह बहुत है। *3.* वह नहीं थी. *4.* उन्होंने नहीं किया. *5.* मैंने नहीं किया. *6.* मैंने क्या किया? *7.* मैंने बहुत किया। *8.* मैंने वह किया। *9.* नहीं मैंने किया।

• *1.* That's good enough. *2.* It's a lot. *3.* She wasn't. *4.* They didn't. *5.* I didn't. *6.* What did I do? *7.* I've had enough. *8.* I did that. *9.* No, I did.

[7] *1.* मैंने उसे किया। *2.* मैंने कुछ किया। *3.* वह मैंने किया। *4.* कुछ और है. *5.* और मैंने किया। *6.* और उसने किया. *7.* किया और किया। *8.* और मैं हूँ। *9.* एक और है।
• *1.* I've done that. *2.* I did something. *3.* That I did. *4.* There's something else. *5.* And I did. *6.* And he did. *7.* Done and done. *8.* And I am. *9.* There's one more.

[8] *1.* और यह है। *2.* और तुम हो? *3.* तुम ठीक हो? *4.* मैं ठीक हूँ। *5.* यह ठीक है। *6.* वह ठीक है। *7.* मैं ठीक हूं। *8.* आप ठीक हैं। *9.* नहीं ठीक है। *10.* हम ठीक हैं। *11.* ठीक है मैं। *12.* यह ठीक था।
• *1.* And it is. *2.* And are you? *3.* Are you okay? *4.* I'm fine. *5.* It's fine. *6.* That's okay. *7.* I'll be fine. *8.* You're okay. *9.* No, it's fine. *10.* We're fine. *11.* Okay, I will. *12.* It was okay.

[9] *1.* वह ठीक हैं। *2.* वह ठीक था। *3.* वह ठीक थी। *4.* क्या ऐसा है? *5.* ऐसा किया था। *6.* उसने ऐसा किया। *7.* ऐसा नहीं है? *8.* हो सकता है। *9.* नहीं हो सकता। *10.* कर सकता है। *11.* मैं भी नहीं। *12.* मैं भी हूँ।
• *1.* He's doing fine. *2.* He was fine. *3.* She was fine. *4.* Is that so? *5.* It did. *6.* That does it. *7.* It isn't? *8.* Could be. *9.* Can't be. *10.* Can do. *11.* I don't either. *12.* I am, too.

[10] *1.* और तुम भी। *2.* मैंने भी किया। *3.* तो मैंने किया। *4.* तो आप हैं। *5.* तो क्या आप। *6.* कुछ तो है। *7.* तो मैं हूँ। *8.* यह बात है। *9.* क्या बात है? *10.* कि बात है। *11.* एक बात है। *12.* कोई बात नहीं।
• *1.* And so do you. *2.* I did, too. *3.* So did I. *4.* So are you. *5.* So do you. *6.* There's something. *7.* So I am. *8.* This is it. *9.* What's the point? *10.* That's the thing. *11.* There is one thing. *12.* It's okay.

[11] *1.* कोई नहीं है। *2.* वे ठीक हैं। *3.* क्या वे हैं? *4.* क्या वे नहीं? *5.* वे नहीं हैं? *6.* वे क्या हैं? *7.* वे मेरे हैं। *8.* तुम मेरे हो। *9.* मेरे पास है। *10.* आपको एक चाहिए? *11.* तुम्हें कुछ चाहिए? *12.* आपको क्या चाहिए?
• *1.* Nobody is. *2.* They're fine. *3.* Are they? *4.* Don't they? *5.* They're not? *6.* They're what? *7.* They're mine. *8.* You're mine. *9.* I have. *10.* You want one? *11.* Do you want some? *12.* What you want?

[12] *1.* आपको कुछ चाहिए? *2.* मुझे कुछ चाहिए। *3.* तुम्हें क्या चाहिए? *4.* तुम्हें भी चाहिए। *5.* आपको वह चाहिए? *6.* इसे क्या दिया? *7.* मुझे क्या

दिया? *8.* अच्छा ऐसा है। *9.* मैं अच्छा हूँ।
• *1.* You need something? *2.* I need something. *3.* Who do you want? *4.* You should, too. *5.* You want what? *6.* What gave it away? *7.* What gave me away? *8.* I see. *9.* I'm good.

**[13]** *1.* यह अच्छा है। *2.* वह अच्छा है। *3.* यह अच्छा था। *4.* वह अच्छा था। *5.* बहुत अच्छा था। *6.* क्या अच्छा है? *7.* मैं अच्छा था। *8.* ऐसा नहीं होगा। *9.* यह क्या होगा?
• *1.* That's nice. *2.* He's good. *3.* It was good. *4.* That was good. *5.* It was very good. *6.* What's good? *7.* I was good. *8.* It won't. *9.* What'll it be?

**[14]** *1.* यह अच्छा होगा। *2.* यह ठीक होगा। *3.* और क्या होगा? *4.* यह नहीं होगा। *5.* और वह होगा? *6.* अब क्या है? *7.* यह अब है। *8.* मैं अब हूँ। *9.* अब हम भी। *10.* मैं अब भी। *11.* अब ठीक है. *12.* तुम अब हो।
• *1.* That'd be nice. *2.* It'll be OK. *3.* What else would it be? *4.* It won't be. *5.* And that would be? *6.* What is it now? *7.* It is now. *8.* I am now. *9.* Now we're even. *10.* I still am. *11.* It's okay now. *12.* You are now.

**[15]** *1.* वह अब है। *2.* क्या उसने अब? *3.* अब तुम हो। *4.* यह आप थे। *5.* वह आप थे? *6.* तुम नहीं थे। *7.* आप ठीक थे. *8.* वे नहीं थे। *9.* आप क्या थे? *10.* क्या करना है? *11.* मुझे करना होगा। *12.* आपको करना होगा।
• *1.* He is now. *2.* Did he now? *3.* Now you are. *4.* It was you. *5.* That was you? *6.* You weren't. *7.* You were fine. *8.* They weren't. *9.* What were you? *10.* Do what? *11.* I have to. *12.* You have to.

**[16]** *1.* उसे करना है। *2.* मेरे साथ हो। *3.* मैं यहाँ हूँ। *4.* यहाँ हम हैं। *5.* वे यहाँ हैं। *6.* यहाँ हैं हम। *7.* वह यहाँ है। *8.* यह यहाँ है। *9.* यहाँ वह है। *10.* वह यहाँ था। *11.* हम यहाँ हैं। *12.* वह यहाँ थी।
• *1.* She has to. *2.* Be with me. *3.* I'm here. *4.* Here we are. *5.* They're here. *6.* There we are. *7.* She's here. *8.* It's here. *9.* Here he is. *10.* He was here. *11.* We are here. *12.* She was here.

**[17]** *1.* तुम यहाँ हो? *2.* कोई यहाँ है? *3.* यहाँ क्या है? *4.* वे यहाँ थे। *5.* यहाँ कुछ है. *6.* यह यहाँ था। *7.* यहाँ कोई है. *8.* आप यहाँ थे। *9.* ऐसा ही हो। *10.* ऐसा ही होगा। *11.* ऐसा ही है। *12.* आप ही हैं।
• *1.* You're here? *2.* Is anyone here? *3.* What's in here? *4.* They were here. *5.* Here's something. *6.* It was here. *7.* There's someone here. *8.* You were here. *9.* I hope so. *10.* So be it. *11.* That's the way it is. *12.* It is you.

**[18]** *1.* आपको लगता है? *2.* मुझे लगता है। *3.* ऐसा लगता है. *4.* तुम्हें लगता है? *5.* मुझे नहीं लगता। *6.* अच्छा लगता है। *7.* तुम्हें नहीं लगता? *8.* ठीक लगता है। *9.* मुझे पता है।
● *1.* You think? *2.* I think. *3.* Looks that way. *4.* You feel that? *5.* I suppose not. *6.* That sounds nice. *7.* You don't think? *8.* Sounds cool. *9.* I know.

**[19]** *1.* आपको पता है? *2.* मुझे नहीं पता। *3.* मुझे पता नहीं। *4.* मुझे क्या पता? *5.* पता क्या है? *6.* पता था क्या? *7.* तुम्हें पता नहीं! *8.* ठीक से करो। *9.* इसे ठीक करो।
● *1.* You know? *2.* I do not know. *3.* Beats me. *4.* What do I know? *5.* What's the address? *6.* Knew what? *7.* You don't know! *8.* Do it right. *9.* Fix this.

**[20]** *1.* अब क्या करें? *2.* आप उसे करें। *3.* तो इसे करें। *4.* इसे ठीक करें। *5.* नहीं आप करें। *6.* कुछ और करें। *7.* आप भी करें। *8.* कुछ अच्छा करें। *9.* अब यह करें।
● *1.* What do we do now? *2.* You do that. *3.* Then do it. *4.* Fix it. *5.* No, you do. *6.* Do something else. *7.* You do, too. *8.* Make a fist. *9.* Now do it.

**[21]** *1.* यह बस है। *2.* वे आपके हैं। *3.* आपने क्या किया? *4.* आपने नहीं किया। *5.* आपने अच्छा किया। *6.* आपने यह किया। *7.* वह आपने किया? *8.* आपने भी नहीं. *9.* तो आपने किया।
● *1.* It just is. *2.* They're yours. *3.* What did you do? *4.* You didn't. *5.* You did good. *6.* You did this. *7.* You did that? *8.* Neither did you. *9.* So you did.

**[22]** *1.* जा रहे थे। *2.* तुम जा रहे? *3.* मैं करता हूं। *4.* वह करता है। *5.* कोई नहीं करता। *6.* क्या करता है? *7.* वह नहीं करता? *8.* मैं करता हूँ। *9.* ठीक है, चलो.
● *1.* We're going. *2.* You going? *3.* I do. *4.* He does. *5.* Nobody does. *6.* What does? *7.* He doesn't? *8.* I do it. *9.* All right, come on.

**[23]** *1.* मेरे साथ चलो। *2.* चलो उसे करें। *3.* चलो ठीक है. *4.* नहीं, नहीं, चलो. *5.* चलो, बात करो! *6.* दो कर दो। *7.* उसे मुझे दो। *8.* वह दो हैं. *9.* वह मुझे दो। *10.* मुझे कुछ दो। *11.* मुझे और दो। *12.* मुझे दो दो।
● *1.* Walk with me. *2.* Let's get to it. *3.* Come on, it's okay. *4.* No, no, come on. *5.* Come on, talk! *6.* Make it two. *7.* Give him to me. *8.* That's two. *9.* Give that to me. *10.* Give me something. *11.* Give me more. *12.* Give me two.

**[24]** *1.* यह काम है। *2.* काम नहीं करता. *3.* वह काम किया। *4.* ऐसा मत करो! *5.* तो मत करो. *6.* बस मत करो. *7.* मत भी करो. *8.* बात मत करो! *9.* हाँ मैंने किया। *10.* हाँ यह है। *11.* हाँ वह है। *12.* हाँ यह था।

● *1.* It's work. *2.* Doesn't work. *3.* That worked. *4.* Don't do it! *5.* Then don't. *6.* Just don't. *7.* Don't even. *8.* Don't talk! *9.* Yes, I did. *10.* Yeah, it is. *11.* Yes, he is. *12.* Yes, it was.

**[25]** *1.* हाँ वह था। *2.* हाँ मैं था। *3.* हाँ उसने किया। *4.* हाँ, हम हैं। *5.* हाँ, वे हैं। *6.* हाँ यह होगा। *7.* हाँ मैं हूँ! *8.* हाँ वह थी। *9.* यह हाँ है। *10.* हाँ, उन्होंने किया। *11.* मैंने किया, हाँ. *12.* हाँ वे थे।

● *1.* Yes, he did. *2.* Yes, I was. *3.* Yes, she did. *4.* Yeah, we are. *5.* Yeah, they are. *6.* Yes, it would. *7.* Yes, I am! *8.* Yes, she was. *9.* That's a yes. *10.* Yeah, they did. *11.* I did, yeah. *12.* Yes, they were.

**[26]** *1.* हाँ, आप थे. *2.* हाँ, ऐसा करो. *3.* हाँ, हम थे। *4.* मैं हूँ, हाँ. *5.* यह है, हाँ. *6.* हाँ, यह करो. *7.* आपको क्या हुआ? *8.* क्या हुआ है? *9.* उसे क्या हुआ?

● *1.* Yeah, you were. *2.* Yes, do that. *3.* Yeah, we were. *4.* I am, yeah. *5.* It is, yeah. *6.* Yeah, do it. *7.* What happened to you? *8.* What's happened? *9.* What happened to him?

**[27]** *1.* तो क्या हुआ? *2.* कुछ हुआ क्या? *3.* अच्छा ही हुआ। *4.* यह क्या हुआ। *5.* अच्छा, क्या हुआ? *6.* और क्या हुआ? *7.* ऐसा नहीं हुआ. *8.* किया हुआ है। *9.* हमें क्या हुआ?

● *1.* So what happened? *2.* Did something happen? *3.* Thank goodness. *4.* That's what happened. *5.* Well, what happened? *6.* And what happened? *7.* It didn't. *8.* Already done. *9.* What happened to us?

**[28]** *1.* हाँ, ऐसा हुआ। *2.* क्या हुआ था? *3.* यह हुआ है। *4.* क्या कुछ हुआ? *5.* अब क्या हुआ? *6.* बस बहुत हुआ। *7.* यह मेरा है। *8.* वह मेरा है। *9.* यह मेरा था। *10.* वह मेरा था। *11.* उन्हें क्या हुआ? *12.* उन्हें लगता है।

● *1.* Yeah, it did. *2.* What did happen? *3.* It's happened. *4.* Did anything happen? *5.* Now, what happened? *6.* OK, that's enough. *7.* It's mine. *8.* That's mine. *9.* It was mine. *10.* That was mine. *11.* What happened to them? *12.* Find them.

**[29]** *1.* उन्हें करने दो। *2.* उन्हें करना है। *3.* मैं नहीं चाहता. *4.* मैं चाहता हूँ। *5.* मैं चाहता हूं। *6.* एक चाहता हूं? *7.* मैं चाहता था। *8.* वह मेरी है। *9.* सब ठीक होगा।

● *1.* Let them. *2.* They have to. *3.* I don't want to. *4.* I want to. *5.* I wish. *6.* Want one? *7.* I wanted to. *8.* She's mine. *9.* It's going to be okay.

**[30]** *1.* सब ठीक है। *2.* हम सब थे. *3.* यह सब है। *4.* ठीक है जाओ। *5.* चलो बस जाओ। *6.* जाओ उन्हें जाओ। *7.* नहीं, तुम जाओ. *8.* इस पर था। *9.* क्यों किया था? *10.* ऐसा क्यों था? *11.* तुम क्यों हो? *12.* ऐसा क्यों होगा?
● *1.* All is well. *2.* We all were. *3.* That's the stuff. *4.* Okay, go. *5.* Let's just go. *6.* Go get 'em. *7.* No, you go. *8.* We're on. *9.* Why did you do it? *10.* Why was that? *11.* Why are you? *12.* Why would it?

**[31]** *1.* इसे ले जाओ। *2.* यह सब ले। *3.* कृपया, मत करो. *4.* नहीं, नहीं, कृपया! *5.* कृपया, बस जाओ। *6.* नहीं, कृपया, नहीं! *7.* कृपया यहाँ पर। *8.* कृपया एक और। *9.* हाँ कृपया करो।
● *1.* Take her. *2.* Take it all. *3.* Please, don't. *4.* No, no, please! *5.* Please, just go. *6.* No, please, no! *7.* Over here, please. *8.* One more, please. *9.* Yes, please do.

**[32]** *1.* ठीक है, कृपया. *2.* वे करते हैं। *3.* वे नहीं करते. *4.* आप क्या करते? *5.* कुछ करते हैं। *6.* कुछ चाहते हैं? *7.* आप नहीं चाहते? *8.* आपका क्या है? *9.* आप कैसे हैं?
● *1.* Okay, please. *2.* They do. *3.* They don't. *4.* What would you have done? *5.* Some do. *6.* Want some? *7.* You don't want to? *8.* What's yours? *9.* How are you?

**[33]** *1.* यह कैसे हुआ? *2.* तुम कैसे हो'? *3.* तुम्हें कैसे पता? *4.* वह कैसे हुआ? *5.* कैसे था कि? *6.* हम कैसे हैं? *7.* वे कैसे हैं? *8.* ऐसा कैसे हुआ? *9.* मैंने कैसे किया?
● *1.* How did it go? *2.* How you doin'? *3.* How'd you know? *4.* How did that happen? *5.* How was that? *6.* How are we doing? *7.* How are they? *8.* How'd that happen? *9.* How'd I do?

**[34]** *1.* मैं कैसे हूँ? *2.* वह कैसे गया? *3.* वह कैसे होगा? *4.* हाँ आ जाओ। *5.* आ रहा है। *6.* क्या मैं आ? *7.* अब आ जाओ। *8.* आ रहे थे! *9.* कृपया आ जाओ। *10.* बस आ जाओ। *11.* उसके पास है। *12.* उसके पास जाओ।
● *1.* How am I? *2.* How did that go? *3.* How would that be? *4.* Yeah, come on. *5.* Coming up. *6.* Can I come? *7.* Come now. *8.* We're coming! *9.* Please, come on. *10.* Just come. *11.* He has. *12.* Go to her.

**[35]** *1.* उसके साथ जाओ। *2.* उसके साथ क्या? *3.* यह समय है। *4.* समय लगता है। *5.* मुझे समय दो। *6.* उसे समय दो। *7.* समय नहीं है. *8.* समय नहीं था. *9.* यह समय था। *10.* अब समय है। *11.* उसने कर लिया। *12.* अभी क्या हुआ?

• *1.* Go with it. *2.* What's with that? *3.* It's time. *4.* It takes time. *5.* Give me time. *6.* Give him time. *7.* There isn't time. *8.* There wasn't time. *9.* It was time. *10.* The time is now. *11.* He's done. *12.* What just happened?

**[36]** *1.* अभी और है। *2.* मैंने अभी किया। *3.* यह अभी हुआ। *4.* मुझे अभी चाहिए। *5.* अभी भी हो! *6.* अभी भी हूँ। *7.* हम अभी हैं। *8.* कृपया अभी नहीं। *9.* ओह, यह है। *10.* ओह तुम भी। *11.* ओह, मैं हूं। *12.* ओह, अब चलो।
• *1.* There's more. *2.* I just did. *3.* It just happened. *4.* I need it now. *5.* Be still! *6.* Still am. *7.* We are now. *8.* Not now, please. *9.* Oh, it is. *10.* Oh, you do? *11.* Oh, I am. *12.* Oh, come on, now.

**[37]** *1.* ओह क्या तुम? *2.* ओह ठीक है। *3.* ओह, नहीं, कृपया. *4.* ओह, मैंने किया। *5.* ओह तो तुम? *6.* ओह, कृपया करें। *7.* ओह, यह क्या? *8.* ओह, वह है. *9.* ओह, क्या मैं?
• *1.* Oh, do you? *2.* Oh, that's fine. *3.* Oh, no, please. *4.* Oh, I did. *5.* Oh, you are? *6.* Oh, please do. *7.* Oh, what is this? *8.* Oh, he is. *9.* Oh, do I?

**[38]** *1.* कहाँ है वह? *2.* वह कहाँ है? *3.* मैं कहाँ हूँ? *4.* आप कहाँ रहे? *5.* कहाँ था मैं? *6.* हम कहाँ थे? *7.* सब कहाँ हैं? *8.* तुम कहाँ थे? *9.* और कहाँ जाओ? *10.* कहाँ क्या है? *11.* वह कहाँ था? *12.* वह कहाँ थी?
• *1.* Where is he? *2.* Where is she? *3.* Where am I? *4.* Where you been? *5.* Where was I? *6.* Where were we? *7.* Where is everyone? *8.* Where've you been? *9.* And go where? *10.* Where's what? *11.* Where was that? *12.* Where was she?

**[39]** *1.* वह कहाँ गया? *2.* तुम कहाँ हो? *3.* मैं कहाँ था? *4.* कभी नहीं हुआ। *5.* क्या कहा आपने? *6.* उसने क्या कहा? *7.* मैंने क्या कहा? *8.* मैंने कहा नहीं। *9.* आप यह कहा।
• *1.* Where does it go? *2.* Where are ya? *3.* Where have I been? *4.* Never happened. *5.* What did you say? *6.* What did he say? *7.* What did I say? *8.* I said no. *9.* You said it.

**[40]** *1.* आपने कुछ कहा? *2.* उन्होंने कहा कि? *3.* उसने कहा की? *4.* उसने नहीं कहा. *5.* उन्होंने क्या कहा? *6.* मैंने कहा जाओ! *7.* तो आपने कहा. *8.* उन्होंने नहीं कहा. *9.* उसने हाँ कहा।
• *1.* Did you say something? *2.* He said that? *3.* She said that? *4.* She didn't say. *5.* What'd they say? *6.* I said go! *7.* So you said. *8.* They didn't say. *9.* She said yes.

**[41]** *1.* उन्होंने कहा हाँ। *2.* मैंने कुछ कहा? *3.* मैं कहा हाँ। *4.* उसने यह कहा.

*5.* उन्होंने यह कहा. *6.* मैंने नहीं कहा. *7.* मैंने कहा था। *8.* उसने कहा क्या? *9.* मुझे पसंद है।

● *1.* He said yes. *2.* Something I said? *3.* I say yes. *4.* She said it. *5.* He said it. *6.* I didn't say. *7.* I told ya. *8.* He said what? *9.* I'd love to.

**[42]** *1.* हम जानते हैं। *2.* आप जानते थे? *3.* सब जानते हैं। *4.* उसे नहीं जानते. *5.* वे जानते थे। *6.* तुम जानते हो। *7.* यहाँ वापस जाओ! *8.* काम पर वापस। *9.* मुझे वापस ले।

● *1.* We know. *2.* You knew? *3.* Everybody knows. *4.* Don't know him. *5.* They knew. *6.* You do know. *7.* Get back here! *8.* Back to work. *9.* Take me back.

**[43]** *1.* लेकिन मैं नहीं. *2.* लेकिन यह है। *3.* लेकिन ऐसा हुआ. *4.* लेकिन हुआ क्या? *5.* लेकिन आपको चाहिए। *6.* लेकिन तुम्हें चाहिए। *7.* लेकिन यह होगा. *8.* मैं जानता था। *9.* वह जानता है।

● *1.* But I don't. *2.* But it is. *3.* But it did. *4.* But what happened? *5.* But you should. *6.* But you must. *7.* But it will. *8.* I knew it. *9.* He knows.

**[44]** *1.* कोई नहीं जानता। *2.* मैं जानता हूँ। *3.* वह जानता था। *4.* आप कौन हैं? *5.* यह कौन है? *6.* कौन जानता है? *7.* वह कौन था? *8.* कौन हैं वे? *9.* वह कौन है? *10.* मैं कौन हूँ? *11.* कौन नहीं करता? *12.* वह कौन थी?

● *1.* No one knows. *2.* I'm aware. *3.* He knew. *4.* Who are you? *5.* Who is this? *6.* Who knows? *7.* Who was that? *8.* Who are they? *9.* Who's he? *10.* Who am I? *11.* Who doesn't? *12.* Who was she?

**[45]** *1.* वे कौन थे? *2.* कौन करता है? *3.* 'हम' कौन हैं? *4.* वे कौन हैं? *5.* कौन नहीं है? *6.* और कौन होगा? *7.* आप कौन हो? *8.* कौन नहीं होगा? *9.* यहाँ कौन था? *10.* कौन कहाँ है? *11.* वह कौन होगा? *12.* मैं कौन हूं?

● *1.* Who were they? *2.* Who does? *3.* Who's 'we'? *4.* Who's they? *5.* Who isn't? *6.* Who else would it be? *7.* Who're you? *8.* Who wouldn't be? *9.* Who was here? *10.* Where is who? *11.* Who would that be? *12.* Who I am?

**[46]** *1.* यहाँ कौन है? *2.* कौन क्या है? *3.* कौन जानता होगा? *4.* हमें मदद चाहिए। *5.* मेरी मदद करो। *6.* कृपया मदद करें! *7.* कुछ मदद चाहिए? *8.* मदद करो, कोई! *9.* मैंने मदद की।

● *1.* Who's in here? *2.* Who's what? *3.* Who would know? *4.* We need help. *5.* Help me up. *6.* Help, please! *7.* Want some help? *8.* Help, somebody! *9.* I helped.

**[47]** *1.* ओह, मदद करो! *2.* वह हो गई. *3.* फिर कैसे हैं? *4.* फिर क्या हुआ? *5.* फिर क्या था? *6.* फिर से जाओ। *7.* ऐसा फिर हुआ. *8.* अच्छा आपको धन्यवाद। *9.* ठीक है धन्यवाद।

● *1.* Oh, help! *2.* She's done. *3.* How are ya? *4.* What happened then? *5.* Then what was it? *6.* Go again. *7.* It happened again. *8.* Well, thank you. *9.* Okay, thank you.

**[48]** *1.* फिर से धन्यवाद। *2.* ओह, नहीं, धन्यवाद. *3.* नहीं, नहीं, धन्यवाद. *4.* ओह, धन्यवाद, धन्यवाद. *5.* ओह, हाँ, धन्यवाद. *6.* कुछ नहीं, धन्यवाद. *7.* फिर भी धन्यवाद। *8.* बहुत अच्छा धन्यवाद। *9.* मुझे धन्यवाद दो?

● *1.* Thank you again. *2.* Oh, no, thank you. *3.* No, no, thank you. *4.* Oh, thank you, thank you. *5.* Oh, yes, thank you. *6.* Nothing, thank you. *7.* Thank you anyway. *8.* Very good, thank you. *9.* Thank me?

**[49]** *1.* हाँ तुमने किया। *2.* तुमने यह किया। *3.* तुमने क्या किया? *4.* लेकिन तुमने किया. *5.* तुमने नहीं किया. *6.* तो क्या तुमने. *7.* और तुमने किया? *8.* क्यों तुमने किया? *9.* अच्छा, तुमने किया।

● *1.* Yes, you did. *2.* You did it. *3.* What'd you do? *4.* But you did. *5.* You did not. *6.* So did you. *7.* And did you? *8.* Why did you? *9.* Well, you did.

**[50]** *1.* ओह, तुमने किया? *2.* नहीं, तुमने किया. *3.* तुमने कैसे किया? *4.* अच्छा, क्या तुमने? *5.* कौन है ये? *6.* ये हम हैं। *7.* ये वे हैं। *8.* वह ये थी। *9.* ये है पता.

● *1.* Oh, you did? *2.* No, you did. *3.* How did you? *4.* Well, did you? *5.* Who is he? *6.* That's us. *7.* It's them. *8.* It was her. *9.* Here's the address.

**[51]** *1.* आपको ये चाहिए। *2.* ये करना चाहिए. *3.* ये कैसे हुआ? *4.* ये मेरे हैं। *5.* ये क्या किया? *6.* जो क्या है? *7.* जो यह है? *8.* क्या यही है? *9.* यही है क्या? *10.* यही हमें चाहिए। *11.* तुमने यही कहा? *12.* यही तुम हो।

● *1.* This is what you want. *2.* This should do it. *3.* How'd this happen? *4.* These are mine. *5.* What did this? *6.* Which is what? *7.* Which is it? *8.* Is that it? *9.* Is this it? *10.* That's what I want. *11.* You mean it? *12.* That's what you are.

**[52]** *1.* यही वह है। *2.* तो यही है? *3.* उन्होंने यही कहा. *4.* हमें यही चाहिए. *5.* और यही है. *6.* यही तो है. *7.* आप यही हैं. *8.* आओ इसे करें। *9.* फिर से आओ? *10.* मेरे पास आओ। *11.* उसे ले आओ! *12.* चलो, चलो, आओ!

● *1.* That is it. *2.* So this is it? *3.* That's what they said. *4.* That's what we need. *5.* And this is it. *6.* That's what that is. *7.* This is who you are. *8.* Let's do this. *9.* Come again? *10.*

Come to me. *11.* Get her! *12.* Come on, come on, come on!

**[53]** *1.* मेरे साथ आओ। *2.* ले आओ उसे। *3.* ओह, यहाँ आओ. *4.* आओ करते हैं। *5.* हाँ चलो आओ। *6.* ओह, अब आओ. *7.* आप यहाँ आओ। *8.* अब साथ आओ। *9.* अब यहाँ आओ। *10.* आओ, तुम सब। *11.* यहाँ, यहाँ आओ। *12.* हाँ, यहाँ आओ।

• *1.* Come with me, please. *2.* Bring him. *3.* Oh, come here. *4.* Yes, let's. *5.* Yes, come on. *6.* Oh, come now. *7.* You, come here. *8.* Come along now. *9.* Now come here. *10.* Come on, y'all. *11.* Here, come here. *12.* Yeah, come here.

**[54]** *1.* क्या तुमने देखा? *2.* आपने क्या देखा? *3.* मैंने उसे देखा। *4.* मैंने देखा है। *5.* तो मैंने देखा। *6.* तुमने उसे देखा। *7.* तुमने मुझे देखा। *8.* उसे नहीं देखा। *9.* उसने मुझे देखा।

• *1.* Did you see that? *2.* What did you see? *3.* I saw it. *4.* I've seen it. *5.* So I see. *6.* You saw it. *7.* You saw me. *8.* Haven't seen him. *9.* He saw me.

**[55]** *1.* मैंने नहीं देखा। *2.* मैंने इसे देखा। *3.* उसने हमें देखा। *4.* उसने क्या देखा? *5.* यह उसकी है। *6.* उसकी मदद करो! *7.* अपना काम करो। *8.* हाँ, मिल गया। *9.* आपको मिल गया?

• *1.* I didn't see. *2.* I seen it. *3.* He saw us. *4.* What did he see? *5.* It's her. *6.* Help him! *7.* Do your job. *8.* Yeah, got it. *9.* You got one?

**[56]** *1.* उसे मिल गया? *2.* मुझे मिल गया। *3.* मैं बाहर हूँ। *4.* वह बाहर है। *5.* तुम बाहर हो। *6.* मुझे बाहर चाहिए। *7.* यह बाहर है। *8.* बाहर आ जाओ। *9.* बाहर तुम जाओ।

• *1.* Got her? *2.* I got in. *3.* I'm out. *4.* He's out. *5.* You're out. *6.* I want out. *7.* It's out. *8.* Come outside. *9.* Out you go.

**[57]** *1.* यहाँ बाहर आओ। *2.* वे बाहर हैं। *3.* अब बाहर आओ! *4.* यह उसका है। *5.* उसका क्या होगा? *6.* मुझे ऐसा लगा। *7.* आपको क्या लगा? *8.* अच्छा लगा मुझे। *9.* यह अच्छा लगा।

• *1.* Come out here. *2.* They're outside. *3.* Come out now! *4.* That's her. *5.* What will happen to him? *6.* I thought so. *7.* What did you think? *8.* I liked it. *9.* It felt good.

**[58]** *1.* मुझे लगा कि। *2.* मुझे लगा की। *3.* ओह, वह देखो। *4.* आओ और देखो। *5.* ओह, यह देखो। *6.* इस को देखो। *7.* अच्छा, तुम देखो। *8.* बस मुझे देखो। *9.* ओह, तुम देखो।

• *1.* I figured that. *2.* I felt that. *3.* Oh, look at that. *4.* Come and see. *5.* Oh, look at this. *6.* Look at this one. *7.* Well, look at you. *8.* Just look at me. *9.* Oh, look at you.

**[59]** *1.* और ये देखो. *2.* यहाँ, इसे देखो. *3.* अब ये देखो. *4.* ये सब देखो. *5.* बस उसे देखो. *6.* अच्छा, ये देखो. *7.* अब, यहाँ देखो. *8.* लेकिन ये देखो. *9.* उसे देखो जाओ.

• *1.* And look at this. *2.* Here, look at this. *3.* Now watch this. *4.* Look at all this. *5.* Just look at him. *6.* Well, look at this. *7.* Now, look here. *8.* But look at this. *9.* Look at him go.

**[60]** *1.* बस इसे देखो. *2.* और तुम देखो. *3.* देखो क्या हुआ. *4.* और मुझे देखो. *5.* अब आप देखो? *6.* आओ, मुझे देखो. *7.* अब, यह देखो. *8.* इसके लिए धन्यवाद। *9.* मुझे जाना होगा।

• *1.* Just look at it. *2.* And look at you. *3.* Look what happened. *4.* And look at me. *5.* Now, you see? *6.* Come on, look at me. *7.* Now, watch this. *8.* Thank you for this. *9.* I gotta go.

**[61]** *1.* मुझे जाना चाहिए। *2.* हमें जाना है। *3.* मुझे जाना है। *4.* तुम्हें जाना चाहिए। *5.* हमें जाना होगा। *6.* तुम्हें जाना होगा। *7.* जाना अच्छा है। *8.* काम पर जाना। *9.* जाना चाहता हूँ?

• *1.* I should go. *2.* We gotta go. *3.* Gotta go. *4.* You have to go. *5.* We got to go. *6.* You gotta go. *7.* Nice going. *8.* Go to work. *9.* Want to go?

**[62]** *1.* हमें जाना चाहिए. *2.* यहां वापस आओ! *3.* यहां क्या हुआ? *4.* तुम यहां आओ। *5.* मैं यहां हूं! *6.* यहां कौन है? *7.* मैं यहां था। *8.* यहां एक है। *9.* आप यहां हैं।

• *1.* We should be going. *2.* Come back here! *3.* What happened here? *4.* Come here, you. *5.* Here I am! *6.* Who's here? *7.* I was here. *8.* Here's one. *9.* You are here.

**[63]** *1.* यहां क्या है? *2.* वह यहां है। *3.* मुझे घर जाना। *4.* घर मेरा है। *5.* आप घर जाओ। *6.* अब घर जाओ। *7.* यह घर है। *8.* मैं घर गया। *9.* बस घर आओ। *10.* घर वापस जाओ। *11.* उससे क्या चाहिए? *12.* मैंने उससे कहा।

• *1.* What's here? *2.* She is here. *3.* I have to go home. *4.* It's my house. *5.* You go home. *6.* Go home now. *7.* This is home. *8.* I went home. *9.* Just come home. *10.* Go back home. *11.* What does she want? *12.* I told him.

**[64]** *1.* किसी ने किया. *2.* प्यार में थे। *3.* वह प्यार है। *4.* यह प्यार है। *5.* धन्यवाद मेरे प्यार। *6.* आपने मुझसे कहा। *7.* मुझसे कहा क्या? *8.* मुझसे बात करो। *9.* तुम वहाँ जाओ।

• *1.* Somebody did. *2.* We're in love. *3.* That's love. *4.* It's love. *5.* Thank you, my love. *6.* You told me. *7.* Told me what? *8.*

Speak to me. *9.* There you go.

**[65]** *1.* वहाँ कौन है? *2.* वहाँ है वह। *3.* हाँ वहाँ है। *4.* तुम वहाँ थे। *5.* वह वहाँ है. *6.* वह वहाँ थी। *7.* वहाँ पर जाना। *8.* वहाँ क्या हुआ? *9.* वहाँ कुछ है. *10.* वहाँ वापस जाओ. *11.* यह वहाँ था। *12.* वहाँ कौन था?
● *1.* Who's there? *2.* There she is. *3.* Yes, there is. *4.* You were there. *5.* He's in there. *6.* She was there. *7.* Go over there. *8.* What happened out there? *9.* There's something out there. *10.* Get back there. *11.* It was there. *12.* Who was there?

**[66]** *1.* हम वहाँ थे। *2.* वहाँ वह है. *3.* हाँ वहाँ था। *4.* वे वहाँ थे। *5.* मैं वहाँ गया। *6.* वहाँ कोई है. *7.* वहां आप हैं। *8.* वे वहां हैं। *9.* मैं वहां था। *10.* वहां क्या है? *11.* यह वहां है। *12.* वह वहां था।
● *1.* We were there. *2.* There's that. *3.* Yes, there was. *4.* They were there. *5.* I went there. *6.* There's someone in there. *7.* There you are. *8.* There they are. *9.* I was there. *10.* What's in there? *11.* It's there. *12.* He was there.

**[67]** *1.* वहां कौन है? *2.* वह वहां है. *3.* तुम वहां जाओ। *4.* वहां नहीं है। *5.* वहां है अभी। *6.* आप वहां हैं। *7.* हम ऐसा करेंगे। *8.* क्या करेंगे आप? *9.* आप क्या करेंगे?
● *1.* Who's in there? *2.* She's in there. *3.* There ya go. *4.* There's not. *5.* There is now. *6.* You're there. *7.* We will. *8.* What will you do? *9.* What would you do?

**[68]** *1.* हम क्या करेंगे? *2.* हाँ आप करेंगे। *3.* वे नहीं करेंगे। *4.* हम बात करेंगे। *5.* हाँ हम करेंगे। *6.* आप अच्छा करेंगे. *7.* लेकिन आप करेंगे। *8.* और हम करेंगे। *9.* आप ऐसा करेंगे?
● *1.* What shall we do? *2.* Yes, you will. *3.* They won't. *4.* We'll talk. *5.* Yes, we will. *6.* You'll do fine. *7.* But you will. *8.* And we will. *9.* You would do that?

**[69]** *1.* आप नहीं करेंगे? *2.* हम नहीं करेंगे? *3.* ओह, आप करेंगे. *4.* लेकिन हम करेंगे. *5.* तो आप करेंगे। *6.* ओह, हम करेंगे. *7.* अच्छा, हम करेंगे? *8.* हम यही करेंगे. *9.* आप यह करेंगे?
● *1.* You wouldn't? *2.* Won't we? *3.* Oh, you will. *4.* But we will. *5.* So will you. *6.* Oh, we will. *7.* Well, shall we? *8.* Here's what we'll do. *9.* You'll do it?

**[70]** *1.* अच्छा, आप करेंगे. *2.* यह सही है। *3.* वह सही है. *4.* वह सही था. *5.* सही है आप. *6.* वे सही हैं. *7.* मैं सही हूँ। *8.* आप सही हैं। *9.* सही काम करो। *10.* आपने सही किया. *11.* सही लगता है. *12.* तुम पहले जाओ।
● *1.* Well, you will. *2.* That's right. *3.* He's right. *4.* He was

right. *5.* Right you are. *6.* They're right. *7.* I'm right. *8.* You are correct. *9.* Do the right thing. *10.* You did right. *11.* Sounds right. *12.* You go first.

**[71]** *1.* वह पहले था. *2.* आप पहले हैं. *3.* इसका क्या हुआ? *4.* मदद की जरूरत? *5.* जरूरत नहीं है. *6.* तुम अभी तक। *7.* ये आ गए। *8.* वे कहाँ गए? *9.* तुम तो गए। *10.* हम कहाँ गए? *11.* मेरा यह मतलब। *12.* इसका मतलब है।
● *1.* That was before. *2.* You're the first. *3.* What happened to it? *4.* Need a hand? *5.* Don't need to. *6.* You still are. *7.* Here they come. *8.* Where'd they go? *9.* You're gone. *10.* Where we headed? *11.* I meant it. *12.* That's mean.

**[72]** *1.* नहीं मतलब नहीं। *2.* मेरा मतलब आप। *3.* आपको यह मिला। *4.* आपको क्या मिला? *5.* मुझे यह मिला। *6.* क्या आपको मिला *7.* हमें क्या मिला? *8.* तुम्हें क्या मिला? *9.* मुझे कुछ मिला।
● *1.* No means no. *2.* I meant you. *3.* You got it. *4.* What have you got? *5.* I found it. *6.* Did you get it? *7.* What do we got? *8.* What'd you find? *9.* I found something.

**[73]** *1.* तुम्हें कुछ मिला? *2.* हमें कुछ मिला. *3.* मैं उससे मिला। *4.* मुझे एक मिला। *5.* यही है ना *6.* ना ही मैं। *7.* अच्छा, है ना? *8.* वह अंदर है। *9.* अच्छा, अंदर आओ।
● *1.* You got something? *2.* We got something. *3.* I met him. *4.* I found one. *5.* Isn't it? *6.* Neither will I. *7.* Well, aren't you? *8.* He's in. *9.* Well, come on in.

**[74]** *1.* हाँ, अंदर आओ। *2.* ठीक अंदर आओ। *3.* वापस अंदर जाओ। *4.* अंदर क्या है? *5.* ओह, अंदर आओ। *6.* अंदर कौन है? *7.* वे अंदर हैं। *8.* अंदर मत आओ. *9.* वापस अंदर आओ।
● *1.* Yeah, come on in. *2.* Come right in. *3.* Go back inside. *4.* What's inside? *5.* Oh, come in. *6.* Who's in? *7.* They're in. *8.* Don't come in. *9.* Come back inside.

**[75]** *1.* यह अंदर है। *2.* वहाँ अंदर जाओ। *3.* नहीं, अंदर आओ। *4.* इसे महसूस करें। *5.* उसे महसूस करें? *6.* मुझे महसूस करो? *7.* कुछ महसूस हुआ? *8.* तुम्हारे पास है। *9.* हमारे साथ आओ।
● *1.* It's in. *2.* Go in there. *3.* No, come in. *4.* Feel it. *5.* Feel that? *6.* Feel me? *7.* Feel anything? *8.* You have it. *9.* Come with us.

**[76]** *1.* हमारे पास है। *2.* इसे बंद करें! *3.* यह बंद है। *4.* इसे बंद करो! *5.* बंद कर दो। *6.* उसे बंद करो. *7.* यह बंद करो! *8.* अभी बंद करो! *9.* वे बंद हैं. *10.*

अब बंद करें! *11.* तुमसे कहा था। *12.* तुमसे यह होगा?
● *1.* We have. *2.* Turn it off! *3.* It's locked. *4.* Shut it! *5.* Shut it down. *6.* Turn that off. *7.* Come off it! *8.* Stop right now! *9.* They're closed. *10.* Stop now! *11.* Told you. *12.* Would you do it?

**[77]** *1.* आगे क्या होगा? *2.* आगे क्या हुआ? *3.* तो आगे आओ। *4.* नाम क्या है? *5.* कृपया अपना नाम? *6.* और आपका नाम? *7.* नाम क्या था? *8.* कोई नाम मिला? *9.* आपका नाम है?
● *1.* What's next? *2.* What happened next? *3.* So come on. *4.* What's the name? *5.* Your name, please? *6.* And your name is? *7.* What was the name? *8.* Got a name? *9.* Your name is?

**[78]** *1.* मुझे नाम चाहिए। *2.* मैं नहीं करूंगा। *3.* मैं क्या करूंगा? *4.* मैं ऐसा करूंगा। *5.* मैं क्यों करूंगा? *6.* फिर मैं करूंगा। *7.* मैं यह करूंगा। *8.* मैं बात करूंगा। *9.* हाँ मैं करूंगा।
● *1.* I want names. *2.* I won't. *3.* What am I gonna do? *4.* I'll do that. *5.* Why would I? *6.* Then I will. *7.* I will do it. *8.* I'll do the talking. *9.* Yes, it will.

**[79]** *1.* अब में करूंगा। *2.* नहीं, मैं करूंगा। *3.* क्या मैं करूंगा? *4.* धन्यवाद मैं करूंगा। *5.* मैं इसे करूंगा। *6.* अच्छा, मैं करूंगा। *7.* अरे, मुझे देखो। *8.* अरे, ये देखो। *9.* अरे क्या हुआ?
● *1.* Now I do. *2.* No, I will. *3.* Will I? *4.* Thank you, I will. *5.* I must be. *6.* Well, I would. *7.* Hey, look at me. *8.* Hey, look at this. *9.* Hey, what happened?

**[80]** *1.* अरे, इसे देखो! *2.* अरे, अंदर आओ। *3.* अरे, वापस आओ! *4.* अरे बाहर देखो! *5.* अरे, वह देखो! *6.* अरे, तुम देखो। *7.* अरे, अरे, चलो। *8.* मुझे याद है। *9.* मुझे याद करो?
● *1.* Hey, watch it! *2.* Hey, come on in. *3.* Hey, come back! *4.* Hey, look out! *5.* Hey, look at that! *6.* Hey, look at you. *7.* Hey, hey, come on. *8.* I remember. *9.* Remember me?

**[81]** *1.* आपको याद है? *2.* तुम्हें याद नहीं? *3.* तुम्हें याद किया। *4.* मुझे याद नहीं. *5.* याद है क्या? *6.* उसे याद है? *7.* ये याद हैं? *8.* यह याद करो। *9.* मुझे याद किया।
● *1.* You remember? *2.* You don't remember? *3.* You missed. *4.* I don't recall. *5.* Remember what? *6.* Remember her? *7.* Remember these? *8.* Remember it. *9.* Missed me.

**[82]** *1.* खैर, वह है. *2.* खैर, मैं था. *3.* खैर, यह था. *4.* खैर, मुझे देखो. *5.* खैर, वह था. *6.* यह होना चाहिए। *7.* आपको होना चाहिए। *8.* यहाँ होना

चाहिए। 9. अच्छा होना चाहिए।

• 1. Well, he is. 2. Well, I was. 3. Well, it was. 4. Well, look at me. 5. Well, he was. 6. It must be. 7. You should have. 8. There has to be. 9. Must be nice.

[83] 1. वहाँ पर होना। 2. इसे होना चाहिए? 3. यह होना था। 4. उन्हें होना चाहिए। 5. वहाँ होना चाहिए। 6. पता होना चाहिए। 7. कि मुझे दे। 8. यह वापस दे! 9. उसे दे दो।

• 1. Getting there. 2. Should it? 3. It had to be. 4. They should be. 5. There must be. 6. Should have known. 7. Give me that. 8. Give it back! 9. Hand it over.

[84] 1. मुझे जाने दो! 2. उसे जाने दो। 3. जाने का समय। 4. उन्हें जाने दो। 5. चलो जाने दो। 6. बस जाने दो। 7. तुम्हारे जाने में। 8. जाने भी दो। 9. क्षमा चाहता हूँ।

• 1. Let me go! 2. Let her go. 3. Time to go. 4. Let them go. 5. Let's go, come on. 6. Just let it go. 7. In you go. 8. Let it be. 9. Forgive me.

[85] 1. मुझे क्षमा करें। 2. हमें क्षमा करें। 3. उसे क्षमा करें। 4. अरे, क्षमा करें! 5. मैंने कोशिश की। 6. ये कोशिश करें। 7. कोशिश मत करो। 8. उसकी कोशिश करो। 9. आप कोशिश करें।

• 1. Pardon me. 2. Excuse us. 3. Forgive him. 4. Hey, excuse me! 5. I tried. 6. Try this. 7. Save your breath. 8. Try that. 9. You try.

[86] 1. और कोशिश करें। 2. आपने कोशिश की। 3. बस कोशिश करें। 4. कुछ कोशिश करो। 5. मैं कोशिश करूंगा। 6. हम कोशिश करेंगे। 7. क्या कोशिश की? 8. ऐसा होता है। 9. क्या होता है?

• 1. Try harder. 2. You tried. 3. Just try. 4. Try some. 5. I'm gonna try. 6. We'll try. 7. Try what? 8. It does. 9. What happens?

[87] 1. मुझे पता होता। 2. मेरा विश्वास है। 3. विश्वास नहीं होता। 4. मुझे विश्वास है। 5. वह बेहतर है। 6. बेहतर महसूस करना? 7. यह बेहतर है। 8. यह बेहतर होगा। 9. आपने बेहतर किया।

• 1. I would know. 2. I believe it. 3. Hard to believe. 4. I believe. 5. That's better. 6. Feel better? 7. It's better. 8. It better be. 9. You'd better.

[88] 1. आप बेहतर हो। 2. बेहतर समय रहे। 3. बहुत बेहतर, धन्यवाद. 4. वह बेहतर था. 5. यही बेहतर है। 6. वह बेहतर होगा. 7. ये बेहतर है। 8. मैं बेहतर करूंगा। 9. मैं वापस आया।

• *1.* You better be. *2.* Have a great time. *3.* Much better, thank you. *4.* That was better. *5.* This is more like it. *6.* He'd better. *7.* That is better. *8.* I'll do better. *9.* I came back.

**[89]** *1.* मुझे याद आया। *2.* मैं यहां आया। *3.* बस इतना ही। *4.* लेकिन इतना ही। *5.* तुमने इतना कहा। *6.* बिल्कुल सही किया। *7.* बिल्कुल तुम हो। *8.* मतलब क्या, बिल्कुल? *9.* बिल्कुल मैंने किया!
• *1.* I remembered. *2.* I came here. *3.* That's all. *4.* But that's it. *5.* Told you so. *6.* Nailed it. *7.* Sure, you are. *8.* Meaning what, exactly? *9.* Of course I did!

**[90]** *1.* आओ तुम लोग. *2.* सब लोग आओ। *3.* तुम लोग आओ। *4.* तुम लोग जाओ. *5.* हमने यह किया। *6.* हाँ हमने किया। *7.* हमने क्या किया? *8.* हमने नहीं किया. *9.* तो हमने किया।
• *1.* Come on, you guys. *2.* Come on, everybody. *3.* You guys, come on. *4.* You guys go. *5.* We did it. *6.* Yes, we did. *7.* What did we do? *8.* We haven't. *9.* So did we.

**[91]** *1.* हमने कैसे किया? *2.* हमने कर लिया। *3.* हमने अभी किया. *4.* हमने यहां किया? *5.* और हमने किया। *6.* लेकिन हमने किया. *7.* हमने इसे देखा. *8.* हमने अच्छा किया. *9.* रुको और देखो।
• *1.* How'd we do? *2.* We are done. *3.* We just did. *4.* We done here? *5.* And we did. *6.* But we did. *7.* We saw it. *8.* We did good. *9.* Wait and see.

**[92]** *1.* नहीं, रुको, रुको. *2.* ठीक है, रुको. *3.* ओह, रुको, रुको. *4.* नहीं, रुको मत. *5.* अरे, रुको, रुको. *6.* तुम यहीं रुको. *7.* वह यहीं है. *8.* बस यहीं रुको। *9.* यह यहीं है.
• *1.* No, wait, wait. *2.* All right, hold on. *3.* Oh, wait, wait. *4.* No, don't stop. *5.* Hey, wait, wait. *6.* You wait here. *7.* He's right here. *8.* Just stay here. *9.* It's in here.

**[93]** *1.* हम यहीं हैं. *2.* यह यहीं था. *3.* वे यहीं हैं. *4.* यहीं ये हुआ. *5.* यहीं मिल गया. *6.* आप यहीं हैं. *7.* यहीं आप हैं. *8.* वह यहीं था. *9.* उनके पास है। *10.* मैंने सचमुच किया. *11.* मैं सचमुच हूं. *12.* आपने सचमुच किया.
• *1.* We're right here. *2.* It was right here. *3.* They're right here. *4.* This is where it happened. *5.* Got it right here. *6.* You're right here. *7.* This is where you belong. *8.* He was right here. *9.* They have. *10.* I really did. *11.* I truly am. *12.* You really do.

**[94]** *1.* यह सचमुच था. *2.* अच्छी बात है. *3.* वह अच्छी है. *4.* वह अच्छी थी. *5.* नीचे मत देखो. *6.* इसे नीचे ले. *7.* वह नीचे है. *8.* यहाँ नीचे आओ. *9.* नीचे तुम जाओ.

• *1.* It really was. *2.* That's good. *3.* She's good. *4.* She was nice. *5.* Don't look down. *6.* Take it down. *7.* He's downstairs. *8.* Come on down here. *9.* Down you go.

[95] *1.* काम करते रहो। *2.* तुम यहीं रहो. *3.* नहीं, यहीं रहो. *4.* और बाहर रहो! *5.* ठीक नीचे रहो। *6.* बिल्कुल बाहर रहो. *7.* नहीं, तुम रहो. *8.* एक आदमी था। *9.* वह आदमी है.
• *1.* Keep working. *2.* You stay right here. *3.* No, stay here. *4.* And stay out! *5.* Be right down. *6.* Be right out. *7.* No, you stay. *8.* There was a man. *9.* That's the man.

[96] *1.* मुझे किस करो। *2.* मैं तैयार हूं। *3.* तैयार हो जाओ। *4.* हम तैयार हैं। *5.* तुम तैयार हो। *6.* यह तैयार है। *7.* मैं तैयार हूँ। *8.* वह तैयार है. *9.* वे तैयार हैं।
• *1.* Kiss me. *2.* I'm ready. *3.* Get ready. *4.* We're ready. *5.* You're up. *6.* It's ready. *7.* I am ready. *8.* He's ready. *9.* They're ready.

[97] *1.* आप तैयार हैं। *2.* मैं तैयार था। *3.* यह हमेशा है. *4.* हमेशा होना चाहिए। *5.* मैं हमेशा करूंगा। *6.* आपने हमेशा किया. *7.* हमेशा से है. *8.* वहाँ हमेशा है. *9.* उसे छोड़ दो।
• *1.* You're ready. *2.* I was ready. *3.* It always is. *4.* Always have. *5.* I always will. *6.* You always did. *7.* Always has. *8.* There always is. *9.* Leave him.

[98] *1.* मुझे छोड़ दो! *2.* जाना छोड़ दिया! *3.* बस इसे छोड़। *4.* उसने छोड़ दिया. *5.* उन्हें छोड़ दो। *6.* यहां छोड़ दो। *7.* बस इसकी कोशिश। *8.* इसकी कोशिश करें। *9.* हम दोस्त हैं।
• *1.* Leave me! *2.* Go left! *3.* Just drop it. *4.* She quit. *5.* Leave them. *6.* Leave it here. *7.* Just try it. *8.* Give it a go. *9.* We're friends.

[99] *1.* हम दोस्त थे। *2.* धन्यवाद मेरे दोस्त। *3.* यहाँ आओ, दोस्त. *4.* वे दोस्त हैं। *5.* चलो दोस्त, चलो. *6.* मेरे दोस्त हैं। *7.* यह माँ है. *8.* आपको धन्यवाद माँ। *9.* वह चला गया।
• *1.* We were friends. *2.* Thank you, my friend. *3.* Come here, buddy. *4.* They're friends. *5.* Let's go, buddy. *6.* I have friends. *7.* It's Mom. *8.* Thank you, Mom. *9.* It's gone.

[100] *1.* क्या चला गया? *2.* कौन चला गया? *3.* इसमें क्या है? *4.* उसे ले लो? *5.* यह ले लो। *6.* लो वह चला। *7.* लो मैं चला। *8.* इसे ले लो! *9.* जाओ, ले लो. *10.* उन्हें ले लो! *11.* खैर, यह लो। *12.* मुझसे यह लो।
• *1.* What's gone? *2.* Who's gone? *3.* What's in it? *4.* Get it? *5.* Here, take this. *6.* There he goes. *7.* Here I go. *8.* Grab it!

*9.* Go on, take it. *10.* Get 'em! *11.* Well, there you have it. *12.* Take it from me.

**[101]** *1.* कुछ और लो। *2.* उसे वापस लो। *3.* चलो, ले लो. *4.* फिर ले लो. *5.* आप कहां हैं? *6.* आप कहां थे? *7.* वे कहां हैं? *8.* वह कहां गया? *9.* वह कहां है? *10.* वह कहां गई? *11.* यह कहां गया? *12.* वह कहां था?
● *1.* Have some more. *2.* Take that back. *3.* Come on, take it. *4.* Then take it. *5.* Where are you? *6.* Where have you been? *7.* Where are they? *8.* Where'd he go? *9.* Where's that? *10.* Where'd she go? *11.* Where'd it go? *12.* Where was he?

**[102]** *1.* यह कहां है? *2.* ये कहां था? *3.* यह कहां हुआ? *4.* उनकी मदद करो। *5.* उन्हें दूर करें। *6.* अब दूर जाओ। *7.* इस पर विचारो। *8.* क्या विचार है? *9.* यही विचार था।
● *1.* Where is this? *2.* Where was this? *3.* Where did it happen? *4.* Help them. *5.* Take them off. *6.* Now go away. *7.* Think it over. *8.* What's the idea? *9.* That was the idea.

**[103]** *1.* न ही मैं। *2.* ऐसा न करें! *3.* क्या न है? *4.* शायद मैं हूँ। *5.* शायद यह है। *6.* शायद मैंने किया। *7.* शायद वह है। *8.* शायद वहाँ है। *9.* शायद यह था। *10.* शायद उसने किया। *11.* वह करती है। *12.* वह नहीं करती।
● *1.* Neither do I. *2.* Do not! *3.* Is that a no? *4.* Maybe I am. *5.* Maybe it is. *6.* Maybe I did. *7.* Maybe he is. *8.* Maybe there is. *9.* Maybe it was. *10.* Maybe he did. *11.* She does. *12.* She doesn't.

**[104]** *1.* आप अच्छे हो। *2.* वे अच्छे थे। *3.* आप अच्छे हैं। *4.* वे अच्छे है। *5.* अच्छे से कहा। *6.* ये अच्छे हैं. *7.* ख़ैर, मैंने किया। *8.* मेरे साथ आइए। *9.* कृपया, अंदर आइए।
● *1.* You're good. *2.* We're good. *3.* You are good. *4.* They're nice. *5.* Well put. *6.* These are good. *7.* Well, I did. *8.* Come with me. *9.* Please, come on in.

**[105]** *1.* मैं समझ गया। *2.* समझ आ गया। *3.* आप समझ गए? *4.* आपको समझ आया? *5.* अब समझ आया। *6.* आया समझ में? *7.* वह कैसा है? *8.* यह कैसा था? *9.* यह कैसा है? *10.* वह कैसा था? *11.* आपको कैसा लगा? *12.* मैं कैसा था?
● *1.* I got it. *2.* I've got it. *3.* You understand that? *4.* Do you get it? *5.* Now I get it. *6.* Did you understand? *7.* How is he? *8.* How was it? *9.* What's it like? *10.* What was that like? *11.* How did you find it? *12.* How was I?

**[106]** *1.* यह सच है। *2.* ये सच है। *3.* क्या सच में? *4.* वह सच है। *5.* सच

कहा आपने। 6. सच तो है। 7. आपने मुझे सुना। 8. सुना है कि? 9. आपने उसे सुना. 10. हाँ, मैंने सुना। 11. तुमने उसे सुना। 12. मैंने यह सुना।

• 1. It's true. 2. It is true. 3. Did you really? 4. That is the truth. 5. Yes, you are right. 6. It is the truth. 7. You heard me. 8. Hear that? 9. You heard him. 10. Yeah, I heard. 11. You heard her. 12. I heard it.

[107] 1. तुमने क्या सुना? 2. मैंने कुछ सुना। 3. हाँ मैं सुना। 4. तो मैंने सुना. 5. तुमने नहीं सुना? 6. तुमने सुना नहीं? 7. मैंने इसे सुना। 8. मैंने उसे सुना. 9. मैंने सुना है।

• 1. What did you hear? 2. I heard something. 3. Yes, I heard. 4. So I heard. 5. You haven't heard? 6. You didn't hear? 7. I hear it. 8. I heard him. 9. I've heard.

[108] 1. आपने सही सुना. 2. तुमने कुछ सुना? 3. मैंने नहीं सुना. 4. मैंने सुना था। 5. मैंने उन्हें सुना. 6. अरे, तुमने सुना? 7. आपने उन्हें सुना. 8. मुझे सच बताओ। 9. मुझे क्या बताओ?

• 1. You heard right. 2. You hear something? 3. I didn't hear. 4. I was listening. 5. I heard them. 6. Hey, you hear that? 7. You heard them. 8. Tell me the truth. 9. Tell me what?

[109] 1. बस मुझे बताओ। 2. और कुछ बताओ। 3. तो मुझे बताओ। 4. मुझे बताओ क्यों। 5. मुझे फिर बताओ। 6. कृपया मुझे बताओ। 7. उसे बताओ क्या? 8. मुझे अभी बताओ। 9. नहीं मुझे बताओ।

• 1. Just tell me. 2. Tell me something. 3. So tell me. 4. Tell me why. 5. Tell me again. 6. Please tell me. 7. Tell him what? 8. Tell me now. 9. No, tell me.

[110] 1. उन्हें बताओ क्या? 2. उसे सच बताओ. 3. उसे बताओ कि। 4. उसे मत बताओ. 5. मुझे बताओ कि। 6. आप उसे बताओ। 7. अच्छा, तुम बताओ. 8. हमें बताओ क्या? 9. मुझे मत बताओ!

• 1. Tell them what? 2. Tell her the truth. 3. Tell him that. 4. Don't tell him. 5. Tell me that. 6. You tell her. 7. Well, you tell me. 8. Tell us what? 9. Don't tell me!

[111] 1. मुझे बताओ कैसे। 2. उन्हें सच बताओ. 3. चलो, मुझे बताओ. 4. अब मुझे बताओ। 5. मुझे बताओ कहाँ। 6. बस उसे बताओ। 7. फिर भी बताओ. 8. बस हमें बताओ. 9. कह नहीं सकता।

• 1. Tell me how. 2. Tell them the truth. 3. Go on, tell me. 4. Now tell me. 5. Tell me where. 6. Just tell him. 7. Tell me anyway. 8. Just tell us. 9. Can't say.

[112] 1. यह जल्दी था। 2. उसे जल्दी करो। 3. अभी जल्दी है। 4. बेहतर जल्दी

करो। 5. बस जल्दी करो. 6. कृपया जल्दी करो। 7. इसे जल्दी करो। 8. चलो, जल्दी से. 9. मैं जल्दी हूं।
- *1.* That was quick. *2.* Hurry it up. *3.* It's early. *4.* Better hurry. *5.* Just hurry. *6.* Hurry, please. *7.* Do it quickly. *8.* Come on, quickly. *9.* I'm early.

[113] *1.* वह जल्दी है. *2.* यहाँ आओ, जल्दी! *3.* मैं जल्दी करूंगा. *4.* वह वही है। *5.* यह वही है। *6.* हाँ, वही है. *7.* वही मैंने किया। *8.* वह वही था. *9.* आप वही हैं.
- *1.* He's early. *2.* Come here, quick! *3.* I'll hurry. *4.* That's him. *5.* It's him. *6.* Yeah, that's the one. *7.* That's what I did. *8.* That was him. *9.* That's who you are.

[114] *1.* वही मुझे मिला. *2.* मैंने वही देखा. *3.* आज क्या है? *4.* आज क्या हुआ? *5.* आज यह है। *6.* भगवान को धन्यवाद। *7.* भगवान का धन्यवाद। *8.* बच्चे कहां हैं? *9.* बच्चे कैसे हैं?
- *1.* That's what I got. *2.* That's what I saw. *3.* What's today? *4.* What happened today? *5.* It's today. *6.* Thank you, God. *7.* Thanks be to God. *8.* Where are the kids? *9.* How are the kids?

[115] *1.* क्या हुआ बच्चे? *2.* तुम्हारे बच्चे हैं? *3.* आपके बच्चे हैं? *4.* तुम बच्चे हो. *5.* आपके बच्चे है? *6.* वे बच्चे हैं. *7.* मेरे बच्चे हैं। *8.* यहाँ आओ, बच्चे. *9.* यहाँ जाता है।
- *1.* What's up, baby? *2.* You got kids? *3.* You have kids? *4.* You're a child. *5.* You have children? *6.* They're children. *7.* I have kids. *8.* Come here, kid. *9.* Here goes.

[116] *1.* कोई नहीं जाता. *2.* वह दिन होगा। *3.* मेरी बात सुनो। *4.* आप मुझे सुनो? *5.* इस बात सुनो। *6.* सुनो, यहां आओ। *7.* ठीक है, सुनो. *8.* अब मुझे सुनो। *9.* सुनो, सब लोग।
- *1.* Nobody leaves. *2.* That'll be the day. *3.* Listen to me. *4.* You hear me? *5.* Listen to this. *6.* Hey, come here. *7.* Okay, listen. *8.* Listen to me now. *9.* Listen up, everybody.

[117] *1.* अब यह सुनो! *2.* क्या सभी तैयार? *3.* यह जगह है। *4.* ध्यान से सुनो। *5.* मैंने ध्यान दिया. *6.* ओह, चलो, यार। *7.* अरे, चलो यार. *8.* क्या हुआ यार? *9.* कैसे हो यार?
- *1.* Now hear this! *2.* Is everything ready? *3.* This is the place. *4.* Listen carefully. *5.* I noticed. *6.* Oh, come on, man. *7.* Hey, come on, man. *8.* What happened, man? *9.* How are you, dear?

[118] *1.* तुमने सुना यार! *2.* मुझे देखो, यार. *3.* उसने मुझे बताया। *4.* आपने

उसे बताया? 5. तुम्हें क्या बताया? 6. आपने उन्हें बताया? 7. उन्होंने मुझे बताया। 8. कार कहाँ है? 9. कार ले आओ.

- *1.* You heard the man! *2.* Look at me, man. *3.* He told me. *4.* You told her? *5.* Told you what? *6.* You told them? *7.* They told me. *8.* Where's the car? *9.* Get the car.

**[119]** *1.* कार में रुको. *2.* चिंता मत करो। *3.* चिंता न करें। *4.* उस ओर देखो। *5.* यह तुम्हारा है। *6.* वह तुम्हारा है. *7.* मैं तुम्हारा हूँ *8.* तुम्हारा मतलब है? *9.* मैं तुम्हारा हूं।

- *1.* Wait in the car. *2.* Don't worry. *3.* Do not worry. *4.* Look at that. *5.* It's yours. *6.* He's yours. *7.* I'm yours. *8.* You mean? *9.* I am yours.

**[120]** *1.* यह तुम्हारा था. *2.* पिता कौन है? *3.* मैं पिता हूं. *4.* आपने क्या सोचा? *5.* वह कब था? *6.* ये कब था? *7.* वह कब हुआ? *8.* यह कब है? *9.* यह कब था? *10.* वह कब होगा? *11.* वह कब गया? *12.* वह कब है?

- *1.* It was yours. *2.* Who's the father? *3.* I'm the father. *4.* What'd you think? *5.* When was that? *6.* When was this? *7.* When did that happen? *8.* When is it? *9.* When was it? *10.* When will that be? *11.* When did he leave? *12.* When is that?

**[121]** *1.* वह ऊपर है. *2.* यह ऊपर है. *3.* यहाँ ऊपर आओ. *4.* ऊपर तुम जाओ. *5.* वे ऊपर हैं. *6.* वह तुम्हारी है. *7.* तुम्हारी कैसे थी? *8.* शुरू मत करो. *9.* चलो शुरू करें।

- *1.* He's upstairs. *2.* It's upstairs. *3.* Come on up here. *4.* Up you get. *5.* They're upstairs. *6.* She's yours. *7.* How was yours? *8.* Don't start. *9.* Let's begin.

**[122]** *1.* चलो शुरू करो। *2.* मैं शुरू करूंगा। *3.* शुरू हो जाओ। *4.* हम शुरू करें? *5.* जैसा आपको पसंद। *6.* जैसा मैं हूं. *7.* जैसा मैंने कहा। *8.* जैसा भी हो। *9.* जैसा आपने कहा.

- *1.* Let's start. *2.* I'll start. *3.* Get started. *4.* Shall we start? *5.* As you like. *6.* As am I. *7.* Like I said. *8.* Whatever it is. *9.* Just like you said.

**[123]** *1.* जैसा मैंने किया. *2.* जैसा होना चाहिए। *3.* जैसा लगता है। *4.* मुझे कॉल करो। *5.* मैंने कॉल किया। *6.* मैं कॉल करूंगा. *7.* से अधिक थे। *8.* अधिक चाहते हैं? *9.* बहुत अधिक है।

- *1.* As did I. *2.* As it should be. *3.* Seems to be. *4.* Call me. *5.* I called. *6.* I'll make the call. *7.* We're over. *8.* Want more? *9.* Are too.

**[124]** *1.* आपको खेद है? *2.* उसे खेद है. *3.* नहीं, धन्यवाद सर. *4.* ओह,

धन्यवाद सर. 5. मैंने किया, सर. 6. अच्छा, धन्यवाद सर। 7. मैं करूंगा, सर. 8. तुम पागल हो। 9. यह पागल है।
• 1. You're sorry? 2. He's sorry. 3. No, thank you, sir. 4. Oh, thank you, sir. 5. I did, sir. 6. Well, thank you, sir. 7. I will, sir. 8. You're crazy. 9. This is crazy.

[125] 1. वह पागल है। 2. आप पागल हैं। 3. वे पागल हैं. 4. पागल हो जाना। 5. ये पागल है। 6. योजना क्या है? 7. वह योजना है। 8. यहाँ योजना है. 9. यही योजना थी.
• 1. That's crazy. 2. You're insane. 3. They're crazy. 4. Go nuts. 5. That's nuts. 6. What's the plan? 7. That's the plan. 8. Here's the plan. 9. That was the plan.

[126] 1. ये है योजना 2. क्या थी योजना? 3. यह कल है। 4. वह सुंदर है। 5. वे सुंदर हैं। 6. यह सुंदर है। 7. आप सुंदर हो। 8. यह सुंदर था। 9. तुम सुंदर हो। 10. यह सुंदर होगा। 11. आप बहुत सुंदर। 12. सुंदर, है ना?
• 1. This is the plan. 2. What was the plan? 3. It's tomorrow. 4. She's beautiful. 5. They're beautiful. 6. It's pretty. 7. You're cute. 8. That was beautiful. 9. You are beautiful. 10. That would be lovely. 11. You're so handsome. 12. Beautiful, isn't she?

[127] 1. अपना बुरा करें। 2. मुझे बुरा लगा। 3. बस काफ़ी है। 4. मैंने काफी कहा! 5. मुझे यकीन है। 6. आपको यकीन है? 7. मैं सिर्फ सुना। 8. आराम से लो। 9. बस आराम करो।
• 1. Do your worst. 2. I felt bad. 3. That's enough. 4. I said enough! 5. I'm sure. 6. You are sure? 7. I just heard. 8. Take it easy. 9. Just relax.

[128] 1. ओह, आराम करो. 2. अरे, आराम करो. 3. तुम्हें आराम चाहिए। 4. अब आराम करो. 5. आराम करो, बच्चे. 6. वह ऐसा करेगा। 7. यह काम करेगा. 8. वह काम करेगा. 9. कौन नहीं करेगा?
• 1. Oh, relax. 2. Hey, relax. 3. You need rest. 4. Take it easy, now. 5. Relax, kid. 6. That'll do. 7. It'll work. 8. That'll work. 9. Who wouldn't?

[129] 1. वह यह करेगा. 2. ऐसा कौन करेगा? 3. वह क्यों करेगा? 4. हाँ, वह करेगा. 5. लेकिन वह करेगा. 6. ओह, वह करेगा. 7. उनका उपयोग करें. 8. मुझे उपयोग करें। 9. निश्चित तुम हो।
• 1. That'll do it. 2. Who would do that? 3. Why would he? 4. Yes, he would. 5. But he will. 6. Oh, he will. 7. Use them. 8. Use me. 9. Of course you are.

**[130]** *1.* यह निश्चित है। *2.* यह निश्चित ही। *3.* आप निश्चित हैं? *4.* एक कारण है. *5.* मुझे करना पड़ा. *6.* हमें करना पड़ा. *7.* शांत हो जाओ। *8.* यह शांत है। *9.* मैं शांत हूं।
● *1.* It sure is. *2.* It certainly is. *3.* You're certain? *4.* There's a reason. *5.* I had to. *6.* We had to. *7.* Just calm down. *8.* It's quiet. *9.* I am calm.

**[131]** *1.* बस शांत रहो. *2.* मैं शांत हूँ। *3.* हम शांत हैं? *4.* वह शांत है। *5.* आप शांत हैं. *6.* शांत हो जाना. *7.* तो शांत रहो। *8.* देखना है कि? *9.* देखना चाहते हैं?
● *1.* Just stay calm. *2.* I'm calm. *3.* We cool? *4.* That is cool. *5.* You're quiet. *6.* Simmer down. *7.* So relax. *8.* See that? *9.* Want to see?

**[132]** *1.* देखना चाहता हूँ? *2.* समस्या क्या है? *3.* समस्या यहीं है. *4.* समस्या क्या थी? *5.* इसे नीचे रखें। *6.* उसे नीचे रखें। *7.* अपना ध्यान रखें। *8.* इसे वापस रखें। *9.* उसे दूर रखें।
● *1.* Wanna see? *2.* What's the problem? *3.* Here's the problem. *4.* What was the problem? *5.* Put it down. *6.* Put that down. *7.* You take care. *8.* Put it back. *9.* Put that away.

**[133]** *1.* उन्हें नीचे रखें। *2.* इसे वहां रखें। *3.* इसे बाहर रखें! *4.* मुझसे दूर रखें। *5.* उन्हें बंद रखें. *6.* यह हमारा है। *7.* हमारा हो गया? *8.* वह हमारा है. *9.* हमारा क्या होगा?
● *1.* Put them down. *2.* Put it there. *3.* Put it out! *4.* Keep away from me. *5.* Keep them closed. *6.* It's ours. *7.* We done? *8.* He's ours. *9.* What will happen to us?

**[134]** *1.* हमने इसे बनाया। *2.* मैंने इसे बनाया। *3.* यह तुमने बनाया? *4.* उसने वह बनाया। *5.* मैं तुम्हें बनाया। *6.* इसे आपने बनाया? *7.* मैंने उन्हें बनाया। *8.* यही जीवन है। *9.* जीवन अच्छा रहे।
● *1.* We made it. *2.* I made it up. *3.* You made this? *4.* He made it. *5.* I made you. *6.* Did you make it? *7.* I made them. *8.* That's life. *9.* Have a nice life.

**[135]** *1.* जीवन अच्छा है। *2.* यह जीवन है। *3.* इस जीवन है। *4.* मेरे पीछे आओ। *5.* आपने पीछे देखो। *6.* वह पीछे है. *7.* उसके पीछे जाओ. *8.* फिर से कहना। *9.* कुछ कहना है?
● *1.* Life is good. *2.* It's life. *3.* This is life. *4.* Follow me. *5.* Look behind you. *6.* He's in the back. *7.* Go after him. *8.* Say it again. *9.* Anything to say?

**[136]** *1.* आप मुझे दें। *2.* इसे यहां दें. *3.* इसे उसे दें। *4.* मुझे यह दें। *5.* इसे

छोड़ दें! 6. कृपया ध्यान दें। 7. इसे समय दें। 8. मुझे कुछ दें। 9. वहाँ छोड़ दें।
• 1. You owe me. 2. Give it here. 3. Give it to him. 4. Give me this. 5. Quit it! 6. Attention, please. 7. Give it time. 8. Give me some. 9. Leave it there.

[137] 1. अब छोड़ दें! 2. इसे होने दें। 3. आपको कितना चाहिए? 4. वह कितना है? 5. आपको कितना मिला? 6. कितना अच्छा हुआ। 7. यह कितना था? 8. वहाँ कितना है? 9. यह कितना है?
• 1. Leave now! 2. Let go of it. 3. How much do you need? 4. How much is that? 5. How much you got? 6. This is so good. 7. How much was it? 8. How much is there? 9. How much is this one?

[138] 1. सब चले गए। 2. चले जाओ बस। 3. कृपया आगे चले। 4. कृपया चले जाओ। 5. आप चले गए। 6. वह चले गए। 7. यह कठिन है। 8. वह कठिन है। 9. समय कठिन है। 10. आप परेशान हैं। 11. वह परेशान है। 12. कोई परेशान नहीं।
• 1. All gone. 2. Just go away. 3. Go ahead, please. 4. Go away, please. 5. You left. 6. He moved. 7. That's tough. 8. That's rough. 9. Times are tough. 10. You're upset. 11. She's upset. 12. No bother.

[139] 1. मैं परेशान हूँ। 2. वह परेशान थी। 3. अरे परेशान हो। 4. मिल कर रहना। 5. मुझे रहना होगा। 6. तुम्हें रहना होगा। 7. यह झूठ है। 8. वह झूठ था। 9. यह झूठ था।
• 1. I'm upset. 2. She was upset. 3. Oh, bother. 4. Get on. 5. I have to be. 6. You have to stay. 7. That's a lie. 8. That was a lie. 9. It was a lie.

[140] 1. उसने गलती की. 2. आप डॉक्टर हैं. 3. मैं डॉक्टर हूं. 4. डॉक्टर कहाँ है? 5. डॉक्टर कहां है? 6. अजीब बात है. 7. यह अजीब है। 8. ये अजीब है. 9. आप अजीब हो।
• 1. She made a mistake. 2. You're a doctor. 3. I'm the Doctor. 4. Where's the doctor? 5. Where is the doctor? 6. That's funny. 7. It's funny. 8. This is weird. 9. You're weird.

[141] 1. अजीब है ना? 2. वह अजीब है। 3. वह अजीब था। 4. मैं खुश हूं। 5. खुश हो जाओ। 6. मैं खुश हूँ। 7. मैं खुश था। 8. वह खुश है। 9. तुम खुश हो। 10. वह खुश था। 11. वहां कौन जाएगा? 12. वह समझ जाएगा।
• 1. Strange, isn't it? 2. That is weird. 3. That was awkward. 4. I'm happy. 5. Cheer up. 6. I am happy. 7. I was happy. 8. He's happy. 9. You're happy. 10. He was happy. 11. Who goes there? 12. He'll understand.

**[142]** *1.* इससे हो जाएगा। *2.* इससे चल जाएगा। *3.* क्या हो जाएगा? *4.* वह हो जाएगा। *5.* यह हो जाएगा। *6.* यह किया जाएगा। *7.* वह वहीं है. *8.* बस वहीं रहो. *9.* तुम वहीं रहो।

● *1.* That will do. *2.* This will do. *3.* What will happen? *4.* He will be. *5.* It will be done. *6.* It shall be done. *7.* He's right there. *8.* Just stay there. *9.* You stay right there.

**[143]** *1.* वह वहीं था. *2.* मैं वहीं था. *3.* यह वहीं था. *4.* वे वहीं हैं. *5.* यह पानी है। *6.* यहाँ इंतजार करें। *7.* मेरा इंतजार करना! *8.* अभी इंतजार करो। *9.* खैर इंतजार करो।

● *1.* He was right there. *2.* I was right there. *3.* It was right there. *4.* They're right there. *5.* It's water. *6.* Wait here. *7.* Wait for me! *8.* Just hold on. *9.* We'll wait.

**[144]** *1.* हम इंतजार करेंगे. *2.* मैंने इंतजार किया। *3.* मैं इंतजार करूंगा। *4.* कोई इंतजार नहीं। *5.* ठीक इंतजार करो। *6.* हम दोनों हैं। *7.* हम दोनों थे. *8.* वे दोनों हैं. *9.* यह पुलिस है।

● *1.* We'll be waiting. *2.* I waited. *3.* I will wait. *4.* No, hang on. *5.* OK, wait. *6.* We both are. *7.* We both were. *8.* They both are. *9.* It's the police.

**[145]** *1.* ये पुलिस है। *2.* पुलिस यहाँ हैं. *3.* हम पुलिस हैं. *4.* मैं भूल गया। *5.* भूल जाओ कि। *6.* उसे भूल जाओ। *7.* आप भूल गए? *8.* भूल गए कुछ? *9.* जब यह हुआ? *10.* मुझे बताओ जब। *11.* यह अलग है। *12.* वह अलग था।

● *1.* This is the police. *2.* The police are here. *3.* We're the police. *4.* I forgot. *5.* Forget that. *6.* Forget him. *7.* You forgot? *8.* Forget something? *9.* When did it happen? *10.* Tell me when. *11.* That's different. *12.* That was different.

**[146]** *1.* तुम अलग हो। *2.* वह अलग है. *3.* मैं अलग हूँ। *4.* यह अलग था. *5.* वे अलग हैं. *6.* ये अलग था. *7.* क्या स्पष्ट है? *8.* हम स्पष्ट हैं. *9.* यह स्पष्ट है। *10.* आप स्पष्ट हैं. *11.* मैं स्पष्ट हूं। *12.* कृपया शांत रहें।

● *1.* You're different. *2.* He's different. *3.* I'm different. *4.* It was different. *5.* They're different. *6.* This was different. *7.* Is that clear? *8.* We're clear. *9.* It's clear. *10.* You're clear. *11.* I'm clear. *12.* Please be quiet.

**[147]** *1.* आप शांत रहें? *2.* आप अच्छे रहें। *3.* वो कौन है? *4.* वो रहा वो। *5.* वो यहां है। *6.* वो ठीक है? *7.* ये रही वो। *8.* यह वो था। *9.* वो सुंदर है। *10.* वो सही थी। *11.* वो क्या है? *12.* ये वो हैं।

● *1.* You cool? *2.* You be good. *3.* Who's that? *4.* There he is. *5.* He's here. *6.* Is he okay? *7.* Here she is. *8.* It was him. *9.* That's lovely. *10.* She was right. *11.* What is he? *12.* That's them.

**[148]** *1.* खैर, वो देखो। *2.* यह वो है। *3.* आपने देखा वो? *4.* वो वहां है। *5.* वो मेरे हैं। *6.* वो दिन थे। *7.* और वो मैं। *8.* हम वो करेंगे. *9.* वो में करूंगा। *10.* मुझे फोन आया। *11.* वह फोन करेगा। *12.* यह महत्वपूर्ण है।

• *1.* Well, look at that. *2.* This is him. *3.* You saw that? *4.* She's over there. *5.* Those are mine. *6.* Those were the days. *7.* And that's me. *8.* We'll do that. *9.* That I do. *10.* I got a call. *11.* He'll call. *12.* It's important.

**[149]** *1.* वह महत्वपूर्ण है। *2.* यही महत्वपूर्ण है. *3.* इसे कम करें। *4.* यह पिताजी हैं. *5.* आशा करते है। *6.* मैं गलत था। *7.* वह गलत है. *8.* आपने गलत सोचा। *9.* वे गलत थे।

• *1.* That's important. *2.* That's what's important. *3.* Turn it down. *4.* It's Dad. *5.* Let's hope so. *6.* I was mistaken. *7.* She's wrong. *8.* You thought wrong. *9.* They were wrong.

**[150]** *1.* यह गलत है! *2.* क्योंकि मैं हूँ। *3.* क्योंकि मैं नहीं। *4.* क्योंकि मैंने किया. *5.* क्योंकि तुम हो। *6.* आओ, प्रयास करें. *7.* यहाँ आओ, प्रिये। *8.* प्रिये, यहाँ आओ। *9.* क्षमा करें, प्रिये।

• *1.* It's wrong! *2.* Because I am. *3.* Because I'm not. *4.* Because I did. *5.* Because you are. *6.* Come on, try. *7.* Come here, sweetie. *8.* Come here, honey. *9.* Excuse me, honey.

**[151]** *1.* ओह, चलो प्रिये। *2.* घर छोड़ देना! *3.* ये बात सुन। *4.* आप कब आये? *5.* मुझे आने दो। *6.* उन्हें आने दो। *7.* उसे आने दो. *8.* कहीं मत जाओ. *9.* मैं भी शामिल।

• *1.* Oh, come on, honey. *2.* Move out! *3.* Listen to it. *4.* When did you get in? *5.* Let me through. *6.* Let them come. *7.* Let him come. *8.* Don't go anywhere. *9.* I'm in.


## Difficulty Level: 3

**[1]** *1.* नहीं, यह नहीं है। *2.* नहीं आप नहीं हैं। *3.* क्या यह आप है? *4.* नहीं, वह नहीं है। *5.* यह एक नहीं है. *6.* नहीं, मैं नहीं था. *7.* क्या यह वह था? *8.* क्या यह आप हो? *9.* क्या यह मैं हूं?

• *1.* No, it is not. *2.* No, you're not. *3.* Is it you? *4.* No, he's not. *5.* That's a no. *6.* No, I wasn't. *7.* Was it him? *8.* Is this you? *9.* Is it me?

**[2]** *1.* क्या वह तुम हो? *2.* क्या हो रहा है? *3.* मैं कर रहा हूं! *4.* वह यह है कि। *5.* हम कर रहे हैं? *6.* यह तुम पर है। *7.* यह हो गया है। *8.* कुछ हो रहा है. *9.* मैं कुछ नहीं हूँ।

• *1.* Is that you? *2.* What's happening? *3.* I'm on it! *4.* That's that. *5.* Are we done? *6.* It's on you. *7.* It has to be. *8.* Something's happening. *9.* I'm nothing.

**[3]** *1.* उसने क्या किया है? *2.* यह वह नहीं थी. *3.* नहीं, मैंने नहीं किया. *4.* और यह था कि? *5.* और वह क्या है? *6.* क्या कुछ और है? *7.* और तुम क्या हो? *8.* और तुम नहीं हो? *9.* तुम कुछ और हो.
• *1.* What's he done? *2.* It wasn't her. *3.* No, I didn't. *4.* And what's that? *5.* And what is that? *6.* Is there anything else? *7.* And what are you? *8.* And you're not? *9.* You're something else.

**[4]** *1.* और कुछ नहीं है. *2.* और मैं क्या हूँ? *3.* और वह तुम हो. *4.* वह कुछ और है. *5.* क्या आप ठीक हैं? *6.* नहीं, मैं ठीक हूँ। *7.* नहीं, यह ठीक है. *8.* नहीं वह ठीक है। *9.* वह ठीक से गया।
• *1.* There's nothing else. *2.* And what am I? *3.* And that's you. *4.* That's something else. *5.* Are you OK? *6.* No, I'm fine. *7.* No, that's okay. *8.* No, that's fine. *9.* That went well.

**[5]** *1.* तुम ठीक नहीं हो. *2.* वह ठीक नहीं है. *3.* और यह ठीक है. *4.* मैं ठीक नहीं हूँ। *5.* नहीं, तुम ठीक हो. *6.* नहीं, ऐसा नहीं है. *7.* क्या उसने ऐसा किया? *8.* क्या मैंने ऐसा किया? *9.* मैं कर सकता हूँ।
• *1.* You're not fine. *2.* She's not well. *3.* And that's okay. *4.* I'm not okay. *5.* No, you're fine. *6.* No, it isn't. *7.* Did he do it? *8.* Did I do it? *9.* I can.

**[6]** *1.* ऐसा नहीं हो सकता. *2.* यह नहीं हो सकता! *3.* यह हो सकता था। *4.* यह हो सकता है। *5.* वह हो सकता है। *6.* क्या हो सकता है? *7.* ऐसा हो सकता है। *8.* कुछ भी नहीं है। *9.* और हम भी हैं.
• *1.* This can't be happening. *2.* It can't be! *3.* It could be. *4.* It might. *5.* He might. *6.* What could it be? *7.* That may be. *8.* There's nothing. *9.* And so are we.

**[7]** *1.* क्या और भी हैं? *2.* तो यह क्या है? *3.* क्या बात क्या बात? *4.* तो यह बात है? *5.* यह एक बात है. *6.* कुछ तो बात है। *7.* बात नहीं कर रहे! *8.* एक और बात है. *9.* एक बात और है।
• *1.* Are there more? *2.* So what is it? *3.* What's the matter? *4.* So that's it? *5.* It's a thing. *6.* There is something. *7.* No talking! *8.* There's one other thing. *9.* There is one more thing.

**[8]** *1.* वह बात नहीं थी. *2.* क्या वह कोई हैं? *3.* कोई नहीं कर सकता। *4.* कोई और नहीं है. *5.* क्या वे नहीं हैं? *6.* आप नहीं कर सकते. *7.* यह मेरे लिए है. *8.* वे मेरे नहीं हैं. *9.* यह मेरे पास है।

• *1.* That wasn't it. *2.* Is anyone there? *3.* No can do. *4.* There's no one else. *5.* Aren't they? *6.* You can't. *7.* It is to me. *8.* They're not mine. *9.* I have it.

**[9]** *1.* क्या तुम्हें कुछ चाहिए? *2.* आप को यह चाहिए? *3.* मुझे यह चाहिए था। *4.* यह बहुत अच्छा है। *5.* नहीं, मैं अच्छा हूं। *6.* अच्छा कर रहे हो। *7.* क्या वह अच्छा था? *8.* आपको कुछ नहीं होगा। *9.* और वह क्या होगा?
• *1.* You want anything? *2.* You want this? *3.* I needed it. *4.* That's great. *5.* No, I'm good. *6.* Doing good. *7.* Was that good? *8.* You're gonna be fine. *9.* And what would that be?

**[10]** *1.* यह बहुत अच्छा होगा. *2.* मेरे पास एक होगा. *3.* आप के लिए होगा। *4.* वह बहुत अच्छा होगा. *5.* अब तुम्हें क्या चाहिए? *6.* अब बहुत हो गया. *7.* मैं अब ठीक हूं। *8.* अब और बात नहीं. *9.* अब तुम मेरे हो।
• *1.* This is gonna be great. *2.* I'll have one. *3.* You'll have to. *4.* That would be very nice. *5.* What do you want now? *6.* That's enough now. *7.* I'm fine now. *8.* No more talking. *9.* You're mine now.

**[11]** *1.* मैं अब और नहीं. *2.* क्या वह आप थे? *3.* बात कर रहे थे. *4.* हम कर सकते थे? *5.* नहीं, वे नहीं थे. *6.* मुझे क्या करना चाहिए? *7.* तुम्हें यह करना होगा। *8.* आपको कुछ करना होगा. *9.* तुम्हें कुछ करना होगा.
• *1.* I don't anymore. *2.* Was it you? *3.* We're talking. *4.* Could we? *5.* No, they weren't. *6.* What should I do? *7.* You have to do it. *8.* You have to do something. *9.* You gotta do something.

**[12]** *1.* वह मेरे साथ है. *2.* हम एक साथ हैं। *3.* हम एक साथ रहे. *4.* अब हम साथ हैं. *5.* यह करने के लिए। *6.* क्या वह यहाँ है? *7.* मैं अब यहाँ हूँ। *8.* वे यहाँ नहीं हैं. *9.* और हम यहाँ हैं.
• *1.* He's with me. *2.* We belong together. *3.* We stick together. *4.* We're together now. *5.* Get to it. *6.* Is he here? *7.* I'm here now. *8.* They're not here. *9.* And here we are.

**[13]** *1.* यहाँ कुछ भी नहीं। *2.* तो हम यहाँ हैं। *3.* और आप यहाँ हैं. *4.* अब आप यहाँ हैं. *5.* अच्छा, आप यहाँ हैं. *6.* आप यहाँ नहीं थे. *7.* हम अब यहाँ हैं. *8.* तो मैं यहाँ हूँ. *9.* हम यहाँ पर हैं!
• *1.* Here goes nothing. *2.* So here we are. *3.* And here you are. *4.* You're here now. *5.* Good, you're here. *6.* You weren't here. *7.* We're here now. *8.* So, here I am. *9.* We're over here!

**[14]** *1.* तो आप यहाँ हैं. *2.* और मैं यहाँ हूँ. *3.* यह मैं ही हूं। *4.* इसे करना ही होगा। *5.* हम एक ही हैं। *6.* आप एक ही हो। *7.* तुम ही एक हो। *8.* तो ऐसा ही होगा। *9.* आपको ऐसा लगता है?

• *1.* So here you are. *2.* And I'm here. *3.* This is me. *4.* Make it happen. *5.* We're the same. *6.* You're the one. *7.* You're the only one. *8.* Then so be it. *9.* You think so?

**[15]** *1.* नहीं, मुझे नहीं लगता. *2.* मुझे लगता मैं था। *3.* यह अच्छा नहीं लगता. *4.* तुम्हें पता है क्या? *5.* मुझे नहीं पता था. *6.* मुझे नहीं पता होगा. *7.* आपको पता था कि। *8.* मुझे कुछ पता नहीं। *9.* कोई तो कुछ करो!
• *1.* No, I suppose not. *2.* I wish I were. *3.* That doesn't look good. *4.* You know what? *5.* I didn't know. *6.* I wouldn't know. *7.* You knew that. *8.* I've got no idea. *9.* Somebody do something!

**[16]** *1.* मेरे लिए यह करो. *2.* ठीक है, ऐसा करो. *3.* अच्छा तुम करो अब। *4.* तो हम क्या करें? *5.* बस ऐसा ही है. *6.* यह आपके लिए है। *7.* आपके पास क्या होगा? *8.* आपके पास मैं हूं। *9.* क्या वे आपके हैं?
• *1.* Do this for me. *2.* Okay, do it. *3.* Well, you do now. *4.* So what do we do? *5.* That's just how it is. *6.* This is for you. *7.* What'll you have? *8.* You've got me. *9.* Are they yours?

**[17]** *1.* नहीं, आपने नहीं किया. *2.* मैं जा रहा हूं। *3.* आप जा सकते हैं। *4.* तुम जा रहे हो? *5.* तुम जा सकते हो। *6.* वे जा रहे हैं. *7.* आप जा रहे हैं। *8.* हम जा सकते हैं। *9.* हम नहीं जा सकते.
• *1.* No, you didn't. *2.* I'm leaving. *3.* You can go. *4.* You're leaving? *5.* You may go. *6.* They're leaving. *7.* You're going. *8.* We can go. *9.* We can't leave.

**[18]** *1.* तुम नहीं जा सकते! *2.* नहीं, वह नहीं करता. *3.* मैं बस करता हूं। *4.* मैं भी करता हूं. *5.* मैं किया करता था। *6.* और मैं करता हूँ. *7.* मैं बात करता हूँ। *8.* अब भी करता हूं. *9.* हमें करना ही होगा।
• *1.* You can't go! *2.* No, he doesn't. *3.* I just do. *4.* I do, too. *5.* I used to be. *6.* And I do. *7.* I'll talk. *8.* Still do. *9.* We have to.

**[19]** *1.* हमें तुम चाहिए हो। *2.* बस अपने आप हो। *3.* ठीक है, चलो, चलो। *4.* मुझे यह करने दो। *5.* यह काम करता है। *6.* काम करने के लिए। *7.* मैं काम पर हूं। *8.* काम कर रहे थे। *9.* इसे काम करना होगा।
• *1.* We want you. *2.* Just be yourself. *3.* Okay, come on, come on. *4.* Let me do this. *5.* It works. *6.* To work. *7.* I'm on duty. *8.* We're working. *9.* It has to work.

**[20]** *1.* मुझे वह मत दो! *2.* नहीं, नहीं, मत करो. *3.* नहीं, ऐसा मत करो. *4.* मत करो, ठीक है? *5.* हाँ मुझे पता है। *6.* हाँ मैं ठीक हूँ. *7.* हाँ, मैं अच्छा हूँ. *8.* हाँ यह मैं हूं। *9.* हाँ, मैं यहाँ हूँ।
• *1.* Don't give me that! *2.* No, no, don't. *3.* No, don't do this. *4.* Don't, okay? *5.* Yes, I know. *6.* Yeah, I'm fine. *7.* Yeah, I'm

good. *8.* Yeah, it's me. *9.* Yeah, I'm here.

[21] *1.* हाँ वह मैं हूँ। *2.* हाँ, हम ठीक हैं। *3.* हाँ, आपको करना चाहिए। *4.* हाँ, हमें करना चाहिए। *5.* हाँ, यह अच्छा था। *6.* मैं करता हूँ, हाँ। *7.* हाँ मैं करता हूँ। *8.* हाँ, हम यहाँ हैं। *9.* क्या कुछ हुआ है?
● *1.* Yes, that's me. *2.* Yeah, we're fine. *3.* Yeah, you should. *4.* Yeah, we should. *5.* Yeah, it was good. *6.* I do, yeah. *7.* I do, yes. *8.* Yeah, we're here. *9.* Has something happened?

[22] *1.* नहीं, ऐसा नहीं हुआ. *2.* मेरा काम हो गया। *3.* यह मेरा नहीं है। *4.* मेरा पास दो हैं। *5.* वह क्या चाहता है? *6.* मैं तुम्हें चाहता हूँ। *7.* मैं ऐसा नहीं चाहता. *8.* मैं उसे चाहता हूँ। *9.* मैं चाहता हूँ कि।
● *1.* No, it didn't. *2.* I'm done. *3.* It's not mine. *4.* I have two. *5.* What does he want? *6.* I want you. *7.* I don't want that. *8.* I want him. *9.* I want that.

[23] *1.* मैं यह चाहता हूँ। *2.* मैं एक चाहता हूँ। *3.* नहीं, मैं चाहता हूँ. *4.* बात करना चाहता हूं? *5.* यह मेरी बात है. *6.* यह सब ठीक है। *7.* सब कुछ अच्छा होगा। *8.* सब कुछ कर दिया। *9.* वह सब क्या था?
● *1.* I want this. *2.* I want one. *3.* No, I want to. *4.* Want to talk? *5.* That's my thing. *6.* That's all right. *7.* Everything's gonna be fine. *8.* All done. *9.* What was all that about?

[24] *1.* क्या हम सब नहीं? *2.* हम सब यहाँ हैं. *3.* वे सब यहाँ हैं. *4.* क्या वह सब था? *5.* चलो ठीक है जाओ। *6.* मैं इस पर हूँ। *7.* आपने ऐसा क्यों किया? *8.* मुझे पता है क्यों। *9.* तुम क्यों नहीं हो?
● *1.* Don't we all? *2.* We're all here. *3.* They're all here. *4.* Was that all? *5.* Alright, let's go. *6.* I'm over it. *7.* Why did you do that? *8.* I know why. *9.* Why aren't you?

[25] *1.* क्यों क्या बात है? *2.* आपको क्यों चाहिए होगा? *3.* वह उसे ले गया. *4.* नहीं, नहीं, नहीं, कृपया। *5.* चलो यह करते हैं। *6.* आप ऐसा नहीं करते. *7.* नहीं, वे नहीं करते. *8.* हम भी नहीं करते। *9.* और आप नहीं करते?
● *1.* Why, what's the matter? *2.* Why would you want to? *3.* He took her. *4.* No, no, no, please. *5.* Let's do it. *6.* You don't. *7.* No, they don't. *8.* Neither do we. *9.* And you don't?

[26] *1.* हम बात करते है। *2.* आप काम करते हो? *3.* आप क्या चाहते हैं? *4.* तुम चाहते हो एक? *5.* तुम कुछ चाहते हो? *6.* तुम वह चाहते हो? *7.* तुम उसे चाहते हो? *8.* तुम यह चाहते हो। *9.* तुम मुझे चाहते थे?
● *1.* We talk. *2.* You working? *3.* What do you want? *4.* Do you want one? *5.* You want something? *6.* You want that? *7.* You want her? *8.* If you want it. *9.* You wanted me?

**[27]** *1.* आपका पता क्या है? *2.* आपका काम हो गया। *3.* यह कैसे हो गया? *4.* मुझे कैसे पता होगा? *5.* मुझे नहीं पता कैसे. *6.* आपने ऐसा कैसे किया? *7.* तो आप कैसे हैं? *8.* उसने ऐसा कैसे किया? *9.* सब कुछ कैसे है?

• *1.* What's your address? *2.* You're through. *3.* How did this happen? *4.* How would I know? *5.* I don't know how. *6.* How'd you do that? *7.* So how are you? *8.* How could he? *9.* How is everything?

**[28]** *1.* आपको पता है कैसे? *2.* अच्छा, तुम्हें कैसे पता? *3.* आप सब कैसे हैं? *4.* अच्छा आप कैसे हैं? *5.* उसने वह कैसे किया? *6.* वे आ रहे हैं। *7.* वह आ रहा है। *8.* वह आ गया है। *9.* कोई आ रहा है।

• *1.* Do you know how? *2.* Well, how do you know? *3.* How y'all doing? *4.* Good, how are you? *5.* How did she do that? *6.* They're coming. *7.* He's coming. *8.* Here he comes. *9.* Someone's coming.

**[29]** *1.* क्या बात है आ? *2.* मैं आ रहा हूं। *3.* में आ रहा है। *4.* कुछ आ रहा है. *5.* आप नहीं आ सकते. *6.* उसके साथ क्या है? *7.* मुझे और समय चाहिए। *8.* समय क्या हुआ है? *9.* समय आ गया है।

• *1.* What is the matter? *2.* I'm coming over. *3.* Coming in. *4.* Something's coming. *5.* You can't come. *6.* What's with him? *7.* I need more time. *8.* What's the time? *9.* It is time.

**[30]** *1.* अब समय क्या है? *2.* कुछ समय हुआ है। *3.* क्या समय हो गया? *4.* नहीं, समय नहीं है. *5.* यह समय नहीं है. *6.* मेरे पास समय है। *7.* उसने इसे ले लिया। *8.* मैंने कर लिया है। *9.* उन्होंने यह कर लिया।

• *1.* What time is it now? *2.* Been a while. *3.* Is it time? *4.* No, there's no time. *5.* This isn't the time. *6.* I have time. *7.* He took it. *8.* I am done. *9.* They made it.

**[31]** *1.* वह आ रही है। *2.* अभी भी समय है। *3.* आपने अभी क्या किया? *4.* यह मुझे दो, अभी। *5.* ओह, मुझे पता है। *6.* ओह यह आप हैं। *7.* ओह मैं ठीक हूँ। *8.* ओह, हाँ, आप हैं. *9.* ओह, वह मैं हूं।

• *1.* She's coming. *2.* There's still time. *3.* What did you just do? *4.* Give it to me now. *5.* Oh, I know. *6.* Oh, it's you. *7.* Oh, I'm fine. *8.* Oh, yes, you are. *9.* Oh, that's me.

**[32]** *1.* ओह, मैं अच्छा हूँ. *2.* ओह क्या आपने किया? *3.* ओह, क्या मैं हूं? *4.* ओह, क्या आप हैं? *5.* ओह, तुम यहाँ हो। *6.* ओह, मैं ठीक हूं. *7.* ओह, हम यहाँ हैं। *8.* ओह, यह ठीक था. *9.* ओह, आप कैसे हैं?

• *1.* Oh, I'm good. *2.* Oh, did you? *3.* Oh, am I? *4.* Oh, are you? *5.* Oh, you're here. *6.* Oh, I'm okay. *7.* Oh, here we are. *8.* Oh, it was fine. *9.* Oh, how do you do?

**[33]** *1.* आप कहाँ से हैं? *2.* वह अब कहाँ है? *3.* अब, हम कहाँ थे? *4.* अच्छा, वह कहाँ है? *5.* तो वह कहाँ है? *6.* यह अब कहाँ है? *7.* अब, मैं कहाँ था? *8.* वह कहाँ रही है? *9.* और वह कहाँ है?

● *1.* Where are you from? *2.* Where is she now? *3.* Now, where were we? *4.* Well, where is he? *5.* So where is he? *6.* Where is it now? *7.* Now, where was I? *8.* Where has she been? *9.* And where is he?

**[34]** *1.* तो हम कहाँ थे? *2.* अब, वह कहाँ है? *3.* और तुम कहाँ थे? *4.* और तुम कहाँ हो? *5.* मैंने कभी नहीं किया। *6.* कि उसने क्या कहा। *7.* आपने उसे कहा था? *8.* मैंने तुम्हें कहा है। *9.* मैंने यह कहा था।

● *1.* So, where were we? *2.* Now, where is he? *3.* And where were you? *4.* And where are you? *5.* I never did. *6.* That's what she said. *7.* You told him? *8.* I've told you. *9.* I said it.

**[35]** *1.* आपने कुछ नहीं कहा। *2.* आपने कभी नहीं कहा। *3.* आपने ऐसा क्यों कहा? *4.* मैंने ऐसा नहीं कहा! *5.* आपने ऐसा कहा था। *6.* मैंने कुछ नहीं कहा। *7.* तो आपने कहा है। *8.* मैंने कहा ठीक है। *9.* आपने ऐसा नहीं कहा।

● *1.* You didn't say anything. *2.* You never said. *3.* Why'd you say that? *4.* I didn't say that! *5.* You said so. *6.* I didn't say nothing. *7.* So you've said. *8.* I said okay. *9.* That's not what you said.

**[36]** *1.* मुझे यह पसंद है। *2.* क्या पसंद नहीं करना? *3.* आप जानते हैं कि। *4.* तुम जानते हो क्यों। *5.* वे यह नहीं जानते। *6.* तो तुम जानते हो। *7.* तुम मुझे नहीं जानते? *8.* कृपया वापस आ जाओ। *9.* मुझे वह वापस चाहिए।

● *1.* I like it. *2.* What's not to like? *3.* You know that. *4.* You know why. *5.* They don't know that. *6.* So you know. *7.* You don't know me? *8.* Please come back. *9.* I want him back.

**[37]** *1.* लेकिन मैं करता हूं। *2.* लेकिन तुम ... नहीं हो। *3.* लेकिन यह ठीक है। *4.* लेकिन ऐसा नहीं था। *5.* लेकिन ऐसा नहीं हुआ। *6.* लेकिन कोई बात नहीं। *7.* लेकिन यह है क्या? *8.* लेकिन वह नहीं है। *9.* लेकिन उसने ऐसा किया।

● *1.* But I do. *2.* But you're not. *3.* But that's okay. *4.* But it wasn't. *5.* But it didn't. *6.* But it's okay. *7.* But what is it? *8.* But he's not. *9.* But he did.

**[38]** *1.* लेकिन मैंने यह किया. *2.* लेकिन आप यहाँ हैं। *3.* लेकिन उन्होंने ऐसा किया. *4.* ओह, लेकिन यह है. *5.* लेकिन वे करते हैं. *6.* लेकिन आपको करना होगा. *7.* लेकिन आपके पास है. *8.* लेकिन मुझे पता है। *9.* लेकिन मेरे पास है।

● *1.* But I did it. *2.* But here you are. *3.* But they did. *4.* Oh, but it is. *5.* But they do. *6.* But you have to. *7.* But you have. *8.* But I know. *9.* But I have.

**[39]** *1.* लेकिन वह नहीं था. *2.* मैं तुम्हें जानता हूं। *3.* क्या वह जानता है? *4.* वह क्या जानता है? *5.* में उन्हें जानता हूँ। *6.* वह मुझे जानता है। *7.* वह यह जानता है. *8.* वह कुछ जानता है. *9.* वह कैसे जानता है?

● *1.* But he wasn't. *2.* I know you. *3.* Does he know? *4.* What does he know? *5.* I know them. *6.* He knows me. *7.* He knows that. *8.* He knows something. *9.* How does he know?

**[40]** *1.* वह यह नहीं जानता. *2.* कोई नहीं जानता क्यों. *3.* और आप कौन है? *4.* लेकिन तुम कौन हो? *5.* अच्छा, तुम कौन हो? *6.* कृपया मेरी मदद करें। *7.* में मदद करता हूँ। *8.* आपको कुछ मदद चाहिए? *9.* यह मदद करता है।

● *1.* He doesn't know that. *2.* Nobody knows why. *3.* And who are you? *4.* But who are you? *5.* Well, who are you? *6.* Please help me. *7.* Let me help. *8.* You need some help? *9.* It helps.

**[41]** *1.* आपको कोई मदद चाहिए? *2.* मदद आ रही है. *3.* हमें कुछ मदद चाहिए. *4.* इसे फिर से करें। *5.* और फिर क्या हुआ? *6.* फिर आपने क्या किया? *7.* फिर आप कौन हैं? *8.* फिर तुम क्या हो? *9.* तो फिर क्या है?

● *1.* You need any help? *2.* Help is coming. *3.* We need some help. *4.* Do it again. *5.* And then what happened? *6.* What did you do then? *7.* Who are you again? *8.* Then what are you? *9.* Then what is?

**[42]** *1.* अच्छा, तो फिर चलो। *2.* फिर आप क्या हैं? *3.* तो फिर कौन है? *4.* तो फिर तुम जाओ. *5.* और फिर यह है. *6.* फिर यह क्या है? *7.* और फिर ऐसा हुआ. *8.* यह फिर क्या था? *9.* यह फिर क्या है?

● *1.* Well, come on, then. *2.* Who are you, then? *3.* Then who is? *4.* Off you go, then. *5.* And then there's this. *6.* What's this then? *7.* And then it happened. *8.* What was it again? *9.* What is it again?

**[43]** *1.* तो फिर क्या हुआ? *2.* आपका बहुत-बहुत धन्यवाद। *3.* धन्यवाद मैं ठीक हूं। *4.* मैं ठीक हूं धन्यवाद। *5.* मैं अच्छा हूँ, धन्यवाद। *6.* ओह, ठीक है, धन्यवाद। *7.* ऐसा तुमने क्यों किया? *8.* तुमने मुझे क्या दिया? *9.* तुमने उसे क्या दिया?

● *1.* So then what happened? *2.* Thank you very much. *3.* I'm fine, thanks. *4.* I'm fine, thank you. *5.* I'm good, thanks. *6.* Oh, well, thank you. *7.* What did you do that for? *8.* What did you give me? *9.* What did you give her?

**[44]** *1.* और ये हो गया। *2.* क्या ये ठीक है? *3.* ये सब आपका है। *4.* ये आपके लिए हैं। *5.* ये आप पर है। *6.* क्या तुमने ये किया? *7.* मेरे लिए ये करो। *8.* ये सब कौन है? *9.* ये अच्छा नहीं है।

● *1.* Here you are. *2.* Is that okay? *3.* It's all yours. *4.* These are for you. *5.* That's up to you. *6.* Did you do this? *7.* Do it for me. *8.* Who are all these people? *9.* This isn't good.

**[45]** *1.* तुमने ये क्यों कहा? *2.* उन्होंने ये कर दिया। *3.* तो ये बात है। *4.* लेकिन बात ये है. *5.* ये अच्छा नहीं लगता. *6.* मुझे ये करना है। *7.* ये जा रहा है। *8.* नहीं ये ठीक है। *9.* क्या ये आपके हैं?
● *1.* Why did you say that? *2.* They did it. *3.* It's like this. *4.* But here's the thing. *5.* This doesn't look good. *6.* I need to do this. *7.* It's going. *8.* No, that's OK. *9.* Are these yours?

**[46]** *1.* नहीं, ये अच्छा है. *2.* हमें ये करना होगा. *3.* ये सब क्या है? *4.* ये अच्छा लगता है. *5.* मुझे ये अभी चाहिए। *6.* नहीं ये मेरा है! *7.* ये मेरे लिए है? *8.* तो ये करते है। *9.* अब ये क्या है?
● *1.* No, this is good. *2.* We have to do this. *3.* What's all this stuff? *4.* This feels good. *5.* I want it now. *6.* No, it's mine! *7.* It's for me? *8.* So let's do it. *9.* What's this now?

**[47]** *1.* तुमने ये सब किया? *2.* जो एक आप हैं? *3.* जो कुछ भी है। *4.* जो मैं चाहता हूं? *5.* यही तो बात है। *6.* यही उसने कहा था। *7.* मैं यही करता हूं। *8.* मुझे यही सब चाहिए। *9.* क्या वह यही था?
● *1.* You did all this? *2.* Which one are you? *3.* Whatever that is. *4.* What I want? *5.* That's the point. *6.* That's what he said. *7.* It's what I do. *8.* That's all I need. *9.* Was that it?

**[48]** *1.* वे यही करते हैं. *2.* आप यही करते हैं. *3.* और वह यही था. *4.* हमें बस यही चाहिए। *5.* वे यही चाहते हैं. *6.* हम यही करते हैं। *7.* हम यही चाहते हैं. *8.* क्या तुमने यही किया? *9.* आप मेरे साथ आओ।
● *1.* That's what they do. *2.* That's what you do. *3.* And that was it. *4.* That's all we need. *5.* That's what they want. *6.* Here's what we do. *7.* That's what we want. *8.* Is that what you did? *9.* You come with me.

**[49]** *1.* चलो, आओ, आओ, चलो। *2.* ठीक है, यहाँ आओ. *3.* उसे यहाँ ले आओ. *4.* चलो उसे ले आओ. *5.* आओ और इसे करो! *6.* आओ, मेरी मदद करो. *7.* तुम यहाँ वापस आओ! *8.* यहाँ आओ, यहाँ आओ! *9.* चलो, आओ, आओ, आओ!
● *1.* Come on, come on, come on, come on. *2.* Okay, come here. *3.* Bring him here. *4.* Let's go get him. *5.* Come on, do it! *6.* Come on, help me. *7.* You come back here! *8.* Come here, come here! *9.* Come on, come on, come on, come on!

**[50]** *1.* इसे यहाँ ले आओ. *2.* आपने इसे देखा था? *3.* क्या अपने उसे देखा? *4.* क्या तुमने उसे देखा? *5.* क्या तुमने कुछ देखा? *6.* क्या तुमने उन्हें देखा? *7.* क्या उसने तुम्हें देखा? *8.* मैंने उसे देखा है. *9.* मैंने सब कुछ देखा.

● *1.* Bring it over here. *2.* Did you see it? *3.* Have you seen her? *4.* Did you see her? *5.* Did you see anything? *6.* Did you see them? *7.* Did he see you? *8.* I've seen him. *9.* I saw everything.

**[51]** *1.* मैंने देखा है कि। *2.* मैंने यह सब देखा। *3.* मैंने अभी उसे देखा. *4.* हाँ, मैंने वह देखा। *5.* और तुमने क्या देखा? *6.* क्या तुमने देखा है? *7.* तुमने उसे देखा है? *8.* क्या तुमने नहीं देखा? *9.* तुमने उसे कहाँ देखा?
● *1.* I noticed that. *2.* I saw it all. *3.* I just saw him. *4.* Yeah, I saw that. *5.* And what did you see? *6.* Have you seen? *7.* You've seen her? *8.* Didn't you see? *9.* Where did you see him?

**[52]** *1.* हाँ, मैंने उसे देखा। *2.* क्या वह उसकी है? *3.* कृपया उसकी मदद करें. *4.* आपने अपना समय लिया. *5.* बस अपना काम करो. *6.* मैंने अपना काम किया. *7.* मुझे यह मिल गया। *8.* इसे बाहर ले जाओ! *9.* बाहर आ रहा है।
● *1.* Yeah, I saw him. *2.* Is that her? *3.* Please help him. *4.* You took your time. *5.* Just do your job. *6.* I did my part. *7.* I got this. *8.* Move it out! *9.* Coming out.

**[53]** *1.* और हम बाहर हैं. *2.* यही उसका काम है. *3.* मुझे लगा तुम थे। *4.* अपने आप को देखो। *5.* तुम यह देखो कि? *6.* देखो तुमने क्या किया. *7.* मुझे देखो, मुझे देखो। *8.* ठीक है तुम देखो। *9.* देखो यह कौन है!
● *1.* And we're out. *2.* That's his job. *3.* I thought it was you. *4.* Look at you. *5.* You see that? *6.* Look what you did. *7.* Look at me, look at me. *8.* Okay, see you. *9.* Look who it is!

**[54]** *1.* अब मुझे ही देखो। *2.* देखो, मुझे पता है. *3.* देखो, मैं ठीक हूं. *4.* की तरह लगता है। *5.* मैं आपकी तरह हूं। *6.* यह इसके बारे में। *7.* आप इसके साथ थे? *8.* अब मुझे जाना होगा। *9.* मैं जाना चाहता हूँ।
● *1.* Now look at me. *2.* Look, I know. *3.* Look, I'm fine. *4.* Looks like. *5.* I'm like you. *6.* That's about it. *7.* Who were you with? *8.* I have to go now. *9.* I want to go.

**[55]** *1.* आप जाना चाहते हैं? *2.* हमें कहाँ जाना चाहिए? *3.* क्या हमें जाना चाहिए? *4.* मैं जाना चाहता हूं। *5.* तुम्हें क्यों जाना है? *6.* तुम जाना चाहते हो? *7.* तुम यहां क्यों हो? *8.* क्या आप यहां हैं? *9.* मैं यहां पर हूं।
● *1.* You want to go? *2.* Where should we go? *3.* Should we go? *4.* I wanna go. *5.* Why do you have to go? *6.* You wanna leave? *7.* Why are you here? *8.* Are you here? *9.* I'm over here.

**[56]** *1.* क्या यह यहां है? *2.* क्या यहां और है? *3.* मैं यहां ठीक हूं। *4.* यह यहां

253

पर है। 5. अब मैं यहां हूं। 6. लेकिन हम यहां हैं। 7. यह मेरा घर है। 8. मुझे घर ले चलो। 9. मेरे साथ घर चलो।

● 1. Is it here? 2. Is there more? 3. I'm fine here. 4. It is here. 5. Now I'm here. 6. But here we are. 7. This is my home. 8. Take me home. 9. Come home with me.

[57] 1. मैं घर पर हूं। 2. मैं घर पर था। 3. उसे घर ले जाओ। 4. घर में आ जाओ! 5. आप घर पर हैं। 6. मैं घर गया था। 7. उसे घर ले आओ. 8. कृपया घर आ जाओ। 9. मुझे घर जाना चाहिए.

● 1. I'm at home. 2. I was at home. 3. Take her home. 4. Get in the house! 5. You are home. 6. I was home. 7. Bring her home. 8. Please come home. 9. I should go home.

[58] 1. आपने उससे क्या कहा? 2. जाओ उससे बात करो. 3. बस उससे बात करो. 4. उससे बात मत करो. 5. तुमने उससे बात की? 6. मैंने उससे बात की. 7. किसी ने नहीं किया. 8. मैंने उससे प्यार किया. 9. प्यार करने के लिए।

● 1. What did you say to him? 2. Go talk to him. 3. Just talk to him. 4. Don't talk to him. 5. You talked to her? 6. I spoke to her. 7. No one did. 8. I would love that. 9. To love.

[59] 1. वह प्यार में है. 2. मेरे साथ प्यार करो। 3. हम प्यार में थे। 4. वे प्यार में हैं। 5. तुमने मुझसे क्या कहा? 6. अभी मुझसे बात करें। 7. कृपया मुझसे बात करें। 8. यह वहाँ पर है। 9. अच्छा, तुम वहाँ जाओ।

● 1. He's in love. 2. Make love to me. 3. We were in love. 4. They're in love. 5. What did you say to me? 6. Just talk to me. 7. Please talk to me. 8. It's over there. 9. Well, there you go.

[60] 1. हाँ, तुम वहाँ जाओ। 2. वहाँ वापस क्या हुआ? 3. ओह, तुम वहाँ जाओ। 4. वहाँ कोई नहीं हैं। 5. क्या वहाँ कोई हैं? 6. वहाँ से बाहर आओ! 7. ओह, वे वहाँ हैं। 8. चलो वहाँ से बाहर. 9. और तुम वहाँ हो।

● 1. Yeah, there you go. 2. What happened back there? 3. Oh, there you go. 4. There aren't any. 5. Is anybody out there? 6. Come out of there! 7. Oh, there they are. 8. Come on out of there. 9. And there you are.

[61] 1. वे सब वहाँ हैं. 2. तुम वहाँ नहीं थे! 3. हाँ, मैं वहाँ था। 4. और तुम वहाँ जाओ. 5. देखो वहां कौन है। 6. आप वहां नहीं थे. 7. वहां क्या हुआ था? 8. मैं वहां नहीं था. 9. क्या तुम वहां थे?

● 1. They're all there. 2. You weren't there! 3. Yeah, I was there. 4. And there you go. 5. Look who's here. 6. You weren't there. 7. What happened there? 8. I wasn't there. 9. Were you there?

**[62]** *1.* वहां, मैंने यह कहा. *2.* वहां से बाहर आओ. *3.* वह वहां नहीं थी. *4.* क्या हम वहां हैं? *5.* और यह वहां था. *6.* क्या वह वहां था? *7.* वे वहां नहीं हैं. *8.* तुम वहां नहीं हो. *9.* वहां हम नहीं हैं.

● *1.* There, I said it. *2.* Come out of there. *3.* She wasn't there. *4.* Are we there? *5.* And there it was. *6.* Was he there? *7.* They're not there. *8.* You're not there. *9.* There is no us.

**[63]** *1.* तो आप वहां हैं. *2.* वहां कभी नहीं गया। *3.* वह रूप क्या है? *4.* आप क्या पसंद करेंगे? *5.* नहीं, वे नहीं करेंगे. *6.* नहीं, हम नहीं करेंगे. *7.* हम ऐसा क्यों करेंगे? *8.* वे ऐसा क्यों करेंगे? *9.* हम ऐसा कैसे करेंगे?

● *1.* So there you are. *2.* Never been there. *3.* What's that look? *4.* What would you like? *5.* No, they won't. *6.* No, we won't. *7.* Why would we do that? *8.* Why would they? *9.* How are we gonna do that?

**[64]** *1.* हम आपकी मदद करेंगे. *2.* हम कुछ काम करेंगे. *3.* वे ऐसा नहीं करेंगे. *4.* हम इसे कैसे करेंगे? *5.* हम क्यों नहीं करेंगे? *6.* क्या वह सही है? *7.* आप सब सही हैं। *8.* नहीं, आप सही हैं. *9.* आपने सही काम किया।

● *1.* We'll help you. *2.* We'll work something out. *3.* They wouldn't. *4.* How do we do it? *5.* Why wouldn't we? *6.* Is that right? *7.* You're all right. *8.* No, you're right. *9.* You did the right thing.

**[65]** *1.* सही में उसने किया। *2.* और आप सही हैं. *3.* लेकिन आप सही हैं. *4.* ओह, आप सही हैं. *5.* और आप सही थे. *6.* नहीं, आप सही थे. *7.* लेकिन आप सही थे. *8.* मैंने सही काम किया. *9.* ये सही नहीं लगता.

● *1.* Of course he does. *2.* And you're right. *3.* But you're right. *4.* Oh, you're right. *5.* And you were right. *6.* No, you were right. *7.* But you were right. *8.* I did the right thing. *9.* This doesn't feel right.

**[66]** *1.* उसके साथ सही हुआ। *2.* मैं सही नहीं हूँ। *3.* और मैं सही था. *4.* आप पहले से ही। *5.* मैं यहां पहले था। *6.* आपने पहले क्या किया? *7.* नहीं, पहले तुम जाओ. *8.* उसने आपसे क्या कहा? *9.* तुम्हें मेरी जरूरत है।

● *1.* Serves him right. *2.* I'm not perfect. *3.* And I was right. *4.* You already have. *5.* I was here first. *6.* What did you do before? *7.* No, you go first. *8.* What did she say to you? *9.* You need me.

**[67]** *1.* कुछ मदद की जरूरत? *2.* मुझे उसे जरूरत हैं। *3.* मुझे उसकी जरूरत हैं। *4.* मुझे इससे प्यार है। *5.* उस के लिए धन्यवाद। *6.* हम उस पर रहे। *7.* उस तरह क्या है? *8.* मैं उस पर हूँ. *9.* उस पर मत देखो.

● *1.* Need some help? *2.* I need him. *3.* I need that. *4.* I love it.

*5.* Thank you for that. *6.* We're on it. *7.* What's that like? *8.* I'm on him. *9.* Don't look at that.

**[68]** *1.* तुम मुझे मिल गए। *2.* आप वापस आ गए। *3.* वे वापस आ गए। *4.* क्या आप गए थे? *5.* हम आ गए हैं। *6.* आप वहां गए हैं? *7.* आपका क्या मतलब है? *8.* इसका मतलब कुछ नहीं। *9.* तुम यहाँ कैसे मिला?
• *1.* I got you. *2.* You came back. *3.* They're back. *4.* Did you go? *5.* We've arrived. *6.* You've been there? *7.* What do you mean? *8.* It means nothing. *9.* How did you get here?

**[69]** *1.* तुम्हें वहाँ क्या मिला? *2.* देखो मुझे क्या मिला। *3.* क्या आपको कुछ मिला? *4.* तुम्हें वहां क्या मिला? *5.* तुम्हें और क्या मिला? *6.* क्या तुम्हें वह मिला? *7.* क्या आपको वह मिला? *8.* मुझे बस यही मिला। *9.* आपके लिए कुछ मिला.
• *1.* What have you got there? *2.* Look what I found. *3.* Did you find anything? *4.* What you got there? *5.* What else you got? *6.* Did you find him? *7.* Did you get that? *8.* That's all I got. *9.* Got something for you.

**[70]** *1.* हमें कुछ नहीं मिला. *2.* मैं किसी से मिला। *3.* तुम्हें कुछ नहीं मिला. *4.* मुझे कुछ नहीं मिला. *5.* क्या तुम्हें कुछ मिला? *6.* आपको क्या समय मिला? *7.* वह सब तुम्हें मिला? *8.* मुझे यह नहीं मिला. *9.* तुम्हें कोई पता मिला?
• *1.* We got nothing. *2.* I met someone. *3.* You got nothing. *4.* I got nothin'. *5.* Did you get anything? *6.* What time you got? *7.* That all you got? *8.* I haven't got it. *9.* You got an address?

**[71]** *1.* तो, हमें क्या मिला? *2.* मुझे समय नहीं मिला. *3.* हमें कुछ मिला है. *4.* मैंने कहा था ना। *5.* यह काम ना करें। *6.* तुमने किया, है ना? *7.* मैं हूं, है ना? *8.* अंदर आओ, अंदर आओ. *9.* आपके अंदर क्या है?
• *1.* So, what do we got? *2.* I haven't got time. *3.* We've got something. *4.* I told you so. *5.* Just stop it. *6.* You did, didn't you? *7.* I am, aren't I? *8.* Come in, come in. *9.* What's got into you?

**[72]** *1.* क्या आप अंदर हैं? *2.* क्या वह अंदर है? *3.* मैं अंदर चाहता हूँ *4.* बस अंदर आ जाओ. *5.* हाँ, मैं अंदर हूँ। *6.* आप अंदर चाहते हैं? *7.* वापस अंदर आ जाओ. *8.* हमें अंदर ले चलो. *9.* क्या अंदर कोई है?
• *1.* Are you in? *2.* Is he in? *3.* I want in. *4.* Just get in. *5.* Yeah, I'm in. *6.* You want in? *7.* Get back inside. *8.* Take us in. *9.* Is there anybody there?

**[73]** *1.* चलो, वहाँ अंदर जाओ. *2.* अच्छा लग रहा है. *3.* मैं महसूस करता हूँ। *4.* मैंने यह महसूस किया। *5.* आप महसूस करते हो? *6.* इसे कैसे महसूस किया?

*7.* मैंने कुछ महसूस किया। *8.* मैं तुम्हारे साथ हूं। *9.* तुम्हारे पास क्या है?
● *1.* Come on, get in there. *2.* Looks good. *3.* I feel it. *4.* I felt it. *5.* You feel it? *6.* How did it feel? *7.* I feel something. *8.* I'm with you. *9.* What do you have?

**[74]** *1.* वे सब तुम्हारे हैं. *2.* यह हुई ना बात। *3.* हमारे यहाँ क्या है? *4.* हमारे पास वापस आओ. *5.* आप हमारे साथ हैं. *6.* वह हमारे पास था. *7.* बात करना बंद करें। *8.* बंद करो बंद करो! *9.* यह बंद हो गया।
● *1.* They're all yours. *2.* That's more like it. *3.* What have we here? *4.* Come back to us. *5.* You're with us. *6.* We had him. *7.* Stop talking. *8.* Stop, stop! *9.* It's off.

**[75]** *1.* अब इसे बंद करो. *2.* मैं बाहर बंद हूं. *3.* इसे अभी बंद करो! *4.* मुझे तुमसे प्यार है। *5.* उसने तुमसे क्या कहा? *6.* तो अब आगे क्या? *7.* मुझे आगे जाना है. *8.* उसका नाम क्या है? *9.* मुझे एक नाम दो।
● *1.* Now stop it. *2.* I'm locked out. *3.* Stop this now! *4.* I love you. *5.* What did he say to you? *6.* So what happens now? *7.* I'm moving. *8.* What's his name? *9.* Give me a name.

**[76]** *1.* मुझे एक नाम चाहिए. *2.* नहीं, मैं नहीं करूंगा. *3.* अब में क्या करूंगा? *4.* अरे यह मैं हूँ। *5.* अरे आप कैसे हैं? *6.* अरे! कोई बात नहीं। *7.* अरे, तुम ठीक हो? *8.* अरे, वह क्या है? *9.* अरे, क्या बात है?
● *1.* I need a name. *2.* No, I won't. *3.* What am I going to do now? *4.* Hey, it's me. *5.* Hey, how are you? *6.* Oh, it's okay. *7.* Hey, are you okay? *8.* Hey, what's that? *9.* Hey, what's the matter?

**[77]** *1.* अरे क्या हो गया? *2.* अरे तुम कहाँ हो? *3.* अरे, तुम वहाँ हो. *4.* अरे, वह वहाँ है। *5.* अरे! आप कौन है? *6.* अरे, तुम कहाँ थे? *7.* अरे, सब ठीक है? *8.* अरे, यहाँ वापस आओ! *9.* अरे, वह मेरा है.
● *1.* Hey, what's wrong? *2.* Hey, where are you? *3.* Hey, there you are. *4.* Hey, there he is. *5.* Hey, who are you? *6.* Hey, where you been? *7.* Hey, is everything okay? *8.* Hey, get back here! *9.* Hey, that's mine.

**[78]** *1.* अरे, वह कौन है? *2.* अरे, वह क्या था? *3.* अरे आपको क्या हुआ? *4.* क्या तुम्हें याद नहीं? *5.* मुझे आप याद हैं। *6.* ओह, मुझे याद है. *7.* मुझे यह याद है। *8.* मुझे वह याद है। *9.* आपको यह याद है?
● *1.* Hey, who's that? *2.* Hey, what was that? *3.* Hey, man, what's up? *4.* Don't you remember? *5.* I remember you. *6.* Oh, I remember. *7.* I remember this. *8.* I remember it. *9.* You remember this?

**[79]** *1.* मैंने उसे याद किया। *2.* तुमने मुझे याद किया? *3.* अरे, मुझे याद है? *4.* खैर, हम यहाँ हैं। *5.* खैर, यह वहाँ है। *6.* खैर, ये बात है. *7.* खैर, मुझे जाना चाहिए. *8.* खैर, उसने ऐसा किया। *9.* खैर, बात ये है.

● *1.* I missed him. *2.* Have you missed me? *3.* Hey, remember me? *4.* Well, here we are. *5.* Well, there it is. *6.* Well, that's the thing. *7.* Well, I should go. *8.* Well, he did. *9.* Well, here's the thing.

**[80]** *1.* खैर, ऐसा नहीं था। *2.* खैर, वह नहीं है। *3.* खैर, मैं नहीं करूंगा। *4.* खैर, यह मैं हूं। *5.* खैर, मैं नहीं था। *6.* खैर, यह अब है। *7.* आपको पता होना चाहिए। *8.* यह होना नहीं था। *9.* उसे होना ही होगा.

● *1.* Well, it wasn't. *2.* Well, he's not. *3.* Well, I won't. *4.* Well, this is me. *5.* Well, I wasn't. *6.* Well, it is now. *7.* You should know. *8.* It wasn't meant to be. *9.* He has to be.

**[81]** *1.* मैं देख नहीं सकता. *2.* आप देख सकते हैं। *3.* इसे मुझे दे दो। *4.* जाने के लिए मिला। *5.* बस मुझे जाने दो। *6.* यहाँ, मुझे जाने दो। *7.* बस उसे जाने दो. *8.* मैंने उसे जाने दिया। *9.* नहीं, मुझे जाने दो।

● *1.* I can't see. *2.* You can check. *3.* Give it to me. *4.* Got to go. *5.* Just let me go. *6.* Here, let me. *7.* Just let him go. *8.* I let him go. *9.* No, let me.

**[82]** *1.* उसे बाहर जाने दो! *2.* पहले मुझे जाने दो। *3.* मैं क्षमा चाहता हूँ? *4.* कृपया हमें क्षमा करें। *5.* कृपया मुझे क्षमा करें। *6.* आप मुझे क्षमा करें? *7.* मुझे कोशिश करने दो। *8.* फिर से कोशिश करें। *9.* मैं कोशिश करता हूँ।

● *1.* Let him out! *2.* Let me go first. *3.* I beg your pardon? *4.* Excuse us, please. *5.* Please, excuse me. *6.* You forgive me? *7.* Let me try. *8.* Try it again. *9.* I try.

**[83]** *1.* आओ कोशिश करते हैं। *2.* कोशिश करना चाहते हैं? *3.* मैंने वह कोशिश की. *4.* कोशिश भी मत करो. *5.* अब आप कोशिश करो। *6.* कोशिश करना चाहता हूं? *7.* आपने कोशिश की है? *8.* हाँ ऐसा होता है। *9.* मैंने यह किया होता।

● *1.* Let's try. *2.* Want to try? *3.* I tried that. *4.* Don't even try. *5.* Now you try. *6.* Wanna try? *7.* Have you tried? *8.* Yes, it does. *9.* I would have.

**[84]** *1.* मैं और कहाँ होता? *2.* मुझे ऐसा विश्वास है। *3.* इस पर विश्वास करो। *4.* कृपया मेरा विश्वास करो। *5.* आप बेहतर महसूस करेंगे। *6.* हाँ, यह बेहतर है। *7.* वहां, यह बेहतर है। *8.* ओह, यह बेहतर है। *9.* मैंने बेहतर देखा है।

● *1.* Where else would I be? *2.* I believe so. *3.* Believe it. *4.* Please believe me. *5.* You'll feel better. *6.* Yeah, that's better. *7.* There, that's better. *8.* Oh, that's better. *9.* I've seen better.

**[85]** *1.* यह बहुत बेहतर है। *2.* खैर, यह बेहतर है. *3.* मेरे पास बेहतर है. *4.* आपको वह पसंद आया? *5.* मुझे अब याद आया। *6.* अब मुझे याद आया। *7.* मुझे क्या याद आया? *8.* आपके अंदर क्या आया? *9.* में अभी आया हूँ।

• *1.* This is much better. *2.* Well, that's better. *3.* I've had better. *4.* You like that? *5.* I remember now. *6.* Now I remember. *7.* What'd I miss? *8.* What got into you? *9.* I just arrived.

**[86]** *1.* बस इतना ही था। *2.* मुझे इतना पता है। *3.* यह इतना अच्छा है। *4.* इतना समय क्या लगा? *5.* मैं बिल्कुल यहाँ हूँ। *6.* बिल्कुल नहीं लिया गया। *7.* आप बिल्कुल सही हैं। *8.* यह बिल्कुल ठीक है। *9.* यह बिल्कुल सही है।

• *1.* That was it. *2.* I know so. *3.* It feels so good. *4.* What took so long? *5.* I'm right here. *6.* None taken. *7.* You're damn right. *8.* It's quite all right. *9.* That's exactly right.

## Difficulty Level: 4

**[1]** *1.* नहीं, यह आप नहीं हैं. *2.* क्या वह वह नहीं है? *3.* यह वह है, यह वह है! *4.* नहीं, यह मैं नहीं था. *5.* वह था, क्या वह था? *6.* वह आप में से एक है. *7.* यह मैं हूं, यह मैं हूं! *8.* नहीं, वह मैं नहीं हूं. *9.* मैं आप में से एक हूं.

• *1.* No, it's not you. *2.* Isn't that him? *3.* It's him, it's him! *4.* No, it wasn't me. *5.* He was, was he? *6.* He's one of yours. *7.* It's me, it's me. *8.* No, that's not me. *9.* I am one of you.

**[2]** *1.* मैं नहीं हूं, मैं नहीं हूं. *2.* नहीं, नहीं, तुम नहीं हो. *3.* वह क्या कर रहा है? *4.* मैं आप में से एक हूं. *5.* मैं यह नहीं कर रहा हूँ. *6.* मैं क्या कर रहा हूँ? *7.* नहीं, मैं यह कर रहा हूँ. *8.* मैं यह कर रहा हूँ. *9.* कि क्या हो रहा है।

• *1.* I'm not, I'm not. *2.* No, no, you're not. *3.* What's he doing? *4.* I'm one of you. *5.* I ain't doing it. *6.* What am I doin'? *7.* No, I'm doing it. *8.* I'm doin' it. *9.* That's what's up.

**[3]** *1.* वह हम में से एक है. *2.* नहीं, नहीं, हम नहीं हैं. *3.* उसे क्या हो रहा है? *4.* यह आप के लिए है। *5.* आप क्या कर रहे हो? *6.* यह आप पर नहीं है. *7.* उसे क्या हो गया है? *8.* नहीं, यह नहीं किया गया है. *9.* क्या वह कुछ नहीं है?

• *1.* He's one of us. *2.* No, no, we're not. *3.* What's happening to him? *4.* It's for you. *5.* What are you doing? *6.* It's not on you. *7.* What's happened to him? *8.* No, it's not done. *9.* Isn't that something?

**[4]** *1.* मैं कुछ नहीं कर रहा था. *2.* हम कुछ नहीं कर रहे हैं. *3.* हम कुछ कर रहे हैं. *4.* मैं कुछ कर रहा हूँ। *5.* क्या आप कुछ कर रहे हैं? *6.* मैं कुछ नहीं कर रहा हूं। *7.* आप कुछ नहीं कर रहे हैं! *8.* मैं कुछ नहीं कर रहा हूँ. *9.* उसने कुछ नहीं किया है.

• 1. I wasn't doing anything. 2. We're not doing anything. 3. We are doing something. 4. I am doing something. 5. Are you doing anything? 6. I'm doing nothing. 7. You're not doing anything! 8. I ain't doing nothing. 9. He hasn't done anything.

[5] 1. उन्होंने कुछ नहीं किया है. 2. आप ने कुछ नहीं किया। 3. मैंने कुछ नहीं किया है. 4. मैंने यह किया, मैंने यह किया. 5. और आप कर रहे हैं? 6. और वह यह है कि? 7. नहीं, यह कुछ और है. 8. और मैंने क्या किया है? 9. और मैं क्या कर रहा हूँ?

• 1. They haven't done anything. 2. You do nothing. 3. I've done nothing. 4. I did it, I did it. 5. And you are? 6. And that is? 7. No, it's something else. 8. And what have I done? 9. And what am I doing?

[6] 1. और यह मैं नहीं हूं. 2. यह ठीक है, यह ठीक है. 3. आप ठीक कर रहे हैं? 4. मैं ठीक हूं, मैं ठीक हूं. 5. क्या तुम ठीक कर रहे हो? 6. मैं ठीक हो गया हूं. 7. मैं ठीक हूँ, ठीक है? 8. कुछ नहीं मैं ठीक हूँ। 9. तुम ठीक हो, तुम ठीक हो.

• 1. And it's not me. 2. It's okay, it's okay. 3. You doing okay? 4. I'm fine, I'm fine. 5. Are you doing okay? 6. I'm cured. 7. I'm fine, okay? 8. Nothing, I'm fine. 9. You're okay, you're okay.

[7] 1. तुम ठीक हो, ठीक है? 2. ठीक है, वह क्या है? 3. नहीं, नहीं, नहीं, मैं ठीक हूं. 4. मैं ठीक हो रहा हूं. 5. नहीं, मैं ठीक नहीं हूँ! 6. नहीं, नहीं, मैं ठीक हूं. 7. ठीक है, तुम ठीक हो. 8. ठीक है तुम क्या कर रहे हो? 9. क्या तुम ठीक नहीं हो?

• 1. You're okay, right? 2. Okay, what's that? 3. No, no, no, I'm fine. 4. I'm in recovery. 5. No, I'm not okay! 6. No, no, I'm okay. 7. Okay, you're okay. 8. Okay, what are you doing? 9. Aren't you well?

[8] 1. वह ठीक है, वह ठीक है। 2. क्या आप ठीक कर रहे हैं? 3. वह ठीक हो गया है. 4. क्या, क्या तुम ठीक हो? 5. ठीक है, मैं ठीक हूं. 6. नहीं, मैं ठीक हूं, मैं ठीक हूं। 7. ठीक है, मुझे बहुत हो गया। 8. हम ठीक कर रहे हैं. 9. क्या मैंने ठीक किया है?

• 1. That's fine, that's fine. 2. Are you doing OK? 3. He's cured. 4. What, are you okay? 5. Okay, I'm fine. 6. No, I'm fine, I'm fine. 7. Okay, I've had enough. 8. We're doing okay. 9. Did I do the right thing?

[9] 1. मैं ठीक हूं, ठीक हूं. 2. नहीं, नहीं, वह ठीक है. 3. मैं ठीक हो रहा हूँ. 4. वह ठीक हो रहा है। 5. मैं कर रहा हूं ठीक है। 6. ठीक है, क्या हो रहा है? 7. नहीं, तुम ठीक नहीं हो. 8. मैं ठीक हो गया हूँ! 9. नहीं, उसने ऐसा नहीं किया.

• 1. I'm fine, fine. 2. No, no, he's fine. 3. I'm healing. 4. He's in recovery. 5. I'm doing ok. 6. Okay, what's happening? 7. No, you're not okay. 8. I'm healed! 9. No, he didn't.

[10] 1. हम ऐसा नहीं कर रहे हैं. 2. आप ऐसा नहीं कर रहे हैं. 3. क्या आप ऐसा कर रहे हैं? 4. क्या हम ऐसा कर रहे हैं? 5. क्या ऐसा हो रहा है? 6. नहीं, हम ऐसा नहीं कर रहे हैं.
• 1. We're not doing this. 2. You're not doing this. 3. Are you doing this? 4. Are we doing this? 5. Is this happening? 6. No, we're not doing that.

[11] 1. नहीं, नहीं, नहीं, ऐसा नहीं है. 2. मैं ऐसा नहीं कर रहा हूं. 3. वह ऐसा नहीं कर रहा है. 4. मैं ऐसा नहीं कर रहा था. 5. आप ऐसा कर रहे हैं? 6. नहीं, मैं नहीं कर सकता.
• 1. No, no, no, it's not. 2. I am not doing that. 3. He's not doing it. 4. I wasn't doing that. 5. You're doing that? 6. No, I can't.

[12] 1. यह और क्या हो सकता है? 2. और वह क्या हो सकता है? 3. यह क्या हो सकता है? 4. क्या वह ऐसा कर सकता है? 5. वह क्या हो सकता है? 6. हो सकता है यह आप हो. 7. वह और क्या कर सकता है? 8. और क्या हो सकता है? 9. क्या ऐसा हो सकता है?
• 1. What else could it be? 2. And what might that be? 3. What can it be? 4. Can he do that? 5. What could that be? 6. Maybe it's you. 7. What else can he do? 8. What else could there be? 9. Could that be it?

[13] 1. क्या यह वह हो सकता है? 2. यह कुछ हो सकता है. 3. यह और क्या हो सकता था? 4. वह इसे ठीक कर सकता है. 5. हो सकता है, हो सकता है. 6. वह कुछ हो सकता है. 7. यह वह हो सकता है. 8. नहीं, नहीं, ऐसा नहीं हो सकता. 9. आपको क्या हो रहा है?
• 1. Could it be him? 2. This might be something. 3. What else could it have been? 4. He can fix it. 5. Could be, could be. 6. That could be something. 7. It could be him. 8. No, no, it can't be. 9. What is happening to you?

[14] 1. मैं कुछ भी कर सकता हूं? 2. कुछ भी नहीं हो रहा है। 3. नहीं यह कुछ भी नहीं है। 4. क्या कुछ और भी था? 5. और कुछ और भी है. 6. यह कुछ भी नहीं है. 7. यह कुछ भी नहीं है क्या। 8. वह कुछ भी नहीं है. 9. क्या और भी कुछ है?
• 1. Anything I can do? 2. Nothing's happening. 3. No, it's nothing. 4. Was there anything else? 5. And there's something else. 6. It's not nothing. 7. It is nothing. 8. He's nothing. 9. Are there any more?

**[15]** *1.* नहीं, यह कुछ भी नहीं था. *2.* आप भी कर रहे हैं। *3.* नहीं, कुछ भी नहीं है. *4.* वह कुछ भी नहीं था. *5.* और भी बहुत कुछ है. *6.* और भी हो सकता है. *7.* नहीं, ऐसा कुछ भी नहीं है. *8.* यह भी हो सकता है। *9.* तुम कर भी क्या रहे हो?

• *1.* No, it was nothing. *2.* You are, too. *3.* No, there's nothing. *4.* He was nothing. *5.* There's a lot more. *6.* There could be more. *7.* No, that's nothing. *8.* It could have been. *9.* What are you even doing?

**[16]** *1.* क्या वह कुछ भी नहीं है? *2.* हम भी कर रहे हैं। *3.* यह कुछ भी नहीं था. *4.* और कुछ भी नहीं है. *5.* कुछ तो हो रहा है. *6.* तो हम क्या कर रहे हैं? *7.* तो मैं भी कर सकता था. *8.* तो आप क्या कर रहे हैं? *9.* तो मैं नहीं कर सकता.

• *1.* Is that nothing? *2.* We are even. *3.* It was nothin'. *4.* And there's nothing. *5.* Something's going on. *6.* So what are we doing? *7.* So could I. *8.* So, what are you up to? *9.* So I can't.

**[17]** *1.* तो मैं क्या कर रहा हूँ? *2.* तो क्या हम ठीक हैं? *3.* तो क्या आप ठीक हैं? *4.* ठीक है, तो यह क्या है? *5.* तो क्या मैं ऐसा कर सकता हूँ? *6.* मैं आप से बात कर रहा हूँ। *7.* ठीक है, यह बात है. *8.* एक बात और भी है। *9.* वह बात नहीं कर सकता.

• *1.* So what am I doing? *2.* So are we okay? *3.* So are you okay? *4.* Okay, so what is it? *5.* May I, then? *6.* I'm talking to you. *7.* Okay, that's it. *8.* There is one other thing. *9.* He can't talk.

**[18]** *1.* क्या वह बात कर सकता है? *2.* नहीं, वह बात नहीं है. *3.* और एक बात और है. *4.* हम क्या बात कर रहे हैं? *5.* नहीं, वह बात नहीं थी. *6.* वह बात कर सकता है. *7.* हम बात कर रहे हैं। *8.* क्या बात कर रहे हो? *9.* क्या उसने बात की है?

• *1.* Can he talk? *2.* No, that's not the point. *3.* And there's one more thing. *4.* What are we talking? *5.* No, that wasn't it. *6.* He can talk. *7.* We are talking. *8.* What are talking about? *9.* Has he spoken?

**[19]** *1.* तो हम क्या बात कर रहे हैं? *2.* बात तो कुछ भी नहीं है. *3.* यह कोई नहीं कर सकता। *4.* क्या कोई और भी है? *5.* कोई बात नहीं कोई बात नहीं। *6.* वह कोई भी हो सकता है. *7.* मैं कोई भी हो सकता हूं. *8.* वे क्या कर रहे हैं? *9.* आप यह कर सकते हैं।

• *1.* So what are we talking? *2.* Nothing is the matter. *3.* Nobody can. *4.* Is there anyone else? *5.* Never mind, never mind. *6.* That could be anybody. *7.* I could be anyone. *8.* What are they doing? *9.* You can do it.

**[20]** *1.* क्या तुम कुछ नहीं कर सकते? *2.* नहीं, हम ऐसा नहीं कर सकते. *3.* क्या हम कुछ नहीं कर सकते? *4.* क्या हम बात नहीं कर सकते? *5.* तुम भी हो सकते हो। *6.* तो हम कुछ नहीं कर सकते?
● *1.* Can't you do anything? *2.* No, we can't do that. *3.* Is there nothing we can do? *4.* Can't we talk? *5.* You might as well. *6.* So there's nothing we can do?

**[21]** *1.* नहीं वे ऐसा नहीं कर सकते। *2.* क्या यह मेरे लिए है? *3.* वह मेरे में से एक है. *4.* तुम मेरे लिए कुछ भी नहीं हो. *5.* आप मेरे लिए कुछ नहीं कर सकते. *6.* आप मेरे लिए कुछ कर सकते हैं।
● *1.* No, they cannot. *2.* Is it for me? *3.* He's one of mine. *4.* You're nothing to me. *5.* There's nothing you can do for me. *6.* There's something you can do for me.

**[22]** *1.* मेरे पास कुछ नहीं है. *2.* क्या मैं पास हो गया? *3.* आप पास हो सकते हैं. *4.* क्या मैं पास हो सकता हूँ? *5.* क्या वह पास हो गया? *6.* क्या आप को कुछ चाहिए? *7.* यह मुझे दिया गया था. *8.* क्या उसने तुम्हें कुछ दिया? *9.* मैंने उसे ठीक कर दिया.
● *1.* I've got nothing. *2.* Did I pass? *3.* You may pass. *4.* Can I pass? *5.* Did he pass? *6.* Do you want anything? *7.* It was given to me. *8.* Did he give you anything? *9.* I fixed him.

**[23]** *1.* मैंने तुम्हें कुछ नहीं दिया. *2.* तुम बहुत अच्छा कर रहे हो। *3.* ठीक है वह अच्छा है। *4.* क्या यह अच्छा नहीं है? *5.* नहीं, यह बहुत अच्छा है. *6.* यह अच्छा नहीं हो सकता. *7.* मैं अच्छा हूँ, मैं अच्छा हूँ. *8.* ठीक है, यह बहुत अच्छा है. *9.* वह अच्छा है, वह अच्छा है।
● *1.* I gave you nothing. *2.* You're doing great. *3.* Okay, that's good. *4.* Isn't this nice? *5.* No, it's great. *6.* This can't be good. *7.* I'm good, I'm good. *8.* Okay, that's great. *9.* That's good, that's good.

**[24]** *1.* अच्छा, मैं क्या कर सकता हूँ? *2.* ठीक है, यह अच्छा है। *3.* वह अच्छा कर रहा है. *4.* नहीं, नहीं, मैं अच्छा हूँ. *5.* क्या वह कोई अच्छा है? *6.* नहीं, यह अच्छा नहीं है. *7.* ठीक है, मैं अच्छा हूँ. *8.* यह मेरे लिए अच्छा है। *9.* अच्छा, आप क्या कर सकते हैं?
● *1.* Well, what can I do? *2.* All right, that's good. *3.* He's doing well. *4.* No, no, I'm good. *5.* Is he any good? *6.* No, that's no good. *7.* Okay, I'm good. *8.* It's good for me. *9.* Well, what can you do?

**[25]** *1.* और यह बहुत अच्छा था. *2.* मैं बहुत अच्छा नहीं हूं। *3.* और यह बहुत

अच्छा है. *4.* क्या वह अच्छा नहीं था? *5.* यह अच्छा है, यह अच्छा है. *6.* अच्छा, आप कर सकते हैं। *7.* अच्छा, क्या यह अच्छा नहीं है? *8.* वह मेरे लिए अच्छा था. *9.* नहीं, नहीं, नहीं, मैं अच्छा हूँ।
• *1.* And it was great. *2.* I'm not very good. *3.* And it's great. *4.* Wasn't that good? *5.* It's good, it's good. *6.* Well, you can. *7.* Well, isn't that nice? *8.* He was nice to me. *9.* No, no, no, I'm good.

**[26]** *1.* नहीं, नहीं, यह अच्छा है. *2.* अच्छा, क्या हो रहा है? *3.* क्या वह अच्छा नहीं है? *4.* यह अच्छा हो सकता है. *5.* क्या वह कोई अच्छा था? *6.* यह बहुत अच्छा नहीं है. *7.* नहीं, नहीं, यह बहुत अच्छा है. *8.* नहीं, मैं अच्छा हूँ, मैं अच्छा हूँ। *9.* अच्छा यह कुछ नहीं है।
• *1.* No, no, it's cool. *2.* Well, what's happening? *3.* Isn't he good? *4.* That might be nice. *5.* Was he any good? *6.* This is so not good. *7.* No, no, it's great. *8.* No, I'm good, I'm good. *9.* Well, that's nothing.

**[27]** *1.* यह बहुत अच्छा नहीं था. *2.* अच्छा, क्या मैं कुछ कर सकता हूँ? *3.* यह अच्छा है, बहुत अच्छा है. *4.* वह मेरे लिए बहुत अच्छा रहा है. *5.* मैं अच्छा कर रहा हूँ. *6.* यह बहुत, बहुत अच्छा है.
• *1.* It wasn't very good. *2.* Well, is there anything I can do? *3.* That's good, very good. *4.* He's been very good to me. *5.* I'm doin' good. *6.* It's very, very nice.

**[28]** *1.* क्या यह कोई अच्छा है? *2.* अच्छा, आप हो सकते हैं। *3.* वह बहुत अच्छा नहीं था. *4.* अच्छा, क्या आप कर सकते हैं? *5.* अच्छा, आप और क्या कर सकते हैं? *6.* अच्छा, क्या मैं कर सकता हूँ?
• *1.* Is this any good? *2.* Well, you could be. *3.* That was not very nice. *4.* Well, can you? *5.* Well, what else can you do? *6.* Well, may I?

**[29]** *1.* अच्छा, क्या वह ठीक है? *2.* और यह बहुत अच्छा रहा. *3.* क्या मैं अच्छा नहीं हूँ? *4.* अच्छा, क्या कुछ और भी है? *5.* क्या यह अच्छा नहीं होगा? *6.* मेरे पास एक और होगा. *7.* मेरे पास कुछ और होगा. *8.* मेरे पास भी एक होगा. *9.* मेरे पास भी कुछ होगा.
• *1.* Well, is she okay? *2.* And it's been great. *3.* Aren't I nice? *4.* Well, is there anything else? *5.* Wouldn't that be nice? *6.* I'll have another. *7.* I'll have some more. *8.* I'll have one, too. *9.* I'll have some too.

**[30]** *1.* आपको कुछ तो चाहिए होगा. *2.* मैं अब ऐसा नहीं कर सकता. *3.* अब तुम्हें और क्या चाहिए? *4.* अब आप बात कर रहे हैं। *5.* अब बहुत हो गया है। *6.* अब हम बात कर रहे हैं। *7.* अब तुम कर सकते हो। *8.* अब आप और हम हैं।

264

*9.* अब आप क्या कर रहे हैं?

• *1.* You must want something. *2.* I can't do this anymore. *3.* What more do you want? *4.* Now you're talking. *5.* Enough is enough. *6.* Now we're talking. *7.* Now you do. *8.* It's you and me. *9.* Now what are you doing?

**[31]** *1.* अब उसने क्या किया है? *2.* अब हम बात कर सकते हैं। *3.* अब क्या हो रहा है? *4.* मेरे पास वह अब भी है। *5.* अब वे क्या कर रहे है? *6.* क्या अब आप ठीक हैं? *7.* मैं अब भी मैं हूं. *8.* अब और नहीं, तुम नहीं हो. *9.* यह अब हो रहा है.

• *1.* What's he done now? *2.* Now we can talk. *3.* What's going on now? *4.* I still have it. *5.* What are they doing now? *6.* Are you all right now? *7.* I'm still me. *8.* Not anymore, you're not. *9.* It's happening now.

**[32]** *1.* अब और कुछ नहीं है. *2.* क्या अब हम बात कर सकते हैं? *3.* वह अब क्या कर रहा है? *4.* अब आप कर सकते हैं। *5.* मेरे लिए अब बहुत हो गया है। *6.* और अब आप क्या कर रहे हो? *7.* तुम अब भी तुम हो. *8.* अब यह हो गया है. *9.* तो आप अब क्या कर रहे हैं?

• *1.* There's no more. *2.* Can we talk now? *3.* What is he doing now? *4.* Now you can. *5.* I have had enough. *6.* And what are you doing now? *7.* You're still you. *8.* Now it's done. *9.* So what are you doing now?

**[33]** *1.* और अब मेरे पास है. *2.* अब, क्या कुछ और है? *3.* अब यह मेरे पास है. *4.* वे अब यह कर रहे हैं. *5.* अब तुम मेरे पास हो. *6.* मुझे अब भी भी है। *7.* अब हम क्या कर सकते हैं? *8.* तुम अब क्या कर रहे हो? *9.* अब वह क्या कर रहा है?

• *1.* And now I have. *2.* Now, is there anything else? *3.* Now I have it. *4.* They're doing it now. *5.* Now I have you. *6.* I still have. *7.* What can we do now? *8.* What're you doing now? *9.* What the hell is he doing now?

**[34]** *1.* हम अब भी इसे कर सकते हैं। *2.* और मैं अब भी हूं. *3.* अब वे मेरे पास नहीं हैं. *4.* क्या वह अब ठीक है? *5.* अब आप बात कर सकते हैं. *6.* मेरे पास अब कुछ भी नहीं है. *7.* अब तुम्हें क्या हो गया है? *8.* अब कुछ भी नहीं है. *9.* और अब आप क्या हैं?

• *1.* We can still do it. *2.* And I still am. *3.* I don't have them anymore. *4.* Is he okay now? *5.* You can talk now. *6.* I have nothing now. *7.* What's wrong with you now? *8.* Now there's nothing. *9.* And what are you now?

**[35]** *1.* अब यह क्या कर रहा है? *2.* अब तुम यह कर सकते हो। *3.* क्या अब

आप कर सकते हैं? *4.* उसने अब क्या किया है? *5.* अब आप यह कर रहे हैं. *6.* अब हम कर सकते हैं. *7.* वे क्या कर रहे थे? *8.* हम कुछ नहीं कर सकते थे। *9.* नहीं, यह तुम नहीं थे.

● *1.* What's it doing now? *2.* You can now. *3.* Can you do it now? *4.* What's she done now? *5.* You're doing it now. *6.* Now we can. *7.* What were they? *8.* There was nothing we could do. *9.* No, it wasn't you.

[36] *1.* क्या मुझे ऐसा करना चाहिए? *2.* मैं बहुत कुछ करना है। *3.* आपको इसे ठीक करना होगा. *4.* तुम्हें मेरे लिए यह करना होगा. *5.* नहीं, आपको यह करना होगा. *6.* आप के साथ क्या है?

● *1.* Should I? *2.* I have a lot to do. *3.* You need to fix this. *4.* You gotta do this for me. *5.* No, you have to do it. *6.* What's up with you?

[37] *1.* तुम मेरे साथ ऐसा नहीं कर सकते! *2.* अब तुम मेरे साथ हो. *3.* हम अब साथ नहीं हैं. *4.* उसने मेरे साथ ऐसा किया. *5.* हम यह एक साथ कर रहे हैं. *6.* तुम मेरे साथ क्या कर रहे हो?

● *1.* You can't do this to me! *2.* You're with me now. *3.* We're not together anymore. *4.* She did this to me. *5.* We're doing this together. *6.* What are you doing with me?

[38] *1.* मेरे साथ कोई बात नहीं है. *2.* वह मेरे साथ नहीं था. *3.* मेरे साथ ऐसा नहीं हो रहा है. *4.* तुम मेरे साथ ऐसा कर रहे हो. *5.* उन्होंने मेरे साथ कुछ किया. *6.* हम इसे एक साथ कर रहे हैं.

● *1.* There's nothing the matter with me. *2.* He wasn't with me. *3.* This isn't happening to me. *4.* You're doing this to me. *5.* They did something to me. *6.* We're doing it together.

[39] *1.* क्या वे अब भी साथ हैं? *2.* उसने मेरे साथ ऐसा नहीं किया. *3.* वह मेरे साथ ऐसा नहीं कर सकता. *4.* बात करने को कुछ नहीं. *5.* आप से बात करने के लिए। *6.* ऐसा करने के लिए बहुत कुछ है।

● *1.* Are they still together? *2.* He didn't do this to me. *3.* He can't do this to me. *4.* Nothing to talk about. *5.* To talk to you. *6.* There's a lot to do.

[40] *1.* बात करने के लिए और क्या है? *2.* मुझे कोई बात करने के लिए चाहिए। *3.* वह यहाँ क्या कर रहा है? *4.* तुम यहाँ के नहीं हो. *5.* ठीक है, यह यहाँ है। *6.* यहाँ कुछ भी नहीं है.

● *1.* What else is there to talk about? *2.* I need someone to talk to. *3.* What's he doing here? *4.* You don't belong here. *5.* Okay, here it is. *6.* There's nothing in here.

[41] *1.* मैं यहाँ हूँ, मैं यहाँ हूँ. *2.* ठीक है, मैं यहाँ हूँ. *3.* ठीक है, हम यहाँ हैं। *4.* तुम यहाँ मेरे साथ हो. *5.* अच्छा, अब आप यहाँ हैं। *6.* यहाँ कोई और नहीं है. *7.* और अब आप यहाँ हैं. *8.* यहाँ बहुत कुछ करने को है। *9.* मुझे यहाँ क्या करना होगा?

● *1.* I'm here, I'm here. *2.* Okay, I'm here. *3.* Okay, here we are. *4.* You're here with me. *5.* Well, you're here now. *6.* There's no one else here. *7.* And now you're here. *8.* There's so much to do. *9.* What am I supposed to do here?

[42] *1.* यह यहाँ बहुत अच्छा है. *2.* आप यहाँ से नहीं हैं. *3.* मैं यहाँ का नहीं हूँ! *4.* वे मेरे लिए यहाँ हैं. *5.* अच्छा है कि आप यहाँ हैं. *6.* यहाँ यह है, यहाँ यह है. *7.* यह अच्छा है कि आप यहाँ हैं. *8.* ठीक है, यहाँ कुछ नहीं होगा। *9.* आप यहाँ नहीं हो सकते!

● *1.* It's so nice here. *2.* You're not from around here. *3.* I don't belong here! *4.* They're here for me. *5.* Good that you're here. *6.* Here it is, here it is. *7.* It's good you're here. *8.* All right, here goes nothing. *9.* You can't be here!

[43] *1.* क्या आप भी यहाँ हैं? *2.* यहाँ और भी बहुत कुछ है. *3.* यहाँ पर और भी बहुत कुछ है. *4.* यहाँ कुछ ठीक नहीं है. *5.* नहीं, मैं यहाँ अच्छा हूँ. *6.* मैं यहाँ हूँ, ठीक है? *7.* तुम यहाँ भी नहीं हो. *8.* मेरे पास वे यहाँ हैं। *9.* नहीं, मैं यहाँ ठीक हूँ।

● *1.* Are you here too? *2.* Here's more. *3.* There's more over here. *4.* Something isn't right here. *5.* No, I'm good here. *6.* I'm here, okay? *7.* You're not even here. *8.* I have them here. *9.* No, I'm fine here.

[44] *1.* आप यहाँ के नहीं हैं! *2.* ठीक है, यहाँ एक है। *3.* मैं यहाँ हूँ, यह ठीक है. *4.* ठीक है, वे यहाँ हैं। *5.* क्या वे अब यहाँ हैं? *6.* यह यहाँ अच्छा नहीं है. *7.* मैं भी ऐसा ही था. *8.* तुम्हें यह करना ही है। *9.* आप ऐसा कर ही नहीं सकते।

● *1.* You do not belong here! *2.* Okay, here's one. *3.* I'm here, it's okay. *4.* Okay, they're here. *5.* Are they here now? *6.* It's no good here. *7.* So was I. *8.* You have to do this. *9.* You cannot do this.

[45] *1.* वह तो बहुत ही अच्छा था। *2.* वह तो अच्छा ही होगा. *3.* कुछ और ही बात थी. *4.* यह बहुत ही अच्छा है। *5.* तो यह आप ही हैं. *6.* तुम्हें यह करना ही होगा. *7.* यह एक ही बात है. *8.* नहीं, वह आप ही थे. *9.* आपको कुछ तो करना ही होगा.

● *1.* That was so good. *2.* That must be nice. *3.* There was something else. *4.* It's good enough. *5.* So it is you. *6.* You got to do it. *7.* It amounts to the same thing. *8.* No, that was you. *9.*

You must do something.

**[46]** *1.* यह तो करना ही होगा. *2.* मुझे यह करना ही होगा. *3.* यह हम ही हो सकते थे. *4.* तुम्हें कुछ करना ही होगा! *5.* वह मैं ही हो सकता हूं. *6.* मुझे भी ऐसा ही लगता है। *7.* वह बहुत अच्छा लगता है। *8.* क्या आपको वह ठीक लगता है? *9.* क्या यह अच्छा लगता है?
● *1.* It's got to be done. *2.* I've got to do it. *3.* It could have been us. *4.* You must do something! *5.* That could be me. *6.* I think so. *7.* That sounds great. *8.* Are you okay with that? *9.* Does that sound good?

**[47]** *1.* तुम्हें लगता है मैंने यह किया? *2.* यह बहुत अच्छा लगता है। *3.* मुझे नहीं लगता मैंने किया. *4.* आपको क्या लगता है क्या होगा? *5.* नहीं, मुझे नहीं लगता कि मैं हूं. *6.* क्या आपको लगता है मैं हूं?
● *1.* You think I did it? *2.* It feels great. *3.* I don't think I did. *4.* What do you think will happen? *5.* No, I don't think I am. *6.* Do you think I am?

**[48]** *1.* तुम्हें क्या लगता है तुम क्या हो? *2.* आपको क्या लगता है मैंने क्या किया? *3.* मुझे बहुत अच्छा लगता हैं। *4.* तुम्हें लगता है वह ठीक है? *5.* तुम्हें लगता है कि यह वह है? *6.* तुम्हें लगता है मैं हूँ?
● *1.* What do you think you are? *2.* What do you think I did? *3.* Sounds pretty good to me. *4.* You think he's okay? *5.* You think it's him? *6.* You think I am?

**[49]** *1.* मुझे नहीं लगता कि वे हैं. *2.* यह आप पर अच्छा लगता है. *3.* आपको क्या लगता है वह क्या था? *4.* क्या यह अच्छा नहीं लगता? *5.* क्या आपको लगता है वह ठीक है? *6.* तुम्हें लगता है कि यह मैं था?
● *1.* I don't think they are. *2.* It suits you well. *3.* What do you think that was? *4.* Doesn't that sound nice? *5.* Do you think she's okay? *6.* You think it was me?

**[50]** *1.* नहीं, यह बहुत अच्छा लगता है. *2.* तुम्हें लगता है मैं कर सकता हूँ? *3.* यह बहुत अच्छा नहीं लगता. *4.* क्या आपको लगता है यह अच्छा है? *5.* तुम्हें लगता है मैंने किया? *6.* ठीक है, यह अच्छा लगता है।
● *1.* No, that sounds great. *2.* You think I can? *3.* That doesn't sound too good. *4.* You think it's good? *5.* You think I did? *6.* Okay, that sounds good.

**[51]** *1.* नहीं, मुझे नहीं लगता कि आप हैं. *2.* ठीक है, अच्छा लगता है। *3.* नहीं, नहीं, मुझे नहीं लगता. *4.* मुझे नहीं लगता कि वह मैं था. *5.* यह क्या है, क्या आपको लगता है? *6.* तुम्हें यह अच्छा लगता था.
● *1.* No, I don't think you are. *2.* All right, sounds good. *3.* No,

no, I guess not. *4.* I don't think that was me. *5.* What is it, do you think? *6.* You used to like it.

**[52]** *1.* यह आप पर बहुत अच्छा लगता है. *2.* तुम्हें यह अच्छा लगता है? *3.* नहीं, यह अच्छा लगता है. *4.* क्या आपको लगता है आपको करना चाहिए? *5.* मुझे नहीं लगता कि वह थी. *6.* और क्या आपको पता है?
● *1.* It suits you very well. *2.* You feel good about that? *3.* No, it feels good. *4.* Do you think you should? *5.* I don't think she was. *6.* And you know what?

**[53]** *1.* तुम्हें पता है कि मैंने किया। *2.* मुझे लगता है तुम्हें पता है। *3.* मुझे पता है तुम कर सकते हो। *4.* मुझे तो पता ही नहीं. *5.* मुझे पता था यह होगा। *6.* तुम्हें पता है, मुझे नहीं पता.
● *1.* You know I do. *2.* I think you know. *3.* I know you can. *4.* I don't even know. *5.* I knew this would happen. *6.* You know, I don't know.

**[54]** *1.* नहीं, मुझे नहीं पता था. *2.* मुझे पता है मेरे पास है. *3.* मुझे अब कुछ नहीं पता. *4.* मैं-मैं-मुझे नहीं पता. *5.* मुझे पता है वह यहाँ है. *6.* नहीं, मुझे पता है, मुझे पता है.
● *1.* No, I didn't know. *2.* I know I have. *3.* I don't know anything anymore. *4.* I-I-I don't know. *5.* I know he's here. *6.* No, I know, I know.

**[55]** *1.* तुम्हें पता है मैं नहीं हूँ. *2.* तुम्हें तो पता ही नहीं. *3.* मुझे पता है तुम यहाँ हो! *4.* मुझे नहीं पता वह क्या था. *5.* तुम्हें पता है मैं कर सकता हूँ. *6.* तुम्हें यह पता नहीं होगा.
● *1.* You know I'm not. *2.* You don't even know. *3.* I know you're here! *4.* I don't know what that was. *5.* You know I can. *6.* You wouldn't know it.

**[56]** *1.* मुझे पता है हम कर सकते हैं. *2.* तुम्हें पता है तुम कर सकते हो. *3.* मुझे नहीं लगता, मुझे पता है. *4.* तुम्हें पता था कि ऐसा होगा. *5.* अच्छा, तुम्हें तो पता ही होगा. *6.* मुझे पता था कि कुछ तो है.
● *1.* I know we can. *2.* You know you can. *3.* I don't think, I know. *4.* You knew this would happen. *5.* Well, you would know. *6.* I knew there was something.

**[57]** *1.* मुझे पता था ऐसा होगा. *2.* तुम्हें यह पता ही नहीं है. *3.* मुझे पता था कि ऐसा कुछ होगा. *4.* तुम्हें पता है, यह बहुत अच्छा है. *5.* मुझे नहीं पता उसने क्या किया. *6.* तुम्हें पता है मेरे पास है.
● *1.* I knew it would happen. *2.* You just don't know it. *3.* I knew something like this would happen. *4.* You know, this is great. *5.*

I don't know what he did. *6.* You know I have.

[58] *1.* मैं- मुझे कुछ पता नहीं. *2.* तुम्हें पता है, यह ठीक है. *3.* मैं- मुझे नहीं पता था. *4.* तुम्हें पता है मैंने नहीं किया. *5.* तुम्हें पता है, यह अच्छा है. *6.* तुम्हें पता है, मैं ठीक हूँ.
• *1.* I-I have no idea. *2.* You know, it's okay. *3.* I-I didn't know. *4.* You know I haven't. *5.* You know, this is good. *6.* You know, I'm fine.

[59] *1.* उसे कुछ पता नहीं था. *2.* मुझे यह तो पता था. *3.* मुझे नहीं पता था कि मैं था. *4.* मुझे पता था कि यह क्या था. *5.* तुम्हें पता है मैं नहीं कर सकता. *6.* तुम्हें पता था कि यह मैं था.
• *1.* She had no idea. *2.* I did know that. *3.* I didn't know I was. *4.* I knew what it was. *5.* You know I cannot. *6.* You knew it was me.

[60] *1.* तुम्हें पता है उसने किया था. *2.* कुछ नहीं, मुझे नहीं पता. *3.* मुझे पता है, मुझे भी नहीं. *4.* मुझे पता था कि यह तुम हो! *5.* अब मुझे कुछ नहीं पता. *6.* तुम्हें पता है वह यहाँ नहीं है.
• *1.* You know he did. *2.* Nothing, I don't know. *3.* I know, me neither. *4.* I knew it was you! *5.* I don't know anything any more. *6.* You know he's not here.

[61] *1.* मुझे यह नहीं पता होगा. *2.* मुझे नहीं पता कि मुझे क्या चाहिए! *3.* नहीं, मुझे यह पता था. *4.* मुझे पता है कुछ हो रहा है. *5.* तुम्हें पता है, तुम्हें पता है. *6.* मुझे नहीं पता था कि ऐसा होगा.
• *1.* I wouldn't know that. *2.* I don't know what I want! *3.* No, I knew that. *4.* I know something's going on. *5.* You know, you know. *6.* I didn't know this would happen.

[62] *1.* तो तुम्हें कुछ तो पता है. *2.* यह ठीक है, तुम्हें पता है? *3.* हो सकता है उसे कुछ पता हो. *4.* अब तो मुझे कुछ भी नहीं पता. *5.* मुझे कुछ भी पता नहीं है. *6.* ठीक है, तुम ऐसा करो.
• *1.* So you do know something. *2.* It's okay, you know? *3.* She may know something. *4.* I don't even know any more. *5.* Nothing I know of. *6.* Okay, you do that.

[63] *1.* अच्छा, अब आप ऐसा करें। *2.* हो सकता है कि आप यह करें। *3.* ठीक है, तो हम क्या करें? *4.* ठीक है, हम क्या करें? *5.* ठीक है, तो अब हम क्या करें? *6.* ठीक है, अब हम क्या करें?
• *1.* Well, now you do. *2.* Maybe you will. *3.* Okay, so what do we do? *4.* Okay, what do we do? *5.* Okay, so what do we do now? *6.* Okay, what do we do now?

**[64]** *1.* हो सकता है हम करें। *2.* यह बस आप और मैं हैं। *3.* हम बस बात कर रहे थे. *4.* मुझे बस पता करना है. *5.* आप बस नहीं कर सकते. *6.* मैंने बस कर ही दिया था। *7.* मैं बस नहीं कर सकता! *8.* बस एक बात और है. *9.* मैं तो बस बात कर रहा हूं.

● *1.* Maybe we will. *2.* It's just you and me. *3.* We were just talking. *4.* I just want to know. *5.* You just can't. *6.* I was so close. *7.* I just can't! *8.* There's just one more thing. *9.* I'm just talking.

**[65]** *1.* क्या यह बस नहीं है? *2.* मैं तो बस बात कर रहा था. *3.* वे बस बात कर रहे हैं. *4.* मैं बस ऐसा कर सकता हूं. *5.* वह बस हो सकता है. *6.* क्या हम बस बात कर सकते हैं? *7.* मैं बस कर सकता हूँ। *8.* बस मेरे लिए यह करो. *9.* यह बस अच्छा हो रहा है.

● *1.* Isn't it just? *2.* I was just talking. *3.* They're just talking. *4.* I just might do that. *5.* He just might. *6.* Can we just talk? *7.* I just can. *8.* Just do this for me. *9.* It's just getting good.

**[66]** *1.* मुझे तो बस करना ही था. *2.* मेरे पास बस यह था। *3.* यह मेरे बस की बात नहीं है. *4.* आपके लिए यह क्या है? *5.* मैं आपके लिए कुछ कर सकता हूँ? *6.* मुझे लगता है आपके पास है।

● *1.* I just had to. *2.* I just had it. *3.* It is not in my power. *4.* What's it to you? *5.* Something I can do for you? *6.* I think you have.

**[67]** *1.* आपके साथ भी ऐसा ही है। *2.* वे आपके साथ क्या कर रहे हैं? *3.* क्या उसने आपके साथ कुछ किया? *4.* आपके पास एक हो सकता है. *5.* मैं आपके लिए वह कर सकता हूं. *6.* और आपके साथ भी ऐसा ही है.

● *1.* So is yours. *2.* What are they doing to you? *3.* Did he do something to you? *4.* You can have one. *5.* I can do that for you. *6.* And so have you.

**[68]** *1.* नहीं, आपके पास नहीं होगा. *2.* मुझे आपके साथ क्या करना चाहिए? *3.* क्या उन्होंने आपके साथ ऐसा किया? *4.* आपके पास एक भी नहीं है? *5.* आपके पास कुछ भी नहीं है. *6.* वह आपके पास हो सकता है.

● *1.* No, you wouldn't have. *2.* What am I supposed to do with you? *3.* Did they do this to you? *4.* You don't have one? *5.* You don't have anything. *6.* You can have that.

**[69]** *1.* क्या उसने आपके साथ ऐसा किया? *2.* क्या आपके पास कुछ नहीं होगा? *3.* आपके पास है, है आपके पास? *4.* आपके पास यह नहीं हो सकता! *5.* आपके पास कुछ भी हो सकता है. *6.* उन्होंने आपके साथ कुछ नहीं किया है.

● *1.* Did he do that to you? *2.* Won't you have some? *3.* You have, have you? *4.* You can't have it! *5.* You can have anything.

*6.* They've done nothing to you.

**[70]** *1.* आपके पास कुछ हो सकता है. *2.* आपके पास भी हो सकता है. *3.* उसने आपके साथ ऐसा किया? *4.* क्या उन्होंने आपके साथ कुछ किया? *5.* उन्होंने आपके साथ ऐसा किया? *6.* आपने मेरे साथ क्या किया?
● *1.* You can have some. *2.* You might as well have. *3.* He did this to you? *4.* Did they do something to you? *5.* They did that to you? *6.* What did you do to me?

**[71]** *1.* आपने इसे ठीक कर दिया? *2.* मुझे लगता है आपने यह किया. *3.* आपने मुझे ठीक कर दिया. *4.* मुझे पता है आपने नहीं किया. *5.* तुम क्या करने जा रहे हो? *6.* मैं आप के साथ जा रहा हूं।
● *1.* You fixed it? *2.* I think you did it. *3.* You healed me. *4.* I know you haven't. *5.* What are you gonna do? *6.* I'm going with you.

**[72]** *1.* आप अब जा सकते हैं। *2.* क्या मैं जा सकता हूँ? *3.* क्या अब हम जा सकते हैं? *4.* क्या हम जा सकते हैं? *5.* मैं बस जा रहा था. *6.* और क्या किया जा सकता है? *7.* हम अब जा रहे हैं. *8.* मैं नहीं जा रहा हूँ! *9.* यह यहाँ जा रहा है।
● *1.* You can go now. *2.* Can I go? *3.* Can we go now? *4.* Can we go? *5.* I was just leaving. *6.* What else can I do? *7.* We're leaving now. *8.* I'm not going! *9.* Here it goes.

**[73]** *1.* मैं अब जा रहा हूँ. *2.* मैं करने जा रहा था। *3.* हम बस जा रहे थे. *4.* हम अब जा सकते हैं. *5.* क्या मैं अब जा सकता हूँ? *6.* ठीक है, मैं जा रहा हूँ। *7.* आप नहीं जा रहे हैं. *8.* मैं ऐसा करने जा रहा हूं। *9.* क्या हम बस जा सकते हैं?
● *1.* I'm gonna go now. *2.* I was going to. *3.* We were just leaving. *4.* We can go now. *5.* May I go now? *6.* All right, I'm going. *7.* You're not leaving. *8.* I'm going to do it. *9.* Can we just go?

**[74]** *1.* मैं बस जा रहा हूं. *2.* अच्छा मैं जा रहा हूँ। *3.* क्या किया जा सकता है? *4.* अब हम जा सकते हैं. *5.* आप तो नहीं जा रहे हैं? *6.* ठीक है, आप जा सकते हैं. *7.* वह बस जा रहा था. *8.* मैं अब जा रहा हूं। *9.* तो मैं जा रहा हूँ.
● *1.* I'm just leaving. *2.* OK, I'm going. *3.* What can be done? *4.* Now we can go. *5.* You're not leaving, are you? *6.* Okay, you can go. *7.* He was just leaving. *8.* I'll be going now. *9.* So I'm gonna go.

**[75]** *1.* नहीं, मैं नहीं जा रहा हूँ. *2.* हम साथ जा सकते थे. *3.* नहीं, मैं जा रहा हूँ. *4.* हम साथ जा सकते हैं. *5.* मैं नहीं जा रहा हूं. *6.* नहीं, आप जा सकते हैं. *7.* अब आप जा सकते हैं. *8.* कुछ भी नहीं किया जा सकता है। *9.* ठीक है, हम

272

जा रहे हैं.

● *1.* No, I'm not leaving. *2.* We could go together. *3.* No, I'm going. *4.* We can go together. *5.* I am not leaving. *6.* No, you can go. *7.* You may leave now. *8.* Nothing can be done. *9.* Okay, we're going.

**[76]** *1.* कुछ किया जा सकता था। *2.* अब आप जा रहे हैं? *3.* अब क्या हम जा सकते हैं? *4.* क्या हम अब जा सकते हैं? *5.* मैं इसे ठीक करने जा रहा हूं. *6.* तो मैं जा सकता हूँ? *7.* वह नहीं जा रहा है. *8.* क्या आप बस जा सकते हैं? *9.* हम नहीं जा रहे हैं.

● *1.* Something had to be done. *2.* You're leaving now? *3.* Now can we go? *4.* Can we leave now? *5.* I'm going to fix it. *6.* So I can go? *7.* He's not going to. *8.* Can you just go? *9.* We're not going to.

**[77]** *1.* क्या मैं जा रहा हूं? *2.* तो आप जा रहे हैं? *3.* वह अब जा रहा है. *4.* क्या अब आप जा सकते हैं? *5.* बस पास से जा रहा। *6.* मुझे लगता है मैं जा रहा हूँ. *7.* मैं जा रहा हूँ, ठीक है? *8.* मैं साथ जा रहा हूँ. *9.* यह नहीं किया जा सकता.

● *1.* Am I going? *2.* So you're going? *3.* He's leaving now. *4.* Can you go now? *5.* Just passing by. *6.* I guess I'll be going. *7.* I'm gonna go, okay? *8.* I'm going with. *9.* It cannot be done.

**[78]** *1.* क्या मैं भी जा सकता हूँ? *2.* वह यह करने जा रहा है. *3.* मैं बस जा रहा हूँ. *4.* हम बस जा रहे हैं. *5.* क्या यह किया जा सकता है? *6.* तो आप जा सकते हैं. *7.* यह किया जा रहा है. *8.* और मैं नहीं जा रहा हूँ. *9.* अब क्या मैं जा सकता हूँ?

● *1.* Can I go too? *2.* He's going to do it. *3.* I'm just going. *4.* We're just leaving. *5.* Can it be done? *6.* So you can go. *7.* It's being done. *8.* And I'm not going to. *9.* Now can I go?

**[79]** *1.* मैं यह करने जा रहा हूं. *2.* वे नहीं जा रहे हैं. *3.* यह किया जा सकता है. *4.* नहीं, मैं तो बस जा रहा था. *5.* क्या कुछ नहीं किया जा सकता? *6.* ठीक है, अब आप जा सकते हैं।

● *1.* I'm going to do this. *2.* They're not leaving. *3.* It could be done. *4.* No, I was just leaving. *5.* Can nothing be done? *6.* All right, you can go now.

**[80]** *1.* क्या यह जा रहा है? *2.* वह किया जा रहा है। *3.* क्या ऐसा किया जा सकता है? *4.* ठीक है, अब हम जा सकते हैं। *5.* बस, मैं जा रहा हूं। *6.* वे बस जा रहे थे. *7.* मैं कुछ नहीं करने जा रहा हूं. *8.* नहीं, आप नहीं जा सकते. *9.* क्या आप जा सकते हैं?

● *1.* Is it going? *2.* He seems to be. *3.* Can that be done? *4.*

Okay, we can go now. *5.* That's it, I'm leaving. *6.* They were just leaving. *7.* I'm not going to do anything. *8.* No, you can't leave. *9.* Could you leave?

**[81]** *1.* मुझे लगता है वे जा रहे हैं. *2.* वे अब जा रहे हैं. *3.* तो क्या हम जा सकते हैं? *4.* ठीक है, मैं अब जा रहा हूँ. *5.* हम तो जा ही रहे थे. *6.* मुझे लगता है, मैं ऐसा करता हूं।
* *1.* I think they're leaving. *2.* They're leaving now. *3.* So can we go? *4.* Okay, I'm going now. *5.* We were just going. *6.* I think I do.

**[82]** *1.* मैं यह किया करता था। *2.* यह मेरे साथ करता है. *3.* नहीं, नहीं, मैं नहीं करता. *4.* और वह क्या करता है? *5.* तो वह क्या करता है? *6.* मैं करता हूँ, क्या मैं? *7.* और अब मैं करता हूँ. *8.* नहीं, नहीं, मैं करता हूँ। *9.* तुम्हें पता है वह क्या करता है?
* *1.* I used to. *2.* It does to me. *3.* No, no, I don't. *4.* And what does he do? *5.* So what does he do? *6.* I do, do I? *7.* And now I do. *8.* No, no, I do. *9.* You know what he does?

**[83]** *1.* क्या वह बात करता है? *2.* वह अब भी करता है. *3.* यह मेरे लिए करता है. *4.* नहीं, मैं-मैं नहीं करता. *5.* वह करता है, करता है? *6.* मैं यहाँ क्या करता हूँ? *7.* अच्छा, यह क्या करता है? *8.* वह और क्या करता है? *9.* यह मेरे लिए कुछ करता है.
* *1.* Does he talk? *2.* He still does. *3.* It does for me. *4.* No, I-I don't. *5.* He does, does he? *6.* What do I do here? *7.* Well, what does it do? *8.* What else does he do? *9.* It does something to me.

# Difficulty Level: 5

**[1]** *1.* क्या हो रहा है क्या हो रहा है? *2.* आप क्या हैं-- आप क्या कर रहे हैं? *3.* क्या मैं इसे ठीक से कर रहा हूं? *4.* नहीं, नहीं, यह ठीक है, यह ठीक है। *5.* यह कुछ भी नहीं है, यह कुछ भी नहीं है. *6.* नहीं तो यह क्या बात कर रहे है?
* *1.* What's up, what's up? *2.* What are you-- what are you doing? *3.* Am I doing it right? *4.* No, no, it's okay, it's okay. *5.* It's nothing, it's nothing. *6.* Then what are you talking about?

**[2]** *1.* क्या आप कुछ भी ठीक से नहीं कर सकते? *2.* आप यह कर सकते हैं, आप यह कर सकते हैं. *3.* क्या आप मेरे लिए कुछ कर सकते हैं? *4.* यह बहुत अच्छा है, यह बहुत अच्छा है। *5.* आप बहुत अच्छा कर रहे हैं, ठीक है? *6.* ठीक है, आप बहुत अच्छा कर रहे हैं।
* *1.* Can't you do anything right? *2.* You can do it, you can do it.

*3.* Can you do something for me? *4.* That's great, that's great.
*5.* You're doing great, okay? *6.* All right, you're doing great.

**[3]** *1.* ठीक है, यह अच्छा है, यह अच्छा है। *2.* अच्छा, क्या आप इसे ठीक कर सकते हैं? *3.* क्या हम अब भी ऐसा कर रहे हैं? *4.* नहीं, तुम मेरे साथ ऐसा नहीं कर सकते! *5.* हम एक साथ कुछ भी कर सकते हैं। *6.* मेरे पास करने के लिए बहुत कुछ है।

- *1.* Okay, that's good, that's good. *2.* Well, can you fix it?
*3.* Are we still doing this? *4.* No, you can't do this to me! *5.* Together, we can do anything. *6.* I got stuff to do.

**[4]** *1.* तुम क्या हो--तुम यहाँ क्या कर रहे हो? *2.* मैं यहाँ से नहीं हूँ, क्या मैं हूँ? *3.* यहाँ करने के लिए और कुछ नहीं है। *4.* यहाँ करने के लिए कुछ भी नहीं है। *5.* क्या यह ठीक है कि मैं यहाँ हूँ? *6.* आपको क्या लगता है कि आप क्या कर रहे हैं?

- *1.* What are you-- what are you doing here? *2.* I'm not from here, am I? *3.* There's nothing more to do here. *4.* There's nothing to do around here. *5.* Is it okay that I'm here? *6.* What do you think you're doing?

**[5]** *1.* मुझे नहीं लगता कि मैं कर सकता हूं. *2.* तुम्हें क्या लगता है मैं क्या कर रहा हूँ? *3.* मुझे लगता है कि यह मेरे पास है। *4.* मुझे नहीं लगता कि मैं अब ऐसा कर सकता हूं. *5.* मुझे नहीं लगता कि उसने ऐसा किया है. *6.* मुझे नहीं लगता कि आपको ऐसा करना चाहिए.

- *1.* I don't think I can. *2.* What do you think I'm doing? *3.* I think I have it. *4.* I don't think I can do this anymore. *5.* I don't think he did it. *6.* I don't think you should.

**[6]** *1.* तुम्हें नहीं लगता कि मैं कर सकता हूँ? *2.* तुम्हें नहीं लगता कि मैं यह कर सकता हूँ? *3.* तुम्हें क्या लगता है मैं यहाँ क्या कर रहा हूँ? *4.* आपको क्या लगता है क्या हो रहा है? *5.* अच्छा, मुझे लगता है आपको ऐसा करना चाहिए। *6.* नहीं, मुझे नहीं लगता कि मैं कर सकता हूँ।

- *1.* You don't think I can? *2.* You don't think I can do it? *3.* What do you think I'm doing here? *4.* What do you think's going on? *5.* Well, I think you should. *6.* No, I don't think I can.

**[7]** *1.* मुझे लगता है कि यह बहुत अच्छा होगा. *2.* तो आपको क्या लगता है मुझे क्या करना चाहिए? *3.* मुझे लगता है कि यह हो गया है. *4.* मुझे नहीं लगता कि मैं यह कर सकता हूं. *5.* मुझे लगता है मैं ऐसा कर सकता हूं. *6.* मुझे लगता है कि यह बहुत अच्छा है।

- *1.* I think that would be great. *2.* So what do you think I should do? *3.* I think it's done. *4.* I just don't think I can do it. *5.* I guess I could do that. *6.* I think this is great.

**[8]** *1.* नहीं, मुझे लगता है आप नहीं कर सकते। *2.* क्या आपको नहीं लगता कि आपको ऐसा करना चाहिए? *3.* और तुम्हें लगता है कि यह मैं था? *4.* मुझे लगता है आपको भी ऐसा करना चाहिए. *5.* तुम्हें लगता है मैं यह नहीं कर सकता? *6.* नहीं, मुझे नहीं लगता कि मेरे पास है।

● *1.* No, I guess you can't. *2.* Don't you think you should? *3.* And you think it was me? *4.* I think you should, too. *5.* You think I can't do it? *6.* No, I don't think I have.

**[9]** *1.* तुम्हें क्या लगता है कि क्या हो रहा है? *2.* मुझे लगता है मेरे पास कुछ हो सकता है. *3.* मुझे लगता है मैं इसे ठीक कर सकता हूं. *4.* मुझे लगता है कि वह मैं ही हूं. *5.* मुझे लगता है कि मैं ऐसा कर सकता हूं. *6.* आपको क्या लगता है यह यहाँ क्या है?

● *1.* What do you think is happening? *2.* I think I might have something. *3.* I think I can fix it. *4.* I think that's me. *5.* I think I can make that happen. *6.* What do you think this is here?

**[10]** *1.* तुम्हें लगता है मैं यह कर सकता हूँ? *2.* आपको क्या लगता है मुझे क्या करना चाहिए? *3.* नहीं, मुझे नहीं लगता कि उसने ऐसा किया। *4.* मुझे लगता है कि वह कुछ कर रहा है। *5.* आपको क्या लगता है आपको क्या करना चाहिए? *6.* मुझे लगता है हम इसे ठीक कर सकते हैं.

● *1.* You think I can do it? *2.* What do you think I ought to do? *3.* No, I don't think he did. *4.* I think he's onto something. *5.* What do you think you should do? *6.* I think we can fix it.

**[11]** *1.* मुझे नहीं लगता कि वह कर सकता है. *2.* क्या तुम्हें लगता है तुम कर सकते हो? *3.* तुम्हें क्या लगता है कि मैंने कुछ किया? *4.* और आपको लगता है कि यह अच्छा है? *5.* मुझे लगता है कि यह आप ही थे. *6.* क्या आपको लगता है मुझे यह करना चाहिए?

● *1.* I don't think he can. *2.* Do you think you could? *3.* What makes you think I did anything? *4.* And you think that's good? *5.* I think it was you. *6.* You think I should do it?

**[12]** *1.* मुझे नहीं लगता कि उन्होंने ऐसा किया है. *2.* नहीं, मुझे लगता है यह बहुत अच्छा है. *3.* अच्छा, आपको क्या लगता है मुझे क्या करना चाहिए? *4.* मुझे लगता है कि वे मेरे पास हैं। *5.* क्या आपको पता है कि यह क्या है? *6.* मुझे पता है तुम क्या कर रहे हो.

● *1.* I don't think they did it. *2.* No, I think it's great. *3.* Well, what do you think I should do? *4.* I think they're on to me. *5.* Do you know what this is? *6.* I know what you're doing.

**[13]** *1.* आप को पता है की यह क्या है? *2.* मुझे पता है कि आप यह कर सकते हैं। *3.* तुम्हें पता है तुम क्या कर रहे हो? *4.* तुम्हें पता है कि यह तुम्हें चाहिए है। *5.* तुम्हें पता नहीं है कि तुम क्या कर रहे हो. *6.* क्या तुम्हें पता है कि मैं क्या हूं।

● *1.* You know what it is? *2.* I know you can do it. *3.* You know what you're doing? *4.* You know you want it. *5.* You have no idea what you're doing. *6.* You know what I am.

[14] *1.* मुझे पता है वे क्या कर रहे हैं। *2.* मुझे पता था कि मैं क्या कर रहा हूं. *3.* ठीक है, ठीक है, तुम्हें पता है क्या? *4.* मुझे ठीक-ठीक पता है कि क्या करना है. *5.* तुम्हें पता था कि तुम क्या कर रहे हो. *6.* मुझे नहीं पता कि मैं क्या कर सकता हूं.
● *1.* I know what they are. *2.* I knew what I was doing. *3.* Okay, well, you know what? *4.* I know exactly what to do. *5.* You knew what you were doing. *6.* I don't know what I can do.

[15] *1.* तुम्हें पता है मैं क्या कर रहा हूं. *2.* मुझे पता है वह क्या कर रहा है. *3.* मुझे नहीं पता कि मैं क्या कर रहा था. *4.* तुम्हें पता है तुम क्या कर सकते हो? *5.* मुझे ठीक-ठीक पता है कि मुझे क्या चाहिए. *6.* मुझे पता है तुम क्या कर रहे थे.
● *1.* You know what I'm doing. *2.* I know what he's doing. *3.* I don't know what I was doing. *4.* You know what you can do? *5.* I know exactly what I want. *6.* I know what you were doing.

[16] *1.* मुझे पता है मैं क्या कर रहा हूं. *2.* मुझे कुछ पता नहीं है कि वह क्या है। *3.* मुझे पता है तुम क्या कर सकते हो. *4.* तुम्हें पता है वे क्या कर रहे हैं? *5.* मुझे नहीं पता तुम क्या कर रहे हो। *6.* मुझे नहीं पता था कि क्या हो रहा है.
● *1.* I know what I'm doin'. *2.* I have no idea what that is. *3.* I know what you can do. *4.* You know what they're doing? *5.* I have no idea what you're saying. *6.* I didn't know what was happening.

[17] *1.* मुझे नहीं पता कि मैं और क्या कर सकता हूं. *2.* मुझे यह भी नहीं पता कि मैंने क्या किया. *3.* उसे यह भी नहीं पता कि मैं यहाँ हूँ. *4.* मुझे पता है कि अब मुझे क्या करना है. *5.* तुम्हें पता है मैं ऐसा नहीं कर सकता! *6.* मुझे नहीं पता था कि आप यहाँ थे।
● *1.* I don't know what else I can do. *2.* I don't even know what I did. *3.* He doesn't even know I'm here. *4.* I know what I have to do now. *5.* You know I can't do that! *6.* I didn't know you were in here.

[18] *1.* और मुझे नहीं पता कि मैं क्या कर रहा हूं. *2.* मुझे नहीं पता था कि वे क्या थे. *3.* मुझे पता था कि हम यह कर सकते हैं. *4.* मुझे ठीक-ठीक पता है कि तुम्हें क्या चाहिए. *5.* उसे कुछ पता नहीं कि वह क्या कर रहा है। *6.* ठीक है, मुझे पता है, मुझे पता है।
● *1.* And I don't know what I'm doing. *2.* I didn't know what they were. *3.* I knew we could do it. *4.* I know exactly what you need.

*5.* He has no idea what he's doing. *6.* Okay, I know, I know.

**[19]** *1.* मुझे पता है कि मेरे लिए क्या अच्छा है. *2.* मुझे पता था कि मैं कर सकता हूं. *3.* तुम्हें पता है मैं क्या कर रहा हूँ? *4.* मुझे ठीक-ठीक पता है कि क्या हो रहा है. *5.* मुझे पता है तुम यहाँ क्या कर रहे हो. *6.* तुम्हें पता है यहाँ क्या हो रहा है.

• *1.* I know what's good for me. *2.* I knew I could. *3.* You know what I'm doing? *4.* I know exactly what is going on. *5.* I know what you're doing here. *6.* You know what's going on here.

**[20]** *1.* मुझे नहीं पता था कि तुम यहाँ थे। *2.* मुझे लगता है मुझे पता है कि तुम्हें क्या चाहिए. *3.* तुम्हें नहीं पता कि क्या हो रहा है? *4.* मुझे पता है वह क्या कर सकता है. *5.* उसे ठीक-ठीक पता होगा कि क्या करना है। *6.* मुझे नहीं पता कि क्या हो सकता था.

• *1.* I didn't know you were down here. *2.* I think I know what you need. *3.* You don't know what's going on? *4.* I know what he can do. *5.* She'll know exactly what to do. *6.* I don't know what could have happened.

**[21]** *1.* तुम्हें पता है, यह कुछ भी नहीं है. *2.* मुझे लगता है मुझे पता है कि क्या करना है. *3.* मुझे नहीं पता कि मैं क्या कर रहा हूं। *4.* ठीक है, मुझे पता है तुम क्या कर रहे हो। *5.* मैं क्या कर रहा था मुझे कुछ पता नहीं था। *6.* तुम्हें पता है मैं यह कर सकता हूं.

• *1.* You know, it's nothing. *2.* I think I know what to do. *3.* I don't know what the hell I'm doing. *4.* Okay, I know what you're doing. *5.* I had no idea what I was doing. *6.* You know I can do this.

**[22]** *1.* मुझे कुछ पता नहीं क्या हो रहा है. *2.* मुझे नहीं पता कि अब क्या करना है. *3.* नहीं, हम तो बस बात कर रहे थे. *4.* क्या मैं आपके लिए कुछ कर सकता हूँ? *5.* मैं यह आपके लिए नहीं कर रहा हूं. *6.* हो सकता है मेरे पास आपके लिए कुछ हो.

• *1.* I have no idea what's happening. *2.* I just don't know what to do now. *3.* No, we were just talking. *4.* Is there anything I can do for you? *5.* I'm not doing it for you. *6.* I might have something for you.

**[23]** *1.* हम आपके लिए कुछ भी कर सकते हैं? *2.* क्या आपके पास करने को कुछ नहीं है? *3.* मुझे लगता है कि यह आपके लिए है. *4.* अब, हम आपके लिए क्या कर सकते हैं? *5.* हम आपके लिए और कुछ भी कर सकते हैं? *6.* मेरे पास आपके लिए कुछ हो सकता है.

• *1.* Anything we can do for you? *2.* Don't you have anything to do? *3.* I think it's for you. *4.* Now, what can we do for you? *5.*

Anything else we can do for you? *6.* I may have something for you.

**[24]** *1.* ठीक है, आपके साथ क्या हो रहा है? *2.* आपने नहीं किया है, क्या आपके पास है? *3.* नहीं, मुझे नहीं लगता कि आपने ऐसा किया होगा। *4.* मुझे नहीं पता कि मैं क्या करने जा रहा हूं। *5.* तुम मेरे साथ क्या करने जा रहे हो? *6.* मैं जा रहा हूँ, मैं जा रहा हूँ.
- *1.* Okay, what's going on with you? *2.* You haven't, have you? *3.* No, I don't suppose you did. *4.* I don't know what I'm gonna do. *5.* What are you going to do to me? *6.* I'm going, I'm going.

**[25]** *1.* तो अब आप क्या करने जा रहे हैं? *2.* हम आपके साथ क्या करने जा रहे हैं? *3.* क्या आप कुछ नहीं करने जा रहे हैं? *4.* अब, यहाँ हम क्या करने जा रहे हैं। *5.* हम जा रहे हैं, हम जा रहे हैं. *6.* तो यहाँ हम क्या करने जा रहे हैं।
- *1.* So what are you going to do now? *2.* What are we going to do with you? *3.* Aren't you going to do something? *4.* Now, here's what we're gonna do. *5.* We're going, we're going. *6.* So here's what we're gonna do.

**[26]** *1.* ठीक है, ठीक है, मैं जा रहा हूँ। *2.* तो, अब हम क्या करने जा रहे हैं? *3.* और अब आप क्या करने जा रहे हैं? *4.* ठीक है, मैं यह करने जा रहा हूँ। *5.* तुम्हें पता है हम क्या करने जा रहे हैं? *6.* हम इसे एक साथ करने जा रहे हैं।
- *1.* Okay, okay, I'm going. *2.* So, what are we gonna do now? *3.* And what are you going to do now? *4.* All right, I'm gonna do it. *5.* You know what we're going to do? *6.* We're gonna do this together.

**[27]** *1.* मैं यह करता हूं, मैं यह करता हूं। *2.* मुझे नहीं लगता कि मैं ऐसा करता हूं। *3.* मुझे नहीं लगता कि वह ऐसा करता है। *4.* तुम्हें क्या लगता है मैं क्या करता हूँ? *5.* तुम्हें क्या लगता है कि मैं क्या करता हूँ? *6.* मुझे लगता है मैं भी ऐसा करता हूं.
- *1.* I do, I do. *2.* I don't think I do. *3.* I don't think he does. *4.* What do you think I do? *5.* What makes you think I do? *6.* I think I do, too.

**[28]** *1.* तो तुम्हें पता है मैं क्या करता हूँ? *2.* मुझे लगता है मैं अब ऐसा करता हूँ। *3.* मुझे नहीं लगता कि हमें ऐसा करना चाहिए. *4.* तो, आपको क्या लगता है हमें क्या करना चाहिए? *5.* क्या आप अपने आप से बात कर रहे हैं? *6.* मैं यह अपने लिए नहीं कर रहा हूं.
- *1.* So you know what I do? *2.* I guess I do now. *3.* I don't think we should do this. *4.* So, what do you think we should do? *5.* Are you talking to yourself? *6.* I'm not doing this for me.

[29] *1.* मुझे लगता है यह काम कर रहा है. *2.* मैं यह काम अपने आप कर सकता हूं. *3.* काम करने के लिए कुछ भी नहीं है. *4.* क्या आप काम पर नहीं जा रहे हैं? *5.* हो सकता है यह काम कर गया हो. *6.* मेरे पास आपके लिए एक और काम है.

• *1.* I think it's working. *2.* I can do this on my own. *3.* There's nothing to work out. *4.* Aren't you going to work? *5.* It might have worked. *6.* I have another job for you.

[30] *1.* आप काम के लिए क्या कर रहे हैं? *2.* मैं यह काम अपने आप करने जा रहा हूं। *3.* तुम्हें पता था कि मैं यहाँ काम करता हूँ। *4.* हाँ, मुझे लगता है मैं कर सकता हूँ। *5.* हाँ, ठीक है, यह काम कर रहा है। *6.* हाँ, मुझे नहीं पता कि यह क्या है।

• *1.* What are you doing for work? *2.* I'm going to do this on my own. *3.* You knew I worked here. *4.* Yes, I think I can. *5.* Yeah, well, it's working. *6.* Yeah, I don't know what it is.

[31] *1.* हाँ, मुझे लगता है उसने ऐसा किया था। *2.* हाँ, हाँ, मुझे पता है, मुझे पता है। *3.* हाँ, ठीक है, मैंने भी ऐसा ही किया। *4.* हम तो बस आपके बारे में बात कर रहे थे. *5.* मैं अपने बारे में बात नहीं कर रहा हूं. *6.* मैं अपने बारे में बात कर रहा था.

• *1.* Yeah, I guess he did. *2.* Yeah, yeah, I know, I know. *3.* Yeah, well, so did I. *4.* We were just talking about you. *5.* I'm not talking about me. *6.* I was talking about me.

[32] *1.* मैं अपने बारे में बात नहीं कर रहा था. *2.* वह मेरे बारे में बात कर रहा है. *3.* मैं अपने बारे में बात कर सकता हूं. *4.* क्या आपके साथ भी ऐसा ही हुआ है? *5.* मुझे यह भी नहीं पता कि क्या हुआ. *6.* मुझे लगता है मुझे पता है क्या हुआ.

• *1.* I wasn't talking about me. *2.* He's talking about me. *3.* I can talk for myself. *4.* Is that what happened to you? *5.* I don't even know what happened. *6.* I think I know what happened.

[33] *1.* मुझे लगता है कि यह बहुत अच्छा हुआ। *2.* मुझे ठीक-ठीक पता है कि क्या हुआ था. *3.* मुझे नहीं पता कि मुझे क्या हुआ है. *4.* तुम्हें पता है मुझे क्या लगता है क्या हुआ? *5.* क्या आप मेरा एक काम कर सकते हैं? *6.* उन्हें क्या लगता है कि वे क्या कर रहे हैं?

• *1.* I think that went very well. *2.* I know exactly what happened. *3.* I don't know what's happened to me. *4.* You know what I think happened? *5.* Can you do me a favor? *6.* What do they think they're doing?

[34] *1.* उन्हें लगता है कि आपने यह किया है. *2.* उन्हें नहीं पता कि क्या हो रहा है. *3.* मैं चाहता हूं कि यह आपके पास हो. *4.* मैं चाहता हूं कि आप मेरे

लिए कुछ करें. 5. आपको क्या लगता है वह क्या चाहता है? 6. मैं चाहता हूं कि तुम मेरे साथ चलो.

- *1.* They think you did it. *2.* They don't know what's going on. *3.* I want you to have it. *4.* I want you to do something for me. *5.* What do you think he wants? *6.* I want you to move in with me.

**[35]** *1.* तुम्हें क्या लगता है मैं क्या चाहता हूँ? *2.* क्या आपको लगता है कि मैं यह करना चाहता हूँ? *3.* मुझे पता है मैं क्या करना चाहता हूं. *4.* मैं चाहता हूं कि आप मेरे लिए काम करें. *5.* मैं आपके बारे में बात करना चाहता हूं. *6.* मुझे ठीक-ठीक पता है कि वह क्या चाहता है।

- *1.* What do you think I want? *2.* You think I want to do this? *3.* I know what I want to do. *4.* I want you to work for me. *5.* I want to talk about you. *6.* I know exactly what he wants.

**[36]** *1.* क्या आपको लगता है मैं यह चाहता हूँ? *2.* मैं चाहता हूं कि आप भी ऐसा ही करें. *3.* मैं चाहता हूं कि आप इसे ठीक करें. *4.* मैं भी नहीं चाहता कि तुम ऐसा करो। *5.* तुम्हें लगता है मैं यह करना चाहता हूँ? *6.* क्या आपको लगता है मैं वह चाहता हूँ?

- *1.* Do you think I want this? *2.* I want you to do the same. *3.* I want you to fix it. *4.* I don't want you to, either. *5.* You think I wanna do this? *6.* Do you think I want that?

**[37]** *1.* मैं आपके लिए भी ऐसा ही करना चाहता हूं. *2.* मुझे यह सब कुछ साथ में पता था. *3.* ऐसा लगता है कि आप सब ठीक कर रहे हैं। *4.* क्या आपको लगता है यह सब ठीक है? *5.* क्या आपको लगता है कि यह सब ठीक है? *6.* मैं यह सब अपने आप से कर सकता हूँ।

- *1.* I want to do the same for you. *2.* I knew it all along. *3.* You seem to be doing all right. *4.* Do you think it's all right? *5.* You think it's all right? *6.* I can do it all by myself.

**[38]** *1.* मुझे लगता है कि अब हम सब ठीक हैं। *2.* मुझे लगता है मेरे पास सब कुछ है. *3.* इस बारे में आप क्या करने जा रहे हैं? *4.* मैं इस बारे में बात नहीं कर रहा हूं। *5.* मैं इस बारे में बात कर रहा हूं. *6.* हाँ, हम इस पर काम कर रहे हैं।

- *1.* I think we're all right now. *2.* I think I have everything. *3.* What are you going to do about it? *4.* That's not what I'm talking about. *5.* I'm talking about this. *6.* Yeah, we're working on it.

**[39]** *1.* हाँ, मैं इस पर काम कर रहा हूँ। *2.* क्या हम इस बारे में बात नहीं कर सकते? *3.* हम इस बारे में बात कर सकते हैं. *4.* मैं इस बारे में अब और बात नहीं कर सकता. *5.* मुझे इस बारे में कुछ भी पता नहीं है. *6.* मैं इस बारे में बात भी नहीं करना चाहता.

- *1.* Yeah, I'm working on it. *2.* Can we not talk about this? *3.*

We can talk about this. *4.* I can't talk about this anymore. *5.* I know nothing of this. *6.* I don't even want to talk about it.

**[40]** *1.* मुझे इस बारे में कुछ नहीं पता था. *2.* मैं इस बारे में बात करना चाहता हूं. *3.* मैं इस पर हूँ, मैं इस पर हूँ. *4.* क्या हम इस पर बात नहीं कर सकते? *5.* क्या हम इस पर काम नहीं कर सकते? *6.* मुझे इस सब के बारे में नहीं पता.
• *1.* I knew nothing about this. *2.* I want to talk about this. *3.* I'm on it, I'm on it. *4.* Can't we talk it over? *5.* Can't we work this out? *6.* I don't know about all this.

**[41]** *1.* हम इस बारे में क्यों बात कर रहे हैं? *2.* और मुझे लगता है मुझे पता है क्यों। *3.* आपको क्या लगता है कि आप यहाँ क्यों हैं? *4.* मुझे इस बारे में क्यों नहीं पता था? *5.* मुझे नहीं पता कि मैंने ऐसा क्यों नहीं किया। *6.* आपको क्या लगता है मैंने ऐसा क्यों किया?
• *1.* Why are we talking about this? *2.* And I think I know why. *3.* Why do you think you're here? *4.* Why didn't I know about this? *5.* I don't know why I didn't. *6.* Why do you think I did that?

**[42]** *1.* क्यों, क्या आपको लगता है मुझे ऐसा करना चाहिए? *2.* मुझे पता है तुम ऐसा क्यों कर रहे हो. *3.* तुम मेरे साथ ऐसा क्यों कर रहे हो? *4.* आपको क्या लगता है उसने ऐसा क्यों किया? *5.* मुझे नहीं पता कि मैंने ऐसा क्यों किया। *6.* तुम्हें लगता है तुम मुझे ले जा सकते हो?
• *1.* Why, do you think I should? *2.* I know why you're doing this. *3.* Why you doing this to me? *4.* Why do you think she did that? *5.* I don't know why I just did that. *6.* You think you can take me?

**[43]** *1.* मैं उसे अपने साथ ले जा रहा हूं. *2.* मैं इसे अपने साथ ले जा रहा हूं. *3.* मैं तुम्हें अपने साथ ले जा रहा हूं. *4.* हम उसे अपने साथ ले जा रहे हैं. *5.* क्या मैं इसे आपके लिए ले जा सकता हूँ? *6.* मैं तुम्हें अपने साथ नहीं ले जा सकता!
• *1.* I'm taking her with me. *2.* I'm taking it with me. *3.* I'm taking you with me. *4.* We're taking him with us. *5.* Can I carry that for you? *6.* I can't take you with me!

**[44]** *1.* मैं चाहता हूं कि तुम मुझे ले जाओ. *2.* आप उसे अपने साथ ले जा सकते हैं. *3.* मुझे नहीं लगता कि मैं इसे ले सकता हूं. *4.* हम इसे अपने साथ ले जा रहे हैं. *5.* आप इसे अपने साथ ले जा सकते हैं. *6.* क्या आप इसे मेरे लिए ले सकते हैं?
• *1.* I want you to take me. *2.* You can take that with you. *3.* I dont think I can take this. *4.* We're taking it with us. *5.* You can take it with you. *6.* Can you grab it for me?

**[45]** *1.* क्या आप इसे यहाँ से ले सकते हैं? *2.* क्या हम कृपया इस बारे में बात

कर सकते हैं? *3.* मुझे नहीं लगता कि आप ऐसा करते हैं. *4.* आप कुछ नहीं के बारे में बात करते हैं. *5.* आपको क्या लगता है हम क्या करते हैं? *6.* हाँ, और आप भी ऐसा ही करते हैं।

● *1.* Can you take it from here? *2.* Can we please talk about this? *3.* I don't think you do. *4.* Thou talk'st of nothing. *5.* What do you think we do? *6.* Yes, and so do you.

**[46]** *1.* आपको क्या लगता है वे क्या चाहते हैं? *2.* आप इस बारे में बात करना चाहते हैं? *3.* क्या आप इस बारे में बात करना चाहते हैं? *4.* क्या आप मेरे लिए काम करना चाहते हैं? *5.* क्या आप एक साथ काम करना चाहते हैं? *6.* आप क्या चाहते हैं कि वे क्या करें?

● *1.* What do you think they want? *2.* You want to talk about this? *3.* Do you want to talk about this? *4.* You want to work for me? *5.* You want to work together? *6.* What do you want them to do?

**[47]** *1.* हम चाहते हैं कि यह आपके पास हो। *2.* आप इस बारे में कुछ करना चाहते हैं? *3.* क्या आप चाहते हैं कि वह ऐसा हो? *4.* क्या मैं आपका कुछ ठीक कर सकता हूँ? *5.* मुझे नहीं लगता कि यह आपका कोई काम है। *6.* आप मेरे साथ ऐसा कैसे कर सकते हैं?

● *1.* We want you to have it. *2.* You want to do something about this? *3.* Do you want him to be? *4.* Can I fix you something? *5.* I don't think that's any of your business. *6.* How could you do this to me?

**[48]** *1.* मुझे पता है यह कैसे काम करता है. *2.* और आप यह कैसे करने जा रहे हैं? *3.* यह सब मुझे पता है कि कैसे करना है। *4.* मुझे नहीं पता कि और कुछ कैसे करना है. *5.* तुम्हें कैसे पता कि यह मैं ही था? *6.* यह आपके लिए कैसे काम कर रहा है?

● *1.* I know how it works. *2.* And how are you going to do that? *3.* It's all I know how to do. *4.* I don't know how to do anything else. *5.* How do you know it was me? *6.* How's that working for you?

**[49]** *1.* और मुझे लगता है मुझे पता है कैसे। *2.* मुझे नहीं पता कि मैं यह कैसे करता हूं. *3.* अच्छा, आप ऐसा कैसे करने जा रहे हैं? *4.* मुझे नहीं पता कि ऐसा कैसे हुआ होगा. *5.* मुझे नहीं पता कि यह कैसे करना है। *6.* और हम यह कैसे करने जा रहे हैं?

● *1.* And I think I know how. *2.* I don't know how I do it. *3.* Well, how are you going to do that? *4.* I don't know how this could have happened. *5.* I have no idea how to do that. *6.* And how are we going to do that?

**[50]** *1.* मैं आ रहा हूं, मैं आ रहा हूं. *2.* उन्हें पता था कि हम आ रहे हैं. *3.* मैं आ रहा हूँ, मैं आ रहा हूँ! *4.* मुझे पता था कि वह आ रहा है. *5.* वह आ रहा है, वह आ रहा है. *6.* वे आ रहे हैं, वे आ रहे हैं.

● *1.* I'm coming, I'm coming. *2.* They knew we were coming. *3.* I'm coming, I'm coming! *4.* I knew that was coming. *5.* He's coming, he's coming. *6.* They're coming, they're coming.

**[51]** *1.* यह आ रहा है, यह आ रहा है. *2.* क्या आप कृपया मेरे साथ आ सकते हैं? *3.* उन्हें पता था कि आप आ रहे हैं. *4.* मुझे नहीं पता था कि तुम आ रहे हो. *5.* हाँ, मैं आ रहा हूँ, मैं आ रहा हूँ! *6.* क्या तुम मेरे साथ नहीं आ रहे हो?

● *1.* It's coming, it's coming. *2.* Could you come with me, please? *3.* They knew you were coming. *4.* I didn't know you were coming over. *5.* Yeah, I'm coming, I'm coming. *6.* Aren't you joining me?

**[52]** *1.* मुझे नहीं लगता कि वह आ रहा है. *2.* क्या तुम्हें पता था मैं आ रहा था? *3.* ठीक है, ठीक है, मैं आ रहा हूँ! *4.* क्या उसे पता था कि तुम आ रहे हो? *5.* तुम्हें पता था कि यह आ रहा था. *6.* मुझे उसके बारे में कुछ भी पता नहीं होगा.

● *1.* I don't think he's coming. *2.* Did you know I was coming? *3.* Okay, okay, I'm coming! *4.* Did she know you were coming? *5.* You knew this was coming. *6.* I wouldn't know anything about that.

**[53]** *1.* आप उसके साथ क्या करने जा रहे हैं? *2.* आपको क्या लगता है उसके साथ क्या हुआ? *3.* हम उसके साथ क्या करने जा रहे हैं? *4.* मैं तुम्हें उसके पास ले जा सकता हूं. *5.* आप उसके साथ ऐसा कैसे कर सकते हैं? *6.* हम उसके बारे में क्या करने जा रहे हैं?

● *1.* What are you going to do with him? *2.* What do you think happened to him? *3.* What are we going to do with him? *4.* I can take you to him. *5.* How could you do this to him? *6.* What are we gonna do about her?

**[54]** *1.* क्या आप मुझे उसके पास ले जा सकते हैं? *2.* मैं उसके बारे में बात कर रहा हूं. *3.* मैं उसके साथ क्या करने जा रहा हूँ? *4.* मैं उसके बारे में बात नहीं कर रहा हूं. *5.* अब हम उसके लिए कुछ नहीं कर सकते। *6.* आप उसके बारे में क्या करने जा रहे हैं?

● *1.* Can you take me to him? *2.* I'm talking about him. *3.* What am I going to do with her? *4.* I'm not talking about her. *5.* There's nothing we can do for him now. *6.* What are you going to do about him?

**[55]** *1.* मैं उसके बारे में बात नहीं करना चाहता. *2.* मैं उसके लिए और कुछ

नहीं कर सकता। 3. क्या आप उसके लिए कुछ कर सकते हैं? 4. यह मेरे लिए नहीं है, यह उसके लिए है। 5. हम तो बस उसके बारे में बात कर रहे थे। 6. अब आप उसके लिए कुछ नहीं कर सकते।
● 1. I don't wanna talk about her. 2. There's nothing more I can do for him. 3. Can you do anything for him? 4. It's not for me, it's for him. 5. We were just talking about him. 6. There's nothing you can do for him now.

[56] 1. मैं उसके बारे में बात नहीं कर रहा था। 2. उसके पास आप पर कुछ भी नहीं है। 3. मैं उसके बारे में बात कर रहा था। 4. क्या आप उसके साथ काम कर सकते हैं? 5. और तुम उसके साथ क्या कर रहे हो? 6. आपको पता है कि समय क्या हुआ है?
● 1. I wasn't talking about her. 2. He's got nothing on you. 3. I was talking about him. 4. Can you work with that? 5. And what are you doing with her? 6. You know what time it is?

[57] 1. मुझे लगता है कि अब समय आ गया है। 2. तुम इस समय यहाँ क्या कर रहे हो? 3. मुझे लगता है कि समय आ गया है। 4. क्या यह बात करने का अच्छा समय है? 5. हम समय पर कैसे काम कर रहे हैं? 6. मैंने कुछ समय से काम नहीं किया है।
● 1. I think it's time. 2. What are you doing here at this hour? 3. I think the time has come. 4. Is this a good time to talk? 5. How we doing on time? 6. I haven't worked in a while.

[58] 1. मैं बहुत समय से ऐसा करना चाहता था। 2. क्या अब आपके पास मेरे लिए समय है? 3. मैंने कुछ समय से ऐसा नहीं किया है। 4. क्या यह समय के बारे में नहीं है? 5. क्या आपके पास बात करने के लिए समय है? 6. मुझे लगता है कि आपने बहुत कुछ कर लिया है।
● 1. I've wanted to do that for so long. 2. Do you have time for me now? 3. I haven't done this in a while. 4. Isn't it about time? 5. Do you have time to talk? 6. I think you've had enough.

[59] 1. आपको क्या लगता है वह क्या कर रही है? 2. वह मेरे बारे में बात कर रही है। 3. अभी भी इस पर काम कर रहा है। 4. मैं अभी इस बारे में बात नहीं कर सकता। 5. क्या आप अभी भी ऐसा कर रहे हैं? 6. क्या आपको लगता है कि वह अभी भी यहाँ है?
● 1. How do you think she's doing? 2. She's talking about me. 3. Still working on it. 4. I can't talk about it right now. 5. You're still doing that? 6. You think he's still here?

[60] 1. क्या हम अभी इस बारे में बात नहीं कर सकते? 2. क्या आप अभी भी बात कर रहे हैं? 3. तुम अभी भी यहाँ क्या कर रहे हो? 4. मैं अभी भी यहाँ क्या कर रहा हूँ? 5. हम अभी भी यहाँ क्या कर रहे हैं? 6. मुझे लगता है कि

हमें इसे अभी करना चाहिए.
- *1.* Can we not talk about this right now? *2.* Are you still talking? *3.* What the hell are you still doing here? *4.* What am I still doing here? *5.* What are we still doing here? *6.* I think we should do it now.

**[61]** *1.* मैं अभी भी इसे ठीक कर सकता हूं. *2.* तुम्हें पता है कि मुझे अभी क्या चाहिए? *3.* मैं अभी इस बारे में बात नहीं करना चाहता. *4.* हम अभी ऐसा नहीं करने जा रहे हैं. *5.* क्या आप अभी भी काम कर रहे हैं? *6.* क्या हम अभी बात नहीं कर रहे हैं?
- *1.* I can still fix this. *2.* You know what I'd like right now? *3.* I don't wanna talk about it right now. *4.* We're not gonna do this right now. *5.* Are you still working? *6.* Aren't we talking now?

**[62]** *1.* क्या आप अभी इस बारे में बात करना चाहते हैं? *2.* क्या आप अभी भी यहाँ काम करते हैं? *3.* ओह, मुझे लगता है आप ऐसा करते हैं। *4.* ओह, आपके पास है, क्या आपके पास है? *5.* ओह, मुझे पता है मैं कर सकता हूँ। *6.* तुम्हें पता है तुम कहाँ जा रहे हो?
- *1.* You want to talk about this now? *2.* You still work here? *3.* Oh, I think you do. *4.* Oh, you have, have you? *5.* Oh, I know I can. *6.* You know where you're going?

**[63]** *1.* और आपको क्या लगता है आप कहाँ जा रहे हैं? *2.* तुम्हें क्या लगता है मैं कहाँ जा रहा हूँ? *3.* मुझे पता है वह कहाँ जा रहा है. *4.* हाँ, मुझे पता है कि यह कहाँ है। *5.* मुझे पता है मैं कहाँ जा रहा हूँ. *6.* आपको क्या लगता है कि आप कहाँ जा रहे हैं?
- *1.* And where do you think you're going? *2.* Where do you think I'm going? *3.* I know where he's going. *4.* Yeah, I know where it is. *5.* I know where I'm going. *6.* Where you think you're going?

**[64]** *1.* आपको क्या लगता है हम कहाँ जा रहे हैं? *2.* आपको क्या लगता है आप कहाँ जा रहे हैं? *3.* मुझे ठीक-ठीक पता है कि वह कहाँ है। *4.* आपको क्या लगता है वे कहाँ जा रहे हैं? *5.* हाँ, मुझे पता है कि मैं कहाँ जा रहा हूँ। *6.* उन्हें क्या लगता है कि वे कहाँ जा रहे हैं?
- *1.* Where do you think we're going? *2.* Where you think you going? *3.* I know exactly where he is. *4.* Where do you think they're going? *5.* Yes, I know where I'm going. *6.* Where do they think they're going?

**[65]** *1.* आपको क्या लगता है वह कहाँ जा रहा है? *2.* आपको क्या लगता है आप अभी कहाँ हैं? *3.* ठीक है, यह कहाँ से आ रहा है? *4.* आप कभी भी अपने बारे में बात नहीं करते. *5.* मैं कभी नहीं चाहता था कि ऐसा हो। *6.* आप कभी

भी मेरे पास आ सकते हैं.

● *1.* Where do you think he's going? *2.* Where do you think you are right now? *3.* Okay, where is this coming from? *4.* You never talk about yourself. *5.* I never meant for this to happen. *6.* You can always come to me.

**[66]** *1.* क्या उसने कभी मेरे बारे में बात की? *2.* मैं ऐसा कभी नहीं चाहता था कि ऐसा हो। *3.* आपने कहा कि आप बात करना चाहते हैं। *4.* मुझे नहीं पता कि मैंने ऐसा क्यों कहा। *5.* मैंने यह नहीं कहा कि ऐसा नहीं था। *6.* ओह, ठीक है, आपने ऐसा क्यों नहीं कहा?

● *1.* Did she ever talk about me? *2.* I never meant for that to happen. *3.* You said you wanted to talk. *4.* I don't know why I just said that. *5.* I didn't say it wasn't. *6.* Oh, well, why didn't you say so?

**[67]** *1.* मैंने कहा, तुम यहाँ क्या कर रहे हो? *2.* क्या उसने मेरे बारे में कुछ कहा है? *3.* मुझे यह करने के लिए कहा गया था। *4.* क्या मैंने कहा कि आप जा सकते हैं? *5.* आपने कहा था कि मैं जा सकता हूं. *6.* उन्होंने कहा कि यह नहीं किया जा सकता।

● *1.* I said, what are you doing here? *2.* Has she said anything about me? *3.* I was told to do it. *4.* Did I say you could leave? *5.* You said I could go. *6.* They said it couldn't be done.

**[68]** *1.* मैंने कभी नहीं कहा कि आपने ऐसा नहीं किया। *2.* मैंने यह नहीं कहा कि आपने नहीं कहा। *3.* आपने कहा था कि वह नहीं आ रहा है। *4.* क्या तुम्हें पता है कि मैंने क्या कहा? *5.* मैंने कभी नहीं कहा कि मैं नहीं था। *6.* क्या उसने उसके बारे में और कुछ कहा?

● *1.* I never said you didn't. *2.* I didn't say you didn't. *3.* You said he wasn't coming. *4.* Do you know what I said? *5.* I never said I wasn't. *6.* Did she say anything else about him?

**[69]** *1.* मैंने यह नहीं कहा कि आपने ऐसा किया है। *2.* आपको क्या लगता है उसने ऐसा क्यों कहा? *3.* मैंने कभी नहीं कहा कि आप नहीं थे। *4.* मुझे यह भी नहीं पता कि मैंने क्या कहा. *5.* मुझे लगता है वह तुम्हें पसंद करता है. *6.* मुझे लगता है कि मैं इसे पसंद किया।

● *1.* I didn't say that you did. *2.* Why do you think he said that? *3.* I never said you weren't. *4.* I don't even know what I said. *5.* I think he likes you. *6.* I think I like it.

**[70]** *1.* मुझे पता था कि मैं तुम्हें पसंद करता हूं. *2.* मुझे यह पसंद है, मुझे यह पसंद है। *3.* क्या तुम अब भी मुझे पसंद करते हो? *4.* आप उसे पसंद करते हैं, वह आपको पसंद करता है। *5.* क्या आपको लगता है मुझे यह पसंद है? *6.* आप इस बारे में क्या पसंद करते हो?

- *1.* I knew I liked you. *2.* I like it, I like it. *3.* Do you still like me? *4.* You like him, he likes you. *5.* You think I like this? *6.* What do you love about it?

**[71]** *1.* हाँ, ठीक है, मुझे यह पसंद नहीं है। *2.* वह इस बारे में बात करना पसंद नहीं करते. *3.* मुझे पसंद है कि आप कहाँ जा रहे हैं। *4.* तुम्हें पता था कि मैं उसे पसंद करता हूँ। *5.* मैं चाहता हूं कि आप उसे पसंद करें. *6.* मुझे नहीं लगता कि उसे यह पसंद है.
- *1.* Yeah, well, I don't like it. *2.* He doesn't like to talk about it. *3.* I like where you're going. *4.* You knew I liked her. *5.* I want you to like him. *6.* I don't think she likes it.

**[72]** *1.* क्या आपको लगता है कि मुझे ऐसा करना पसंद है? *2.* मुझे नहीं लगता कि मुझे यह पसंद है. *3.* मैं चाहता था कि तुम मुझे पसंद करो. *4.* ऐसा नहीं है कि मुझे यह पसंद नहीं है. *5.* तुम जानते हो कि तुम्हें क्या करना है। *6.* क्या आप जानते हैं कि वह क्या है?
- *1.* You think I like doing this? *2.* I don't think I like that. *3.* I wanted you to like me. *4.* It's not that I don't like it. *5.* You know what to do. *6.* Do you know what that is?

**[73]** *1.* क्या आप जानते हैं कि यह क्या है! *2.* क्या आप जानते हैं कि आप क्या कर रहे हैं? *3.* क्या आप जानते हैं कि आपने क्या किया है? *4.* हम जानते हैं कि हम क्या कर रहे हैं. *5.* क्या आप जानते हैं कि आप यहाँ क्यों हैं? *6.* क्या आप जानते हैं कि आप क्या हैं?
- *1.* Do you know what it is? *2.* Do you know what you're doing? *3.* Do you know what you've done? *4.* We know what we're doing. *5.* Do you know why you're here? *6.* Do you know what you are?

**[74]** *1.* आप नहीं जानते कि आप क्या कर रहे हैं! *2.* क्या आप इस बारे में कुछ भी जानते हैं? *3.* वे जानते हैं कि वे क्या कर रहे हैं. *4.* क्या आप जानते हैं क्या हो रहा है? *5.* आप जानते हैं कि यह कैसे काम करता है. *6.* आप भी यह जानते हैं और मैं भी।
- *1.* You don't know what you're doing! *2.* Do you know anything about this? *3.* They know what they're doing. *4.* Do you know what's going on? *5.* You know how this works. *6.* You know that as well as I do.

**[75]** *1.* क्या आप जानते हैं कि आप कहाँ जा रहे हैं? *2.* आप मेरे बारे में सब कुछ जानते हैं. *3.* आप जानते हैं कि आप ऐसा करते हैं। *4.* आप जानते हैं कि हम यहाँ क्यों हैं। *5.* आप जानते हैं कि हम क्या कर सकते हैं? *6.* क्या आप जानते है कि मुझे क्या पसंद है?
- *1.* Do you know where you're going? *2.* You know everything

about me. *3.* You know you do. *4.* You know why we're here.
*5.* You know what we could do? *6.* You know what I like?

**[76]** *1.* क्या आप जानते हैं हम यहाँ क्यों हैं? *2.* आप जानते हैं कि हम ऐसा नहीं कर सकते. *3.* क्या आप जानते हैं उसके साथ क्या हुआ? *4.* क्या आप उसके बारे में कुछ जानते हैं? *5.* आप जानते हैं कि हम क्या चाहते हैं. *6.* आप जानते हैं कि यह कैसे करना है.
• *1.* Do you know why we're here? *2.* You know we can't do that. *3.* Do you know what happened to him? *4.* Do you know anything about him? *5.* You know what we want. *6.* You know how to do that.

**[77]** *1.* आप उसके बारे में और क्या जानते हैं? *2.* आप जानते हैं कि आपको क्या करना चाहिए. *3.* हम उसके बारे में और क्या जानते हैं? *4.* अच्छा, क्या आप जानते हैं वह कहाँ है? *5.* आपको क्या लगता है आप क्या जानते हैं? *6.* क्या आप जानते हैं कि यह क्या था?
• *1.* What else do you know about him? *2.* You know what you must do. *3.* What else do we know about him? *4.* Well, do you know where he is? *5.* What do you think you know? *6.* Do you know what it was?

**[78]** *1.* क्या वे जानते हैं कि हम यहाँ हैं? *2.* क्या आप जानते हैं वह क्या कर रहा है? *3.* आप भी इसे जानते हैं और मैं भी। *4.* क्या आप जानते हैं कि यह कैसे काम करता है? *5.* क्या आप इस बारे में कुछ जानते हैं? *6.* क्या आप जानते हैं वह कहाँ हो सकता है?
• *1.* Do they know we're here? *2.* Do you know what he's doing? *3.* You know it as well as I do. *4.* Do you know how it works? *5.* Did you know anything about this? *6.* Do you know where he might be?

**[79]** *1.* तो आप जानते हैं कि मैंने क्या किया? *2.* क्या आपको लगता है कि वे जानते हैं? *3.* क्या आप जानते हैं वह कहाँ जा रहा था? *4.* आप कैसे जानते हैं कि यह वह थी? *5.* आप जानते हैं हम क्या कर सकते हैं? *6.* तो क्या आप उसके बारे में जानते हैं?
• *1.* So you know what I did? *2.* You think they know? *3.* Do you know where he was going? *4.* How do you know it was her? *5.* You know what we can do? *6.* So you know about that?

**[80]** *1.* और आप जानते हैं कि मैं यह कर सकता हूं. *2.* क्या आप जानते हैं कि वे क्या कर रहे हैं? *3.* आप मेरे बारे में और क्या जानते हैं? *4.* क्या आप जानते हैं कि आपने क्या किया? *5.* क्या आप जानते हैं कि मैं क्या चाहता हूँ? *6.* आप नहीं जानते कि आप कहाँ जा रहे हैं।
• *1.* And you know I can do it. *2.* Do you know what they're

doing? *3.* What else do you know about me? *4.* Do you know what you did? *5.* Do you know what I wish? *6.* You don't know where you're going.

**[81]** *1.* वे नहीं जानते कि वे क्या चाहते हैं. *2.* क्या आप जानते हैं कि वे क्या चाहते हैं? *3.* हम आपके बारे में सब कुछ जानते हैं. *4.* क्या आप जानते हैं कि आपके साथ क्या हुआ? *5.* आप जानते हैं कि मैं यहाँ क्या कर रहा हूँ। *6.* आप कैसे जानते हैं कि यह कैसे करना है?

• *1.* They don't know what they want. *2.* Do you know what they want? *3.* We know all about you. *4.* Do you know what happened to you? *5.* You know what I'm doing here. *6.* How do you know how to do this?

**[82]** *1.* क्या आप जानते हैं कि अभी क्या हुआ? *2.* क्या आप जानते हैं उसने ऐसा क्यों किया? *3.* क्या आप जानते हैं कि आपने अभी क्या कहा? *4.* क्या आप जानते हैं कि आपने अभी क्या किया? *5.* और आप जानते हैं कि उसने क्या किया? *6.* आप जानते हैं कि वे ऐसा करते हैं।

• *1.* Do you know what just happened? *2.* Do you know why he did it? *3.* Do you know what you just said? *4.* Do you know what you just did? *5.* And you know what he did? *6.* You know they do.

**[83]** *1.* आप नहीं जानते कि वह कहाँ गया है। *2.* क्या आप जानते हैं कि वे क्या करते हैं? *3.* क्या आप जानते हैं मैं क्या करना चाहता हूँ? *4.* आप जानते हैं कि आप ऐसा नहीं कर सकते. *5.* आप जानते हैं कि मैं यहाँ क्यों हूँ। *6.* आप कैसे जानते हैं कि वह नहीं है?

• *1.* You don't know where he's been. *2.* Do you know what they do? *3.* Do you know what I want to do? *4.* You know you can't do that. *5.* You know why I am here. *6.* How do you know he isn't?

**[84]** *1.* हम जानते हैं कि हम क्या चाहते हैं. *2.* क्या आप जानते हैं कि आपको क्या चाहिए? *3.* आप जानते हैं कि हम क्या करते हैं. *4.* आप नहीं जानते कि मैंने क्या किया है. *5.* क्या आप जानते हैं कि वह क्या कर रहा था? *6.* क्या आप जानते हैं कि उन्होंने मेरे साथ क्या किया?

• *1.* We know what we want. *2.* Do you know what you need? *3.* You know what we do. *4.* You don't know what I've done. *5.* Do you know what he was doing? *6.* Do you know what they did to me?

**[85]** *1.* क्या हम जानते हैं कि हम क्या कर रहे हैं? *2.* आप जानते हैं कि हमें क्या करना चाहिए? *3.* उन्हें लगता है कि आप कुछ जानते हैं. *4.* और क्या आप जानते हैं उन्होंने क्या कहा? *5.* वे जानते हैं कि हम आ रहे हैं. *6.* आप जानते हैं

कि आप क्या कर सकते हैं.

• *1.* Do we know what we're doing? *2.* You know what we ought to do? *3.* They think you know something. *4.* And do you know what he said? *5.* They know we're coming. *6.* You know what you can do.

**[86]** *1.* आप इस सब के बारे में क्या जानते हैं? *2.* वे जानते थे कि वे क्या कर रहे हैं। *3.* और क्या आप जानते हैं कि उसने क्या किया? *4.* क्या आप इस सब के बारे में जानते थे? *5.* हम जानते हैं कि वे क्या कर सकते हैं. *6.* आप नहीं जानते कि इसे कैसे काम करना है।

• *1.* What do you know about all this? *2.* They knew what they were getting into. *3.* And do you know what he did? *4.* Did you know about all this? *5.* We know what they can do. *6.* You don't know how to work it.

**[87]** *1.* वे नहीं जानते कि वे क्या करते हैं. *2.* मुझे लगता है कि वे यह जानते हैं. *3.* क्या आप जानते हैं कि वे कहाँ जा रहे थे? *4.* तो आप जानते हैं कि उसने क्या किया? *5.* क्या वे जानते हैं कि हम कहाँ हैं? *6.* क्या वे जानते हैं कि आप यहाँ हैं?

• *1.* They know not what they do. *2.* I think they know that. *3.* Do you know where they were headed? *4.* So you know what he did? *5.* Do they know where we are? *6.* Do they know you're here?

**[88]** *1.* और मुझे लगता है कि आप यह जानते हैं. *2.* आप कुछ और हैं, यह आप जानते हैं? *3.* क्या आप जानते हैं कि वे कहाँ हो सकते हैं? *4.* क्या हम जानते हैं कि वे क्या चाहते हैं? *5.* आप जानते हैं कि मैं क्या कर सकता हूं. *6.* क्या आप जानते थे कि यह आ रहा था?

• *1.* And I think you know that. *2.* You're something else, you know that? *3.* Do you know where they might be? *4.* Do we know what they want? *5.* You know what I can do. *6.* Did you know this was coming?

**[89]** *1.* क्या आप जानते हैं वह कहाँ जा रहा है? *2.* क्या आप जानते हैं कि यह कैसे हुआ? *3.* क्या आप जानते हैं कि आपके पास क्या है? *4.* आप कैसे जानते हैं कि वह क्या चाहता है? *5.* क्या आप जानते भी हैं कि वह क्या है? *6.* हम जानते हैं कि वह कहाँ जा रहा है।

• *1.* Do you know where he's going? *2.* Do you know how it happened? *3.* Do you know what you're having? *4.* How do you know what he wants? *5.* Do you even know what that is? *6.* We know where he's headed.

**[90]** *1.* आप जानते हैं, हमें ऐसा नहीं करना है. *2.* क्या आप जानते हैं वह यहाँ

क्यों है? *3.* आप नहीं जानते कि यह कैसे काम करता है। *4.* यह सब मेरे लिए अब वापस आ रहा है। *5.* क्या हम काम पर वापस आ सकते हैं? *6.* मुझे नहीं लगता कि वे वापस आ रहे हैं.

● *1.* You know, we don't have to do this. *2.* Do you know why he's here? *3.* You don't know how it works. *4.* It's all coming back to me now. *5.* Can we get back to work? *6.* I don't think they're coming back.

[91] *1.* क्या आप मुझे वापस ले जा सकते हैं? *2.* मुझे लगता है वह वापस आ गया है. *3.* क्या आप काम पर वापस जा रहे हैं? *4.* क्या आपको लगता है वह वापस आ रहा है? *5.* क्या मैं अब काम पर वापस आ सकता हूँ? *6.* मुझे पता था कि तुम वापस आ रहे हो.

● *1.* Can you take me back? *2.* I guess he's back. *3.* You going back to work? *4.* Do you think he's coming back? *5.* Can I get back to work now? *6.* I knew you were coming back.

[92] *1.* लेकिन मैं इस पर काम कर रहा हूं. *2.* लेकिन आपने ऐसा नहीं किया, क्या आपने किया? *3.* लेकिन मैं आपके लिए क्या कर सकता हूँ? *4.* लेकिन मुझे लगता है कि आप यह जानते हैं. *5.* लेकिन मुझे नहीं पता कि और क्या करना है. *6.* लेकिन मुझे पता है कि मुझे क्या चाहिए.

● *1.* But I'm working on it. *2.* But you didn't, did you? *3.* But what can I do for you? *4.* But I guess you know that. *5.* But I don't know what else to do. *6.* But I know what I want.

[93] *1.* मुझे नहीं पता क्यों, लेकिन मुझे पता है। *2.* लेकिन मैं ऐसा नहीं करने जा रहा हूं. *3.* मैंने नहीं किया, लेकिन अब मैं करता हूं. *4.* लेकिन उसने ऐसा नहीं किया, क्या उसने ऐसा किया? *5.* लेकिन मुझे लगता है आप ऐसा करते हैं. *6.* मुझे पता है, लेकिन आप नहीं कर सकते।

● *1.* I don't know why, but I do. *2.* But I'm not going to do that. *3.* I didn't, but now I do. *4.* But she didn't, did she? *5.* But I think you do. *6.* I know, but you can't.

[94] *1.* मैं जानता हूँ कि मैं कर रहा सकता हूँ। *2.* वह जानता है कि वह क्या कर रहा है। *3.* मैं जानता था कि यह तुम ही हो। *4.* मैं जानता हूं कि यह आप ही हैं। *5.* मैं जानता हूं आप यह कर सकते हैं. *6.* मैं यह जानता था, मैं यह जानता था।

● *1.* I know I am. *2.* He knows what he's doing. *3.* I knew it was you. *4.* I know it's you. *5.* I know you can do this. *6.* I knew it, I knew it.

[95] *1.* मैं आपके बारे में बहुत कुछ जानता हूं. *2.* मैं जानता हूं आप ऐसा कर सकते हैं. *3.* मैं नहीं जानता कि हम क्या कर रहे हैं. *4.* क्या वह जानता है कि मैं यहाँ हूँ? *5.* वह नहीं जानता कि वह क्या चाहता है. *6.* क्या वह जानता है कि आप यहाँ हैं?

- *1.* I know a lot about you. *2.* I know you could. *3.* I don't know what we're doing. *4.* Does he know I'm here? *5.* He doesn't know what he wants. *6.* Does he know you're here?

**[96]** *1.* मैं जानता हूं कि मुझे क्या करना चाहिए. *2.* तुम्हें पता है मैं यह कैसे जानता हूँ? *3.* क्या आपको नहीं लगता कि मैं जानता हूँ? *4.* मैं नहीं जानता, लेकिन मुझे यह पसंद नहीं है। *5.* मुझे लगता है कि मैं तुम्हें जानता हूँ। *6.* आप इसे जानते हैं, मैं इसे जानता हूं।

- *1.* I know what I must do. *2.* You know how I know that? *3.* Don't you think I know? *4.* I don't know, but I don't like it. *5.* I think I know you. *6.* You know it, I know it.

**[97]** *1.* आप यह जानते हैं और मैं यह जानता हूं। *2.* क्या वह जानता है कि आप कहाँ हैं? *3.* क्या वह जानता है कि वह क्या कर रहा है? *4.* मैं जानता हूं कि आप उन्हें पसंद करते हैं. *5.* मैं जानता हूं कि हम क्या कर सकते हैं. *6.* मैं जानता हूं कि आप ऐसा करते हैं।

- *1.* You know that and I know that. *2.* Does he know where you are? *3.* Does he know what he's doing? *4.* I know you like them. *5.* I know what we can do. *6.* I know that you do.

**[98]** *1.* मैं नहीं जानता था कि वह तुम हो। *2.* मैं इसे जानता हूं, मैं इसे जानता हूं। *3.* मैं जानता हूं कि आपके पास यह है। *4.* मैं जानता हूं कि आप ऐसा कर सकते हैं. *5.* वह जानता है कि क्या हो रहा है. *6.* मैं जानता हूँ कि यह तुम ही थे!

- *1.* I didn't know that was you. *2.* I know it, I know it. *3.* I know you have it. *4.* I know you can do that. *5.* He knows what's going on. *6.* I know it was you!

**[99]** *1.* मुझे पता था कि मैं तुम्हें जानता हूं. *2.* मैं उसके बारे में सब कुछ जानता हूं. *3.* मैं जानता हूं तुम्हें यह पसंद नहीं है. *4.* मैं नहीं जानता कि आप ऐसा कैसे करते हैं। *5.* वह जानता था कि हम आ रहे हैं। *6.* मैं जानता हूं कि मुझे ऐसा नहीं करना चाहिए।

- *1.* I knew I knew you. *2.* I know everything about him. *3.* I know you don't like it. *4.* I don't know how you do that. *5.* He knew we were coming. *6.* I know I shouldn't have.

**[100]** *1.* और आप जानते हैं कि मैं कैसे जानता हूं? *2.* मैं जानता हूं कि आपके लिए क्या अच्छा है. *3.* वह जानता है कि वह कहाँ जा रहा है। *4.* वह आपके बारे में सब कुछ जानता है. *5.* मैं जानता हूं, लेकिन मैं क्या कर सकता हूं? *6.* आप क्या जानते हैं कि मैं नहीं जानता?

- *1.* And you know how I know? *2.* I know what's good for you. *3.* He knows where he's going. *4.* He knows all about you. *5.* I know, but what can I do? *6.* What do you know that I don't?

**[101]** *1.* मैं जानता हूं आप यह कैसे करते हैं. *2.* तुम्हें क्या लगता है कि मैं जानता हूँ? *3.* क्या आप जानते हैं मैं कैसे जानता हूँ? *4.* मुझे लगता है कि वह यह जानता है। *5.* मैं नहीं जानता कि आप यहाँ क्यों हैं। *6.* क्या आपको लगता है कि मैं यह नहीं जानता?

• *1.* I know how you do it. *2.* What makes you think I know? *3.* Do you know how I know? *4.* I think he knows that. *5.* I don't know why you're here. *6.* Think I don't know that?

**[102]** *1.* और आप जानते हैं कि मैं जानता हूं। *2.* मैं जानता हूं कि यह आ रहा है। *3.* मैं जानता हूं कि यह सब क्या है। *4.* मैं यह जानता हूं, आप यह जानते हैं। *5.* मैं जानता था कि कुछ ठीक नहीं है। *6.* मैं यह भी नहीं जानता कि वह क्या था।

• *1.* And you know I do. *2.* I know it's coming. *3.* I know what this is all about. *4.* I know that, you know that. *5.* I knew something wasn't right. *6.* I don't even know what that was.

**[103]** *1.* मैं जानता हूं कि हम यह कर सकते हैं. *2.* मैं जानता था कि यह कुछ ऐसा ही था। *3.* मैं जानता हूं कि वे ऐसा नहीं करते। *4.* क्या कोई और जानता है कि आप यहाँ हैं? *5.* मैं जानता था कि वह तुम ही हो। *6.* मैं जानता हूं कि हमें क्या करना चाहिए.

• *1.* I know we can do it. *2.* I knew it was something like that. *3.* I know they don't. *4.* Does anyone else know you're here? *5.* I knew that was you. *6.* I know what we must do.

**[104]** *1.* मैं ठीक-ठीक जानता हूं कि यह क्या है। *2.* मैं यह जानता हूं, लेकिन वह नहीं जानता। *3.* मैं जानता हूं मैं तुम्हें पसंद करता हूं. *4.* मैं जानता था कि तुम यह नहीं कर सकते। *5.* वह जानता था कि तुम आ रहे हो। *6.* वह जानता है कि हम आ रहे हैं।

• *1.* I know exactly what it is. *2.* I know that, but he doesn't. *3.* I know I like you. *4.* I knew you couldn't do it. *5.* He knew you were coming. *6.* He knows we're coming.

**[105]** *1.* मैं जानता था कि तुम ऐसा कर सकते हो। *2.* मैं जानता हूं कि मुझे ऐसा नहीं करना चाहिए था. *3.* वह जानता था कि अब समय आ गया है। *4.* मैं नहीं जानता कि हम और क्या कर सकते हैं. *5.* हाँ, मैं जानता हूँ कि आप नहीं जानते। *6.* क्या वह जानता है कि आप जानते हैं?

• *1.* I knew that you could. *2.* I know I shouldn't have done it. *3.* He knew it was time. *4.* I don't know what else we can do. *5.* Yeah, I know you don't. *6.* Does he know you know?

**[106]** *1.* मुझे लगता है मैं जानता हूं कि वह क्या है। *2.* कोई नहीं जानता कि उसके साथ क्या हुआ. *3.* वह जानता था कि वे आ रहे हैं। *4.* कोई नहीं जानता कि क्या हो रहा है. *5.* मैं जानता हूं आप कैसे काम करते हैं. *6.* मैं जानता हूं कि

वे आपके पास हैं।

● *1.* I think I know what that is. *2.* No one knows what happened to her. *3.* He knew they were coming. *4.* Nobody knows what's going on. *5.* I know how you work. *6.* I know you have them.

**[107]** *1.* मैं तो बस एक को ही जानता हूँ। *2.* मैं नहीं जानता कि हम क्या करने जा रहे हैं। *3.* मैं इसे जानता हूं और आप इसे जानते हैं। *4.* मैं जानता हूं कि यह कैसे हो सकता है. *5.* तुम्हें क्या लगता है मैं कैसे जानता हूँ? *6.* क्या वह जानता है कि क्या हो रहा है?

● *1.* I know just the one. *2.* I don't know what we're going to do. *3.* I know it and you know it. *4.* I know how that can be. *5.* How do you think I know? *6.* Does he know what's happening?

**[108]** *1.* मैं यह भी नहीं जानता कि वे क्या हैं। *2.* तुम्हें क्या लगता है कि मैं कुछ भी जानता हूँ? *3.* मैं जानता हूं कि आप कर सकते हैं. *4.* मैं जानता हूं कि उसने ऐसा किया था। *5.* मैं ठीक-ठीक जानता हूं कि तुम क्या हो. *6.* वह जानता है कि यह आप ही थे।

● *1.* I don't even know what they are. *2.* What makes you think I know anything? *3.* I know that you can. *4.* I know that he did. *5.* I know exactly what you are. *6.* He knows it was you.

**[109]** *1.* मैं जानता हूं कि वे कैसे काम करते हैं। *2.* मैं नहीं जानता कि आप यह कैसे करते हैं. *3.* और मैं जानता हूं आप भी ऐसा करते हैं। *4.* वह यह भी नहीं जानता कि हम यहाँ हैं। *5.* तुम्हें नहीं लगता कि मैं यह जानता हूँ? *6.* मैं नहीं जानता, लेकिन यह अच्छा नहीं हो सकता।

● *1.* I know how they work. *2.* I do not know how you do it. *3.* And I know you do, too. *4.* He doesn't even know we're here. *5.* You don't think that I know that? *6.* I don't know, but it can't be good.

**[110]** *1.* क्या आप जानते हैं कि वह कौन है? *2.* हाँ, मैं जानता हूँ कि तुम कौन हो। *3.* मैं ठीक-ठीक जानता हूं कि तुम कौन हो. *4.* और मैं जानता हूं कि तुम कौन हो. *5.* आप को क्या लगता हैं हम कौन हैं? *6.* तुम कौन हो और तुम क्या चाहते हो?

● *1.* Do you know who he is? *2.* Yeah, I know who you are. *3.* I know exactly who you are. *4.* And I know who you are. *5.* Who do you think we are? *6.* Who are you and what do you want?

**[111]** *1.* तुम्हें पता है मैं कौन हूँ, ठीक है? *2.* मुझे लगता है मुझे पता है यह कौन है. *3.* तुम कौन हो, यहाँ क्या कर रहे हो? *4.* तुम्हें लगता है मैं नहीं जानता कि तुम कौन हो? *5.* मैं यह भी नहीं जानता कि वे कौन हैं। *6.* और कौन जानता है कि हम यहाँ हैं?

● *1.* You know who I am, right? *2.* I think I know who it is. *3.*

Who are you, what are you doing here? *4.* You think I don't know who you are? *5.* I don't even know who they are. *6.* Who else knows we're here?

**[112]** *1.* लेकिन मैं जानता हूं कि तुम कौन हो. *2.* मैं ठीक-ठीक जानता हूं कि वह कौन है। *3.* मुझे लगता है मैं जानता हूं वह कौन है. *4.* मुझे नहीं पता था कि मैं कौन हूं. *5.* अब मैं जानता हूं कि तुम कौन हो. *6.* अब हम जानते हैं कि हम कौन हैं।

● *1.* But I know who you are. *2.* I know exactly who he is. *3.* I think I know who he is. *4.* I didn't know who I was. *5.* I know who you are now. *6.* We know who we are now.

**[113]** *1.* वह यह भी नहीं जानता कि मैं कौन हूं। *2.* मैं यह भी नहीं जानता कि वह कौन है. *3.* अब मैं जानता हूं कि मैं कौन हूं। *4.* मुझे नहीं पता था कि वह कौन थी. *5.* मैं नहीं जानता था कि वह कौन था. *6.* मैं मदद के लिए कुछ भी कर सकता हूँ?

● *1.* He doesn't even know who I am. *2.* I don't even know who she is. *3.* I know who I am now. *4.* I had no idea who she was. *5.* I did not know who he was. *6.* Anything I can do to help?

**[114]** *1.* मुझे लगता है मैं आपकी मदद कर सकता हूं. *2.* क्या आप इस के साथ मेरी मदद कर सकते हैं? *3.* कृपया क्या आप मेरी मदद कर सकते हैं? *4.* मुझे लगता है मैं मदद कर सकता हूं. *5.* मैं चाहता हूँ कि तुम मेरी मदद करो। *6.* मैं आपकी मदद नहीं करने जा रहा हूं.

● *1.* I think I can help you. *2.* Can you help me with this? *3.* Can you help me, please? *4.* I think I can help. *5.* I want you to help me. *6.* I'm not going to help you.

**[115]** *1.* आपने कहा कि आप मदद करना चाहते हैं. *2.* क्या हम आपकी कुछ मदद कर सकते हैं? *3.* और आप मेरी मदद करने जा रहे हैं. *4.* क्या आप मेरी कुछ मदद कर सकते हैं? *5.* आपने कहा था कि आप मेरी मदद कर सकते हैं। *6.* क्या आप मेरी मदद करने जा रहे हैं?

● *1.* You said you wanted to help. *2.* Can we help you with something? *3.* And you're going to help me. *4.* Could you help me with something? *5.* You said you could help me. *6.* You're going to help me?

**[116]** *1.* मैं ऐसा करने में आपकी मदद कर सकता हूं. *2.* मुझे लगता है आप मेरी मदद कर सकते हैं. *3.* मैं तो बस आपकी मदद करना चाहता था. *4.* मुझे लगता है वह मदद कर सकता है. *5.* ऐसा लगता है कि आप कुछ मदद ले सकते हैं। *6.* मैं आपकी कुछ मदद करने जा रहा हूं.

● *1.* I can help you do that. *2.* I think you can help me. *3.* I just wanted to help you. *4.* I think he can help. *5.* Looks like you could use some help. *6.* I'm going to get you some help.

**[117]** *1.* आपने कहा था कि आप मेरी मदद करना चाहते हैं। *2.* मैं जानता हूं आप मेरी मदद करना चाहते हैं. *3.* तो आप मेरी मदद क्यों कर रहे हैं? *4.* उन्होंने कहा कि वह मदद कर सकते हैं. *5.* क्या आप यहाँ मेरी मदद कर सकते हैं? *6.* तुम मेरी मदद करो, तुम अपनी मदद करो।
● *1.* You said you wanted to help me. *2.* I know you want to help me. *3.* So why are you helping me? *4.* He said he could help. *5.* Can you help me here? *6.* You help me, you help yourself.

**[118]** *1.* तो, हम आपकी कैसे मदद कर सकते हैं? *2.* क्या आप ऐसा करने में मेरी मदद कर सकते हैं? *3.* और मैं आपकी मदद करने जा रहा हूं. *4.* तो फिर तुम यहाँ क्या कर रहे हो? *5.* तो फिर आप ऐसा क्यों कर रहे हैं? *6.* तो फिर आप क्या करने जा रहे हैं?
● *1.* So, how can we help you? *2.* Can you help me do that? *3.* And I'm going to help you. *4.* Then what are you doing here? *5.* Then why are you doing this? *6.* Then what are you going to do?

**[119]** *1.* तो फिर हम क्या करने जा रहे हैं? *2.* फिर आप जानते हैं कि क्या करना है. *3.* और फिर भी आप अभी भी यहाँ हैं. *4.* यह वह समय फिर से आ गया है! *5.* लेकिन फिर भी मैं तुम्हें पसंद करता हूं. *6.* अच्छा, तो फिर मुझे भी अपने साथ ले चलो।
● *1.* Then what are we going to do? *2.* Then you know what to do. *3.* And yet you're still here. *4.* It's that time again! *5.* But I like you anyway. *6.* Well, then take me with you.

**[120]** *1.* फिर आप मेरी मदद क्यों कर रहे हैं? *2.* तो फिर हम बात क्यों कर रहे हैं? *3.* तो फिर हम ऐसा क्यों कर रहे हैं? *4.* हम फिर से एक साथ हो सकते हैं. *5.* आपने फिर से कहा कि आप कौन थे? *6.* तो फिर हम अभी भी यहाँ क्यों हैं?
● *1.* Then why are you helping me? *2.* Then why are we talking? *3.* Then why are we doing this? *4.* We can be together again. *5.* Who'd you say you were again? *6.* Then why are we still here?

**[121]** *1.* ठीक है, चलो इसे फिर से करते हैं। *2.* हम यह सब फिर से कर सकते हैं! *3.* तुम्हें कुछ पता नहीं कि तुमने क्या किया है. *4.* मैंने कभी नहीं कहा कि तुमने ऐसा किया। *5.* तुमने कहा था कि तुम जा रहे हो. *6.* तुमने कहा था कि तुम नहीं आ रहे हो.
● *1.* All right, let's do it again. *2.* We can do it all again! *3.* You have no idea what you've done. *4.* I never said you did. *5.* You said you were leaving. *6.* You said you weren't coming.

**[122]** *1.* मुझे नहीं लगता कि मैं ये कर सकता हूं. *2.* और आपको पता है कि ये कैसे करना है? *3.* मुझे पता है ये कैसे काम करता है. *4.* मुझे लगता है मुझे पता है ये क्या है. *5.* ऐसा कुछ भी नहीं है जो आप कर सकते हैं. *6.* क्या यह कुछ ऐसा था जो मैंने कहा था?

● *1.* I don't think I can do this. *2.* And you know this how? *3.* I know how this works. *4.* I think I know what this is. *5.* There's nothing you can do. *6.* Was it something I said?

**[123]** *1.* मैंने वह सब कुछ किया जो मैं कर सकता था। *2.* मेरे पास जो कुछ भी है वह सब तुम हो। *3.* मेरे पास वह सब कुछ है जो मुझे चाहिए। *4.* कुछ तो होगा जो मैं कर सकता हूं. *5.* तुम जो चाहते हो वह मेरे पास है। *6.* मैंने तुम्हें वह दिया जो तुम चाहते थे।

● *1.* I did everything I could. *2.* You're all I've got. *3.* I have everything I need. *4.* There must be something I can do. *5.* I have what you want. *6.* I gave you what you wanted.

**[124]** *1.* यह वह नहीं है जो मैं चाहता था। *2.* क्या आपके पास वह सब कुछ है जो आपको चाहिए? *3.* मैं जो चाहता हूं उसके बारे में क्या? *4.* मेरे पास वह सब कुछ है जो मैं चाहता हूं. *5.* मैं मदद के लिए जो भी कर सकता हूं. *6.* मैंने वह सब किया जो मैं कर सकता था।

● *1.* This isn't what I wanted. *2.* You have everything you need? *3.* What about what I want? *4.* I have everything I want. *5.* Whatever I can do to help. *6.* I did all I could.

**[125]** *1.* यह तुम ही हो जो मैं चाहता हूँ। *2.* मेरे पास कुछ है जो तुम चाहते हो. *3.* आपके पास वह सब कुछ है जो आपको चाहिए। *4.* नहीं, यह वह नहीं है जो मैं चाहता हूं। *5.* उसके पास जो कुछ है वह सब मैं ही हूं। *6.* यह वह सब है जो मैं कभी चाहता था।

● *1.* It's you I want. *2.* I have something you want. *3.* You have everything you need. *4.* No, that's not what I want. *5.* I'm all he's got. *6.* It's all I ever wanted.

**[126]** *1.* आपने जो कुछ भी किया उसके लिए धन्यवाद। *2.* आपने वह सब किया जो आप कर सकते थे. *3.* क्या यह कुछ ऐसा है जो मैंने किया है? *4.* आप जो चाहते हैं वह आपके पास है। *5.* यह वह नहीं है जो मैं चाहता हूं। *6.* आप जो करते हैं वह मुझे पसंद है.

● *1.* Thank you for everything you've done. *2.* You did all you could. *3.* Is it something I've done? *4.* You have what you want. *5.* This isn't what I want. *6.* I love what you do.

**[127]** *1.* मैं वह सब कुछ हूं जो आपके पास है। *2.* आपके पास कुछ है जो मैं चाहता हूँ। *3.* यह कुछ ऐसा है जो मुझे करना है। *4.* मुझे कुछ ऐसा करना है जो मुझे करना है। *5.* यह वह नहीं है जो मैं करता हूं। *6.* यह आप ही हैं जो वह

चाहता है।
- *1.* I'm all you've got. *2.* You have something I want. *3.* This is something I have to do. *4.* There's something I need you to do. *5.* It's not what I do. *6.* It's you he wants.

**[128]** *1.* यह वह नहीं है जो आपने कहा था। *2.* यह वह सब कुछ है जो मैं कभी चाहता था। *3.* क्या यह कुछ ऐसा था जो मैंने किया था? *4.* यह वह नहीं है जो मैं चाहता हूँ! *5.* क्या आप जो करते हैं वह आपको पसंद है? *6.* उसके पास ऐसा क्या है जो मेरे पास नहीं है?
- *1.* It's not what you said. *2.* It's everything I ever wanted. *3.* Was it something I did? *4.* That's not what I want! *5.* Do you like what you do? *6.* What does she have that I don't?

**[129]** *1.* मैंने वह सब कुछ किया जो आपने कहा था। *2.* हम वह कर रहे हैं जो हम कर सकते हैं। *3.* मैंने वह सब कुछ किया जो आप चाहते थे। *4.* मैं जो कुछ भी करता हूं वह आपके लिए है। *5.* क्या ऐसा कुछ था जो आप चाहते थे? *6.* मैंने वह सब किया है जो मैं कर सकता था।
- *1.* I did everything you said. *2.* We're doing what we can. *3.* I did everything you wanted. *4.* Everything I do is for you. *5.* Was there something you wanted? *6.* I have done all I can.

**[130]** *1.* मैंने वह सब कुछ किया जो मुझे करना चाहिए था। *2.* मैंने वह किया है जो मैं कर सकता हूं। *3.* तो, वह क्या है जो आप चाहते हैं? *4.* और वह क्या है जो आप चाहते हैं? *5.* आपने मेरे लिए जो किया उसके लिए धन्यवाद। *6.* यह वह नहीं है जो मैंने किया है।
- *1.* I did everything I was supposed to do. *2.* I've done what I can. *3.* So, what is it that you want? *4.* And what is it that you want? *5.* Thank you for what you did for me. *6.* It's not what I've done.

**[131]** *1.* मैं जो कर रहा हूं वह मुझे पसंद है. *2.* मैं वह कर सकता हूं जो मुझे पसंद है. *3.* मेरे पास वह सब कुछ है जो तुम्हें चाहिए। *4.* यह कुछ ऐसा है जो मुझे करना होगा। *5.* यह मैं ही हूं जो तुम चाहते हो। *6.* यह बस कुछ ऐसा है जो मैं करता हूं।
- *1.* I like what I'm doing. *2.* I can do what I like. *3.* I have everything you need. *4.* It's something I gotta do. *5.* It's me that you want. *6.* It's just something I do.

**[132]** *1.* आपने जो कुछ किया है उसके लिए धन्यवाद। *2.* उसके पास जो कुछ भी है वह मेरे पास होगा। *3.* यह कुछ ऐसा था जो मुझे करना था। *4.* क्या यह कुछ ऐसा है जो मैंने किया? *5.* मैंने जो किया वह मुझे नहीं करना चाहिए था। *6.* यह वह सब कुछ है जो मेरे पास है।
- *1.* Thank you for all you have done. *2.* I'll have whatever he's

having. *3.* It was something I had to do. *4.* Is it something I did?
*5.* I shouldn't have done what I did. *6.* It's everything I have.

**[133]** *1.* मैं अब जो हूं वह मुझे पसंद है। *2.* मैंने वह सब कुछ किया जो उसने
कहा था। *3.* मेरे पास वह सब कुछ है जो मैं चाहता था। *4.* यही वह है जो मैं
चाहता हूं कि आप करें। *5.* मुझे लगता है कि यही सब कुछ है। *6.* यही तो मैं
चाहता हूँ कि तुम करो।
• *1.* I like who I am now. *2.* I did everything he asked. *3.* I have
everything I wanted. *4.* Here's what I want you to do. *5.* I think
that's everything. *6.* This is what I want you to do.

**[134]** *1.* ठीक है, हम यही करने जा रहे हैं। *2.* क्या आपको लगता है मैं यही
चाहता था? *3.* मुझे लगता है कि हमें यही करना चाहिए। *4.* यही बात मुझे
उसके बारे में पसंद है। *5.* मुझे लगता है कि उसने यही कहा है। *6.* हाँ, मुझे लगता
है कि यही बात है।
• *1.* Okay, this is what we're gonna do. *2.* Do you think I wanted
this? *3.* Here's what I think we should do. *4.* That's what I like
about him. *5.* I think that's what she said. *6.* Yes, I think that's
it.

**[135]** *1.* मैं जानता हूं कि मैंने यही कहा था। *2.* मुझे लगता है कि मैंने यही कहा
था। *3.* क्या आपको लगता है कि आप यही कर रहे हैं? *4.* बस यही तो मैं कभी
करना चाहता था। *5.* मैं चाहता हूँ कि तुम मेरे साथ आओ। *6.* मुझे चाहिए कि
तुम आओ और मुझे ले आओ।
• *1.* I know that's what I said. *2.* I think that's what I said. *3.* Is
that what you think you're doing? *4.* That's all I ever wanted to
do. *5.* I need you to come with me. *6.* I need you to come and
get me.

**[136]** *1.* मुझे चाहिए कि तुम मेरे लिए कुछ ले आओ। *2.* आपने जो देखा क्या
वह आपको पसंद है? *3.* क्या आपने देखा कि आपने क्या किया है? *4.* मैंने उसे
बहुत समय से नहीं देखा है। *5.* मैंने तुम्हें बहुत समय से नहीं देखा है। *6.* क्या
आपको लगता है कि उन्होंने हमें देखा?
• *1.* I need you to get something for me. *2.* Do you like what
you see? *3.* You see what you've done? *4.* I haven't seen him
for ages. *5.* I haven't seen you for ages. *6.* Do you think they
saw us?

**[137]** *1.* मैंने देखा है कि तुम क्या कर सकते हो। *2.* लेकिन मुझे पता है कि मैंने
क्या देखा। *3.* मैंने देखा है कि वह क्या कर सकता है। *4.* मैंने कुछ समय से ऐसा
नहीं देखा है। *5.* मैंने देखा है कि वे क्या करते हैं। *6.* मैंने उसे कुछ समय से नहीं
देखा है।
• *1.* I've seen what you can do. *2.* But I know what I saw. *3.*

I've seen what he can do. *4.* I haven't seen that in a while. *5.* I've seen what they do. *6.* I haven't seen him for a while.

**[138]** *1.* तुमने कहा था कि तुमने उसे नहीं देखा है। *2.* आपने देखा है कि मैं क्या कर सकता हूँ। *3.* मैं चाहता हूं कि आप उसकी मदद करें. *4.* मुझे लगता है मैं उसकी मदद कर सकता हूं. *5.* आप तो बस अपना काम कर रहे थे. *6.* मुझे पता है कि मुझे अपना काम कैसे करना है।

• *1.* You said you hadn't seen her. *2.* You've seen what I can do. *3.* I want you to help him. *4.* I think I can help him. *5.* You were just doing your job. *6.* I know how to do my job.

**[139]** *1.* मुझे यह मिल गया, मुझे यह मिल गया। *2.* तुम्हें वह मिल गया जो तुम चाहते थे। *3.* मुझे लगता है कि हमें यह मिल गया। *4.* मुझे लगता है मुझे यह मिल गया है. *5.* मुझे लगता है मुझे कुछ मिल गया है. *6.* मुझे लगता है हमें कुछ मिल गया है.

• *1.* I got it, I got it. *2.* You got what you wanted. *3.* I think we got it. *4.* I think I've got it. *5.* I think I've got something. *6.* I think we got something.

**[140]** *1.* मुझे लगता है कि हमें वह मिल गया। *2.* मैं जो चाहता था वह मुझे मिल गया। *3.* आप जो चाहते थे वह आपको मिल गया। *4.* ठीक है, मुझे लगता है मुझे यह मिल गया। *5.* नहीं, मुझे यह मिल गया, मुझे यह मिल गया। *6.* तुम जो चाहते हो वह मुझे मिल गया।

• *1.* I think we got him. *2.* I got what I wanted. *3.* You got what you want. *4.* Okay, I think I got it. *5.* No, I got it, I got it. *6.* I got what you want.

**[141]** *1.* मुझे लगता है कि हमें यह मिल गया है। *2.* मुझे वह सब कुछ मिल गया जो मुझे चाहिए। *3.* हाँ, मुझे यह मिल गया, मुझे यह मिल गया। *4.* उसे वह मिल गया जो वह चाहता था। *5.* मैं जानता हूं कि तुम्हें क्या मिल रहा है। *6.* यह वह सब है जो मुझे मिल सकता है।

• *1.* I think we've got it. *2.* I got everything I need. *3.* Yeah, I got it, I got it. *4.* He got what he wanted. *5.* I know what you're getting at. *6.* It's all I could get.

**[142]** *1.* मुझे लगता है आपको यह मिल गया है। *2.* तुम जो चाहते हो वह मुझे मिल गया है। *3.* तुम्हें यह मिल गया, तुम्हें यह मिल गया। *4.* ठीक है, मुझे यह मिल गया, मुझे यह मिल गया। *5.* मुझे लगता है मुझे कुछ मिल गया होगा. *6.* नहीं, मुझे लगता है मुझे यह मिल गया।

• *1.* I think you've got it. *2.* I've got what you want. *3.* You got it, you got it. *4.* Okay, I got it, I got it. *5.* I think I might have found something. *6.* No, I think I got it.

**[143]** *1.* मैं जानता हूं तुम्हें यह मिल गया है। *2.* आप इसे चाहते थे, आपको यह मिल गया। *3.* मुझे लगता है कि उसे यह मिल गया है। *4.* मुझे लगता है कि उसे एक बात मिल गई है। *5.* आप इसे चाहते हैं, आपको यह मिल गया। *6.* मुझे लगता है मुझे यह मिल रहा है।

● *1.* I know you've got it. *2.* You wanted it, you got it. *3.* I think she's got it. *4.* I think he's got a point. *5.* You want it, you got it. *6.* I think I'm getting it.

**[144]** *1.* उसे वह मिल गया जो वह चाहता है। *2.* तुम जो चाहते थे वह मुझे मिल गया। *3.* यह ठीक है, मैं तुम्हें मिल गया हूँ। *4.* ठीक है, मुझे लगता है हमें यह मिल गया। *5.* उन्हें वह मिल गया जो वे चाहते थे। *6.* आपको वह मिल गया जो आप चाहते थे!

● *1.* He's got what he wants. *2.* I got what you wanted. *3.* It's okay, I've got you. *4.* Okay, I think we got it. *5.* They got what they wanted. *6.* You got what you wanted!

**[145]** *1.* यह सब ठीक है, मैं तुम्हें मिल गया हूँ। *2.* ऐसा लगता है कि वह हमें मिल गया है। *3.* क्या मुझे कृपया एक और मिल सकता है? *4.* मुझे यह मिल गया है, मुझे यह मिल गया है। *5.* मुझे नहीं पता था कि तुम बाहर हो। *6.* आप यहाँ से बाहर नहीं जा रहे हैं!

● *1.* It's all right, I've got you. *2.* Looks like we got him. *3.* Can I have another one, please? *4.* I've got it, I've got it. *5.* I didn't know you were out. *6.* You're not getting out of here!

**[146]** *1.* क्या आप यहाँ से बाहर आ सकते हैं? *2.* ठीक है, अब आप बाहर आ सकते हैं। *3.* मैं कुछ समय के लिए बाहर गया हूं। *4.* मुझे लगता है मैं बाहर जा रहा हूं। *5.* क्या मैं तुम्हें बाहर ले जा सकता हूँ? *6.* यह तुम्हें फिर से देखा तो अच्छा लगा।

● *1.* Can you come out here? *2.* All right, you can come out now. *3.* I've been away for a while. *4.* I think I'm gonna head out. *5.* Can I walk you out? *6.* It's good to see you again.

**[147]** *1.* मुझे लगा कि तुम नहीं आ रहे हो। *2.* मुझे लगा कि आप बात करना चाहते हैं। *3.* मुझे लगा कि आपको ये पसंद आ सकते हैं। *4.* मुझे लगा कि तुम्हें कुछ हो गया है। *5.* मुझे लगा कि आप मदद कर सकते हैं। *6.* मुझे लगा कि हम बाहर जा रहे हैं।

● *1.* I thought you weren't coming. *2.* I thought you wanted to talk. *3.* I thought you might like these. *4.* I thought something happened to you. *5.* I thought you could help. *6.* I thought we were going out.

**[148]** *1.* नहीं, मुझे लगा कि आपने ऐसा किया है। *2.* मुझे लगा कि मैं जानता हूं कि मैं कौन हूं। *3.* मुझे लगा कि मैं आपकी मदद कर रहा हूं. *4.* मुझे लगा कि

आप बाहर जा रहे हैं. 5. मुझे लगा कि आप मेरी मदद करना चाहते हैं. 6. मुझे लगा कि आपको कुछ पसंद आ सकते हैं।

● 1. No, I thought you did. 2. I thought I knew who I was. 3. I thought I was helping you. 4. I thought you were going out. 5. I thought you wanted to help me. 6. I thought you might like some.

[149] 1. मुझे लगा कि आप उन्हें पसंद कर सकते हैं. 2. मुझे लगा कि हम साथ काम कर रहे हैं। 3. मुझे लगा कि तुम वापस नहीं आ रहे हो. 4. मुझे लगा कि आप मेरी मदद कर सकते हैं. 5. मुझे लगा कि आपको यह पसंद आ सकता है. 6. मुझे लगा कि आप बहुत अच्छा कर रहे हैं.

● 1. I thought you might like them. 2. I thought we were working together. 3. I thought you weren't coming back. 4. I thought you could help me. 5. I thought you might like that. 6. I thought you were doing so well.

[150] 1. मुझे लगा कि तुम्हें वह मिल गया है। 2. देखो, मुझे पता है तुम क्या कर रहे हो। 3. आप इस तरह क्यों बात कर रहे हैं? 4. आप इसे इस तरह से नहीं कर सकते. 5. मैं इसे इस तरह से पसंद करता हूं. 6. मैंने उसे इस तरह कभी नहीं देखा था.

● 1. I thought you got that. 2. Look, I know what you're doing. 3. Why are you talking like this? 4. You can't do it that way. 5. I prefer it this way. 6. I'd never seen him like that.

[151] 1. मुझे लगता है कि यह इस तरह का है। 2. मैं इसके बारे में बात नहीं करना चाहता. 3. क्या आप इसके बारे में कुछ जानते हैं? 4. आप इसके बारे में कुछ नहीं कर सकते। 5. इसके बारे में हम कुछ नहीं कर सकते। 6. आप जानते हैं कि मैं इसके लिए अच्छा हूं।

● 1. I guess it kind of is. 2. I don't wanna talk about it. 3. You know anything about that? 4. There's nothing you can do about it. 5. There's nothing we can do about it. 6. You know I'm good for it.

[152] 1. हम इसके बारे में क्या करने जा रहे हैं? 2. आप इसके साथ क्या करने जा रहे हैं? 3. हम इसके बारे में क्या कर सकते हैं? 4. अच्छा, आप इसके बारे में क्या जानते हैं? 5. हम इसके बारे में बात कर सकते हैं. 6. आप इसके बारे में क्या करना चाहते हैं?

● 1. What are we gonna do about it? 2. What are you going to do with that? 3. What can we do about it? 4. Well, what do you know about that? 5. We can talk about it. 6. What do you want to do about it?

[153] 1. आपको इसके बारे में कुछ भी पता नहीं है. 2. आप इसके बारे में क्या

कर सकते हैं? *3.* हम इसके साथ क्या करने जा रहे हैं? *4.* आप को इसके बारे में क्या पसंद है? *5.* क्या हम इसके बारे में बात कर सकते हैं? *6.* हम इसके बारे में कुछ नहीं कर सकते.

• *1.* You don't know anything about it. *2.* What can you do about it? *3.* What are we going to do with it? *4.* What do you like about it? *5.* Can we talk about it? *6.* Nothing we can do about it.

**[154]** *1.* मुझे नहीं पता कि इसके साथ क्या करना है। *2.* अब हम इसके बारे में कुछ नहीं कर सकते। *3.* आप इसके बारे में कुछ भी नहीं कर सकते हैं। *4.* और इसके बारे में हम कुछ नहीं कर सकते। *5.* आप इसके बारे में कुछ भी नहीं जानते। *6.* वह इसके बारे में सब कुछ जानता है।

• *1.* I wouldn't know what to do with it. *2.* There's nothing we can do about it now. *3.* Nothing you can do about it. *4.* And there's nothing we can do about it. *5.* You don't know a damn thing about it. *6.* He knows all about it.

**[155]** *1.* और आप इसके बारे में क्या जानते हैं? *2.* हम इसके बारे में सब कुछ जानते हैं. *3.* अब आप इसके बारे में कुछ नहीं कर सकते। *4.* मैं इसके बारे में कुछ करने जा रहा हूं. *5.* आप इसके बारे में क्या करने जा रहे हैं? *6.* लेकिन हम इसके बारे में क्या कर सकते हैं?

• *1.* And what do you know about it? *2.* We know all about it. *3.* There's nothing you can do about it now. *4.* I'm going to do something about it. *5.* What you going to do about it? *6.* But what can we do about it?

**[156]** *1.* तो हम इसके बारे में क्या करने जा रहे हैं? *2.* क्या आप इसके बारे में बहुत कुछ जानते हैं? *3.* हाँ, मुझे इसके बारे में सब पता है। *4.* मुझे इसके बारे में सब कुछ पसंद है. *5.* अच्छा, मैं इसके बारे में क्या कर सकता हूँ? *6.* इसके बारे में आप कुछ नहीं कर सकते।

• *1.* So what are we gonna do about it? *2.* Do you know much about it? *3.* Yeah, I know all about it. *4.* I like everything about it. *5.* Well, what can I do about it? *6.* There's nothing you can do about that.

**[157]** *1.* हम इसके बारे में बात कर रहे थे. *2.* क्या वह इसके बारे में बात करता है? *3.* हम क्या कर रहे हैं इसके बारे में. *4.* लेकिन आपको इसके बारे में कुछ भी पता नहीं होगा. *5.* क्या आप इसके साथ कुछ भी कर सकते हैं? *6.* ठीक है, चलो इसके बारे में बात करते हैं।

• *1.* We were talking about it. *2.* Does he talk about it? *3.* About what we're doing. *4.* But you wouldn't know anything about that. *5.* Can you do anything with it? *6.* All right, let's talk about it.

**[158]** *1.* क्या आप इसके बारे में कुछ नहीं कर सकते? *2.* अभी मेरे पास इसके लिए समय नहीं है. *3.* ओह, मेरे पास इसके लिए समय नहीं है। *4.* ऐसा नहीं है कि हम इसके बारे में जानते हैं। *5.* तो क्या आपको इसके बारे में पता था? *6.* और आप इसके बारे में क्या कर रहे हैं?

● *1.* Can't you do something about that? *2.* I don't have time for this now. *3.* Oh, I don't have time for this. *4.* Not that we're aware of. *5.* So you knew about this? *6.* And what are you doing about it?

**[159]** *1.* तुम इसके बारे में कुछ कर सकते हैं? *2.* क्या तुम मेरे साथ बाहर जाना चाहते हो? *3.* क्या अब और कुछ नहीं किया जाना चाहिए? *4.* यह वह सब कुछ है जो मैंने कभी जाना है। *5.* मैं जानता था कि मुझे नहीं जाना चाहिए था! *6.* क्या आप जानते हैं कि कहाँ जाना है?

● *1.* Can you do something about it? *2.* Do you want to go out with me? *3.* Must there no more be done? *4.* It's all I've ever known. *5.* I knew I shouldn't have went! *6.* Do you know where to go?

**[160]** *1.* आप जानते हैं कि क्या किया जाना चाहिए. *2.* मैं आपकी मदद करने के लिए यहां हूं. *3.* मुझे पता है यहां क्या हो रहा है. *4.* मुझे पता है मैं यहां क्या कर रहा हूं. *5.* मुझे लगता है मुझे यहां कुछ मिल गया है. *6.* मैं तुम्हें यहां से ले जा रहा हूं.

● *1.* You know what must be done. *2.* I'm here to help you. *3.* I know what's going on here. *4.* I know what I'm doing here. *5.* I think I got something here. *6.* I'm taking you out of here.

**[161]** *1.* मुझे नहीं पता था कि यहां कोई है. *2.* क्या आप यहां काम करना पसंद करते हैं? *3.* हम यहां से बाहर नहीं जा रहे हैं. *4.* यहां वह सब कुछ है जो आपको चाहिए। *5.* क्या आप यहां मेरी मदद कर सकते हैं? *6.* मैं यहां इसके बारे में बात नहीं करना चाहता.

● *1.* I didn't know anyone was in here. *2.* Do you like working here? *3.* We're not getting out of here. *4.* Here's everything you need. *5.* Can you give me a hand here? *6.* I don't want to talk about it here.

**[162]** *1.* मुझे नहीं लगता कि हम यहां के हैं. *2.* लेकिन मैं जानता हूं कि मैं यहां क्यों हूं. *3.* हम यहां आपके बारे में बात करने के लिए हैं. *4.* आप जानते हैं कि यहां क्या करना होगा. *5.* हम सब जानते हैं कि यहां क्या हो रहा है. *6.* मुझे लगता है मैं जानता हूं कि यहां क्या हुआ।

● *1.* I don't think we belong here. *2.* But I know why I'm here. *3.* We're here to talk about you. *4.* You know what has to be done here. *5.* We all know what's going on here. *6.* I think I know what happened here.

**[163]** *1.* तुम मेरे घर में क्या कर रहे हो? *2.* क्या मैं तुम्हें घर ले जा सकता हूँ? *3.* क्या आप मुझे घर ले जा सकते हैं? *4.* क्या आप अपने घर का काम कर रहे हैं? *5.* मुझे लगा कि हम घर जा रहे हैं। *6.* मैं बस यही चाहता हूं कि तुम घर आओ।

● *1.* What are you doing in my house? *2.* Can I take you home? *3.* Can you take me home? *4.* Are you doing your homework? *5.* I thought we were going home. *6.* I just want you to come home.

**[164]** *1.* क्या मैं तुम्हें घर ले जा रहा हूँ? *2.* मैं बस घर जाना चाहता हूँ, ठीक है? *3.* मैं चाहता हूँ कि तुम मेरे साथ घर आओ। *4.* मुझे नहीं लगता कि वह घर पर है. *5.* क्या आपने उससे इस बारे में बात की है? *6.* मैं चाहता हूं कि आप उससे बात करें.

● *1.* Am I taking you home? *2.* I just want to go home, okay? *3.* I want you to come home with me. *4.* I don't think he's home. *5.* Have you talked to him about it? *6.* I want you to talk to her.

**[165]** *1.* आप उससे इस तरह बात नहीं कर सकते. *2.* क्या मैं उससे कुछ बात कर सकता हूँ? *3.* क्या आप अब भी उससे बात करते हैं? *4.* क्या मैं किसी के साथ आपकी मदद कर सकता हूं? *5.* यह किसी के साथ भी हो सकता है. *6.* क्या किसी और को इसके बारे में पता है?

● *1.* You can't talk to her like that. *2.* Could I have a word with him? *3.* Do you still talk to him? *4.* Can I help you with something? *5.* It could happen to anybody. *6.* Does anyone else know about this?

**[166]** *1.* क्या किसी को पता है कि आप यहाँ हैं? *2.* ऐसा लगता है कि किसी को पता नहीं है। *3.* मैं किसी से बात नहीं कर रहा था. *4.* क्या आप किसी से बात कर रहे थे? *5.* मैं किसी भी तरह से मदद करना चाहता हूं। *6.* मुझे लगा कि मैंने किसी को देखा है.

● *1.* Does anyone know you're here? *2.* No one seems to know. *3.* I wasn't talking to anybody. *4.* Were you talking to someone? *5.* I want to help any way I can. *6.* I thought I saw someone.

**[167]** *1.* वह तुम में से किसी का काम नहीं है! *2.* मैं अभी किसी से नहीं मिल रहा हूं. *3.* मैं जानता हूं कि यह किसी के पास है। *4.* आपको लगता है कि आप किसी को जानते हैं. *5.* आप जानते है मैं आपको प्यार करता हूँ। *6.* मुझे लगता है कि मैं प्यार में हूँ।

● *1.* That is none of your business! *2.* I'm not seeing anyone right now. *3.* I know someone has it. *4.* You think you know someone. *5.* You know I love you. *6.* I think I'm in love.

**[168]** *1.* आपने कहा कि आप मुझे प्यार करते हैं। *2.* क्या तुम अब भी उससे प्यार करते हो? *3.* क्या आप अब भी उससे प्यार करते हैं? *4.* आप प्यार के बारे में क्या जानते हैं? *5.* मुझे लगता है कि मुझे प्यार हो रहा है। *6.* और मैं आप के साथ प्यार में हूँ।

• *1.* You said you loved me. *2.* Do you still love her? *3.* Are you still in love with him? *4.* What do you know about love? *5.* I think I'm falling in love. *6.* And I'm in love with you.

**[169]** *1.* मुझे लगता है कि वह प्यार में है। *2.* क्या आप किसी और से प्यार करते हैं? *3.* मैं चाहता हूं कि तुम मुझे प्यार करो। *4.* मुझे लगता है मैं उससे प्यार करता हूं। *5.* मुझे लगा कि मुझे उससे प्यार हो गया है। *6.* मैं प्यार करता हूँ और मैं प्यार करता हूँ।

• *1.* I think he's in love. *2.* Do you love someone else? *3.* I want you to love me. *4.* I think I love him. *5.* I thought I was in love with him. *6.* I love and I'm loved.

**[170]** *1.* मुझे लगता है मुझे उससे प्यार हो गया है। *2.* मैं प्यार के बारे में क्या जानता हूँ? *3.* मैंने कभी किसी और से प्यार नहीं किया। *4.* मुझे पता है तुम उससे प्यार करते हो। *5.* मुझे लगता है तुम उससे प्यार करते हो। *6.* मैंने उससे कहा कि मैं उससे प्यार करता हूं।

• *1.* I think I'm in love with him. *2.* What do I know about love? *3.* I've never loved anyone else. *4.* I know you love him. *5.* I think you love her. *6.* I told her I loved her.

**[171]** *1.* क्या आप अब भी मुझसे प्यार करते हैं? *2.* उसने मुझसे कहा कि वह मुझसे प्यार करता है। *3.* मुझे पता है तुमने मुझसे क्या कहा था। *4.* आप मुझसे इस तरह बात नहीं कर सकते। *5.* तुम मुझसे इस तरह बात क्यों करते हो? *6.* उसने कहा कि वह मुझसे प्यार करता है।

• *1.* Do you still love me? *2.* He told me he loved me. *3.* I know what you told me. *4.* You can't talk to me that way. *5.* Why do you talk to me like that? *6.* He said he loved me.

**[172]** *1.* मुझे पता है वह मुझसे प्यार करता है। *2.* तुम मुझसे इस तरह क्यों बात कर रहे हो? *3.* तुमने मुझसे कहा था कि तुम मुझसे प्यार करते हो। *4.* आप मुझसे बात कर सकते हैं, आप जानते हैं। *5.* क्या आप जानते हैं उसने मुझसे क्या कहा? *6.* उन्होंने मुझसे कहा कि आप आ रहे हैं।

• *1.* I know he loves me. *2.* Why are you talking to me like this? *3.* You told me you loved me. *4.* You can talk to me, you know. *5.* Do you know what he said to me? *6.* They told me you were coming.

**[173]** *1.* तुम मुझसे इस तरह कैसे बात कर सकते हो? *2.* तुम मुझसे इस तरह बात नहीं कर सकते। *3.* मैंने वह सब कुछ किया जो आपने मुझसे कहा था। *4.*

मुझे लगा कि अब तुम मुझसे प्यार नहीं करते। 5. मुझे लगा कि तुम मुझसे बात नहीं कर रहे हो. 6. तुमने कहा था कि तुम मुझसे प्यार करते हो।

● 1. How can you talk to me like that? 2. You can't speak to me like that. 3. I did everything you asked of me. 4. I thought you didn't love me anymore. 5. I thought you weren't talking to me. 6. You said that you loved me.

[174] 1. मैं जानता था कि तुम मुझसे प्यार करते हो। 2. तुम अब भी मुझसे बात नहीं कर रहे हो? 3. क्या तुम मुझसे वापस बात कर रहे हो? 4. मुझे लगता है कि वह मुझसे प्यार करता है. 5. तुमने अभी कहा कि तुम मुझसे प्यार करते हो। 6. मुझे लगा कि वह मुझसे प्यार करता है.

● 1. I knew you loved me. 2. You're still not talking to me? 3. Are you talking back to me? 4. I think he's in love with me. 5. You just said that you love me. 6. I thought he loved me.

[175] 1. मैं नहीं जानता कि तुम मुझसे क्या चाहते हो! 2. आप मुझसे इस बारे में क्यों बात कर रहे हैं? 3. मेरा कभी भी वहाँ जाना नहीं हुआ है। 4. क्या आपको लगता है यह अभी भी वहाँ है? 5. क्या मैं तुम्हें वहाँ ले जा सकता हूँ? 6. क्या आप हमें वहां ले जा सकते हैं?

● 1. I don't know what you want from me! 2. Why are you talking to me about this? 3. I've never been there. 4. Do you think it's still there? 5. Can I take you there? 6. Can you take us there?

[176] 1. तो फिर आप वहां क्या कर रहे थे? 2. क्या आप अभी भी वहां से बाहर हैं? 3. मुझे लगता है कि यह वहां पर है। 4. मैं तुम्हें अभी वहां ले जा सकता हूं. 5. मुझे नहीं पता था कि वे वहां थे. 6. लेकिन वह अभी भी वहां से बाहर है.

● 1. Then what were you doing there? 2. Are you still out there? 3. I think it's over there. 4. I can take you there right now. 5. I didn't know they were there. 6. But he's still out there.

[177] 1. आप वहां से वापस नहीं जा रहे हैं. 2. मैं वहां से वापस नहीं जा रहा हूं. 3. हम वह सब कुछ करेंगे जो हम कर सकते हैं। 4. आपने कहा था कि आप मेरी मदद करेंगे। 5. तुम्हें क्या लगता है वे उसके साथ क्या करेंगे? 6. हम इस बारे में फिर कभी बात करेंगे.

● 1. You're not going back out there. 2. I'm not going back out there. 3. We'll do everything we can. 4. You said you'd help me. 5. What do you think they'll do to him? 6. We'll talk about this another time.

[178] 1. हम इसके बारे में फिर कभी बात करेंगे. 2. क्या आपको लगता है कि वे ऐसा करेंगे? 3. नहीं, मुझे लगता है आप ऐसा नहीं करेंगे। 4. ओह, मुझे नहीं लगता कि आप ऐसा करेंगे। 5. लेकिन मैं जानता हूं आप ऐसा नहीं करेंगे. 6. और

308

आपको लगता है कि वे ऐसा करेंगे?
- *1.* We'll talk about it some other time. *2.* You think they'll do it? *3.* No, I guess you wouldn't. *4.* Oh, I don't think you will. *5.* But I know you won't. *6.* And you think they will?

**[179]** *1.* आपने कहा था कि आप मेरे लिए कुछ भी करेंगे। *2.* मुझे लगा कि मैं सही काम कर रहा हूं। *3.* आप एक बात के बारे में सही थे। *4.* आप एक बात के बारे में सही हैं। *5.* मुझे लगता है की तुम सही हो सकते हो। *6.* मुझे लगता है कि यह करना सही काम है।
- *1.* You said you'd do anything for me. *2.* I thought I was doing the right thing. *3.* You were right about one thing. *4.* You're right about one thing. *5.* I think you may be right. *6.* I think it's the right thing to do.

**[180]** *1.* वह एक बात के बारे में सही थे। *2.* तुम्हें पता है, मुझे लगता है कि तुम सही हो। *3.* मुझे लगता है वह सही हो सकता है। *4.* मुझे लगता है कि आप इस बारे में सही हैं। *5.* क्या आपको लगता है कि यह सही है? *6.* हाँ, मुझे लगता है कि यह सही है।
- *1.* He was right about one thing. *2.* You know, I think you're right. *3.* I think he might be right. *4.* I think you're right about that. *5.* Do you think that's right? *6.* Yes, I think that's right.

**[181]** *1.* मुझे लगता है आप सही काम कर रहे हैं. *2.* यह सही है, मैं वापस आ गया हूँ। *3.* यह सही है, आप ऐसा नहीं कर सकते। *4.* लेकिन मैं जानता हूं कि यह सही है. *5.* ठीक है, आप सही हैं, आप सही हैं। *6.* मैं जानता हूं कि मैं इस बारे में सही हूं।
- *1.* I think you're doing the right thing. *2.* That's right, I'm back. *3.* That's right, you can't. *4.* But I know it's right. *5.* Okay, you're right, you're right. *6.* I know I'm right about this.

**[182]** *1.* लेकिन ये तो बहुत पहले की बात है। *2.* लेकिन आपको यह पहले से ही पता था। *3.* लेकिन आप को यह पहले से ही पता है। *4.* मुझे पहले से ही एक मिल गया है। *5.* मैंने उसे पहले कभी इस तरह नहीं देखा था। *6.* मैं उसे पहले से ही पसंद करता हूं.
- *1.* But that was a long time ago. *2.* But you already knew that. *3.* But you already know that. *4.* I already got one. *5.* I've never seen him like that before. *6.* I like him already.

**[183]** *1.* यह तो मुझे पहले से ही पता है। *2.* यह तो हम पहले से ही जानते थे। *3.* यह पहले से ही काम कर रहा है। *4.* क्या आपने पहले कभी ऐसा कुछ देखा है? *5.* मुझे लगता है आप पहले से ही जानते हैं। *6.* आप पहले से ही बहुत कुछ जानते हैं।
- *1.* I already know it. *2.* We already knew that. *3.* It's working

already. *4.* Have you ever seen anything like this before? *5.* I think you already know. *6.* You already know too much.

**[184]** *1.* क्या आपने पहले कभी ऐसा कुछ किया है? *2.* यह तो हम पहले से ही जानते हैं। *3.* क्या आप पहले से ही जा रहे हैं? *4.* यह मेरे समय से पहले की बात है. *5.* क्या आप पहले से ही घर पर हैं? *6.* मुझे पता था कि मैंने इसे पहले भी देखा है।

• *1.* You ever done anything like this before? *2.* We already know that. *3.* Are you going already? *4.* It's before my time. *5.* Are you home already? *6.* I knew I'd seen it before.

**[185]** *1.* उसके पास पहले से ही सब कुछ है. *2.* मुझे पता था कि मैंने उसे पहले भी देखा है। *3.* ऐसा मेरे साथ पहले कभी नहीं हुआ था. *4.* मुझे लगता है आपके पास पहले से ही है. *5.* मेरे साथ पहले कभी ऐसा कुछ नहीं हुआ. *6.* मुझे लगता है मेरे पास पहले से ही है.

• *1.* He's already got everything. *2.* I knew I'd seen him before. *3.* This never happened to me before. *4.* I think you already have. *5.* Nothing like this ever happened to me before. *6.* I think I already have.

**[186]** *1.* मैं पहले से ही जानता हूं कि तुम कौन हो. *2.* आपको पहले से ही एक मिल गया है. *3.* लेकिन ये तो आप पहले से ही जानते हैं. *4.* ऐसा कुछ भी नहीं जो मैंने पहले कभी देखा हो. *5.* मुझे लगता है मैं पहले से ही हूं. *6.* पहले तो मुझे लगा कि यह आप ही हैं।

• *1.* I already know who you are. *2.* You already got one. *3.* But you already know this. *4.* Nothing I've ever seen before. *5.* I think I already am. *6.* At first I thought it was you.

**[187]** *1.* यह वह नहीं है जो आपने पहले कहा था। *2.* मैं उससे पहले से ही प्यार करता हूं. *3.* कुछ ऐसा करें जो आपने पहले कभी नहीं किया हो. *4.* आपके पास पहले से ही सब कुछ है. *5.* आपने पहले कभी ऐसा नहीं किया है क्या? *6.* आप पहले से ही सब कुछ जानते हैं.

• *1.* That's not what you said before. *2.* I love her already. *3.* Do something you've never done before. *4.* You already have everything. *5.* You haven't done this before, have you? *6.* You already know everything.

**[188]** *1.* पहले कभी किसी ने मेरे लिए ऐसा नहीं किया। *2.* हाँ, मैं पहले से ही इस पर हूँ। *3.* यह तो आप पहले से ही जानते थे. *4.* ओह, मुझे यह पहले से ही पता था। *5.* मुझे लगता है कि मैं इसका पता लगा सकता हूं। *6.* हम अभी भी इसका पता लगा रहे हैं।

• *1.* No one's ever done that for me before. *2.* Yeah, I'm already on it. *3.* You knew that already. *4.* Duh, I already knew that. *5.*

I think I can figure it out. *6.* We're still figuring it out.

**[189]** *1.* मुझे पता है यह आपसे हो सकता है। *2.* मुझे लगता है मैं आपसे प्यार करता हूँ। *3.* क्या मैं आपसे कुछ बात कर सकता हूँ? *4.* क्या मैं आपसे बात कर सकता हूँ, कृपया? *5.* मैं आपसे अब और बात नहीं कर रहा हूं। *6.* कृपया क्या मैं आपसे कुछ बात कर सकता हूँ?
- *1.* I knew you could do it. *2.* I think I love you. *3.* May I have a word with you? *4.* Can I talk to you, please? *5.* I'm not talking to you any more. *6.* May I have a word with you, please?

**[190]** *1.* क्या मैं आपसे बाहर बात कर सकता हूँ? *2.* मैंने आपसे ऐसा करने के लिए कभी नहीं कहा. *3.* कोई भी आपसे बात नहीं कर रहा है. *4.* मुझे लगता है कि वह आपसे प्यार करता है. *5.* मैं इस बारे में आपसे बात नहीं कर सकता. *6.* क्या हम आपसे कुछ बात कर सकते हैं?
- *1.* Can I talk to you outside? *2.* I never asked you to do that. *3.* Nobody's talking to you. *4.* I think he's in love with you. *5.* I can't talk to you about this. *6.* Can we have a word with you?

**[191]** *1.* मुझे लगता है वह आपसे बात कर रही है. *2.* मैंने आपसे ऐसा करने के लिए नहीं कहा था. *3.* नहीं, मैं आपसे बात नहीं कर रहा था. *4.* क्या आप जानते हो कि मैं आपसे प्यार करता हूं? *5.* मैं आपसे प्यार करता हूँ और आपको यह पता है। *6.* क्या मैं अब आपसे बात कर सकता हूँ?
- *1.* I think she's talking to you. *2.* I didn't ask you to do this. *3.* No, I wasn't talking to you. *4.* Do you know that I love you? *5.* I love you and you know it. *6.* Can I talk to you now?

**[192]** *1.* मुझे लगता है वह आपसे बात कर रहा है. *2.* मैं अब भी आपसे बात क्यों कर रहा हूं? *3.* क्या कोई आपसे बात नहीं कर रहा है? *4.* मैं तो बस आपसे बात कर रहा हूं. *5.* मुझे लगता है हमें बात करने की जरूरत है. *6.* आप जानते हैं कि क्या करने की जरूरत है.
- *1.* I think he's talking to you. *2.* Why am I still talking to you? *3.* Ain't nobody talking to you. *4.* I'm just talking to you. *5.* I think we need to talk. *6.* You know what needs to be done.

## Difficulty Level: 6

**[1]** *1.* तुम्हें क्या लगता है तुम मेरे साथ क्या कर रहे हो? *2.* क्या आपको लगता है कि आप इसे ठीक कर सकते हैं? *3.* मुझे ठीक-ठीक पता था कि मैं क्या कर रहा हूं। *4.* क्या तुम्हें पता भी है कि तुम क्या कर रहे हो? *5.* तुम्हें पता है मुझे क्या लगता है तुम्हें क्या करना चाहिए? *6.* मुझे लगता है वह आपके बारे में बात कर रहा है.
- *1.* What do you think you're doing to me? *2.* Think you can

fix it? *3.* I knew exactly what I was doing. *4.* Do you even know what you're doing? *5.* You know what I think you should do? *6.* I think he's talking about you.

**[2]** *1.* मुझे ठीक-ठीक पता है कि उसके साथ क्या करना है। *2.* हम अभी भी इस बारे में बात क्यों कर रहे हैं? *3.* बस आपको क्या लगता है कि आप कहाँ जा रहे हैं? *4.* तुम्हें यह भी नहीं पता कि तुम कहाँ जा रहे हो। *5.* मुझे ठीक-ठीक पता है कि मैं कहाँ जा रहा हूँ। *6.* तुम्हें यह भी पता नहीं कि मैं कहाँ जा रहा हूँ।
• *1.* I know exactly what to do with him. *2.* Why are we still talking about this? *3.* Just where do you think you're going? *4.* You don't even know where you're going. *5.* I know exactly where I'm going. *6.* You don't even know where I'm going.

**[3]** *1.* मुझे लगता है आप जानते हैं कि मैं यहाँ क्यों हूँ। *2.* क्या आप जानते हैं कि आप मेरे साथ क्या कर रहे हैं? *3.* आप ठीक-ठीक जानते हैं कि आप क्या कर रहे हैं। *4.* मैं ठीक-ठीक जानता हूं कि मैं क्या कर रहा हूं। *5.* हाँ, मुझे लगता है मैं जानता हूँ कि क्या करना है। *6.* क्या आपको लगता है कि आप मेरी मदद कर सकते हैं?
• *1.* I think you know why I'm here. *2.* Do you know what you're doing to me? *3.* You know exactly what you're doing. *4.* I know exactly what I'm doing. *5.* Yes, I think I know what to do. *6.* Do you think you can help me?

**[4]** *1.* क्या हम इस बारे में फिर कभी बात कर सकते हैं? *2.* हम वह सब कुछ कर रहे हैं जो हम कर सकते हैं। *3.* ऐसा बहुत कुछ है जो आप मेरे बारे में नहीं जानते। *4.* मैं वह सब कर रहा हूं जो मैं कर सकता हूं। *5.* उसके पास जो कुछ भी है वह सब मैं ही हूं। *6.* मुझे लगता है कि मेरे पास वह सब कुछ है जो मुझे चाहिए।
• *1.* Can we talk about this some other time? *2.* We're doing everything we can. *3.* There's a lot you don't know about me. *4.* I'm doing all I can. *5.* I'm all she has. *6.* I think I have everything I need.

**[5]** *1.* मैं जो कुछ भी करता हूं वह सब तुम्हें पता है। *2.* आपने मेरे लिए जो कुछ भी किया है उसके लिए धन्यवाद। *3.* क्या आपको लगता है कि आप उसकी मदद कर सकते हैं? *4.* क्या आपको वह सब कुछ मिल गया जो आप चाहते थे? *5.* मुझे लगा कि आपने कहा था कि आप उसे नहीं जानते। *6.* इसके बारे में बात करने के लिए और कुछ नहीं है।
• *1.* You know everything I do. *2.* Thank you for everything you've done for me. *3.* You think you can help him? *4.* Got everything you want? *5.* I thought you said you didn't know him. *6.* There's nothing more to talk about.

**[6]** *1.* मुझे लगता है मैं जानता हूं कि यहां क्या हो रहा है। *2.* यह ठीक है, मैं आपकी मदद करने के लिए यहां हूं। *3.* क्या मैं आपकी किसी भी तरह से मदद कर सकता हूँ? *4.* मैं उससे प्यार करता हूँ, और वह मुझसे प्यार करता है। *5.* मैंने वह सब कुछ किया जो आपने मुझसे करने को कहा था। *6.* मैं जानता हूं कि मैं आपके लिए वहां नहीं गया हूं।

• *1.* I think I know what's going on here. *2.* It's okay, I'm here to help you. *3.* Can I help you in any way? *4.* I love him, and he loves me. *5.* I did everything you told me to do. *6.* I know I haven't been there for you.

**[7]** *1.* यह ऐसा कुछ नहीं है जो मैंने पहले नहीं देखा हो। *2.* लेकिन मुझे लगता है कि आप यह पहले से ही जानते हैं। *3.* लेकिन मुझे लगता है कि आप यह पहले से ही जानते थे। *4.* आप जानते हैं कि मैं उस बारे में बात नहीं कर सकता। *5.* मुझे लगता है मैं जानता हूं कि आपका मतलब क्या है। *6.* हाँ, ठीक है, आप जानते हैं कि मेरा क्या मतलब है।

• *1.* It's nothing I haven't seen before. *2.* But I guess you already know that. *3.* But I guess you already knew that. *4.* You know I can't talk about that. *5.* I think I know what you mean. *6.* Yeah, well, you know what I mean.

**[8]** *1.* आपको इसके बारे में कुछ भी पता नहीं होगा, है ना? *2.* तुम्हें पता है कि तुम क्या कर रहे हो, है ना? *3.* आप नहीं जानते कि आप क्या कर रहे हैं, है ना? *4.* लेकिन आप जानते हैं कि मेरा क्या मतलब है, है ना? *5.* ऐसा लग रहा था कि उन्हें यह पसंद आ रहा है। *6.* आप कुछ भी महसूस नहीं कर सकते, क्या आप कर सकते हैं?

• *1.* You wouldn't know anything about that, would you? *2.* You know what you're doing, right? *3.* You don't know what you're doing, do you? *4.* But you know what I mean, right? *5.* They seemed to like it. *6.* You can't feel anything, can you?

**[9]** *1.* तुम्हें पता है कि मुझे तुम्हारे बारे में क्या पसंद है? *2.* हमारे पास जो कुछ भी है वह सब हम ही हैं। *3.* क्या हम इस बारे में बात करना बंद कर सकते हैं? *4.* ऐसा कुछ भी नहीं है जो मैं आपके लिए नहीं करूंगा। *5.* अरे, आपको क्या लगता है कि आप कहाँ जा रहे हैं? *6.* अरे हम तो बस आपके बारे में बात कर रहे थे।

• *1.* You know what I love about you? *2.* We're all we've got. *3.* Can we stop talking about this? *4.* There's nothing I wouldn't do for you. *5.* Hey, where do you think you're going? *6.* Hey, we were just talking about you.

**[10]** *1.* क्या आप देख रहे हैं कि यहाँ क्या हो रहा है? *2.* मैं यह नहीं देख रहा था कि मैं कहाँ जा रहा हूँ। *3.* मैं महसूस कर सकता हूं कि वह मुझे देख रहा है। *4.* मुझे लगता है कि अब आपके जाने का समय हो गया है। *5.* मुझे लगा कि मैंने

313

तुम्हें घर जाने के लिए कहा है। 6. मुझे पता है आप क्या करने की कोशिश कर रहे हैं.

• 1. Do you see what's happening here? 2. I wasn't looking where I was going. 3. I can feel him watching me. 4. I think it's time for you to leave. 5. I thought I told you to go home. 6. I know what you're trying to do.

[11] 1. मुझे यह भी नहीं पता कि मैं कोशिश क्यों करता हूं। 2. मैं विश्वास नहीं कर सकता कि हम ऐसा कर रहे हैं। 3. मुझे विश्वास नहीं हो रहा कि मेरे साथ ऐसा हो रहा है. 4. मैं जो देख रहा हूं उस पर विश्वास नहीं हो रहा. 5. मुझे विश्वास नहीं हो रहा कि आपने मेरे साथ ऐसा किया। 6. जो मैंने अभी देखा उस पर मुझे विश्वास नहीं हो रहा।

• 1. I don't even know why I try. 2. I can't believe we're doing this. 3. I can't believe this is happening to me. 4. I can't believe what I'm seeing. 5. I can't believe you did this to me. 6. I can't believe what I just saw.

[12] 1. मेरा विश्वास करो, मुझे पता है कि मैं क्या कर रहा हूं। 2. मुझे विश्वास ही नहीं हो रहा कि ऐसा हो रहा है। 3. मैं आपकी किसी भी बात पर कैसे विश्वास कर सकता हूँ? 4. मुझे विश्वास नहीं हो रहा कि मैं आपसे मिल रहा हूं. 5. मुझे अब भी विश्वास नहीं हो रहा कि तुम यहाँ हो। 6. मेरा मतलब है, क्या आप उस पर विश्वास कर सकते हैं?

• 1. Believe me, I know what I'm doing. 2. I just can't believe this is happening. 3. How can I believe anything you say? 4. I can't believe I'm meeting you. 5. I still can't believe you're here. 6. I mean, can you believe that?

[13] 1. मैं जो देख रहा हूँ उस पर विश्वास नहीं हो रहा! 2. मैं देख रहा हूं कि आप बेहतर महसूस कर रहे हैं। 3. क्या आपके पास करने के लिए कुछ भी बेहतर नहीं है? 4. हमने वह सब कुछ किया है जो हम कर सकते हैं। 5. उनके पास जो कुछ भी है वह सब मैं ही हूं। 6. ऐसा लगता है कि आप उसे अच्छी तरह से जानते हैं।

• 1. I can't believe what I'm seeing! 2. I see you're feeling better. 3. Haven't you anything better to do? 4. We've done everything we can. 5. I'm all they have. 6. You seem to know him well.

[14] 1. हम इस आदमी के बारे में क्या करने जा रहे हैं? 2. मुझे पता है मैं किस बारे में बात कर रहा हूं. 3. क्या आप जानते हैं कि वह किस पर काम कर रहा था? 4. मैंने तुमसे कहा था कि वह कुछ करने को तैयार है। 5. क्या आप इसके बारे में बात करने के लिए तैयार हैं? 6. मैं हमेशा से जानता था कि आप यह कर सकते हैं।

• 1. What are we gonna do about this guy? 2. I know what I'm talking about. *3.* Do you know what he was working on? *4.* I told you he was up to something. *5.* You ready to talk about it? *6.* I always knew you could do it.

**[15]** *1.* मुझे विश्वास ही नहीं हो रहा कि वह चला गया है। *2.* मुझे लगता है कि मैं इसमें आपकी मदद कर सकता हूं. *3.* वह कहां से आया, इसके बारे में और भी बहुत कुछ। *4.* मुझे लगता है मैं जानता हूं कि वे कहां जा रहे हैं। *5.* मुझे लगता है मैं जानता हूं कि यह कहां जा रहा है। *6.* आप जानते हैं कि मैं इसके साथ कहां जा रहा हूं।

• *1.* I just can't believe he's gone. *2.* I think I can help you with that. *3.* Plenty more where that came from. *4.* I think I know where they're going. *5.* I think I know where this is going. *6.* You know where I'm going with this.

**[16]** *1.* मुझे लगता है मुझे पता है कि वह कहां गया था. *2.* मैं देख रहा हूं कि आप इसके साथ कहां जा रहे हैं। *3.* मुझे लगता है कि मेरे पास एक बहुत अच्छा विचार है. *4.* आप जानते हैं कि मैं किस बारे में बात कर रहा हूँ, है न? *5.* लेकिन वह न तो यहां है और न ही वहां है. *6.* हमें इस काम के लिए एक अच्छे आदमी की जरूरत है.

• *1.* I think I know where he went. *2.* I see where you're going with this. *3.* I think I have a pretty good idea. *4.* You know what I'm talking about, don't you? *5.* But that's neither here nor there. *6.* We need a goodman for this job.

**[17]** *1.* ख़ैर, मुझे लगता है कि यह सब अच्छे के लिए है। *2.* मुझे कुछ समझ नहीं आया कि आप किस बारे में बात कर रहे हैं। *3.* मुझे समझ नहीं आ रहा कि मेरे साथ क्या हो रहा है. *4.* क्या हम इस बारे में बाद में बात कर सकते हैं? *5.* मैंने तुम्हारे लिए जो कुछ भी किया है उसके बाद भी? *6.* मैं वास्तव में नहीं जानता कि मैं क्या कर रहा हूं।

• *1.* Well, I guess it's all for the best. *2.* I got no idea what you're talking about. *3.* I don't understand what's happening to me. *4.* Can we talk about this later? *5.* After everything I've done for you? *6.* I don't really know what I'm doing.

**[18]** *1.* आपको क्या लगता है आप वास्तव में क्या कर रहे हैं? *2.* आप वास्तव में इस आदमी के बारे में क्या जानते हैं? *3.* आपको क्या लगता है आप वास्तव में यहाँ क्या कर रहे हैं? *4.* मुझे पता है कि आप वास्तव में कैसा महसूस कर रहे हैं। *5.* मैं कुछ नहीं कर सकता कि मैं कैसा महसूस कर रहा हूँ। *6.* ऐसा कैसे हुआ कि मैंने उसके बारे में कभी नहीं सुना?

• *1.* What exactly do you think you're doing? *2.* What do you actually know about this guy? *3.* What exactly do you think you're doing here? *4.* I know exactly how you feel. *5.* I can't help how I feel. *6.* How come I've never heard of him?

**[19]** *1.* मुझे लगा कि मैंने तुम्हें किसी से बात करते हुए सुना है। *2.* मुझे समझ नहीं आ रहा कि आप क्या कह रहे हैं। *3.* मैं आपसे कुछ भी करने के लिए नहीं कह रहा हूं। *4.* तुम्हें पता है कि तुम मुझसे क्या करने को कह रहे हो? *5.* क्या आप वही कह रहे हैं जो मुझे लगता है कि आप कह रहे हैं? *6.* मैं बस वही कर रहा था जो मुझसे कहा गया था।

• *1.* I thought I heard you talking to someone. *2.* I don't understand what you're saying. *3.* I'm not asking you to do anything. *4.* You know what you're asking me to do? *5.* Are you saying what I think you're saying? *6.* I was just doing what I was told.

**[20]** *1.* क्या इसका मतलब यह है कि यह ख़त्म हो गया है? *2.* आप भगवान के नाम पर किस बारे में बात कर रहे हैं? *3.* मैं यह भी नहीं जानता कि इसे क्या कहा जाता है। *4.* आपने इस जगह के साथ जो किया है वह मुझे पसंद है। *5.* उसने तुम्हें यह नहीं बताया कि वह कहाँ जा रहा है? *6.* क्या आपने उसे बताया है कि आप कैसा महसूस करते हैं?

• *1.* Does that mean this is over? *2.* What in God's name are you talking about? *3.* I don't even know what it's called. *4.* I love what you've done with the place. *5.* He didn't tell you where he was going? *6.* Have you told him how you feel?

**[21]** *1.* तुम वह नहीं हो जो मैंने सोचा था कि तुम हो। *2.* मुझे लगता है कि मैंने वास्तव में इसके बारे में कभी नहीं सोचा। *3.* मुझे विश्वास नहीं हो रहा कि तुम वापस आ गये हो। *4.* यह ऐसा कुछ है जैसा हमने पहले कभी नहीं देखा है। *5.* अगर आप चाहते हैं तो मैं आपकी मदद कर सकता हूं। *6.* मुझे खेद है कि आप अच्छा महसूस नहीं कर रहे हैं।

• *1.* You're not who I thought you were. *2.* I guess I never really thought about it. *3.* I can't believe you're back. *4.* It's like nothing we've ever seen before. *5.* I can help you if you want. *6.* I'm sorry you're not feeling well.

**[22]** *1.* मुझे पहले से ही उनके लिए खेद महसूस हो रहा है। *2.* मुझे आपके लिए खेद महसूस होता है, वास्तव में मुझे खेद है। *3.* हम वह सब कुछ कर रहे हैं जो हम कर सकते हैं, सर। *4.* आप इसके बारे में क्या करने की योजना बना रहे हैं? *5.* क्या हम कल रात के बारे में बात कर सकते हैं? *6.* जो कुछ हुआ उसके बारे में मुझे बहुत बुरा लग रहा है।

• *1.* I feel sorry for them already. *2.* I feel sorry for you, I really do. *3.* We're doing everything we can, sir. *4.* What do you plan to do about it? *5.* Can we talk about last night? *6.* I feel really bad about what happened.

**[23]** *1.* मुझे लगता है कि आज के लिए इतना ही काफी है। *2.* मुझे यकीन नहीं

है कि मैं जानता हूं कि आपका क्या मतलब है। *3.* मुझे यकीन है कि हम इस पर काम कर सकते हैं। *4.* मुझे यकीन है कि आप यह पहले से ही जानते हैं। *5.* क्या आपको यकीन है कि हम सही काम कर रहे हैं? *6.* मुझे यकीन है कि आप वह सब कुछ कर रहे हैं जो आप कर सकते हैं।

● *1.* I think that's enough for today. *2.* I'm not sure I know what you mean. *3.* I'm sure we can work this out. *4.* I'm sure you already know that. *5.* You sure we're doing the right thing? *6.* I'm sure you're doing everything you can.

**[24]** *1.* मुझे यकीन है कि आपने वह सब कुछ किया जो आप कर सकते थे। *2.* खैर, मुझे लगता है कि यह सिर्फ आप और मैं हैं। *3.* क्या मैं आपसे एक मिनट के लिए बात कर सकता हूँ? *4.* क्या आप कृपया हमें एक मिनट का समय दे सकते हैं? *5.* मुझे एक मिनट के लिए भी इस पर विश्वास नहीं हुआ। *6.* ऐसा लगता है कि आप कुछ का उपयोग कर सकते हैं।

● *1.* I'm sure you did everything you could. *2.* Well, I guess it's just you and me. *3.* Could I talk to you for a minute? *4.* Could you give us a minute, please? *5.* I don't believe that for a minute. *6.* Looks like you could use some.

**[25]** *1.* निश्चित रूप से आप जानते हैं कि आप क्या कर रहे हैं? *2.* मैं निश्चित रूप से आपकी मदद का उपयोग कर सकता हूँ। *3.* मैं वास्तव में निश्चित नहीं हूं कि इसका क्या मतलब है। *4.* मैं पूरी रात तुम्हें कॉल करने की कोशिश कर रहा हूं। *5.* क्या हम किसी और चीज़ के बारे में बात कर सकते हैं? *6.* क्या आप जानते हैं कि उस चीज़ का उपयोग कैसे करना है?

● *1.* Sure you know what you're doing? *2.* I could sure use your help. *3.* I'm not really sure what that means. *4.* I've been trying to call you all night. *5.* Can we talk about something else? *6.* You know how to use that thing?

**[26]** *1.* क्या आप जानते हैं कि किस चीज़ से आपको बेहतर महसूस हो सकता है? *2.* आप जानते हैं कि किस चीज़ से मुझे बेहतर महसूस होगा? *3.* मैं तो बस ये देखना चाहता था कि तुम कैसे हो। *4.* मैंने वह सब देख लिया है जो मुझे देखना चाहिए था। *5.* क्या ऐसा कुछ है जो आप मुझे नहीं बता रहे हैं? *6.* मैंने तुम्हें वह सब कुछ बता दिया जो मैं जानता हूं।

● *1.* You know what might make you feel better? *2.* You know what would make me feel better? *3.* I just wanted to see how you were. *4.* I've seen all I need to see. *5.* Is there something you're not telling me? *6.* I told you everything I know.

**[27]** *1.* मैं तुम्हें वह सब कुछ बता रहा हूं जो मैं जानता हूं। *2.* क्या आप हमें बता सकते हैं कि वास्तव में क्या हुआ था? *3.* क्या मैं उसे बता सकता हूँ कि कौन कॉल कर रहा है? *4.* मैं आपको बस वही बता रहा हूं जो मैं जानता हूं। *5.*

आपको ऐसा क्यों लगता है कि मैं आपको बता रहा हूँ? 6. मैंने उन्हें वह सब कुछ बता दिया जो मैं जानता हूं।

• 1. I'm telling you everything I know. 2. Can you tell us exactly what happened? 3. May I tell him who's calling? 4. I'm just telling you what I know. 5. Why do you think I'm telling you? 6. I told them everything I know.

[28] 1. क्या कोई मुझे बता सकता है कि क्या हो रहा है? 2. ख़ैर, मुझे लगता है कि हमारा काम यहीं ख़त्म हो गया है। 3. क्या आपके पास कुछ है जो आप मुझसे कहना चाहते हैं? 4. प्यार का मतलब है कभी यह न कहना कि आपको खेद है। 5. मैं सिर्फ़ यह कहना चाहता था कि मैं तुमसे प्यार करता हूं। 6. तो मैं सिर्फ़ यह कहना चाहता था कि मुझे क्षमा करें।

• 1. Can someone tell me what's going on? 2. Well, I think we're done here. 3. You got something you wanna say to me? 4. Love means never having to say you're sorry. 5. I just wanted to say I love you. 6. So I just wanted to say I'm sorry.

[29] 1. मुझे यह भी नहीं पता कि यह कितना समय हो गया है। 2. तुम्हें पता है कि मैं तुमसे कितना प्यार करता हूँ, ठीक है? 3. मैं चाहता हूँ कि तुम कल तक यहाँ से चले जाओ। 4. मुझे लगता है कि अब बेहतर होगा कि तुम चले जाओ। 5. मैं चाहता हूं कि तुम्हें पता चले कि मैं तुमसे प्यार करता हूं। 6. यही वह बात नहीं है जो मुझे परेशान कर रही है।

• 1. I don't even know how long it's been. 2. You know how much I love you, right? 3. I want you out of here by tomorrow. 4. I think you'd better leave now. 5. I want you to know I love you. 6. That's not what's bothering me.

[30] 1. क्या तुम लोगों के पास करने के लिए कोई काम नहीं है? 2. मैं तुम लोगों को अपने जीवन से बाहर करना चाहता हूँ! 3. क्या यह सबसे अच्छा काम है जो आप कर सकते हैं? 4. मैं बस वही चाहता हूं जो आपके लिए सबसे अच्छा हो। 5. मुझे लगता है कि मुझे पता है कि सबसे अच्छा क्या है। 6. मुझे लगता है कि अगर तुम चले जाओ तो यह सबसे अच्छा होगा।

• 1. Don't you people have work to do? 2. I want you people out of my life! 3. That's the best you can do? 4. I just want what's best for you. 5. I think I know what's best. 6. I think it'd be best if you left.

[31] 1. मुझे लगता है कि अगर तुम चले जाओ तो यह सबसे अच्छा है। 2. मुझे लगता है कि हमने काफ़ी देर तक इंतजार किया है। 3. और मैं आगे क्या होता है उसका इंतजार कर रहा हूं। 4. मुझे लगता है कि हम दोनों जानते हैं कि यह सच नहीं है। 5. मुझे लगता है कि हमें इस बारे में बात करनी चाहिए. 6. मुझे लगा कि तुम मेरे बारे में सब भूल गए हो।

- *1.* I think it's best if you leave. *2.* I think we've waited long enough. *3.* And I look forward to what comes next. *4.* I think we both know that's not true. *5.* I think we should talk about this. *6.* I thought you'd forgotten all about me.

[32] *1.* मैंने तुमसे इसके बारे में भूल जाने के लिए कहा था। *2.* जब मैं तुमसे बात कर रहा हूँ तो मेरी ओर देखो! *3.* एक बार जब आप अंदर आ गए, तो आप अंदर हो गए। *4.* जब से मैंने यह किया है, काफी समय हो गया है। *5.* खैर, यह कम से कम मैं तो कर ही सकता था। *6.* क्या तुम्हें सचमुच लगता है कि पिताजी के पास कोई योजना है?

- *1.* I told you to forget about it. *2.* Look at me when I'm talking to you! *3.* Once you're in, you're in. *4.* It's been a while since I've done this. *5.* Well, it's the least I could do. *6.* Do you really think dad has a plan?

[33] *1.* पिताजी, मुझे नहीं पता कि आप किस बारे में बात कर रहे हैं। *2.* वह पूरी तरह से पागल की तरह व्यवहार कर रहा है। *3.* मैं आशा करता हूँ कि तुम्हें समझ में आ गया होगा। *4.* मुझे आशा है कि आप जानते हैं कि आप क्या कर रहे हैं। *5.* मैं आशा कर रहा था कि आप मुझे बता सकते हैं। *6.* आशा है आप जानते हैं कि आप क्या कर रहे हैं।

- *1.* Dad, I don't know what you're talking about. *2.* He's acting like a complete whacko. *3.* I hope you understand. *4.* I hope you know what you're doing. *5.* I was hoping you could tell me. *6.* Hope you know what you're doing.

[34] *1.* मुझे आशा है कि वह जानता है कि वह क्या कर रहा है। *2.* मैं आशा कर रहा था कि आप मुझे यह बता सकते हैं। *3.* खैर, मुझे आशा है कि आप जानते हैं कि आप क्या कर रहे हैं। *4.* मैं बस आशा करता हूं कि आप जानते हैं कि आप क्या कर रहे हैं। *5.* मुझे आशा है कि आप मुझे इसके लिए क्षमा कर सकते हैं। *6.* तुम्हें पता है कि तुम मुझ पर भरोसा कर सकते हो।

- *1.* I hope he knows what he's doing. *2.* I was hoping you could tell me that. *3.* Well, I hope you know what you're doing. *4.* I just hope you know what you're doing. *5.* I hope you can forgive me for this. *6.* You know you can trust me.

[35] *1.* मैं आपसे मुझ पर भरोसा करने के लिए कह रहा हूं। *2.* मैं जानता था कि उस पर भरोसा नहीं किया जा सकता। *3.* क्या मैं ऐसा करने के लिए आप पर भरोसा कर सकता हूँ? *4.* मैं बस इतना चाहता हूं कि आप मुझ पर फिर से भरोसा करें। *5.* मैं जानता था कि हमें आप पर भरोसा नहीं करना चाहिए था। *6.* मेरे पास आप पर भरोसा करने का कोई कारण नहीं है।

- *1.* I'm asking you to trust me. *2.* I knew she couldn't be trusted. *3.* Can I trust you to do that? *4.* I just want you to trust me again.

*5.* I knew we shouldn't have trusted you. *6.* I have no reason to trust you.

**[36]** *1.* मैं खुश हूं, क्योंकि मैं जो चाहता था वह मुझे मिल गया। *2.* जो खुद की मदद करता है उसकी भगवान भी मदद करता है। *3.* मुझे आशा है कि मैंने खुद को स्पष्ट कर दिया है। *4.* आपको क्या लगता है मैं क्या करने का प्रयास कर रहा हूँ? *5.* मैं बस आपको हर चीज़ के लिए धन्यवाद देना चाहता था। *6.* क्या आप सुन रहे हैं कि मैं क्या कह रहा हूँ?
● *1.* I'm happy, coz I got what I wanted. *2.* God helps those who help themselves. *3.* I hope I made myself clear. *4.* What do you think I'm trying to do? *5.* I just wanted to thank you for everything. *6.* Are you listening to what I'm saying?

**[37]** *1.* मुझे विश्वास नहीं हो रहा कि मैं यह सुन रहा हूं। *2.* क्या आपको लगता है कि मैं इसका आनंद ले रहा हूं? *3.* मैं आप सभी को आने के लिए धन्यवाद देना चाहता हूँ। *4.* हो सकता है कि आपको कोई ऐसा व्यक्ति मिल गया हो जो आपको बेहतर लगता हो। *5.* मैं तुम्हें कभी मूर्ख नहीं बना सकता, क्या मैं ऐसा कर सकता हूँ? *6.* मैं खुद को पूरी तरह से मूर्ख जैसा महसूस करता हूं।
● *1.* I can't believe I'm hearing this. *2.* Do you think I'm enjoying this? *3.* I want to thank you all for coming. *4.* Maybe you found someone you like better. *5.* I never could fool you, could I? *6.* I feel like a total goofball.

**[38]** *1.* मुझे लगा कि मैंने तुम्हें हमेशा के लिए खो दिया है। *2.* या तो आपको यह मिल गया है या आपको नहीं मिला है। *3.* मुझे यह भी नहीं पता कि मैं तुम्हें पसंद करता हूं या नहीं. *4.* मुझे नहीं पता कि मैं आप पर विश्वास करता हूं या नहीं। *5.* मुझे नहीं पता कि मुझे तुम पर भरोसा है या नहीं। *6.* मुझे नहीं पता था कि आप वापस आ रहे हैं या नहीं।
● *1.* I thought I'd lost you forever. *2.* Either you've got it or you haven't. *3.* I don't even know if I like you. *4.* I don't know if I believe you. *5.* I don't know if I trust you. *6.* I didn't know if you were coming back.

**[39]** *1.* मुझे यकीन नहीं है कि आप मुझे याद करते हैं या नहीं। *2.* आपको किसी भी चीज़ के बारे में चिंता करने की ज़रूरत नहीं है। *3.* अगर तुम्हें किसी चीज़ की ज़रूरत हो तो मैं यहाँ हूं। *4.* ठीक है, अगर तुम्हें मेरी ज़रूरत हो तो मैं यहाँ हूँ। *5.* जब उसे उसकी ज़रूरत थी तो उसने मदद न करने का व्यवहार किया। *6.* सिर्फ एक व्यक्ति आपके जीवन को हमेशा के लिए बदल सकता है।
● *1.* I'm not sure if you remember me. *2.* You don't have to worry about a thing. *3.* I'm here if you need anything. *4.* Well, I'm here if you need me. *5.* He acted unhelpful when she needed him. *6.* Just one person can change your life forever.

**[40]** *1.* मुझे लगता है कि कुछ ऐसा है जो आपको जानना चाहिए। *2.* मैं जानना चाहता हूँ कि तुम यहाँ क्या कर रहे हो। *3.* मैं बस यह जानना चाहता हूं कि क्या हो रहा है। *4.* कुछ ऐसा जो मुझे बहुत पहले ही कर लेना चाहिए था। *5.* मैं जो करता हूं उससे आपका कोई लेना-देना नहीं है। *6.* मैं यह जानता था, और फिर भी मैंने उसे काम पर रख लिया।

● *1.* There's something I think you should know. *2.* I wanna know what you're doing here. *3.* I just wanna know what's going on. *4.* Something I should've done a long time ago. *5.* What I do is none of your business. *6.* I knew it, and I hired him anyway.

**[41]** *1.* मुझे लगता है कि हमारा काम यहीं पूरा हो गया है। *2.* मैं विश्वास नहीं कर सकता कि हमने इसे पूरा कर लिया। *3.* जब हमारा काम पूरा हो जाएगा तो मैं आपको कॉल करूंगा। *4.* मैं सोच रहा था कि क्या आप मेरी मदद कर सकते हैं। *5.* मैं ठीक-ठीक जानता हूँ कि तुम क्या सोच रहे हो। *6.* अरे, मैं तो बस तुम्हारे बारे में ही सोच रहा था।

● *1.* I think we're done here. *2.* I can't believe we pulled it off. *3.* I'll call you when we're done. *4.* I was wondering if you could help me. *5.* I know exactly what you're thinking. *6.* Hey, I was just thinking about you.

**[42]** *1.* मैं किसी भी चीज़ के बारे में नहीं सोच रहा हूं। *2.* तुम्हें पता है, मैं बस तुम्हारे बारे में सोच रहा था। *3.* मुझे ऐसा लग रहा है जैसे मैं पागल हो रहा हूं। *4.* ऐसा लगता है जैसे बहुत समय पहले की बात है, है ना? *5.* ऐसा लगता है जैसे यह सिर्फ आप और मैं हैं, दोस्त। *6.* उसे ऐसा महसूस हुआ जैसे वह पूरी तरह से पागल हो गई हो।

● *1.* I'm not thinking about anything. *2.* You know, I was just thinking about you. *3.* I feel like I'm going crazy. *4.* Seems like a long time ago, doesn't it? *5.* Looks like it's just you and me, bud. *6.* She felt like a complete nincompoop.

**[43]** *1.* क्या आपको लगता है कि आप हमारी मदद कर सकते हैं? *2.* मुझे इसकी परवाह नहीं है कि आप यह कैसे करते हैं। *3.* मुझे डर है कि मैं तुम्हें ऐसा करने नहीं दे सकता। *4.* मैं भी स्थिति के बारे में ऐसा ही महसूस करता हूं। *5.* वह कभी भी उसके या अपने भाई के बारे में बात नहीं करता। *6.* मैं तुमसे मुझसे शादी करने के लिए नहीं कह रहा हूँ।

● *1.* You think you could help us out? *2.* I don't care how you do it. *3.* I'm afraid I can't let you do that. *4.* I feel similarly about the situation. *5.* He never talks about her or his brother. *6.* I'm not asking you to marry me.

**[44]** *1.* इसका मतलब यह नहीं है कि मुझे यह पसंद आना चाहिए। *2.* मैंने तुमसे कहा था कि हमें यहाँ नहीं आना चाहिए था। *3.* क्या आपको लगता है कि आप

यहां खुश रह सकते हैं? *4.* आप कहते हैं कि आप मुझसे प्यार करते हैं, लेकिन आप नहीं करते। *5.* मुझे इसकी परवाह नहीं है कि वे इसे क्या कहते हैं। *6.* यदि आप इस पर काम करते हैं तो यह काम करता है।

● *1.* Doesn't mean I have to like it. *2.* I told you we shouldn't have come here. *3.* You think you could be happy here? *4.* You say you love me, but you don't. *5.* I don't care what they call it. *6.* It works if you work it.

[45] *1.* यदि आप इसे चाहते हैं, तो आप इसे प्राप्त कर सकते हैं। *2.* क्या तुम मेरा इंतज़ार कर रहे हो, क्या आप मेरा इंतज़ार कर रहे हैं? *3.* मैं तुम्हें वह देने के लिए यहां हूं जो तुम चाहते हो। *4.* क्या आप जानते हैं कि मैं उसे कहाँ पा सकता हूँ? *5.* मैं बस यह नहीं समझ पा रहा हूं कि ऐसा क्यों है। *6.* मुझे यकीन नहीं है कि मैं आपका मतलब समझ पा रहा हूं।

● *1.* If you want it, you can have it. *2.* Are you waiting for me? *3.* I'm here to give you what you want. *4.* Do you know where I can find him? *5.* I just don't understand why. *6.* I'm not sure I understand what you mean.

[46] *1.* मैं जो सुन रहा हूं उस पर विश्वास नहीं कर पा रहा हूं। *2.* मैं खुद अब भी इस पर विश्वास नहीं कर पा रहा हूं। *3.* मुझे लगता है कि मैं अपने पिता को देख पा रहा हूं। *4.* हर चीज़ के लिए एक समय और एक जगह होती है। *5.* जब वह यहां होती है तो वह बहुत अच्छी होती है। *6.* मुझे समझ नहीं आता कि यह काम क्यों नहीं कर रहा है।

● *1.* I cannot believe what I'm hearing. *2.* I still can't believe it myself. *3.* Methinks I see my father. *4.* There's a time and a place for everything. *5.* She's great, when she's here. *6.* I don't understand why it's not working.

[47] *1.* क्या आपको लगता है कि यह किसी तरह का मजाक है? *2.* उसे अपने निर्णय पर विचार करने के लिए समय चाहिए था। *3.* मैं उम्मीद कर रहा था कि हम बात कर सकते हैं। *4.* क्या आप सचमुच मुझसे इस बात पर विश्वास करने की उम्मीद करते हैं? *5.* क्या आप मुझसे आप पर विश्वास करने की उम्मीद करते हैं? *6.* मुझे पूरी उम्मीद है कि आप जानते हैं कि आप क्या कर रहे हैं।

● *1.* You think this is some kind of joke? *2.* She needed time to contemplate her decision. *3.* I was hoping we could talk. *4.* Do you really expect me to believe that? *5.* You expect me to believe you? *6.* I sure hope you know what you're doing.

[48] *1.* अच्छा, अगर तुम्हें किसी चीज़ की ज़रूरत हो तो मुझे बताना। *2.* क्या आप मुझे बताना चाहते हैं कि क्या हो रहा है? *3.* क्या आपके पास कुछ है जो आप मुझे बताना चाहते हैं? *4.* क्या आप मुझे बताना चाहते हैं कि यह किस बारे में है? *5.* मैं मदद के लिए जो कुछ भी कर सकता हूँ वह करूँगा। *6.* आप दोनों

के बीच पहले से ही कुछ हुआ है, है ना?

• *1.* Well, let me know if you need anything. *2.* Want to tell me what's going on? *3.* You have something you want to tell me? *4.* Want to tell me what this is about? *5.* I'll do anything I can to help. *6.* Something already happened between you two, hasn't it?

**[49]** *1.* मैं जानता हूं कि आप केवल मदद करने की कोशिश कर रहे थे। *2.* केवल एक ही व्यक्ति है जो मेरी मदद कर सकता है। *3.* मैं केवल एक ही चीज़ के बारे में सोच सकता हूँ। *4.* जब मैं सही होता हूं तो मुझे इससे नफरत होती है। *5.* मैं बस इतना चाहता हूं कि तुम मुझे अकेला छोड़ दो। *6.* दोस्तों के चले जाने के बाद वह अकेला महसूस करने लगा।

• *1.* I know you were only trying to help. *2.* There's only one person who can help me. *3.* I can only think of one thing. *4.* I hate it when I'm right. *5.* I just want you to leave me alone. *6.* He felt lonesome after his friends left.

**[50]** *1.* मुझे इसे ठीक करने के लिए एक विकल्प की आवश्यकता है। *2.* क्या आप सचमुच सोचते हैं कि यह एक अच्छा विचार है? *3.* मैं वह नहीं हूं जो आप सोचते हैं कि मैं हूं। *4.* हम वो नहीं हैं जो आप सोचते हैं कि हम हैं। *5.* आप सोचते हैं कि आप ऐसा करते हैं, लेकिन आप ऐसा नहीं करते। *6.* मुझे आशा है कि आप पसंद करेंगे जो आप देखते हैं।

• *1.* I need an option to fix this. *2.* You really think that's a good idea? *3.* I am not what you think I am. *4.* We're not who you think we are. *5.* You think you do, but you don't. *6.* I hope you like what you see.

**[51]** *1.* मुझे लगता है कि हम एक दूसरे की मदद कर सकते हैं. *2.* मुझे आशा है कि मैं बहुत देर से फ़ोन नहीं कर रहा हूँ। *3.* जब मेरा काम पूरा हो जाएगा तो मैं तुम्हें बता दूंगा। *4.* मुझे लगता है कि मैं इसे एक रात के लिए बंद कर दूंगा। *5.* क्या आपको लगता है कि यह पैसे के बारे में है? *6.* क्या आप निश्चित हैं कि हम पहले कभी नहीं मिले हैं?

• *1.* I think we can help each other. *2.* I hope I'm not calling too late. *3.* I'll let you know when I'm done. *4.* I think I'm gonna call it a night. *5.* You think this is about money? *6.* Are you sure we haven't met before?

**[52]** *1.* दर्द देने वाले और लेने वाले दोनों को परेशान करता है। *2.* जब मैं ऐसा करता हूँ तो क्या मुझे दर्द होता है? *3.* क्या आप मुझे बता सकते हैं कि दर्द कहाँ होता है? *4.* मुझे अब भी आशा है, हे भगवान, मुझे अब भी आशा है। *5.* मुझे लगता है कि आप यहां बहुत बड़ी गलती कर रहे हैं। *6.* मुझे यह देखकर खुशी हुई कि आप बेहतर महसूस कर रहे हैं।

- *1.* Pain ennobles both the giver and the receiver. *2.* Does it hurt when I do this? *3.* Can you tell me where it hurts? *4.* Still I hope, my God, still I hope. *5.* I think you're making a big mistake here. *6.* I'm glad to see you're feeling better.

**[53]** *1.* मैं तुमसे प्यार करता हूँ और मैं तुम्हें याद आती है। *2.* आइए देखें कि हम इसके बारे में क्या कर सकते हैं। *3.* आइए देखें कि आपने अपना काम ठीक से किया है या नहीं। *4.* आप जो कह रहे हैं उसका एक भी शब्द मुझे समझ नहीं आ रहा है। *5.* और यही वह दिन है जो सब कुछ बदल देता है। *6.* क्या आप मुझे यह बताना चाहेंगे कि क्या हो रहा है?
- *1.* I love you, and I miss you. *2.* Let's see what we can do about that. *3.* Let's see if you've done your job properly. *4.* I can't understand a word you're saying. *5.* And this is the day that changes everything. *6.* You mind telling me what's going on?

**[54]** *1.* क्या आपके पास कोई विचार है कि कहां से शुरुआत करें? *2.* ऐसा लग रहा था कि यह कठिन कार्य कभी ख़त्म नहीं होगा। *3.* मैं बस वैसा ही करता हूं जैसा मुझे कहा जाता है। *4.* बेहतर होगा कि हम वैसा ही करें जैसा वह कहते हैं। *5.* मैं सब कुछ वैसा ही वापस चाहता हूँ जैसा वह था। *6.* मुझे बहुत खुशी है कि आप बेहतर महसूस कर रहे हैं।
- *1.* Do you have any idea where to start? *2.* The tedious task felt never-ending. *3.* I just do as I'm told. *4.* We'd better do as he says. *5.* I want everything back the way it was. *6.* I'm so glad you're feeling better.

**[55]** *1.* आख़िर तुम्हें क्या लगता है कि तुम कहाँ जा रहे हो? *2.* मुझे खेद है कि मैं और अधिक मदद नहीं कर सका। *3.* मैं तुम्हें वह सब कुछ बता चुका हूँ जो मैं जानता हूँ। *4.* मैं आपको पहले ही बता चुका हूं कि ऐसा क्यों है। *5.* मैं आपको पहले ही बता चुका हूं कि क्या हुआ था. *6.* मुझे लगता है कि वह पहले से ही ऐसा कर चुका है।
- *1.* Where the hell you think you're going? *2.* I'm sorry I couldn't be more help. *3.* I've told you everything I know. *4.* I already told you why. *5.* I already told you what happened. *6.* I think he already has.

**[56]** *1.* आप जो भी करने जा रहे हैं, उसे तेजी से करें। *2.* मुझे लगा कि मैंने तुम्हें चुप रहने के लिए कहा है। *3.* क्या आप मुझसे पूछ रहे हैं या मुझे बता रहे हैं? *4.* क्या मैं पूछ सकता हूँ कि यह किस बारे में है? *5.* अगर आपको किसी चीज़ की ज़रूरत है, तो बस पूछ लें। *6.* क्या मैं पूछ सकता हूँ कि कौन कॉल कर रहा है?
- *1.* Whatever you're gonna do, do it fast. *2.* I thought I told you to shut up. *3.* Are you asking me or telling me? *4.* Can I ask

what this is about? *5.* If there's anything you need, just ask. *6.* Can I ask who's calling?

**[57]** *1.* मुझे आश्चर्य है कि क्या आप हमारी मदद कर सकते हैं। *2.* क्या आप जानते हैं कि उनमें से किसी एक का उपयोग कैसे करें? *3.* क्या मैं आपसे एक सेकंड के लिए बात कर सकता हूँ? *4.* मुझे लगता है मैं किसी ऐसे व्यक्ति को जानता हूं जो मदद कर सकता है। *5.* मेरे बारे में ऐसे बात मत करो जैसे मैं यहाँ नहीं हूँ। *6.* मुझे यह ऐसे याद है जैसे यह कल की बात हो।

• *1.* I wonder if you could help us. *2.* You know how to use one of those? *3.* Can I talk to you for a sec? *4.* I think I know someone who can help. *5.* Don't talk about me like I'm not here. *6.* I remember it as if it were yesterday.

**[58]** *1.* मैं बता सकता हूँ कि तुम कब झूठ बोल रहे हो। *2.* मैं उन लोगों में से हूं जो बेहतर भुगतान करते हैं। *3.* वह वैसा नहीं है जैसा वह कहता है कि वह है। *4.* वह कहता है कि उसे आपसे बात करने की ज़रूरत है। *5.* मुझे कोई कारण नहीं दिखता कि आपको ऐसा क्यों नहीं करना चाहिए। *6.* क्या आप मुझे बता सकते हैं कि वह कैसा दिखता है?

• *1.* I can tell when you're lying. *2.* I'm the kind that pays better. *3.* He's not who he says he is. *4.* He says he needs to talk to you. *5.* I see no reason why you shouldn't. *6.* Can you tell me what he looks like?

**[59]** *1.* क्या तुम्हें याद है कि मैंने तुमसे क्या वादा किया था? *2.* क्या आपके पास अपने बारे में कहने के लिए कुछ है? *3.* मुझे यह कहने से नफरत है कि मैंने तुमसे ऐसा कहा था। *4.* क्या आप जानते हैं कि आप क्या कहने जा रहे हैं? *5.* मैं वह सब कह चुका हूं जो मैं कहने वाला हूं। *6.* क्या हर कोई जानता है कि यह कौन सा समय है?

• *1.* Do you remember what I promised you? *2.* Do you have anything to say for yourself? *3.* I hate to say I told you so. *4.* Do you know what you're going to say? *5.* I've said all I'm gonna say. *6.* Does everybody know what time it is?

**[60]** *1.* मैं तुम्हें वह सब कुछ बताऊंगा जो तुम जानना चाहते हो। *2.* चलिए इस बारे में बाद में बात करते हैं, ठीक है? *3.* मैं आपके साथ इस पर चर्चा नहीं करने जा रहा हूं। *4.* मुझे ऐसा लग रहा है जैसे मैं बीमार होने वाला हूं। *5.* आप आज रात के खाने के लिए क्या कर रहे हैं? *6.* आप जानते हैं कि बच्चों के साथ यह कैसा होता है।

• *1.* I'll tell you anything you wanna know. *2.* Let's talk about this later, okay? *3.* I'm not going to discuss this with you. *4.* I feel like I'm gonna be sick. *5.* What are you doing for dinner tonight? *6.* You know how it is with kids.

**[61]** *1.* क्या आप निश्चित हैं कि हम सही रास्ते पर जा रहे हैं? *2.* उनके रास्ते अलग-अलग हो गए और वे दो ही रह गए। *3.* एक महिला के रूप में वह खुद को मजबूत महसूस करती हैं।' *4.* क्या मैं जान सकता हूं कि आप कौन बोल रहे हैं? *5.* क्या आप जानते हैं कि आप कितनी तेजी से जा रहे थे? *6.* अगर मैं तुम होते तो मैं उस पर भरोसा नहीं करता।

● *1.* Are you sure we're going the right way? *2.* Their paths diverged, and they remained twain. *3.* She feels strong as a female. *4.* May I ask who's calling? *5.* Do you know how fast you were going? *6.* I wouldn't trust him if I were you.

**[62]** *1.* हम जो भी सहायता प्राप्त कर सकते हैं, हमें वह चाहिए। *2.* क्या आप निश्चित हैं कि आपको सहायता की आवश्यकता नहीं है? *3.* यदि आपको किसी सहायता की आवश्यकता हो तो मुझे कॉल करें। *4.* मैंने तुमसे कहा था कि मुझे तुम्हारी सहायता की आवश्यकता नहीं है। *5.* और इसे करने के लिए मुझे आपकी सहायता की आवश्यकता है। *6.* मैं जानता हूं कि आप इसे लेकर कहां जा रहे हैं।

● *1.* We need all the help we can get. *2.* Are you sure you don't need help? *3.* Call me if you need any help. *4.* I told you I don't need your help. *5.* And I need your help to do it. *6.* I know where you're going with this.

**[63]** *1.* मुझे खुशी है कि आपने मुझसे बाहर जाने के लिए पूछा। *2.* मुझे लगता है कि मैं तुम्हारे दिल के बहुत करीब हूं। *3.* मुझे ऐसा लग रहा है जैसे मेरा दिल टूट रहा है। *4.* उह, आपको क्या लगता है कि आप कहाँ जा रहे हैं? *5.* मुझे आशा है कि आप जो खोज रहे हैं वह आपको मिल जाएगा। *6.* क्या तुमने सचमुच सोचा था कि तुम मुझे रोक सकते हो?

● *1.* I'm glad you asked me out. *2.* I feel so close to you. *3.* I feel like my heart is breaking. *4.* Uh, where do you think you're going? *5.* I hope you find what you're looking for. *6.* Did you really think you could stop me?

**[64]** *1.* मुझे बताएं क्या आपको किसी भी तरह की मदद की ज़रूरत है। *2.* मुझे एक अच्छा कारण बताएं कि मुझे ऐसा क्यों करना चाहिए। *3.* मुझे यह मत बताएं कि आप इस पर विश्वास करते हैं। *4.* मुझे विश्वास ही नहीं हो रहा कि वह चली गयी है। *5.* मुझे लगता है कि हमें एक-दूसरे से मिलना बंद कर देना चाहिए।' *6.* वह किसी चीज़ के लिए मेरा इस्तेमाल करने की कोशिश कर रहा है।

● *1.* Let me know if you need any help. *2.* Give me one good reason why I should. *3.* Don't tell me you believe this. *4.* I just can't believe she's gone. *5.* I think we should stop seeing each other. *6.* He's trying to use me for something.

**[65]** *1.* अगर मैंने तुम्हें बताया तो तुम मुझ पर विश्वास नहीं करोगे। *2.* मैं जानता हूँ कि आप किसी प्रकार की परेशानी में हैं। *3.* उसने तेजी से काम किया,

326

इस प्रकार जल्दी काम पूरा कर लिया। *4.* मुझे ऐसा लग रहा है जैसे मैं सपना देख रहा हूं. *5.* आप जो करने का प्रयास कर रहे हैं मैं उसकी सराहना करता हूँ। *6.* मैं आपकी चिंता की सराहना करता हूं, लेकिन मैं ठीक हो जाऊंगा।

• *1.* You wouldn't believe me if I told you. *2.* I know you're in some kind of trouble. *3.* She worked quickly, thus finishing early. *4.* I feel like I'm dreaming. *5.* I appreciate what you're trying to do. *6.* I appreciate your concern, but I'll be fine.

**[66]** *1.* आपने जो कुछ भी किया है हम उसकी सराहना करते हैं। *2.* क्या आप मुझे एक क्षण के लिए क्षमा कर सकते हैं? *3.* आपने उस स्थान के साथ जो किया है, वह पसंद है। *4.* मुझे आशा है कि मैं इस स्थान पर फिर से आऊंगा। *5.* क्या आप रात के खाने के लिए नहीं रुक रहे हैं? *6.* जब लोग बीच में आते हैं तो मुझे इससे नफरत है।

• *1.* We appreciate everything you've done. *2.* Can you excuse me for a second? *3.* Love what you've done with the place. *4.* I hope to revisit this place. *5.* Aren't you staying for dinner? *6.* I hate it when people interrupt.

**[67]** *1.* मुझे पता था कि मेरे द्वारा आप पर भरोसा किया जा सकता है। *2.* यह मत सोचो कि मैं नहीं जानता कि तुम क्या कर रहे हो। *3.* मुझे नहीं पता कि मैं किस बात को लेकर चिंतित था. *4.* मैं इससे अधिक खतरनाक किसी चीज़ के बारे में नहीं सोच सकता। *5.* वह एक बड़े आदमी की तरह व्यवहार करना पसंद करता है। *6.* मुझे यह भी नहीं पता था कि आपकी एक बेटी भी है।

• *1.* I knew I could count on you. *2.* Don't think I don't know what you're doing. *3.* I don't know what I was worried about. *4.* I can't think of anything more dangerous. *5.* He likes to act like a bigshot. *6.* I didn't even know you had a daughter.

**[68]** *1.* वह उसे धोखा देने के लिए खुद को तैयार नहीं कर सका। *2.* जब तक यह ख़त्म नहीं हो जाता तब तक यह ख़त्म नहीं होता। *3.* हम एक दूसरे को तब से जानते हैं जब हम बच्चे थे। *4.* तब आप जानते हैं कि मैं किस बारे में बात कर रहा हूं। *5.* मैं जब चाहता हूँ तब वही करता हूँ जो मैं चाहता हूँ। *6.* जब से मैंने तुम्हें आखिरी बार देखा था तब से तुम बड़े हो गए हो।

• *1.* He couldn't bring himself to betray her. *2.* It ain't over till it's over. *3.* We've known each other since we were kids. *4.* Then you know what I'm talking about. *5.* I do what I want when I want. *6.* You've grown since I last saw you.

**[69]** *1.* मुझे लगता है कि हम अपना समय बर्बाद कर रहे हैं। *2.* मैं ऐसा इसलिए कह रहा हूं क्योंकि मुझे इसकी परवाह है। *3.* चोट को ठीक करने के लिए डॉक्टर ने आराम की सलाह दी। *4.* मेरे पास बस इतना ही है कि आप बहुत कुछ पा चुके हैं। *5.* मुझे लगा कि हम उन सब से आगे निकल चुके हैं। *6.* इससे कोई फर्क नहीं

पड़ता कि मेरे साथ क्या होता है.

- *1.* I think we're wasting our time. *2.* I say it because I care. *3.* The doctor recommended rest to mend the injury. *4.* I've had just about enough of you. *5.* I thought we were past all that. *6.* It doesn't matter what happens to me.

[70] *1.* मुझे किसी बच्चे की देखभाल करने वाली की जरूरत नहीं है. *2.* मुझे लगता है कि बेहतर होगा कि हम घर चले जाएं। *3.* मुझे ऐसा लग रहा है जैसे मैं अपना दिमाग खो रहा हूं। *4.* क्या आप पूरी तरह से अपने दिमाग से बाहर हो गए हैं? *5.* मुझे लगता है कि आप अपने दिमाग से बाहर हो गए हैं। *6.* वह जानता था कि अपनी बहन को कैसे परेशान करना है।

- *1.* I don't need a baby-sitter. *2.* I think we'd better go home. *3.* I feel like I'm losing my mind. *4.* Are you completely out of your mind? *5.* I think you're out of your mind. *6.* He knew how to aggravate his sister.

[71] *1.* जब वह डरा हुआ होता है तो वह बहुत प्यारा लगता है। *2.* आप जानते हैं कि मैं किसके बारे में बात कर रहा हूं। *3.* किसी महिला के साथ व्यवहार करने का यह कोई तरीका नहीं है। *4.* क्या आप वही सोच रहे हैं जो मैं सोचता हूँ कि आप सोच रहे हैं? *5.* जब मैं किसी को देखता हूं तो मुझे पता चल जाता है। *6.* मैं इसे वैसे ही कहता हूं जैसे मैं इसे देखता हूं।

- *1.* He's so lovable when he's scared. *2.* You know who I'm talking about. *3.* That's no way to treat a lady. *4.* Are you thinking what I think you're thinking? *5.* I know one when I see one. *6.* I call it like I see it.

[72] *1.* आप मुझे दिल का दौरा देने की कोशिश कर रहे हैं? *2.* तुम्हारी माँ ने मुझे तुम्हारे जैसा बनने के लिए काम पर रखा है। *3.* मुझे समझ नहीं आ रहा कि आप इतने परेशान क्यों हैं। *4.* तुम्हें जो कुछ भी अपने आप को बताने की आवश्यकता है। *5.* मुझे लगता है कि वह हमें कुछ बताने की कोशिश कर रहा है। *6.* अजीब बात है कि चीजें कैसे बदल जाती हैं, है ना?

- *1.* You trying to give me a heart attack? *2.* Your mom hired me to be you. *3.* I don't understand why you're so upset. *4.* Whatever you need to tell yourself. *5.* I think he's trying to tell us something. *6.* Funny how things turn out, isn't it?

[73] *1.* मुझे कैसे पता चलेगा कि मैं आप पर भरोसा कर सकता हूँ? *2.* मैं देखूंगा कि मैं इसके बारे में क्या कर सकता हूं। *3.* खैर, जब मैं इसे देखूंगा तो मुझे इस पर विश्वास हो जाएगा। *4.* आपको इतनी देर से परेशान करने के लिए मुझे खेद है। *5.* अब तक उन्हें ऐसी स्थिति का सामना कभी नहीं करना पड़ा था। *6.* मुझे क्षमा करें, मुझे पता है कि देर हो चुकी है।

- *1.* How do I know I can trust you? *2.* I'll see what I can do about that. *3.* Well, I'll believe it when I see it. *4.* I'm sorry to bother you so late. *5.* He had hitherto never encountered such a situation. *6.* I'm sorry, I know it's late.

[74] *1.* मुझे इस नंबर पर कॉल करने के लिए कहा गया था. *2.* मुझे लगता है कि आपने बहुत ज्यादा शराब पी ली है। *3.* मैं पूरे दिन तुम्हें कॉल करने की कोशिश कर रहा हूं। *4.* उसने अपने पेय के साथ एक पीछा करने वाले को आदेश दिया। *5.* क्या आपने सोचा था कि आप मुझसे हमेशा के लिए बच सकते हैं? *6.* क्या मुझे ऐसा लग रहा है जैसे मैं मज़ाक कर रहा हूँ?
● *1.* I was told to call this number. *2.* I think you've had too much to drink. *3.* I've been trying to call you all day. *4.* He ordered a chaser with his drink. *5.* Thought you could elude me forever? *6.* Do I look like I'm joking?

[75] *1.* मुझे लगता है कि यह कलाकार जगह-जगह जा रहा है। *2.* मैं बस इतना चाहता हूं कि आप मुझे माफ कर दें। *3.* यह सबसे पागलपन भरी बात है जो मैंने कभी सुनी है। *4.* क्या आप जानते हैं कि यह कितना पागलपन भरा लगता है? *5.* मैं जानता हूं कि यह पागलपन लगता है, लेकिन यह सच है। *6.* क्या आप अनुमान लगा सकते हैं कि ये क्या हो रहा है?
● *1.* I think this artist is going places. *2.* I just want you to forgive me. *3.* That's the craziest thing I've ever heard. *4.* Do you know how crazy that sounds? *5.* I know it sounds crazy, but it's true. *6.* Can you guess what this is?

[76] *1.* वे केवल कारण के बारे में अनुमान ही लगा सकते थे। *2.* वह एक गड़बड़ करने वाले के रूप में जाने जाते थे। *3.* जब तक आप इसे न देख लें तब तक प्रतीक्षा करें. *4.* क्या मैं तुम्हें दोपहर के भोजन पर ले जा सकता हूँ? *5.* वे दोपहर के भोजन के समय बातचीत के लिए मिलते हैं। *6.* उसने दोपहर के भोजन के लिए एक होगी का ऑर्डर दिया।
● *1.* They could only speculate about the cause. *2.* He was known as a messer. *3.* Wait till you see this. *4.* Can I take you to lunch? *5.* They meet for lunchtime conversation. *6.* He ordered a hoagie for lunch.

[77] *1.* आप देखेंगे कि मैं किस बारे में बात कर रहा हूं। *2.* मुझे पता था कि हम एक-दूसरे को फिर से देखेंगे। *3.* मैंने तुम पर एक क्षण के लिए भी संदेह नहीं किया। *4.* उसके मन में अपने बेटे के बारे में विचार आते रहते हैं। *5.* वह हमेशा किसी न किसी बात को लेकर परेशान रहती है। *6.* मुझे लगता है आप जरूरत से ज्यादा प्रतिक्रिया कर रहे हैं.
● *1.* You'll see what I'm talking about. *2.* I knew we'd see each other again. *3.* I never doubted you for a second. *4.* Thoughts of her son occupy her mind. *5.* She's always in a tizzy about

something. *6.* I think you're overreacting.

**[78]** *1.* जब तक ऐसा कुछ न हो जो आप मुझे नहीं बता रहे हों। *2.* मैं कभी भी किसी भी चीज़ के बारे में इतना आश्वस्त नहीं रहा। *3.* मैं बस अपने दिन की योजना बनाने की कोशिश कर रहा हूं। *4.* मैं आपसे मांग करता हूं कि मुझे बताएं कि आप कौन हैं! *5.* क्या आप वाकई जानते हैं कि आप क्या कर रहे हैं? *6.* जब मैं कहता हूं कि यह खत्म हो गया है तो यह खत्म हो गया है।
• *1.* Unless there's something you're not telling me. *2.* I've never been more sure of anything. *3.* I'm just trying to plan my day. *4.* I demand you tell me who you are! *5.* Are you sure you know what you're doing? *6.* It's over when I say it's over.

**[79]** *1.* जब तक लड़ाई खत्म नहीं हो जाती तब तक लड़ाई खत्म नहीं होती. *2.* यदि आप काम पूरा होने से पहले ही थक जाएं तो क्या होगा? *3.* हम दोपहर के भोजन के बाद बैठक फिर से शुरू करेंगे। *4.* क्या तुम्हें दिखाई नहीं देता कि यहाँ क्या हो रहा है? *5.* उन्होंने उन पर गलत तरीके से काम करने का आरोप लगाया. *6.* उन्होंने इस परियोजना में सभी को शामिल करने का प्रयास किया।
• *1.* The fight isn't over till it's over. *2.* What if you tire before it's done? *3.* We will resume the meeting after lunch. *4.* Don't you see what's happening here? *5.* He accused them of acting unfairly. *6.* He tried to involve everyone in the project.

**[80]** *1.* मुझे लगता है कि अब सोने का समय हो गया है। *2.* जब मुझे तुम्हारी ज़रूरत होती है तो तुम कभी आसपास नहीं होते। *3.* ख़ैर, मैं इसकी कल्पना नहीं कर सकता कि ऐसा क्यों है। *4.* वहां और भी बहुत कुछ है जहां से वह आया है। *5.* हम वहीं वापस आ गए हैं जहां से हमने शुरुआत की थी। *6.* मैं अभी भी इसका पता लगाने की कोशिश कर रहा हूं।
• *1.* I think it's time for bed. *2.* You're never around when I need you. *3.* Well, I can't imagine why. *4.* There's more where that came from. *5.* We're right back where we started. *6.* I'm still trying to figure it out.

**[81]** *1.* मुझे लगता है कि मैं तुम्हें परेशान नहीं कर रहा हूं। *2.* क्या आपको आपके लक्ष्य के बारे में जानकारी दी गई है? *3.* अच्छा, अगर तुम्हें किसी चीज़ की ज़रूरत हो तो मुझे बुला लेना। *4.* वह जानती है कि वह किस बारे में बात कर रही है। *5.* ऐसा लगता है कि आपने सब कुछ नियंत्रण में कर लिया है। *6.* कृपया फोन काट दें और दोबारा कॉल करने का प्रयास करें।
• *1.* I hope I'm not bothering you. *2.* Have you been briefed on your target? *3.* Well, call me if you need anything. *4.* She knows what she's talking about. *5.* You seem to have everything under control. *6.* Please hang up and try your call again.

**[82]** *1.* हमें यह जानने की जरूरत है कि हम किसके साथ काम कर रहे हैं। *2.*

आप ऐसे दिखते हैं जैसे आप पेय का उपयोग कर सकते हैं। 3. मैंने कभी नहीं सोचा था कि मुझे यह दिन देखना पड़ेगा। 4. आप हमसे यह उम्मीद करते हैं कि हम उस पर विश्वास करें? 5. आपको कोई अंदाज़ा नहीं है कि आप किसके साथ काम कर रहे हैं। 6. मुझे एहसास ही नहीं हुआ कि मैं क्या कर रहा हूं.

● 1. We need to know what we're dealing with. 2. You look like you could use a drink. 3. I never thought I'd see the day. 4. You expect us to believe that? 5. You have no idea what you're dealing with. 6. I didn't realize what I was doing.

[83] 1. क्या आप जानते हैं कि आप किससे बात कर रहे हैं? 2. मुझे नहीं लगता कि मैं इतना लंबा इंतज़ार कर सकता हूं. 3. आपको क्या लगता है कि आप किसे मूर्ख बना रहे हैं? 4. यह इस पर निर्भर करता है कि आप क्या खोज रहे हैं। 5. मुझे पता था कि मैं तुम पर निर्भर रह सकता हूँ। 6. जब मैं तुमसे बात कर रहा हूं तो मेरी तरफ देखो।

● 1. Do you know who you're talking to? 2. I don't think I can wait that long. 3. Who do you think you're fooling? 4. Depends on what you're looking for. 5. I knew I could depend on you. 6. Look at me when I'm talking to you.

[84] 1. और मैं इसे इसी तरह बनाए रखने का इरादा रखता हूं। 2. किसी मित्र के साथ व्यवहार करने का यह कोई तरीका नहीं है। 3. आप ऐसे दिखते हैं जैसे आप किसी मित्र का उपयोग कर सकते हैं। 4. मैं देख रहा हूं कि आपने एक मित्र बना लिया है। 5. मैं एक मित्र के रूप में आपके पास आ रहा हूं। 6. आप ही एकमात्र व्यक्ति हैं जो मेरी मदद कर सकते हैं।

● 1. And I intend to keep it that way. 2. That's no way to treat a friend. 3. You look like you could use a friend. 4. I see you've made a friend. 5. I'm coming to you as a friend. 6. You're the only one who can help me.

[85] 1. खैर, अगर मैं ऐसा करता हूं तो मुझे कोई आपत्ति नहीं है। 2. हाँ, मैं शर्त लगा सकता हूँ कि आपने ऐसा किया होगा। 3. मैं कुछ भी साबित करने की कोशिश नहीं कर रहा हूं. 4. मैं बस यही आशा करता हूं कि हमें बहुत देर न हो जाए। 5. जब आपको यह मिल जाए तो बस मुझे कॉल करें, ठीक है? 6. मैं चाहता हूं कि मेरा काम अच्छी तरह से किया जाए।

● 1. Well, I don't mind if I do. 2. Yeah, I'll bet you did. 3. I'm not trying to prove anything. 4. I just hope we're not too late. 5. Just call me when you get this, okay? 6. I prefer mine to be well-done.

[86] 1. आप यह नहीं कर सके, क्या आप ऐसा कर सकते हैं? 2. आइए मैं आपको बताता हूं कि यह कैसे काम करता है। 3. मैं आपको बताता हूँ कि मैं किस बारे में बात कर रहा हूँ। 4. मैं आपको उतना ही प्यार करता हूं जितना कि आप

मुझे करते हैं। 5. ख़ैर, यह कहना जितना आसान है, करना उतना आसान नहीं है।
6. इसमें जितना हमने सोचा था उससे अधिक समय लग सकता है।

• 1. You couldn't do it, could you? 2. Let me tell you how this works. 3. I'll tell you what I'm talking about. 4. I love you as you are. 5. Well, that's easier said than done. 6. That might take longer than we thought.

[87] 1. आप इसे ऐसे कहते हैं जैसे यह एक बुरी बात है। 2. कृपया क्या मैं हर किसी का ध्यान आकर्षित कर सकता हूँ? 3. कभी नहीं सोचा था कि मैं यह दिन देखने के लिए जीवित रहूँगा। 4. मैं विश्वास नहीं कर सकता कि आप इसके लिए गिर गए। 5. मैंने कभी नहीं सोचा था कि मैं इतना नीचे गिर जाऊंगा। 6. वो बातें जो मैं उसके बारे में कभी नहीं जानता था।

• 1. You say it like it's a bad thing. 2. Can I have everyone's attention, please? 3. Never thought I'd live to see the day. 4. I can't believe you fell for that. 5. I never thought I'd stoop so low. 6. Things I never knew about him.

[88] 1. हम एक साथ रहने के लिए सब कुछ जोखिम में डाल देंगे। 2. आखिर वह क्या सोचता है कि वह क्या कर रहा है? 3. उन्होंने किसी भी सुधार को स्वीकार करने से इनकार कर दिया। 4. मुझे पता है कि वह आपके लिए कितना मायने रखता है। 5. मुझे आशा है कि मैं बीच में नहीं पड़ रहा हूँ। 6. उसे अपने दृष्टिकोण पर फिर से काम करने की आवश्यकता महसूस हुई।

• 1. We'll risk it all to be together. 2. What the hell does he think he's doing? 3. He refused to accept any correction. 4. I know how much he meant to you. 5. I hope I'm not interrupting. 6. She felt the need to rework her approach.

[89] 1. मुझे लगता है कि हमने सब कुछ कवर कर लिया है। 2. कोई है जो अपनी आँखों के बिना स्पष्ट रूप से देखता है। 3. यह आगे ही आगे और आगे ही आगे चलता ही जाता है। 4. तुम्हें हमेशा कैसे पता चलता है कि यह मैं हूं? 5. ऐसा लगता है जैसे मैं ठीक समय पर यहाँ पहुँच गया हूँ। 6. मैं विश्वास नहीं कर सकता कि बात यहाँ तक पहुँच गयी है।

• 1. I think we've covered everything. 2. Someone who sees clearly without her eyes. 3. It goes on and on and on. 4. How do you always know it's me? 5. Looks like I got here just in time. 6. I can't believe it's come to this.

[90] 1. के माध्यम से आ रहा है, के माध्यम से आ रहा है। 2. क्या आपको नहीं लगता कि आप ज़रूरत से ज़्यादा प्रतिक्रिया कर रहे हैं? 3. क्या तुम्हें लगता है कि मैं बहुत ज़्यादा बातें करता हूँ? 4. तुम्हें पता है कि मुझे सबसे ज़्यादा क्या याद आता है? 5. क्या आपके पास इसका समर्थन करने के लिए कोई सबूत है? 6. उन्हें परियोजना पर फिर से ध्यान केंद्रित करने की जरूरत थी।

• *1.* Coming through, coming through. *2.* Don't you think you're overreacting? *3.* Do you think I talk too much? *4.* You know what I miss the most? *5.* Do you have any evidence to support that? *6.* They needed to refocus the project.

**[91]** *1.* मैं आपको किसी भी अन्य चीज़ से अधिक प्यार करता हूँ। *2.* केवल एक अन्य व्यक्ति ही जानता है कि मैं क्या करता हूँ। *3.* यह किसी भी अन्य जगह की तरह ही अच्छी जगह है। *4.* मैं आप पर एक एहसान करने की कोशिश कर रहा हूं। *5.* आप कोशिश करने के लिए किसी लड़की को दोष नहीं दे सकते। *6.* उस पर गलत तरीके से अपराध का आरोप लगाया गया था।
• *1.* I love you more than anything. *2.* Only one other person knows what I do. *3.* This is as good a place as any. *4.* I'm trying to do you a favor. *5.* You can't blame a girl for trying. *6.* He was wrongfully accused of the crime.

**[92]** *1.* क्या आप मुझे बता सकते हैं कि वहां कैसे पहुंचा जाए? *2.* मुझे लगता है कि बेहतर होगा कि आप मेरे साथ आएं। *3.* मैं देख रहा हूँ कि आप क्या हासिल कर रहे हैं। *4.* टीम ने खेल में जीत हासिल करने के लिए संघर्ष किया। *5.* हम बहुत सारे पैसे के बारे में बात कर रहे हैं। *6.* मैं आपसे एक दोस्त के तौर पर बात कर रहा हूं.
• *1.* Can you tell me how to get there? *2.* I think you'd better come with me. *3.* I see what you're getting at. *4.* The team fought to prevail in the game. *5.* We're talking about a lot of money. *6.* I'm talking to you as a friend.

**[93]** *1.* आपके पास दोषी महसूस करने के लिए कुछ भी नहीं है। *2.* क्या आप किसी बात को लेकर दोषी महसूस कर रहे हैं? *3.* क्या मैं पूछ सकता हूँ कि आपके मन में क्या बदलाव आया? *4.* इसका मतलब है कि वह अभी भी मुझे ढूंढना बाकी है। *5.* मैं खुद को ठीक करते हुए सैम को ठीक करता हूं। *6.* सैम, तुम्हें पता है कि हम पिताजी को ढूंढ लेंगे, है ना?
• *1.* You have nothing to feel guilty about. *2.* Are you feeling guilty about something? *3.* May I ask what changed your mind? *4.* That means he's still mine to find. *5.* I heal Sam while healing myself. *6.* Sam, you know we're gonna find Dad, right?

**[94]** *1.* नई दवा ने उसकी स्थिति को स्थिर करने में मदद की। *2.* जब तक काम पूरा न हो जाए तब तक मेहनत करें। *3.* क्या आप मुझे बता सकते हैं कि आपकी उम्र कितनी है? *4.* उम्र के साथ कुत्ता और अधिक परेशान करने वाला हो गया। *5.* यह पहली बार है जब मैंने इसके बारे में सुना है। *6.* क्या आपको वह पहली बार याद है जब हम मिले थे?
• *1.* The new medication helped stabilise her condition. *2.* Work hard until the job is done. *3.* Can you tell me how old you are?

*4.* The dog became more troublesome with age. *5.* This is the first I've heard of it. *6.* Remember the first time we met?

**[95]** *1.* मुझे यह भी नहीं पता था कि कहां से शुरू करूं। *2.* मुझे देखने दो कि क्या मैं इसे सीधे समझ पाया हूँ। *3.* मैं बस यह सुनिश्चित करना चाहता था कि आप ठीक हैं। *4.* हमें यह सुनिश्चित करने की ज़रूरत है कि सब कुछ एक साथ हो। *5.* उन्होंने सभी के लिए उचित व्यवहार सुनिश्चित करने का प्रयास किया। *6.* मुझे लगता है कि आप अपने आप पर बहुत ज्यादा सख्त हो रहे हैं।

● *1.* I wouldn't even know where to start. *2.* Let me see if I got this straight. *3.* I just wanted to make sure you're okay. *4.* We need to make sure everything is copacetic. *5.* He tried to ensure fair treatment for all. *6.* I think you're being too hard on yourself.

**[96]** *1.* क्या आपको लगता है कि मैं कोई गेम खेल रहा हूँ? *2.* हमें पूरा करने के लिए एक समय-सीमा स्थापित करने की आवश्यकता है। *3.* उन्होंने समस्या-समाधान के लिए एक कुशल दृष्टिकोण का प्रदर्शन किया।

● *1.* You think I'm playing a game? *2.* We need to establish a timeframe for completion. *3.* She demonstrated a skilful approach to problem-solving.

**[97]** *1.* क्षमा करें, मैं यह सुनकर अपने आप को रोक नहीं सका। *2.* ऐसा लग रहा था कि उसके शब्द विरोध करने के लिए डिज़ाइन किए गए थे। *3.* आप जो चाहें हम उस बारे में बात कर सकते हैं। *4.* क्या आप किसी ऐसे व्यक्ति की तरह लग रहे हैं जिसे आप जानते हैं? *5.* मुझे लगता है कि कुछ ऐसा है जिसे आपको देखना चाहिए। *6.* यह ऐसा कुछ नहीं है जिसे आपने पहले नहीं देखा हो।

● *1.* Excuse me, I couldn't help overhearing. *2.* Her words seemed designed to antagonize. *3.* We can talk about whatever you want. *4.* Sound like anyone you know? *5.* I think there's something you should see. *6.* It's nothing you haven't seen before.

**[98]** *1.* अगर मैंने आपको परेशान किया है तो मैं माफी चाहता हूँ। *2.* मैं जो करने जा रहा हूं उसके लिए माफी चाहता हूं। *3.* क्या मैं आपके लिए ड्रिंक या कुछ और ला सकता हूँ? *4.* ओह, भगवान का शुक्र है कि आप अभी भी यहाँ हैं। *5.* मैं जानता हूं कि यह पूछने के लिए बहुत कुछ है। *6.* क्या आप मुझे एक सेकंड के लिए माफ़ कर सकते हैं?

● *1.* I'm sorry if I disturbed you. *2.* I apologize for what I'm about to do. *3.* Can I get you a drink or something? *4.* Oh, thank God you're still here. *5.* I know it's a lot to ask. *6.* Could you excuse me for one second?

**[99]** *1.* मेरे पास आपको माफ़ करने के लिए कुछ भी नहीं है। *2.* अगर तुम्हें किसी चीज की जरूरत हो तो मुझे फोन करना. *3.* मैं जानता हूं कि किस चीज

से तुम्हें बेहतर महसूस होगा। *4.* क्या मैं ऐसा दिखता हूँ जैसे मेरा जन्म कल ही हुआ हो? *5.* यह वही है जो करने के लिए मेरा जन्म हुआ है। *6.* बच्चे के जन्म की प्रक्रिया हर किसी के लिए अलग-अलग होती है।

• *1.* I have nothing to forgive you. *2.* Call me if you need anything. *3.* I know what'll make you feel better. *4.* Do I look like I was born yesterday? *5.* It's what I was born to do. *6.* The childbirth process is different for everyone.

[100] *1.* मुझे ठंड लग रही है और भूख भी लग रही है। *2.* उसने आने वाली चुनौती के लिए खुद को तैयार कर लिया। *3.* आप क्या सुझाव देते हैं कि हम इसके बारे में क्या करें? *4.* मेरा सुझाव है कि आप सभी अपने आप को तैयार कर लें। *5.* अगर मैं आपके साथ शामिल हो जाऊं तो क्या आपको कोई आपत्ति है? *6.* खैर, मुझे लगता है कि बेहतर होगा कि मैं आगे बढ़ जाऊं।

• *1.* I'm cold and hungry. *2.* She braced herself for the oncoming challenge. *3.* What do you suggest we do about it? *4.* I suggest you all strap yourselves in. *5.* You mind if I join you? *6.* Well, I guess I better get going.

[101] *1.* उसने खुद को एक छोटे से हार से सजाया हुआ था। *2.* आपको अपने लोगों के कौशल पर काम करने की जरूरत है। *3.* उसने परियोजना को पूरा करने के लिए अपने कौशल का उपयोग किया। *4.* उन्होंने भुगतान पर चर्चा करने के लिए कर अधिकारी से मुलाकात की। *5.* उसने जल्दी खराब होने वाले सामान को सावधानी से पैक किया। *6.* आप मेरे लिए किसी भी चीज़ से ज़्यादा मायने रखते हैं।

• *1.* She adorned herself with a bauble necklace. *2.* You need to work on your people skills. *3.* She utilized her skills to complete the project. *4.* They met with the taxman to discuss payments. *5.* She packaged the perishable goods carefully. *6.* You mean more to me than anything.

[102] *1.* मुझे लगता है कि हम पर नजर रखी जा रही है। *2.* उनके बेटे का जन्म लाल सिर वाले बच्चे के रूप में हुआ। *3.* क्या मैं विशेष रूप से कुछ ढूंढने में आपकी सहायता कर सकता हूँ? *4.* हम उसे ढूंढने के लिए हर संभव प्रयास कर रहे हैं। *5.* उन्हें माता-पिता के रूप में अपनी भूमिका के साथ संघर्ष करना पड़ा। *6.* मेरी भाषा के लिए क्षमा करें, लेकिन वह एक मूर्ख है।

• *1.* I think we're being watched. *2.* Their son was born a red-headed baby. *3.* Anything in particular I can help you find? *4.* We're doing everything we can to find him. *5.* He struggled with his role as a parent. *6.* Excuse my language, but he's a dick.

[103] *1.* यदि वह एक महिला का निर्माण कर रहा है तो क्या होगा? *2.* मैं चाहता हूं कि वह पूरी तरह से समझौता कर ले। *3.* क्या आप जानते हैं कि मैंने

आपको अपने ऊपर क्यों खींच लिया? *4.* मुझे लगता है कि हर चीज़ का एक पहला मौका होता है। *5.* यह कई तरह से बहुत ही नाजुक तरीके से किया जाता है। *6.* मैंने इसका नाजुक ढंग से इलाज करने की कोशिश की है।

● *1.* What if he's building a woman? *2.* I want him fully compromised. *3.* Do you know why I pulled you over? *4.* There's a first time for everything, I guess. *5.* This is in ways very delicately done. *6.* I've tried to treat it delicately.

**[104]** *1.* हम जो बेच रहे हैं उसे लोग पसंद कर रहे हैं। *2.* संगीत ने उनकी आत्मा को फिर से जीवंत करने में मदद की। *3.* अगर मैं आपका बाथरूम उपयोग करूँ तो क्या आपको कोई आपत्ति है? *4.* जो आसानी से मिलता है वो आसानी से चला भी जाता है। *5.* हम इस जगह को सचमुच आसानी से खत्म कर सकते हैं। *6.* वह बीमार महसूस कर रही थी और उसे धक्का देना पड़ा।

● *1.* People seem to like what we're selling. *2.* The music helped rejuvenate his spirit. *3.* You mind if I use your bathroom? *4.* Easy come, easy go. *5.* We could knock this place off real easy. *6.* She felt sick and had to hurl.

**[105]** *1.* क्या आपको वही सुनाई दे रहा है जो मुझे सुनाई दे रहा है? *2.* मैं इसके बारे में सुनने के लिए इंतजार नहीं कर सकता। *3.* मुझे लगा कि मैंने तुम्हें वहीं रुकने के लिए कहा है। *4.* तुम मेरी जिंदगी बर्बाद करने की कोशिश क्यों कर रहे हो? *5.* हो सकता है कि हमें यह अवसर दोबारा कभी न मिले। *6.* बीच में रोकने के लिए क्षमा करें, लेकिन यह माइक के बारे में है।

● *1.* Do you hear what I hear? *2.* I can't wait to hear about it. *3.* I thought I told you to stay put. *4.* Why are you trying to ruin my life? *5.* We may never have this opportunity again. *6.* Sorry to interrupt, but it's about Mike.

**[106]** *1.* वे इसे कभी आसान नहीं बनाते, क्या वे ऐसा करते हैं? *2.* क्या आप मुझसे डेट पर जाने के लिए पूछ रहे हैं? *3.* खैर, जो कुछ भी आप सुनते हैं उस पर विश्वास न करें। *4.* मैं उन्हें दोबारा मेरी बातें सुनते हुए नहीं पकड़ने दे सकता। *5.* वे कार्रवाई नहीं करेंगे, इसलिए मैंने फैसला किया कि मैं कार्रवाई करूंगा। *6.* जब लोग थक जाते हैं तो वे शिकायत करने लगते हैं।

● *1.* They never make it easy, do they? *2.* Are you asking me on a date? *3.* Well, don't believe everything you hear. *4.* I can't let them catch me eavesdropping again. *5.* They wouldn't act, so I decided I would. *6.* People tend to grouse when they're tired.

**[107]** *1.* हाल ही में आपमें से बहुत से लोगों को नहीं देखा है। *2.* और वहाँ और भी बहुत कुछ है जहाँ से वह आया है। *3.* वे ऐसी दुनिया में रहते थे जहाँ किसी को परवाह नहीं थी। *4.* जहाँ मुझे कॉफ़ी पसंद है, वहीं मेरे दोस्त को चाय पसंद

है। *5.* क्या आपको लगता है कि आप सब कुछ खरीद सकते हैं? *6.* उनके पिता की विरासत उनके काम के माध्यम से जीवित रही।

* *1.* Haven't seen much of you lately. *2.* And there's plenty more where that came from. *3.* They lived in a world where noone cared. *4.* Whereas I prefer coffee, my friend likes tea. *5.* You think you can buy everything? *6.* His father's legacy lived on through his work.

**[108]** *1.* आपका स्वागत ज़ोर से और स्पष्ट रूप से हो रहा है। *2.* क्या मैं तुम लोगों को पीने के लिए कुछ ला सकता हूँ? *3.* यदि वे असफल होते हैं, तो हर कोई बाहर हो जाएगा। *4.* जादू की चाल कभी भी आश्चर्यचकित करने में असफल नहीं हुई। *5.* कहानी कहने की उनकी प्रतिभा कभी भी आश्चर्यचकित करने में असफल नहीं रही। *6.* क्या आप जानते हैं कि मुझे किस बात पर गुस्सा आता है?

* *1.* Receiving you loud and clear. *2.* Can I get you guys something to drink? *3.* If they fail, everyone's out. *4.* The magic trick never failed to astonish. *5.* His talent for storytelling never failed to astonish. *6.* You know what pisses me off?

**[109]** *1.* शर्म की बात है कि उन्होंने अपनी गलती स्वीकार कर ली। *2.* क्या आप कम से कम जानते हैं कि वह चोरी क्यों करता है? *3.* हालाँकि उसने यह कभी नहीं कहा, लेकिन उसे इसकी परवाह थी। *4.* जब मैं क्रोधित होता हूं तो आप मुझे पसंद नहीं करेंगे। *5.* वे देर से पहुंचे लेकिन किसी भी तरह उन्हें अंदर जाने दिया गया। *6.* लाल बालों वाली लड़की भीड़ में सबसे अलग दिख रही थी।

* *1.* Shamefully, they admitted their mistake. *2.* Do you at least know why he steals? *3.* Though she never said it, she cared. *4.* You wouldn't like me when I'm angry. *5.* They arrived late but were let in anyhow. *6.* The redheaded girl stood out in the crowd.

**[110]** *1.* हाँ, ठीक है, बेहतर होगा कि आप इसकी आदत डाल लें। *2.* वह सप्ताह के दिनों में लंबे समय तक काम करती थी। *3.* क्या ऐसी कोई चीज़ है जिसके बारे में आप बात करना चाहते हैं? *4.* यह वह सब कुछ है जिसके बारे में मैं सोच सकता हूं। *5.* जिसके लिए आप भुगतान करते हैं, आप वही प्राप्त करते हैं। *6.* यह वही लड़का है जिसके बारे में मैंने आपको बताया था।

* *1.* Yeah, well, you better get used to it. *2.* She worked long hours on weekdays. *3.* Is there anything you want to talk about? *4.* It's all I can think about. *5.* You get what you pay for. *6.* This is the guy I told you about.

**[111]** *1.* यह वह सब है जिसके बारे में मैं सोच सकता हूं। *2.* यही वह लड़का है जिसके बारे में मैं आपको बता रहा था। *3.* कुछ पाने में क्या आपकी कुछ मदद की जा सकती है? *4.* मैं पूरी दोपहर से तुम्हें पाने की कोशिश कर रहा हूँ। *5.* हमने

सोचा था कि हम तुम्हें फिर कभी नहीं देख पाएंगे। 6. आइए मैं आपको दिखाता हूं कि यह कैसे किया जाता है।

• 1. It's all I can think of. 2. That's the guy I was telling you about. 3. Can I help you find something? 4. I've been trying to get you all afternoon. 5. We thought we'd never see you again. 6. Let me show you how it's done.

**[112]** 1. वह एक एजेंट के रूप में गुप्त रूप से चली गईं। 2. आप एक सप्ताह के लिए मैदान से बाहर हो गए हैं। 3. ऐसा लग रहा था कि यह गंध रसोई से आ रही है। 4. क्या मैं आपसे एक पल के लिए बात कर सकता हूँ? 5. शांत परिदृश्य ने उसके मन को शांत करने में मदद की। 6. मुझे आपके साथ काम करने के लिए नियुक्त किया गया है।

• 1. She went undercover as an agent. 2. You're grounded for a week. 3. The smell seemed to originate from the kitchen. 4. Can I talk to you for a moment? 5. The serene landscape helped to quieten her mind. 6. I've been assigned to work with you.

**[113]** 1. पानी का उपयोग क्षेत्र को पवित्र करने के लिए किया जाता था। 2. वह अपने माता-पिता द्वारा निर्धारित सीमा का सम्मान करती थी। 3. हममें से कुछ लोग काम करने की कोशिश कर रहे हैं। 4. तुम्हें अंदाज़ा नहीं है कि मैं क्या करने में सक्षम हूं। 5. मुझे आप पर भरोसा करने में सक्षम होने की आवश्यकता है। 6. मैंने सोचा कि आप मदद करने में सक्षम हो सकते हैं.

• 1. The water was used to sanctify the area. 2. She respected the boundary set by her parents. 3. Some of us are trying to work. 4. You have no idea what I'm capable of. 5. I need to be able to trust you. 6. I thought you might be able to help.

**[114]** 1. मुझे विश्वास नहीं हो रहा कि तुम मुझसे रिश्ता तोड़ रहे हो। 2. क्या आप निश्चित हैं कि आप गाड़ी चलाने में सक्षम हैं? 3. मुझे तुम पर अपना जादू चलाने के लिए मत मजबूर करो। 4. वह सुरक्षित रूप से गाड़ी चलाने के लिए बहुत नींद में था। 5. उन्हें नशे में गाड़ी चलाने के आरोप में गिरफ्तार किया गया था. 6. वह प्रस्ताव पर फिर से काम करने के लिए उत्सुक थे।

• 1. I can't believe you're breaking up with me. 2. You sure you're okay to drive? 3. Don't make me use my magic on you. 4. He was too sleepy to drive safely. 5. He was arrested for drunken driving. 6. He was eager to rework the proposal.

**[115]** 1. तुम्हें पता है मुझे कैसे पता चला कि तुम समलैंगिक हो? 2. उन्होंने यह समझने की कोशिश की कि लोगों को क्या आकर्षित करता है। 3. अगर मेरे पास सिगरेट है तो क्या तुम्हें कोई आपत्ति है? 4. उन्होंने खुद को इस प्रोजेक्ट से अलग करने की कोशिश की. 5. मैंने इसके बारे में कभी सपने में भी नहीं सोचा

था. *6.* इस खबर के बाद वह बहुत दुखी महसूस कर रही थीं।

• *1.* You know how I know you're gay? *2.* He sought to understand what fascinated people. *3.* Do you mind if I have a cigarette? *4.* She tried to recuse herself from the project. *5.* I'd never dream of it. *6.* She felt wretched after the news.

**[116]** *1.* मैं ईमानदारी से नहीं जानता कि आप किस बारे में बात कर रहे हैं। *2.* आप ही एकमात्र व्यक्ति हैं जिस पर मैं भरोसा कर सकता हूं। *3.* कुछ ऐसा है जिस पर हमें चर्चा करने की आवश्यकता है। *4.* जिस तरह से उसने ऐसा कहा वह मुझे पसंद नहीं आया। *5.* जिस तरह से यह महसूस होता है वह मुझे पसंद है। *6.* आप जिस पर विश्वास करना चाहते हैं उस पर विश्वास करें।

• *1.* I honestly don't know what you're talking about. *2.* You're the only one I can trust. *3.* There's something we need to discuss. *4.* I don't like the way he said that. *5.* I like the way it feels. *6.* Believe what you want to believe.

**[117]** *1.* यह हमेशा वही होता है जिस पर आपको सबसे कम संदेह होता है। *2.* यह कोई ऐसी चीज़ नहीं है जिस पर मुझे गर्व हो। *3.* जिस कार में वे यात्रा कर रहे थे, वह खराब हो गई। *4.* आपमें से बाकी लोगों के लिए भी यही बात लागू होती है। *5.* यह नियम विशेष रूप से उस स्थिति पर लागू होता है। *6.* मुझे संदेह है कि आप एक अंग्रेजी जासूस हो सकते हैं।

• *1.* It's always the one you least suspect. *2.* It's not something I'm proud of. *3.* The car, wherein they traveled, broke down. *4.* Same goes for the rest of you. *5.* The rule applies specifically to that situation. *6.* I suspect you may be an English spy.

**[118]** *1.* संगीत समारोह ने व्यापक रूप से विविध भीड़ को आकर्षित किया। *2.* उनका कुत्ता बहुत भूखा था और सब कुछ खा जाता था। *3.* कुछ ऐसी बात है जिस पर मैं आपके साथ चर्चा करना चाहूंगा। *4.* मैं जितनी तेजी से काम कर सकता हूं, कर रहा हूं। *5.* उन्होंने एक पेशेवर छत बनाने वाले के रूप में काम किया। *6.* बिना किसी डर के लिए गए फैसले ने सभी को चौंका दिया।

• *1.* The music festival attracted a widely diverse crowd. *2.* Their dog was voracious and ate everything. *3.* There's something I'd like to discuss with you. *4.* I'm working as fast as I can. *5.* He worked as a professional roofer. *6.* The unafraid decision surprised everyone.

**[119]** *1.* मैं यह नहीं कह सकता कि मैं उसे दोषी मानता हूँ। *2.* मैं मानता हूं कि आप जानते हैं कि मैं कौन हूं। *3.* क्या आप जानते हैं कि इस चीज़ को कैसे चलाना है? *4.* उन्हें पुरानी नीति को फिर से लागू करने की जरूरत थी। *5.* मुझे लगता है कि यह उसके दिमाग से फिसल गया होगा। *6.* मैं प्रभु से प्रार्थना करता हूं कि वह मेरी आत्मा को बनाए रखें।

- *1.* Can't say I blame him. *2.* I assume you know who I am. *3.* Do you know how to drive this thing? *4.* They needed to reintroduce the old policy. *5.* I guess it slipped his mind. *6.* I pray the Lord my soul to keep.

**[120]** *1.* दुख की बात है कि पीड़ित का शव कभी नहीं मिला। *2.* खैर, सभी चीजों में से क्या यह वास्तव में हो सकता है? *3.* मुझे लगता है कि आप चीजों की कल्पना कर रहे हैं। *4.* मैं अब चीजों को और अधिक स्पष्ट रूप से देखता हूं। *5.* उसके पास चीजों को व्यवस्थित करने का एक उत्कृष्ट तरीका है। *6.* जब तक आप यह न सुनें कि मेरे साथ क्या हुआ, तब तक प्रतीक्षा करें।
- *1.* Tragically, the victim's body was never found. *2.* Well, of all things Can it be really? *3.* I think you're imagining things. *4.* I see things more clearly now. *5.* She has a nifty way of organizing things. *6.* Wait till you hear what happened to me.

**[121]** *1.* आप जो कुछ भी कहेंगे उसका इस्तेमाल आपके खिलाफ किया जा सकता है। *2.* जैसे हम उन लोगों को माफ कर देते हैं जो हमारे खिलाफ अपराध करते हैं। *3.* मुझे यह जानने की जरूरत है कि मैं किसके खिलाफ हूं।
- *1.* Anything you say may be used against you. *2.* As we forgive those who trespass against us. *3.* I need to know what I'm up against.

**[122]** *1.* क्या आप जानते हैं कि इनमें से किसी एक का उपयोग कैसे करें? *2.* उन्होंने एक प्रश्न के माध्यम से हस्तक्षेप करने का प्रयास किया। *3.* उत्पाद एक सप्ताह के बाद आश्चर्यजनक रूप से विफल हो गया।
- *1.* You know how to use one of these? *2.* He tried to interject with a question. *3.* The product failed shockingly after a week.

**[123]** *1.* वह अपनी बेटी को बाल रोग विशेषज्ञ के पास ले गई। *2.* वह शाम के लिए बच्चों की देखभाल करने के लिए सहमत हो गई। *3.* मैंने सोचा था कि मैं तुम्हें फिर कभी नहीं देख पाऊंगा। *4.* क्या यह वह सर्वोत्तम कार्य है जो आप कर सकते हैं? *5.* बार-बार अपना फोन चेक करना मेरी आदत बन गई है। *6.* क्या आपको वह सब कुछ मिल गया जिसकी आपको आवश्यकता है?
- *1.* She took her daughter to the pediatrician. *2.* She agreed to babysit for the evening. *3.* I thought I'd never see you again. *4.* Is that the best you could do? *5.* It's a habit to check my phone often. *6.* You got everything you need?

**[124]** *1.* उसने वह किया जिसकी कल्पना भी नहीं की जा सकती थी. *2.* क्या हम अभी भी कल रात्रि भोज पर जा रहे हैं? *3.* जिस तरह से उन्होंने उनके बारे में बात की वह अपमानजनक था। *4.* उन्होंने कार्यक्रम के लिए एक ड्राइवर को काम पर रखा था। *5.* शहर भर में होने वाले कार्यक्रम रद्द कर दिए गए हैं. *6.* वह मिलो की तरह अपने विचित्र हास्य के लिए जाने जाते हैं।

- *1.* He did the unthinkable. *2.* Are we still on for dinner to-morrow? *3.* The way he spoke about them was contemptuous. *4.* She hired a chauffeur for the event. *5.* Citywide events are canceled. *6.* He's known for his quirky humor, like Milo.

[125] *1.* उसके विचित्र रंग के बाल लोगों का ध्यान आकर्षित कर रहे थे। *2.* नहीं, यह दो महीने में दो बार होता है, मेरे प्रभु। *3.* उसे उम्मीद थी कि वे उसकी गलती को नजरअंदाज कर देंगे। *4.* तुम्हें क्या लगता है तुम क्या कर रहे हो, जवान आदमी? *5.* जादूगर का कार्य कभी भी आश्चर्यचकित करने में असफल नहीं हुआ। *6.* मेरे पास वह सब कुछ है जो एक आदमी चाह सकता है।
- *1.* His bizarrely colored hair turned heads. *2.* Nay, 'tis twice two months, my lord. *3.* He hoped they would overlook his mis-take. *4.* What do you think you're doing, young man? *5.* The magician's act never failed to astound. *6.* I have everything a man could want.

[126] *1.* वह इस बात से सहमत है कि इससे उसे लाभ होता है। *2.* मुझे ऐसा क्यों लगता है कि मुझसे पूछताछ की जा रही है? *3.* मैंने कभी किसी को इतनी बुरी तरह आहत होते नहीं देखा। *4.* यह पाठ्यक्रम आपके कौशल को समृद्ध करने के लिए डिज़ाइन किया गया है। *5.* टोनी का कहना है कि आप इसे नहीं काट रहे हैं। *6.* ऊपर की ओर देखें और जो चमत्कार मैंने देखा है उसे साझा करें।
- *1.* She agrees insofar as it benefits her. *2.* Why do I feel like I'm being interrogated? *3.* I never saw someone get hurt that bad. *4.* The course is designed to enrich your skills. *5.* Toni says you're not cutting it. *6.* Look upward and share the wonders I've seen.

[127] *1.* आप ऐसे लग रहे हैं जैसे आपने कोई भूत देखा हो। *2.* क्या आप संदेश भेज रहे हैं और गाड़ी चला रहे हैं? *3.* सांस लेने वाले ने अपनी ऊर्जा को फिर से जीवंत कर दिया। *4.* ख़ुशी के गीत इस ख़ुशी के दिन का स्वागत करते हैं! *5.* वे हंसी-मजाक कर रहे थे और इधर-उधर बकवास कर रहे थे। *6.* इसके बाद वे एक-दूसरे के साथ हंसी-मजाक भी करते रहे।
- *1.* You look like you've seen a ghost. *2.* Are you texting and driving? *3.* The breather rejuvenated his energy. *4.* Songs of rejoicing greet this happy day! *5.* They were goofing off and dicking around. *6.* They laughed and joked with each other afterward.

[128] *1.* मानसिक रूप से बीमार मरीज को विशेष देखभाल की जरूरत थी। *2.* उसे जाने के लिए खुद को मानसिक रूप से तैयार करना पड़ा। *3.* मुझे खेद है कि मैं और अधिक मददगार नहीं हो सका। *4.* उन्हें परियोजना को खतरे में न डालने की चेतावनी दी गई। *5.* उसने विशेष रूप से एक लाल कार के लिए

अनुरोध किया। *6.* उसने अनुबंध पर हस्ताक्षर करने के लिए दबाव डालने का विरोध किया।

• *1.* The mentally ill patient needed specialized care. *2.* She had to psych herself into going. *3.* I'm sorry I couldn't be more helpful. *4.* They were warned not to jeopardize the project. *5.* She requested specifically for a red car. *6.* She resisted the coercion to sign the contract.

**[129]** *1.* अगर हम अलग हो गए तो हम और अधिक जमीन कवर कर लेंगे। *2.* ईमानदारी से कहूं तो मुझे इसके बारे में कुछ भी नही पता है। *3.* अगर मैं तुमसे कहूं तो तुम मुझ पर विश्वास नहीं करोगे। *4.* अगर मैं तुमसे कुछ कहूं तो तुम्हें बुरा तो नहीं लगेगा? *5.* पुस्तक लेखक के जीवन के बारे में जानकारी प्रदान करती है। *6.* चाहे कुछ भी हो जाए, मैं हमेशा तुमसे प्यार करता रहूंगा।

• *1.* We'll cover more ground if we split up. *2.* Honestly, I have no idea. *3.* If I told you, you wouldn't believe me. *4.* Do you mind if I tell you something? *5.* The book provides insight into the author's life. *6.* Whatever happens, I will always love you.

**[130]** *1.* अगर मैंने आपकी भावनाओं को ठेस पहुंचाई है तो मुझे खेद है। *2.* वह लंबे दिन के बाद थका हुआ महसूस कर रहा था। *3.* वह अपने गुस्से पर काबू पाने के लिए संघर्ष करती रही। *4.* हो सकता है कि मैंने जरूरत से ज्यादा प्रतिक्रिया व्यक्त की हो। *5.* उन्होंने कला के माध्यम से अपनी भावनाओं को व्यक्त करने की कोशिश की। *6.* उसने किसी भी संदेह को दूर करने की आशा व्यक्त की।

• *1.* I'm sorry if I hurt your feelings. *2.* He felt knackered after the long day. *3.* She struggled to control her temper. *4.* I may have overreacted. *5.* She tried to convey her emotions through art. *6.* She hoped to dispel any doubts.

**[131]** *1.* उसे कभी पता नहीं चला कि उस पर क्या प्रहार हुआ। *2.* अगर मैं ना कहूँ तो क्या आप मुझ पर विश्वास करेंगे? *3.* क्या आप चाहते हैं कि मैं कहूँ कि मुझे खेद है? *4.* क्या आप मुझसे अपेक्षा करते हैं कि मैं आपको धन्यवाद दूं? *5.* यह बिलकुल भी वैसा नहीं है जैसी मैंने अपेक्षा की थी। *6.* उन्हें नियमों का पालन करने वाले व्यक्ति का सामना करना पड़ा।

• *1.* He never knew what hit him. *2.* Would you believe me if I said no? *3.* You want me to say I'm sorry? *4.* Do you expect me to thank you? *5.* It's not at all what I expected. *6.* They encountered a stickler for rules.

**[132]** *1.* उन्हें एक असामान्य रूप से कठिन कार्य का सामना करना पड़ा। *2.* उसे एक चुनौती का सामना करना पड़ा, जिस पर काबू पाना था। *3.* उनके अचानक लिए गए फैसले ने सभी को हैरान कर दिया। *4.* यह ऐसा है जैसे वे कभी अस्तित्व में ही नहीं थे। *5.* इसे किसी प्रकार के जहर के रूप में पढ़ा जाता है। *6.* जो अधिक

करने का साहस करता है वह कोई नहीं है।
- *1.* They encountered an abnormally difficult task. *2.* He faced a challenge to overcome. *3.* Her sudden decision confounded everyone. *4.* It's like they never existed. *5.* It reads out as some sort of poisoning. *6.* Who dares do more is none.

**[133]** *1.* मैं तुम्हें यह बात फिर से कहने का साहस करता हूं। *2.* उन्होंने अपनी स्थिति को वैध बनाने के लिए कड़ी मेहनत की। *3.* यह प्रस्ताव वैध होने के लिए बहुत अच्छा लग रहा था। *4.* लोगों ने इस बात पर बहस की कि इसे वैध बनाया जाए या नहीं। *5.* क्या तुम मेरा करियर बर्बाद करने की कोशिश कर रहे हो? *6.* उन्हें अपने करियर में एक बड़ी चुनौती का सामना करना पड़ा।
- *1.* I dare you to say that again. *2.* He worked hard to legitimize his position. *3.* The offer seemed too good to be legit. *4.* The people debated whether to legalize. *5.* Are you trying to ruin my career? *6.* She faced a monumental challenge in her career.

**[134]** *1.* कला के प्रति उनकी प्रतिभा ने उन्हें खुद को अलग दिखाने में मदद की। *2.* मैं तुम्हारे बारे में नहीं जानता, लेकिन मैं भूख से मर रहा हूँ। *3.* यह तो क्रिसमस की तरह बहुत कुछ देखने की शुरुआत है।
- *1.* His talent for art helped him distinguish himself. *2.* I don't know about you, but I'm starving. *3.* It's beginning to look a lot like Christmas.

**[135]** *1.* उसने रस्सी को लंबा करने के लिए एक उपकरण का उपयोग किया। *2.* ऐसा प्रतीत होता है कि मुझे इसकी कोई परवाह नहीं है। *3.* उसने वहां मौजूद लोगों से इसे नीचे रखने के लिए कहा। *4.* फूल खाने योग्य थे और सलाद में उपयोग किए जाते थे। *5.* वह अपनी स्थिति के आधार पर सम्मान की अपेक्षा करती थी। *6.* क्या ऐसा कुछ है जो मैं कर सकूं मदद के लिए?
- *1.* He used a device to lengthen the rope. *2.* I just can't seem to care. *3.* She asked the occupants to keep it down. *4.* The flowers were edible and used in salads. *5.* She expected deference based on her status. *6.* Is there anything I can do to help?

**[136]** *1.* मैं केवल यही चाहता हूं कि मैं और अधिक कर सकूं। *2.* आप इस पर गंभीरता से विचार नहीं कर रहे हैं, क्या आप हैं? *3.* आप नहीं जानते कि आप किसके साथ खिलवाड़ कर रहे हैं! *4.* मेरा मानना है कि आप दोनों एक दूसरे को जानते हैं। *5.* मेरा मानना है कि इसमें वह लगभग पूरी तरह से शामिल है। *6.* मेरा मानना है कि बातचीत के लिए हमारी देर हो चुकी है।
- *1.* I only wish I could do more. *2.* You're not seriously considering this, are you? *3.* You don't know who you're messing with! *4.* I believe you two know each other. *5.* I think that about

covers it. *6.* I believe we're overdue for a chat.

**[137]** *1.* कर्मचारी अधिक काम के कारण थका हुआ महसूस कर रहे थे। *2.* उसने उसे नाश्ते में से एक टुकड़ा खाने की पेशकश की। *3.* एक संक्षिप्त ब्रेक ने उसे फिर से ध्यान केंद्रित करने में मदद की। *4.* फिल्म में उन्हें एक बदमाश के रूप में दिखाया गया है। *5.* लोग वही मानते हैं जिस पर वे विश्वास करना चाहते हैं। *6.* उसने खुद को अपने अतीत से मुक्त करने की कोशिश की।

● *1.* The employees felt drained from overwork. *2.* She offered him a nibble of the snack. *3.* A brief break helped her refocus. *4.* The film depicts him as a scumbag. *5.* People believe what they want to believe. *6.* He sought to unchain himself from his past.

**[138]** *1.* वह समुद्र तट की ओर जाने वाले मार्ग का अनुसरण करने लगी। *2.* वह किसी भी बातचीत में अपनी ओर से इशारा कर सकता था। *3.* लंबी पैदल यात्रा के दौरान आपके पैर में चोट लग गई। *4.* मनमोहक धुन हर किसी को मंत्रमुग्ध कर देने वाली लग रही थी। *5.* खून की कमी के कारण वह कमजोर महसूस करने लगी थी। *6.* गंदगी की स्थिति के कारण रेस्तरां को बंद कर दिया गया था।

● *1.* She followed the pathway to the beach. *2.* He could winkle his way into any conversation. *3.* Injure your foot while hiking. *4.* The enchanting melody seemed to bewitch everyone. *5.* The anemia left her feeling weak. *6.* The restaurant was shut down for unsanitary conditions.

**[139]** *1.* तेज़ शोर उसकी सुनने की क्षमता को ख़राब कर सकता है। *2.* पूछताछ करने वाले के पास समाचार जानने की क्षमता होती थी। *3.* शरीर को अपने तापमान को नियंत्रित करने की आवश्यकता होती है। *4.* अगली बार, हो सकता है कि हम इतने भाग्यशाली न हों। *5.* वह कमज़ोर दिल वाली है और आसानी से डर जाती है। *6.* उसके सहयोग करने से इनकार करने से स्थिति जटिल हो गई।

● *1.* The loud noise could impair her hearing. *2.* The enquirer had a nose for news. *3.* The body needs to regulate its temperature. *4.* Next time, we might not be so lucky. *5.* She is faint-hearted and easily scared. *6.* Her refusal to cooperate complicated the situation.

**[140]** *1.* मुझे लगता है कि उसकी हालत खराब होती जा रही है। *2.* कार्यक्रम का उद्देश्य स्कूल छोड़ने की दर को कम करना था। *3.* मेरे बाहर निकलने के बाद से वह मेरा पीछा कर रहा है। *4.* नीति परिवर्तन स्वाभाविक रूप से चिंता का कारण बन रहा है। *5.* उन्होंने वर्षों की दूरी के बाद फिर से एक होने की योजना बनाई। *6.* मेरी माँ कहती है कि मुझे कक्षा में भाग लेना चाहिए।

● *1.* I think he's getting worse. *2.* The program aimed to reduce dropout rates. *3.* He's been following me since I got out. *4.*

The policy change is understandably causing concern. *5.* They planned to reunite after years apart. *6.* My mother says I must participate in class.

**[141]** *1.* उन्होंने इस कार्यक्रम को बढ़ावा देने के लिए कड़ी मेहनत की। *2.* नुस्खा के लिए केवल एक कप अधिक सामग्री की आवश्यकता थी। *3.* वह सड़क पर होने वाले अभिनय को मंत्रमुग्ध होकर देखती रही। *4.* मैं कभी भी ऐसा कुछ नहीं करूंगा जिससे आपको ठेस पहुंचे। *5.* मेरे पास कोई है जिससे मैं चाहता हूँ कि तुम मिलो। *6.* यही एकमात्र तरीका है जिससे हम एक साथ रह सकते हैं।

• *1.* She worked hard to promote the event. *2.* The recipe needed just a coupla more ingredients. *3.* She watched the street mime with fascination. *4.* I would never do anything to hurt you. *5.* I have someone I want you to meet. *6.* It's the only way we can be together.

**[142]** *1.* वह दूसरे राज्य में अपने बॉयफ्रेंड से मिलने जा रही है। *2.* सेना ने लाभ हासिल करने के लिए इस रणनीति का इस्तेमाल किया। *3.* अब हमारी रणनीति को पुनः व्यवस्थित करने का समय आ गया है। *4.* हम अपने समय का प्रभावी ढंग से उपयोग कैसे कर सकते हैं? *5.* उनके पास कर्मचारियों की कमी थी और उन्हें अधिक कर्मचारियों की आवश्यकता थी। *6.* उन्होंने पड़ोस के पालतू जानवरों का पालतू जानवर के रूप में स्वागत किया।

• *1.* She's visiting her bf in another state. *2.* The army used the tactic to gain advantage. *3.* It's time to realign our strategy. *4.* How can we leverage our time effectively? *5.* They were short-staffed and needed more staffers. *6.* He greeted the neighborhood pets as a petter.

**[143]** *1.* स्थिति इतनी जटिल थी कि इसे हल करना संभव नहीं था। *2.* उन्होंने स्तर को हल करने के लिए बंदूक का इस्तेमाल किया। *3.* मैं किसी भी चीज़ में बाधा नहीं डाल रहा हूँ, है ना? *4.* बाधा को दूर करने के लिए टीम ने मिलकर काम किया। *5.* बीच की लकड़ी का उपयोग फर्नीचर के लिए किया जाता था। *6.* मशीन घड़ी की कल की सटीकता के साथ काम करती थी।

• *1.* The situation was too complex to solve. *2.* He used gunplay to solve the level. *3.* I'm not interrupting anything, am I? *4.* The team worked together to overcome the obstacle. *5.* The beech wood was used for furniture. *6.* The machine functioned with clockwork accuracy.

**[144]** *1.* ऐसा लगता है जैसे हमारे बीच कोई डील हो गई है। *2.* वह डील पर दोबारा बातचीत करने पर विचार कर रहे हैं। *3.* वे गर्म करने के लिए मिट्टी के तेल का उपयोग करते थे। *4.* क्या आप मुझे नौकरी से निकालने की कोशिश कर रहे हैं? *5.* मैं वास्तव में समय निकालने के लिए आपकी सराहना करता हूँ। *6.*

बेहतर होगा कि जब मैं वापस आऊं तो तुम यहीं रहो।
* *1.* Looks like we have a deal. *2.* He's considering renegoti-
ating the deal. *3.* They used kerosene for heating. *4.* Are you
trying to get me fired? *5.* I really appreciate you taking the time.
*6.* You better be here when I get back.


**[145]** *1.* ऐसा लगता है मानो एक जीवन भर पहले की बात हो. *2.* ऐसा लग
रहा है मानो आपने कोई भूत देख लिया हो. *3.* तुम्हें इससे क्या फ़र्क पड़ता है
कि मैं क्या सोचता हूँ? *4.* उन्होंने एक बाहरी व्यक्ति के रूप में अपनी भूमिका
को अपनाया। *5.* जब तक कामयाब न हो जाओ, कामयाब होने का नाटक करते
रहो। *6.* उन्होंने अपने रोमांचक साहसिक कार्य के बारे में एक किताब लिखी।
* *1.* Seems like a lifetime ago. *2.* Look like you've seen a ghost.
*3.* What do you care what I think? *4.* She embraced her role
as an outsider. *5.* Fake it till you make it. *6.* She wrote a book
about her exciting adventure.


**[146]** *1.* क्या ऐसी कोई चीज़ है जो मैं तुम्हें दिला सकता हूँ? *2.* कंपनी ने अपने
मूल कार्यालय स्थान का विस्तार कर लिया है। *3.* एक स्वस्थ आहार हृदय संबंधी
स्वास्थ्य में सुधार कर सकता है। *4.* उन्होंने अपनी बात स्पष्ट करने के लिए तुलना
का प्रयोग किया। *5.* उसने पहले की तुलना में बाद वाली पोशाक को प्राथमिकता
दी। *6.* जहाज के चालक दल ने जहाज पर सवार सभी लोगों का स्वागत किया।
* *1.* Is there anything I can get you? *2.* The company had
outgrown its original office space. *3.* A healthy diet can improve
cardiovascular health. *4.* They used the comparison to illustrate
their point. *5.* She preferred the latter dress over the former. *6.*
The ship's crew welcomed everyone onboard.


**[147]** *1.* तुम्हें लगता है कि मैं तुम पर हावी हो रहा हूँ? *2.* मैं आपके द्वारा कही
गई बात के बारे में सोच रहा था। *3.* क्या आपने अभी-अभी मेरे द्वारा कही गई
कोई बात सुनी? *4.* मैंने कुछ ऐसी बातें कही जो मुझे नहीं करनी चाहिए थीं। *5.*
कोच ने टीम को प्रेरित करने के लिए संकेत का इस्तेमाल किया। *6.* आप निश्चित
रूप से जानते हैं कि प्रवेश द्वार कैसे बनाया जाता है।
* *1.* You think I'm holding out on you? *2.* I was thinking about
what you said. *3.* Did you hear anything I just said? *4.* I said
some things I shouldn't have. *5.* The coach used goad to motivate the team. *6.* You sure know how to make an entrance.


**[148]** *1.* गाने के बोल एक संकेत के रूप में काम करते थे। *2.* यह स्थान किसी
महिला के स्पर्श का उपयोग कर सकता है। *3.* प्रौद्योगिकी के माध्यम से सब कुछ
हासिल किया जा सकता है। *4.* वे उसे समाज के लिए ख़तरे के रूप में देखते थे।
*5.* बेहतर नींद के लिए सोने के समय की दिनचर्या स्थापित करें। *6.* स्पष्ट संकेत
ने ग्राहकों को अपना रास्ता ढूंढने में मदद की।

346

- *1.* The song's lyrics served as a cue. *2.* This place could use a woman's touch. *3.* Everything is achievable through technology. *4.* They saw him as a menace to society. *5.* Establish a bedtime routine for better sleep. *6.* The clear signage helped customers find their way.

**[149]** *1.* कंपनी ने ग्राहकों को खुश करने के लिए उपहार की पेशकश की। *2.* उन्होंने नए ग्राहकों के लिए एक विशेष डील की पेशकश की। *3.* मुझे नहीं पता कि आप किस बात का जिक्र कर रहे हैं। *4.* उन्हें आगे बढ़ने के लिए एक सहायक वातावरण की आवश्यकता थी। *5.* संगीत की दृष्टि से प्रतिभाशाली समूह ने संगीत कार्यक्रम में प्रस्तुति दी। *6.* मंत्रमुग्ध कर देने वाली प्रस्तुति दर्शकों को मंत्रमुग्ध करती नजर आई।

- *1.* The company offered gifts to placate the customers. *2.* They offered a special deal for new subscribers. *3.* I have no idea what you're referring to. *4.* They needed a supportive environment to thrive. *5.* The musically talented group performed at the concert. *6.* The mesmerizing performance seemed to bewitch the audience.

**[150]** *1.* उनके ठीक होने के लिए देखभाल करने वालों का समर्थन महत्वपूर्ण था। *2.* वह दूर से चिल्लाने की आवाज सुनने के लिए रुक गई। *3.* उसने एक युग की तरह जो महसूस हुआ उसका इंतजार किया। *4.* तब तक रुको जब तक मैं तुम पर अपना हाथ न रख लूं। *5.* अगर मैं शराब पी लूं तो क्या तुम्हें कोई आपत्ति है? *6.* अगर मैं इसे उधार ले लूं तो क्या आपको कोई आपत्ति है?

- *1.* Caregiver support was crucial for their recovery. *2.* She stopped to listen to the distant yipping. *3.* He waited for what felt like an eon. *4.* Wait till I get my hands on you. *5.* Do you mind if I have a drink? *6.* Do you mind if I borrow this?

**[151]** *1.* शारीरिक रूप से सही मॉडल में मानव शरीर को दर्शाया गया है। *2.* मैं सिर्फ हमारे रिश्ते के बारे में बात करने आया था। *3.* वह सहायता प्राप्त आत्महत्या को वैध बनाने में विश्वास करते हैं। *4.* बातचीत के दौरान उन्हें मुंह से दुर्गंध आने की समस्या नजर आई। *5.* मैं कल्पना नहीं कर सकता कि आप किस दौर से गुजर रहे हैं। *6.* मैं आपसे विनती करता हूं कि आप मुझ पर विश्वास करें।

- *1.* The anatomically correct model depicted the human body. *2.* I just came to talk about our relationship. *3.* He believes in the legalization of assisted suicide. *4.* He noticed the halitosis during the conversation. *5.* I can't imagine what you're going through. *6.* I beg you to believe me.

**[152]** *1.* वह कौन है जो मेरे दरवाजे पर दस्तक दे रहा है? *2.* कक्षा में देर से आने के कारण उन्हें हिरासत में ले लिया गया। *3.* उन्हें पानी के भीतर सांस लेने

के लिए संघर्ष करना पड़ा। *4.* क्या आप चाहते हैं कि मैं अपने दोस्त की जासूसी करूँ? *5.* उसने पेंट को तब तक मिलाया जब तक वह नीला न हो गया। *6.* उसने उसे आश्चर्यचकित करने के लिए आंखों पर पट्टी बांध ली।

● *1.* Who's that knocking at my door? *2.* He got detention for being late to class. *3.* They struggled to breathe underwater. *4.* You want me to spy on my friend? *5.* She mixed the paint until it became bluish. *6.* She wore a blindfold to surprise him.

**[153]** *1.* वह हवाई पट्टी पर अपनी सवारी का इंतजार कर रहे थे. *2.* वह लकड़ी के काम में अपनी कुशलता के लिए जाने जाते थे। *3.* हे पिता, मुझे आशीर्वाद दे, क्योंकि मैं ने पाप किया है। *4.* यह हमें वहां पहुंचाने के बारे में है जहां हम जा रहे हैं। *5.* क्या आप थोड़े से इस्तेमाल किए गए कुछ भ्रम खरीदना चाहते हैं? *6.* देर से की गई घोषणा से भ्रम की स्थिति पैदा हो गई।

● *1.* He waited on the airstrip for his ride. *2.* He was known for his skilling in woodworking. *3.* Bless me father, for I have sinned. *4.* It's about getting us to where we're going. *5.* Want to buy some illusions slightly used? *6.* The belated announcement caused confusion.

**[154]** *1.* उन्होंने अपने मंगेतर के परिवार को अपनी सगाई की घोषणा की। *2.* गाना ख़त्म हो गया और यादें हमेशा के लिए ताज़ा हो गईं। *3.* उसने अपने लक्ष्य को प्राप्त करने में बहुत दृढ़ संकल्प दिखाया।

● *1.* They announced their engagement to their fiancee's family. *2.* The song ended, and the memory lingered evermore. *3.* She showed great determination in achieving her goal.

**[155]** *1.* मैंने कभी भी आपको ठेस पहुँचाने वाला कोई काम नहीं किया है। *2.* मैं तुम्हें चोट पहुँचाने के लिए यहाँ नहीं हूँ, ठीक है? *3.* क्या आप जानते हैं कि यह मुझे किसकी याद दिलाता है? *4.* इस उद्देश्य के प्रति उनके जुनून ने दूसरों को प्रेरित किया। *5.* मुझे यह उसी क्षण पता चल गया था जब मैंने तुम्हें देखा था। *6.* मैं आपके द्वारा कही गई बातों के बारे में सोच रहा हूं।

● *1.* I've never done anything to hurt you. *2.* I'm not here to hurt you, okay? *3.* You know what this reminds me of? *4.* His ardour for the cause inspired others. *5.* I knew it the moment I saw you. *6.* I've been thinking about what you said.

**[156]** *1.* उसने वह दिल बेच दिया जिसके बारे में उसने कसम खाई थी कि वह मेरा है! *2.* मैंने उसे तब तक चाकू मारा जब तक उसकी चीख बंद नहीं हो गई। *3.* उन्होंने स्वेच्छा से इस कार्य के लिए स्वेच्छा से भाग लिया।

● *1.* She sold the heart she swore was mine! *2.* I stabbed her until the screaming stopped. *3.* He willingly volunteered for the assignment.

**[157]** *1.* प्रत्येक व्यक्ति की निंदा स्वीकार करें, लेकिन अपना निर्णय सुरक्षित रखें। *2.* उसे ऐसा महसूस हो रहा था जैसे वह किसी गंदे घर में है। *3.* मुझे यह जानने की जरूरत है कि हमारा मुकाबला किससे है।

• *1.* Take each man's censure, but reserve thy judgment. *2.* He felt like he was in a shithouse. *3.* I need to know what we're up against.

**[158]** *1.* विज्ञापन बच्चों को आकर्षित करने के लिए डिज़ाइन किया गया था। *2.* मैं धीरे-धीरे सीख रहा हूं कि ये महिलाएं कौन हैं। *3.* वह अपने क्षितिज का विस्तार करने की योजना बना रही है। *4.* इस जोड़े ने भविष्य में फिर से एक होने की कसम खाई। *5.* उसने लोगों को धोखा देने के लिए गलत दिशा का प्रयोग किया। *6.* मैं सभी लोगों के साथ समान व्यवहार की वकालत करता हूं।

• *1.* The advertisement was designed to appeal to children. *2.* I'm gradually learning who these women are. *3.* She's planning to expand her horizons. *4.* The couple vowed to reunite in the future. *5.* He used misdirection to deceive people. *6.* I advocate for equal treatment of all people.

**[159]** *1.* हम कभी नहीं कभी देश के लिए रवाना हो रहे हैं। *2.* मैं इस समय बहुत ज्यादा सेक्सी महसूस नहीं कर रही हूं। *3.* उनके समय से पहले किये गये कदम के कारण समस्याएँ पैदा हुईं। *4.* उन्होंने सौदे को अंतिम रूप देने से पहले एक चेतावनी का उल्लेख किया। *5.* और हमेशा की तरह, 6:00 बजे से बहस कर रहा हूँ। *6.* कंपनी ने अपनी उत्पाद श्रृंखला में विविधता लाने की कोशिश की।

• *1.* We're in this together. *2.* I don't feel terrifically sexy at the moment. *3.* His premature action caused problems. *4.* He mentioned a caveat before finalizing the deal. *5.* And as usual, arguing since 6:00. *6.* The company sought to diversify its product line.

**[160]** *1.* उन्होंने कार्यस्थल में विविधता को बढ़ावा देने के लिए काम किया। *2.* जब वे चले गये तो वह कमजोर ढंग से हाथ हिला रही थी। *3.* यह बहुत दूर की बात है, लेकिन आप कभी नहीं जान पाते। *4.* वह दूसरों के साथ शालीनता और सम्मान से पेश आती थी। *5.* शहर को व्यवस्था बनाए रखने के लिए एक सतर्क सैनिक की आवश्यकता थी। *6.* उनका व्यवहार एक सतर्क कहानी के रूप में कार्य करता है।

• *1.* They worked to promote diversity in the workplace. *2.* She waved weakly as they left. *3.* It's a long shot, but you never know. *4.* She treated others with decency and respect. *5.* The town needed a vigilante to maintain order. *6.* Their behavior served as a cautionary tale.

**[161]** *1.* मैं अपने बचपन की यादें फिर से ताजा करना चाहता हूं। *2.* पुस्तक

में नायक का चरित्र चित्रण करने का प्रयास किया गया। *3.* उनकी पेंटिंग अक्सर प्रकृति और वन्य जीवन का चित्रण करती हैं। *4.* शिकारी वन्य जीवन के कारण वे इस क्षेत्र से दूर रहते थे। *5.* उन्होंने नौकरी के लिए फिर से आवेदन करने का फैसला किया। *6.* दोपहर के भोजन के मेनू में सैंडविच और सलाद शामिल थे।

● *1.* I want to revisit my childhood memories. *2.* The book sought to characterize the protagonist. *3.* Her paintings often characterize nature and wildlife. *4.* They avoided the area due to predatory wildlife. *5.* They decided to reapply for the job. *6.* The luncheon menu included sandwiches and salads.

[162] *1.* वे पश्चिम की ओर जाने वाली उड़ान में सवार हो गए। *2.* वह एक ऐसा धोखेबाज़ है, जो हमेशा गड़बड़ करता रहता है। *3.* पुलिसकर्मी ने तेज़ गति से गाड़ी चलाने के लिए एक टिकट जारी किया। *4.* मैं देख रहा हूं कि आपको मेरा निमंत्रण मिल गया है। *5.* निमंत्रण में स्पष्ट रूप से बच्चों को बाहर रखने की बात कही गई है। *6.* लेखक ने कहानी कहने के लिए उत्तर आधुनिक दृष्टिकोण का इस्तेमाल किया।

● *1.* They boarded the westbound flight. *2.* He's such a spiller, always making a mess. *3.* The policeman issued a ticket for speeding. *4.* I see you got my invitation. *5.* The invitation explicitly said to exclude children. *6.* The writer used a postmodern approach to storytelling.

[163] *1.* आदेश को याद रखने के लिए उसने एक स्मृति चिन्ह का उपयोग किया। *2.* आप बस मुझे बेहतर महसूस कराने की कोशिश कर रहे हैं। *3.* उन्होंने मंदिर को पवित्र करने के लिए एक समारोह आयोजित किया। *4.* मैं देख रहा हूं कि आपने अपना होमवर्क कर लिया है। *5.* मैंने रात के खाने से पहले अपना होमवर्क पूरा कर लिया। *6.* ऐसा लग रहा था कि शहर पर रहस्य छा गया है।

● *1.* She used a mnemonic to remember the order. *2.* You're just trying to make me feel better. *3.* They held a ceremony to sanctify the temple. *4.* I see you've done your homework. *5.* I finished my homework befor dinner. *6.* The mystery seemed to envelop the town.

[164] *1.* साक्ष्य निर्णायक रूप से उसके अपराध की ओर इशारा करते हैं। *2.* कार्यकर्ता ने दूसरों को बंधन से मुक्त करने के लिए अथक प्रयास किया। *3.* डॉक्टर ने मरीज़ के साथ उपचार के विकल्पों पर चर्चा की।

● *1.* The evidence pointed conclusively to his guilt. *2.* The activist worked tirelessly to unchain others. *3.* The doctor discussed treatment options with the patient.

[165] *1.* उन्होंने फिल्म को बेहतर बनाने के लिए विशेष प्रभावों का इस्तेमाल किया। *2.* हल्के वजन के डिज़ाइन ने इसे ले जाना आसान बना दिया। *3.* दांत के

दर्द के कारण ध्यान केंद्रित करना कठिन हो गया।
- *1.* They used special effects to enhance the movie. *2.* The lightweight design made it easy to carry. *3.* The toothache made it hard to concentrate.

**[166]** *1.* मैं कभी भी ऐसा कुछ नहीं करूँगा जिससे आपको ठेस पहुँचे। *2.* इस आपदा ने शहर को पूरी तरह से नष्ट कर दिया। *3.* आप कमरे को कैसे सुसज्जित करने की योजना बना रहे हैं? *4.* आपने देखा कि कार ने आपके भाई को टक्कर मार दी? *5.* क्या आपको लगता है कि आप इसे प्रबंधित कर सकते हैं? *6.* कार खरीदने के लिए उसे और अधिक पैसे की जरूरत थी।
- *1.* I'd never do anything to hurt you. *2.* The disaster left the town utterly destroyed. *3.* How do you plan to furnish the room? *4.* You saw the car hit your brother? *5.* You think you can manage that? *6.* She needed more dosh to buy the car.

**[167]** *1.* अपने आप को अपने सपनों को प्राप्त करने की कल्पना करें। *2.* मैं अभी तक उस हिस्से का पता नहीं लगा पाया हूं। *3.* बच्चे आइसक्रीम ट्रक के चारों ओर झुंड में इकट्ठा हो गए। *4.* उसने महसूस किया कि भावनाओं का झुंड उस पर हावी हो गया है। *5.* नुस्खा में खाना पकाने के समय को कम करने की आवश्यकता थी। *6.* यह शहर वहां से दो मील की दूरी पर स्थित है।
- *1.* Visualise yourself achieving your dreams. *2.* I haven't figured that part out yet. *3.* The children swarmed around the ice cream truck. *4.* She felt the swarm of emotions overwhelm her. *5.* The recipe called for shortened cooking time. *6.* The town is located two miles whence.

**[168]** *1.* उन्होंने 6 मिनट से कम समय में एक मील दौड़ लगाई। *2.* प्रमुख मील का पत्थर मीलों दूर से दिखाई दे रहा था। *3.* उन्होंने अपने बेटे की स्नातक स्तर की पढ़ाई में भाग लिया। *4.* आवारा ने कठोर परिस्थितियों में जीवित रहने के लिए संघर्ष किया। *5.* इसमें से किसी पर भी उसकी उंगलियों के निशान नहीं हैं। *6.* कट को साफ़ करने के लिए उसने धुंध का उपयोग किया।
- *1.* He ran a mile in under 6 minutes. *2.* The prominent landmark was visible from miles away. *3.* She attended her son's graduation. *4.* The vagrant struggled to survive in harsh conditions. *5.* He has fingerprints on none of this. *6.* She used gauze to clean the cut.

**[169]** *1.* यदि मैं चक से कभी नहीं उबर पाया तो क्या होगा? *2.* वह अभी भी उसके बाद की स्थिति से उबर रहा था। *3.* देवियो और सज्जनो, क्या मैं आपका ध्यान आकर्षित कर सकता हूँ? *4.* पश्चाताप करने वाले चोर ने चोरी का माल वापस कर दिया। *5.* उसे अपने द्वारा पहुंचाई गई चोट के लिए पश्चाताप महसूस हुआ। *6.* उन्होंने एक पेशेवर मालिश करने वाले और मालिश करने वाले को काम

पर रखा।

- *1.* What if I never get over Chuck? *2.* He was still reeling from the aftermath. *3.* Ladies and gentlemen, may I have your attention? *4.* The repentant thief returned the stolen goods. *5.* He felt contrition for the hurt he caused. *6.* They hired a professional masseuse and massager.

**[170]** *1.* गाँव वाले आने वाले तूफ़ान को देखकर थके हुए दिख रहे थे। *2.* बेहद खुश बच्चे ने अपने दादा-दादी को गले लगा लिया। *3.* उसने कार से नाटकीय ढंग से बाहर निकलने की घटना देखी। *4.* मैं जानता हूं कि कौन परिश्रम करता है और कौन रोटी खाता है। *5.* सभी यात्रियों को रात 10 बजे तक जहाज पर पहुंचना होगा। *6.* बच्चे अटारी खेलने के लिए टीवी के आसपास जमा हो गए।

- *1.* The villagers looked wearily at the approaching storm. *2.* The overjoyed child hugged her grandparents. *3.* She witnessed the dramatic ejection from the car. *4.* I know who labors and who loafs. *5.* All passengers must be onboard by 10 PM. *6.* Children gathered around the TV to play atari.

**[171]** *1.* पहाड़ी के नीचे के आवास पहाड़ी के अंदर बनाए गए थे। *2.* वे एक नया प्रबंधक नियुक्त करने की योजना बना रहे हैं। *3.* कुत्ते को यह सीखने की ज़रूरत थी कि कैसे व्यवहार करना है। *4.* यह महज़ एक घटना थी जो उन्हें एक साथ ले आई। *5.* पायलट को बताएं कि विमान का अपहरण कर लिया गया है। *6.* एक बीप ने हमें आने वाले संदेश के प्रति सचेत किया।

- *1.* The underhill dwellings were built into the hillside. *2.* They plan to designate a new manager. *3.* The dog needed to learn how to behave. *4.* It was mere happenstance that brought them together. *5.* Tell the pilot the plane's been hijacked. *6.* A beep alerted us to an incoming message.

**[172]** *1.* उन्हें आशा थी कि वे सभी भय को नष्ट कर देंगे। *2.* यो, अगर मैं तुम्हें जानता हूं, तो एक संदेश छोड़ दो। *3.* उसे नदी को पार करने के लिए उसका सहारा लेना पड़ा। *4.* मुझे ऐसा लग रहा है जैसे मेरा दम घुट रहा है. *5.* क्या आप जानते हैं कि मैं किस दौर से गुजरा हूं? *6.* तुम्हें कोई अंदाज़ा नहीं है कि मैं किस दौर से गुज़र रहा हूँ।

- *1.* They hoped to annihilate all fear. *2.* Yo, if I know you, leave a message. *3.* She had to straddle the stream to cross. *4.* I feel like I'm suffocating. *5.* Do you know what I've been through? *6.* You have no idea what I'm going through.

**[173]** *1.* आप जिस दौर से गुजर रहे हैं, उससे मुझे सहानुभूति है। *2.* ऐसा प्रतीत नहीं होता था कि उसे उससे कोई सहानुभूति है। *3.* उनकी गायन आवाज़ कभी भी आश्चर्यचकित करने में विफल नहीं रही। *4.* वह अपने आत्मविश्वास के

आवरण को मजबूत करने की आशा रखती थी। 5. वह दावा करती है कि उसने एक अलौकिक प्राणी को देखा है। 6. उसने कुत्ते को कमरे के चारों ओर उछल-कूद करते देखा।

• 1. I sympathize with what you're going through. 2. She didn't seem to sympathize with him. 3. Her singing voice never failed to astound. 4. She hoped to strengthen her veneer of confidence. 5. She claims to have seen an extraterrestrial being. 6. She watched the dog prance around the room.

[174] 1. उसने ब्लेड को तेज़ करने के लिए एक पत्थर का इस्तेमाल किया। 2. उसने अपने छात्रों के लिए एक रोमांचक भ्रमण की योजना बनाई। 3. कर्कश स्वर में बोले गए शब्द मुश्किल से सुनाई दे रहे थे। 4. वह वैसी नहीं है जैसा वह कहती है कि वह है। 5. वह अपने करियर के सुनहरे दिनों की प्रतीक्षा कर रही थी। 6. वह टीम का नेतृत्व करने के लिए अयोग्य महसूस करती थीं।

• 1. He used a stone to sharpen the blade. 2. She planned an exciting excursion for her students. 3. The hoarsely spoken words were barely audible. 4. She's not who she says she is. 5. She longed for the heyday of her career. 6. She felt unqualified to lead the team.

[175] 1. मैं दिखने में जितना बड़ा हूं उससे कहीं ज्यादा बड़ा हूं. 2. वे लंबी पैदल यात्रा पर गए और एक विशाल कीड़ा देखा। 3. वह आगे आने वाली संभावित समस्याओं का पूर्वानुमान लगा सकती थी। 4. वह संतान पैदा करने और परिवार शुरू करने की इच्छा रखती थी। 5. चीनी मिट्टी की प्लेट को जटिल रूप से चित्रित किया गया था। 6. पत्नी के कर्तव्यों में खाना बनाना और सफाई करना शामिल था।

• 1. I'm older than I look. 2. They went hiking and saw a giant bug. 3. She could foresee the potential problems ahead. 4. She longed to procreate and start a family. 5. The porcelain plate was intricately painted. 6. Wifey duties included cooking and cleaning.

[176] 1. उन्होंने परियोजना को पूरा करने के लिए पागलों की तरह काम किया। 2. रीढ़ की हड्डी की चोट के लिए सर्जरी की आवश्यकता थी। 3. क्या ऐसी कोई चीज़ है जिसमें मैं आपकी मदद कर सकता हूँ? 4. उन्होंने कई वर्षों तक एक जिज्ञासु के रूप में कार्य किया। 5. उन्होंने समय सीमा को पूरा करने के लिए जुनूनी ढंग से काम किया। 6. उत्कृष्ट रूप से तैयार किए गए आभूषण सूरज की रोशनी में चमक रहे थे।

• 1. He worked maniacally to finish the project. 2. The spinal injury required surgery. 3. Is there something I can help you with? 4. He served as an inquisitor for many years. 5. He worked obsessively to meet the deadline. 6. The exquisitely crafted jewelry sparkled in the sunlight.

**[177]** *1.* जिसने भी यह किया वह जानता था कि वह क्या कर रहा है। *2.* क्या आपको लगता है कि उसका कोई अफेयर चल रहा है? *3.* मुझे लगता है कि मैं इसमें महारत हासिल कर रहा हूं। *4.* इमारत के पिछले हिस्से को नीले रंग से रंगा गया था। *5.* वह नीले रंग की अपेक्षा लाल रंग को अधिक पसंद करता है। *6.* बर्तन धोने वाले तरल पदार्थ से ताजी गंध आ रही थी।

• *1.* Whoever did this knew what they were doing. *2.* Do you think he's having an affair? *3.* I think I'm getting the hang of this. *4.* The backside of the building was painted blue. *5.* He does prefer red over blue. *6.* The dishwashing liquid smelled fresh.

**[178]** *1.* उसने अपने पत्र मित्र के साथ पत्र-व्यवहार का आदान-प्रदान किया। *2.* भले ही वह असभ्य है, फिर भी मैं उसे पसंद करता हूँ। *3.* उन्होंने गांव तक पहुंचने के लिए ऊपर की ओर यात्रा की। *4.* उनकी लापरवाह हरकतें पूरे मिशन को खतरे में डाल सकती हैं। *5.* ऐसा लग रहा था कि उसकी प्रतिभा हर किसी को मात दे रही है। *6.* उन्होंने समय सीमा को पूरा करने के लिए लगन से काम किया।

• *1.* She exchanged correspondence with her pen pal. *2.* I like her even though she's rude. *3.* They traveled upriver to reach the village. *4.* Their reckless actions could jeopardise the entire mission. *5.* Her talent seemed to outshine everyone else's. *6.* He worked diligently to meet the deadline.

**[179]** *1.* उसने अपने बगीचे के लिए एक गार्ड को किराये पर लिया। *2.* टीम ने समस्या के समाधान के लिए समझदारी से काम लिया। *3.* पैदल यात्री से बचने के लिए साइकिल चालक ने गाड़ी मोड़ ली। *4.* वह जो चाहता था उसे पाने के लिए उसने प्रलोभन का सहारा लिया। *5.* कंपनी ने नए कर्मचारियों को आकर्षित करने के लिए प्रलोभन का इस्तेमाल किया। *6.* उन्होंने हास्य का उपयोग ध्यान भटकाने वाली तकनीक के रूप में किया।

• *1.* She hired a gard for her garden. *2.* The team worked sensibly to solve the problem. *3.* The cyclist swerved to avoid the pedestrian. *4.* He used seduction to get what he wanted. *5.* The company used inducement to attract new employees. *6.* He used humor as a distraction technique.

**[180]** *1.* वह संगीत के प्रति अपनी योग्यता का परीक्षण कर रही है। *2.* नौकरी के लिए भाषा के प्रति मजबूत योग्यता की आवश्यकता होती है। *3.* उनकी गर्भाशय संबंधी समस्याओं ने उनकी प्रजनन क्षमता को प्रभावित किया।

• *1.* She's testing her aptitude for music. *2.* The job requires a strong aptitude for language. *3.* Her uterine problems affected her fertility.

**[181]** *1.* ऊंचाई के प्रति उसके भय ने उसे चढ़ने से रोक दिया। *2.* उसके चमड़े वाले हाथों पर उम्र के निशान दिख रहे थे। *3.* जो कोई भी ख़तरा है, उसे ख़त्म किया जा सकता है। *4.* इस वायरस ने जनसंख्या को ख़त्म करने का ख़तरा पैदा कर दिया है। *5.* मैंने मेयर पद के लिए आपके खिलाफ चुनाव लड़ने का फैसला किया है। *6.* उन्होंने रेस्तरां को आपूर्ति करने के लिए एक मछुआरे को काम पर रखा।

• *1.* Her phobia of heights prevented her from climbing. *2.* Her leathery hands showed signs of age. *3.* Anyone that's a threat is expendable. *4.* The virus threatened to decimate the population. *5.* I've decided to run against you for mayor. *6.* They hired a fisher to supply the restaurant.

**[182]** *1.* उसे तेज़ हवा वाले मौसम में चलने में कठिनाई हो रही थी। *2.* उन्होंने उसे अपने कौशल में विविधता लाने के लिए प्रोत्साहित किया। *3.* मालिश करने वाले ने उसकी मांसपेशियों का तनाव दूर कर दिया।

• *1.* She struggled to walk in the windy weather. *2.* She encour-aged him to diversify his skills. *3.* The massager relieved his muscle tension.

**[183]** *1.* एक साइकिल चालक को मजबूत पैर की मांसपेशियों की आवश्यकता होती है। *2.* जब मेरा काम पूरा हो जाएगा तो मैं तुम्हें संदेश भेजूंगा। *3.* उन्होंने संगठन के लिए एक दूत के रूप में कार्य किया। *4.* रिपोर्ट में आर्थिक स्थिति का वर्णन करने का प्रयास किया गया। *5.* उसे एहसास हुआ कि वह एक धोखेबाज का सामना कर रहा था। *6.* आदर्श वाक्य उनके व्यक्तिगत प्रमाण के रूप में कार्य करता था।

• *1.* A cyclist needs strong leg muscles. *2.* I'll text you when I'm done. *3.* She served as an emissary for the organization. *4.* The report sought to characterize the economic situation. *5.* He realized he was facing an imposter. *6.* The motto served as their personal credo.

**[184]** *1.* मैंने कभी नहीं सोचा था कि मैं तुम्हें ऐसा कहते हुए सुनूंगा। *2.* उसने अपने वंश का पता लगाने के लिए अपनी विरासत पर शोध किया। *3.* उन पर आपराधिक गलत काम करने का आरोप लगाया गया था। *4.* मैं आप को भी ऐसा ही करने की सलाह देता हुं। *5.* भेड़ की खाल को गहरे लाल रंग में रंगा गया था। *6.* सीढ़ियाँ उन्हें चढ़ने में मदद करने के लिए डिज़ाइन की गई थीं।

• *1.* I never thought I'd hear you say that. *2.* She researched her heritage to trace her ancestry. *3.* They were accused of criminal wrongdoing. *4.* I recommend you do the same. *5.* The sheepskin was dyed a deep red. *6.* The stairs were designed to help them ascend.

[185] 1. उन्होंने रणनीतिक रूप से खुद को हमले के लिए तैनात किया। 2. मैं जानता हूं कि हम युवा जेमी को कैसे बचा सकते हैं। 3. उसके बारे में अफवाह थी कि वह एक शक्तिशाली जादूगर था। 4. उनके साथियों द्वारा उन्हें उच्च व्यक्ति के रूप में देखा जाता था। 5. उसे अपने साथियों से संबंध बनाने के लिए संघर्ष करना पड़ा। 6. उन्होंने ऐसी कोई भी चीज़ खाने से इंकार कर दिया जो खाने योग्य न हो।

• 1. He tactically positioned himself for the attack. 2. I know how we can save young Jamie. 3. He was rumored to be a powerful sorcerer. 4. They were seen as uppity by their peers. 5. He struggled to relate to his peers. 6. He refused to eat anything that wasn't edible.

[186] 1. प्रलोभन इतना अच्छा था कि इंकार नहीं किया जा सकता था। 2. वह एक गोल्फ खिलाड़ी है जो आपके साथ गंदगी जैसा व्यवहार करता है। 3. उसने धोखाधड़ी को रोकने के लिए एक जवाबी उपाय लागू किया। 4. मैं बिना किसी शर्त के सभी विषयों पर चर्चा करने के लिए यहां हूं। 5. जैसे-जैसे उसकी उम्र बढ़ती गई वह और अधिक कोमल होता गया। 6. प्रयोग ने उस सिद्धांत को निर्णायक रूप से सिद्ध कर दिया।

• 1. The inducement was too good to refuse. 2. He's a golfer who treats you like dirt. 3. She implemented a countermeasure to prevent fraud. 4. I'm here to discuss all topics without reserve. 5. He became more mellow as he aged. 6. The experiment proved conclusively that theory.

[187] 1. तलवार का प्रयोग शरीर की हड्डी तोड़ने के लिए किया गया। 2. वह एक कुख्यात परोपकारी व्यक्ति के रूप में जाने जाते थे। 3. अज्ञात सीटी बजाने वाले ने सभी को रुकने और सुनने पर मजबूर कर दिया।

• 1. The sword was used to disembowel. 2. He was known as a notorious philanderer. 3. The unknown whistler made everyone stop and listen.

[188] 1. उसने प्रतिक्रिया की आशा में घंटी बजाने वाले को फोन किया। 2. डॉक्टर ने मधुमेह को प्रबंधित करने के लिए जीवनशैली में बदलाव पर चर्चा की। 3. क्या हम इस साझा दुश्मन के ख़िलाफ़ एकजुट हो सकते हैं?

• 1. She called the ringer, hoping for a response. 2. The doctor discussed lifestyle changes to manage diabetes. 3. Can we unite against this common enemy?

# Appendix: Essential Verb Conjugations

# 1. होना — *to be*
Used to indicate existence or state of being.

| Person | Pres. | Past | Fut. | Imp. | Cond. |
|---|---|---|---|---|---|
| मैं (I) | हूँ | था / थी | हूँगा / हूँगी | - | होता / होती |
| तुम (You, informal) | हो | थे / थीं | होओगे / होओगी | हो | होते / होती |
| आप (You, formal) | हैं | थे / थीं | होंगे / होंगी | होइए | होते / होती |
| वह / यह (He / She / It) | है | था / थी | होगा / होगी | - | होता / होती |
| हम (We) | हैं | थे / थीं | होंगे / होंगी | - | होते / होती |
| वे / ये (They) | हैं | थे / थीं | होंगे / होंगी | - | होते / होती |

| Person | Pres. Part. | Past Part. |
|---|---|---|
| मैं (I) | होता / होती | हुआ / हुई |
| तुम (You, informal) | होते / होती | हुए / हुई |
| आप (You, formal) | होते / होती | हुए / हुई |
| वह / यह (He / She / It) | होता / होती | हुआ / हुई |
| हम (We) | होते / होती | हुए / हुई |

357

| वे / ये (They) | होते / होती | हुए / हुईं |
|---|---|---|

# 2. करना — *to do*
Used to indicate an action or task.

| Person | Pres. | Past | Fut. | Imp. | Cond. |
|---|---|---|---|---|---|
| मैं (I) | करता हूँ / करती हूँ | किया / की | करूँगा / करूँगी | - | करता / करती |
| तुम (You, infor-mal) | करते हो / करती हो | किया / की | करोगे / करोगी | करो | करते / करती |
| आप (You, formal) | करते हैं / करती हैं | किया / की | करेंगे / करेंगी | करिए | करते / करती |
| वह / यह (He / She / It) | करता है / करती है | किया / की | करेगा / करेगी | - | करता / करती |
| हम (We) | करते हैं / करती हैं | किया / की | करेंगे / करेंगी | - | करते / करती |
| वे / ये (They) | करते हैं / करती हैं | किया / की | करेंगे / करेंगी | - | करते / करती |

| Person | Pres. Part. | Past Part. |
|---|---|---|
| मैं (I) | करता / करती | किया / की |
| तुम (You, informal) | करते / करती | किए / कीं |
| आप (You, formal) | करते / करती | किए / कीं |
| वह / यह (He / She / It) | करता / करती | किया / की |

| | | |
|---|---|---|
| हम (We) | करते / करती | किए / कीं |
| वे / ये (They) | करते / करती | किए / कीं |

# 3. जाना — *to go*

Used to indicate movement from one place to another.

| Person | Pres. | Past | Fut. | Imp. | Cond. |
|---|---|---|---|---|---|
| मैं (I) | जाता हूँ / जाती हूँ | गया / गई | जाऊँगा / जाऊँगी | - | जाता / जाती |
| तुम (You, infor-mal) | जाते हो / जाती हो | गए / गईं | जाओगे / जाओगी | जाओ | जाते / जाती |
| आप (You, formal) | जाते हैं / जाती हैं | गए / गईं | जाएँगे / जाएँगी | जाइए | जाते / जाती |
| वह / यह (He / She / It) | जाता है / जाती है | गया / गई | जाएगा / जाएगी | - | जाता / जाती |
| हम (We) | जाते हैं / जाती हैं | गए / गईं | जाएँगे / जाएँगी | - | जाते / जाती |
| वे / ये (They) | जाते हैं / जाती हैं | गए / गईं | जाएँगे / जाएँगी | - | जाते / जाती |

| Person | Pres. Part. | Past Part. |
|---|---|---|
| मैं (I) | जाता / जाती | गया / गई |
| तुम (You, informal) | जाते / जाती | गए / गईं |
| आप (You, formal) | जाते / जाती | गए / गईं |

| | | |
|---|---|---|
| वह / यह (He / She / It) | जाता / जाती | गया / गई |
| हम (We) | जाते / जाती | गए / गई |
| वे / ये (They) | जाते / जाती | गए / गई |

# 4. आना — *to come*

Used to indicate the action of coming.

| Person | Pres. | Past | Fut. | Imp. | Cond. |
|---|---|---|---|---|---|
| मैं (I) | आता हूँ / आती हूँ | आया / आई | आऊँगा / आऊँगी | - | आता / आती |
| तुम (You, infor-mal) | आते हो / आती हो | आए / आईं | आओगे / आओगी | आओ | आते / आती |
| आप (You, formal) | आते हैं / आती हैं | आए / आईं | आएँगे / आएँगी | आइए | आते / आती |
| वह / यह (He / She / It) | आता है / आती है | आया / आई | आएगा / आएगी | - | आता / आती |
| हम (We) | आते हैं / आती हैं | आए / आईं | आएँगे / आएँगी | - | आते / आती |
| वे / ये (They) | आते हैं / आती हैं | आए / आईं | आएँगे / आएँगी | - | आते / आती |

| Person | Pres. Part. | Past Part. |
|---|---|---|
| मैं (I) | आता / आती | आया / आई |

| | | |
|---|---|---|
| तुम (You, informal) | आते / आती | आए / आई |
| आप (You, formal) | आते / आती | आए / आई |
| वह / यह (He / She / It) | आता / आती | आया / आई |
| हम (We) | आते / आती | आए / आई |
| वे / ये (They) | आते / आती | आए / आई |

# 5. लेना — *to take*
Used to indicate the act of taking or receiving.

| Person | Pres. | Past | Fut. | Imp. | Cond. |
|---|---|---|---|---|---|
| मैं (I) | लेता / लेती हूँ | लिया / ली | लूँगा / लूँगी | - | लेता / लेती |
| तुम (You, infor-mal) | लेते / लेती हो | लिया / ली | लोगे / लोगी | लो | लेते / लेती |
| आप (You, formal) | लेते / लेती हैं | लिया / ली | लेंगे / लेंगी | लीजिए | लेते / लेती |
| वह / यह (He / She / It) | लेता / लेती है | लिया / ली | लेगा / लेगी | - | लेता / लेती |
| हम (We) | लेते / लेती हैं | लिया / ली | लेंगे / लेंगी | - | लेते / लेती |
| वे / ये (They) | लेते / लेती हैं | लिया / ली | लेंगे / लेंगी | - | लेते / लेती |

| Person | Pres. Part. | Past Part. |
|---|---|---|
| मैं (I) | लेता / लेती | लिया / ली |
| तुम (You, informal) | लेते / लेती | लिया / ली |
| आप (You, formal) | लेते / लेती | लिया / ली |
| वह / यह (He / She / It) | लेता / लेती | लिया / ली |
| हम (We) | लेते / लेती | लिया / ली |
| वे / ये (They) | लेते / लेती | लिया / ली |

# 6. देना — *to give*
Used to indicate the act of giving.

| Person | Pres. | Past | Fut. | Imp. | Cond. |
|---|---|---|---|---|---|
| मैं (I) | देता हूँ / देती हूँ | दिया था / दी थी | दूँगा / दूँगी | - | देता / देती |
| तुम (You, infor-mal) | देते हो / देती हो | दिया था / दी थी | दोगे / दोगी | दो | देते / देती |
| आप (You, formal) | देते हैं / देती हैं | दिया था / दी थी | देंगे / देंगी | दीजिए | देते / देती |
| वह / यह (He / She / It) | देता है / देती है | दिया था / दी थी | देगा / देगी | - | देता / देती |
| हम (We) | देते हैं / देती हैं | दिया था / दी थी | देंगे / देंगी | - | देते / देती |
| वे / ये (They) | देते हैं / देती हैं | दिया था / दी थी | देंगे / देंगी | - | देते / देती |

| Person | Pres. Part. | Past Part. |
|---|---|---|
| मैं (I) | देता / देती | दिया / दी |
| तुम (You, informal) | देते / देती | दिया / दी |
| आप (You, formal) | देते / देती | दिया / दी |
| वह / यह (He / She / It) | देता / देती | दिया / दी |
| हम (We) | देते / देती | दिया / दी |
| वे / ये (They) | देते / देती | दिया / दी |

# 7. खाना — *to eat*
Used to indicate the act of eating.

| Person | Pres. | Past | Fut. | Imp. | Cond. |
|---|---|---|---|---|---|
| मैं (I) | खाता हूँ / खाती हूँ | खाया था / खाई थी | खाऊँगा / खाऊँगी | - | खाता / खाती |
| तुम (You, informal) | खाते हो / खाती हो | खाया था / खाई थी | खाओगे / खाओगी | खाओ | खाते / खाती |
| आप (You, formal) | खाते हैं / खाती हैं | खाया था / खाई थी | खाएँगे / खाएँगी | खाइए | खाते / खाती |
| वह / यह (He / She / It) | खाता है / खाती है | खाया था / खाई थी | खाएगा / खाएगी | - | खाता / खाती |
| हम (We) | खाते हैं / खाती हैं | खाया था / खाई थी | खाएँगे / खाएँगी | - | खाते / खाती |

| वे / ये (They) | खाते हैं / खाती हैं | खाया था / खाई थी | खाएँगे / खाएँगी | - | खाते / खाती |
| --- | --- | --- | --- | --- | --- |

| Person | Pres. Part. | Past Part. |
| --- | --- | --- |
| मैं (I) | खाता / खाती | खाया / खाई |
| तुम (You, informal) | खाते / खाती | खाए / खाई |
| आप (You, formal) | खाते / खाती | खाए / खाई |
| वह / यह (He / She / It) | खाता / खाती | खाया / खाई |
| हम (We) | खाते / खाती | खाए / खाई |
| वे / ये (They) | खाते / खाती | खाए / खाई |

# 8. पीना — *to drink*
Used to describe the act of drinking.

| Person | Pres. | Past | Fut. | Imp. | Cond. |
| --- | --- | --- | --- | --- | --- |
| मैं (I) | पीता हूँ / पीती हूँ | पिया था / पी थी | पीऊँगा / पीऊँगी | - | पीता / पीती |
| तुम (You, informal) | पीते हो / पीती हो | पिए थे / पी थीं | पियोगे / पियोगी | पीओ | पीते / पीती |
| आप (You, formal) | पीते हैं / पीती हैं | पिए थे / पी थीं | पिएंगे / पिएंगी | पीजिए | पीते / पीती |

| | Pres. | Past | Fut. | Imp. | Cond. |
|---|---|---|---|---|---|
| वह / यह (He / She / It) | पीता है / पीती है | पिया था / पी थी | पिएगा / पिएगी | - | पीता / पीती |
| हम (We) | पीते हैं / पीती हैं | पिए थे / पी थीं | पिएंगे / पिएंगी | - | पीते / पीती |
| वे / ये (They) | पीते हैं / पीती हैं | पिए थे / पी थीं | पिएंगे / पिएंगी | - | पीते / पीती |

| Person | Pres. Part. | Past Part. |
|---|---|---|
| मैं (I) | पीता / पीती | पिया / पी |
| तुम (You, informal) | पीते / पीती | पिए / पीं |
| आप (You, formal) | पीते / पीती | पिए / पीं |
| वह / यह (He / She / It) | पीता / पीती | पिया / पी |
| हम (We) | पीते / पीती | पिए / पीं |
| वे / ये (They) | पीते / पीती | पिए / पीं |

# 9. सोना — to sleep

Used to describe the act of sleeping.

| Person | Pres. | Past | Fut. | Imp. | Cond. |
|---|---|---|---|---|---|
| मैं (I) | सोता हूँ / सोती हूँ | सोया था / सोई थी | सोऊँगा / सोऊँगी | - | सोता / सोती |
| तुम (You, informal) | सोते हो / सोती हो | सोए थे / सोई थीं | सोओगे / सोओगी | सो | सोते / सोती |

| | | | | | |
|---|---|---|---|---|---|
| आप (You, formal) | सोते हैं / सोती हैं | सोए थे / सोई थीं | सोएँगे / सोएँगी | सोइए | सोते / सोती |
| वह / यह (He / She / It) | सोता है / सोती है | सोया था / सोई थी | सोएगा / सोएगी | - | सोता / सोती |
| हम (We) | सोते हैं / सोती हैं | सोए थे / सोई थीं | सोएँगे / सोएँगी | - | सोते / सोती |
| वे / ये (They) | सोते हैं / सोती हैं | सोए थे / सोई थीं | सोएँगे / सोएँगी | - | सोते / सोती |

| Person | Pres. Part. | Past Part. |
|---|---|---|
| मैं (I) | सोता / सोती | सोया / सोई |
| तुम (You, informal) | सोते / सोती | सोए / सोई |
| आप (You, formal) | सोते / सोती | सोए / सोई |
| वह / यह (He / She / It) | सोता / सोती | सोया / सोई |
| हम (We) | सोते / सोती | सोए / सोई |
| वे / ये (They) | सोते / सोती | सोए / सोई |

## 10. उठना — *to rise, to get up*
Used to indicate the action of rising or getting up.

| Person | Pres. | Past | Fut. | Imp. | Cond. |
|---|---|---|---|---|---|
| मैं (I) | उठता हूँ / उठती हूँ | उठा था / उठी थी | उठूँगा / उठूँगी | - | उठता / उठती |

| | | | | | |
|---|---|---|---|---|---|
| तुम (You, informal) | उठते हो / उठती हो | उठे थे / उठी थीं | उठोगे / उठोगी | उठो | उठते / उठती |
| आप (You, formal) | उठते हैं / उठती हैं | उठे थे / उठी थीं | उठेंगे / उठेंगी | उठिए | उठते / उठती |
| वह / यह (He / She / It) | उठता है / उठती है | उठा था / उठी थी | उठेगा / उठेगी | - | उठता / उठती |
| हम (We) | उठते हैं / उठती हैं | उठे थे / उठी थीं | उठेंगे / उठेंगी | - | उठते / उठती |
| वे / ये (They) | उठते हैं / उठती हैं | उठे थे / उठी थीं | उठेंगे / उठेंगी | - | उठते / उठती |

| Person | Pres. Part. | Past Part. |
|---|---|---|
| मैं (I) | उठता / उठती | उठा / उठी |
| तुम (You, informal) | उठते / उठती | उठे / उठीं |
| आप (You, formal) | उठते / उठती | उठे / उठीं |
| वह / यह (He / She / It) | उठता / उठती | उठा / उठी |
| हम (We) | उठते / उठती | उठे / उठीं |
| वे / ये (They) | उठते / उठती | उठे / उठीं |

# 11. बैठना — *to sit*
Used to indicate the act of sitting.

| Person | Pres. | Past | Fut. | Imp. | Cond. |
|---|---|---|---|---|---|

| | | | | | |
|---|---|---|---|---|---|
| मैं (I) | बैठता हूँ / बैठती हूँ | बैठा था / बैठी थी | बैठूँगा / बैठूँगी | - | बैठता / बैठती |
| तुम (You, informal) | बैठते हो / बैठती हो | बैठे थे / बैठी थीं | बैठोगे / बैठोगी | बैठो | बैठते / बैठती |
| आप (You, formal) | बैठते हैं / बैठती हैं | बैठे थे / बैठी थीं | बैठेंगे / बैठेंगी | बैठिए | बैठते / बैठती |
| वह / यह (He / She / It) | बैठता है / बैठती है | बैठा था / बैठी थी | बैठेगा / बैठेगी | - | बैठता / बैठती |
| हम (We) | बैठते हैं / बैठती हैं | बैठे थे / बैठी थीं | बैठेंगे / बैठेंगी | - | बैठते / बैठती |
| वे / ये (They) | बैठते हैं / बैठती हैं | बैठे थे / बैठी थीं | बैठेंगे / बैठेंगी | - | बैठते / बैठती |

| Person | Pres. Part. | Past Part. |
|---|---|---|
| मैं (I) | बैठता / बैठती | बैठा / बैठी |
| तुम (You, informal) | बैठते / बैठती | बैठे / बैठीं |
| आप (You, formal) | बैठते / बैठती | बैठे / बैठीं |
| वह / यह (He / She / It) | बैठता / बैठती | बैठा / बैठी |
| हम (We) | बैठते / बैठती | बैठे / बैठीं |
| वे / ये (They) | बैठते / बैठती | बैठे / बैठीं |

# 12. चलना — to walk

Used to indicate the action of walking.

| Person | Pres. | Past | Fut. | Imp. | Cond. |
|---|---|---|---|---|---|
| मैं (I) | चलता हूँ / चलती हूँ | चला था / चली थी | चलूँगा / चलूँगी | - | चलता / चलती |
| तुम (You, infor-mal) | चलते हो / चलती हो | चले थे / चली थीं | चलोगे / चलोगी | चलो | चलते / चलती |
| आप (You, formal) | चलते हैं / चलती हैं | चले थे / चली थीं | चलेंगे / चलेंगी | चलिए | चलते / चलती |
| वह / यह (He / She / It) | चलता है / चलती है | चला था / चली थी | चलेगा / चलेगी | - | चलता / चलती |
| हम (We) | चलते हैं / चलती हैं | चले थे / चली थीं | चलेंगे / चलेंगी | - | चलते / चलती |
| वे / ये (They) | चलते हैं / चलती हैं | चले थे / चली थीं | चलेंगे / चलेंगी | - | चलते / चलती |

| Person | Pres. Part. | Past Part. |
|---|---|---|
| मैं (I) | चलता / चलती | चला / चली |
| तुम (You, informal) | चलते / चलती | चले / चलीं |
| आप (You, formal) | चलते / चलती | चले / चलीं |
| वह / यह (He / She / It) | चलता / चलती | चला / चली |
| हम (We) | चलते / चलती | चले / चलीं |
| वे / ये (They) | चलते / चलती | चले / चलीं |

# 13. देखना — *to see*

Used to indicate the act of seeing or observing.

| Person | Pres. | Past | Fut. | Imp. | Cond. |
|---|---|---|---|---|---|
| मैं (I) | देखता हूँ / देखती हूँ | देखा / देखी | देखूँगा / देखूँगी | - | देखता / देखती |
| तुम (You, informal) | देखते हो / देखती हो | देखा / देखी | देखोगे / देखोगी | देखो | देखते / देखती |
| आप (You, formal) | देखते हैं / देखती हैं | देखा / देखी | देखेंगे / देखेंगी | देखिए | देखते / देखती |
| वह / यह (He / She / It) | देखता है / देखती है | देखा / देखी | देखेगा / देखेगी | - | देखता / देखती |
| हम (We) | देखते हैं / देखती हैं | देखा / देखी | देखेंगे / देखेंगी | - | देखते / देखती |
| वे / ये (They) | देखते हैं / देखती हैं | देखा / देखी | देखेंगे / देखेंगी | - | देखते / देखती |

| Person | Pres. Part. | Past Part. |
|---|---|---|
| मैं (I) | देखता / देखती | देखा / देखी |
| तुम (You, informal) | देखते / देखती | देखा / देखी |
| आप (You, formal) | देखते / देखती | देखा / देखी |
| वह / यह (He / She / It) | देखता / देखती | देखा / देखी |
| हम (We) | देखते / देखती | देखा / देखी |
| वे / ये (They) | देखते / देखती | देखा / देखी |

# 14. सुनना — *to listen*

Used to indicate the act of listening.

| Person | Pres. | Past | Fut. | Imp. | Cond. |
|---|---|---|---|---|---|
| मैं (I) | सुनता हूँ / सुनती हूँ | सुना था / सुनी थी | सुनूँगा / सुनूँगी | - | सुनता / सुनती |
| तुम (You, informal) | सुनते हो / सुनती हो | सुने थे / सुनी थीं | सुनोगे / सुनोगी | सुनो | सुनते / सुनती |
| आप (You, formal) | सुनते हैं / सुनती हैं | सुने थे / सुनी थीं | सुनेंगे / सुनेंगी | सुनिए | सुनते / सुनती |
| वह / यह (He / She / It) | सुनता है / सुनती है | सुना था / सुनी थी | सुनेगा / सुनेगी | - | सुनता / सुनती |
| हम (We) | सुनते हैं / सुनती हैं | सुने थे / सुनी थीं | सुनेंगे / सुनेंगी | - | सुनते / सुनती |
| वे / ये (They) | सुनते हैं / सुनती हैं | सुने थे / सुनी थीं | सुनेंगे / सुनेंगी | - | सुनते / सुनती |

| Person | Pres. Part. | Past Part. |
|---|---|---|
| मैं (I) | सुनता / सुनती | सुना / सुनी |
| तुम (You, informal) | सुनते / सुनती | सुने / सुनीं |
| आप (You, formal) | सुनते / सुनती | सुने / सुनीं |
| वह / यह (He / She / It) | सुनता / सुनती | सुना / सुनी |
| हम (We) | सुनते / सुनती | सुने / सुनीं |
| वे / ये (They) | सुनते / सुनती | सुने / सुनीं |

# 15. बोलना — *to speak*
Used to express the act of speaking or talking.

| Person | Pres. | Past | Fut. | Imp. | Cond. |
|---|---|---|---|---|---|
| मैं (I) | बोलता हूँ / बोलती हूँ | बोला / बोली | बोलूँगा / बोलूँगी | - | बोलता / बोलती |
| तुम (You, infor- mal) | बोलते हो / बोलती हो | बोले / बोली | बोलोगे / बोलोगी | बोलो | बोलते / बोलती |
| आप (You, formal) | बोलते हैं / बोलती हैं | बोले / बोली | बोलेंगे / बोलेंगी | बोलिए | बोलते / बोलती |
| वह / यह (He / She / It) | बोलता है / बोलती है | बोला / बोली | बोलेगा / बोलेगी | - | बोलता / बोलती |
| हम (We) | बोलते हैं / बोलती हैं | बोले / बोली | बोलेंगे / बोलेंगी | - | बोलते / बोलती |
| वे / ये (They) | बोलते हैं / बोलती हैं | बोले / बोली | बोलेंगे / बोलेंगी | - | बोलते / बोलती |

| Person | Pres. Part. | Past Part. |
|---|---|---|
| मैं (I) | बोलता / बोलती | बोला / बोली |
| तुम (You, informal) | बोलते / बोलती | बोले / बोली |
| आप (You, formal) | बोलते / बोलती | बोले / बोली |
| वह / यह (He / She / It) | बोलता / बोलती | बोला / बोली |

| हम (We) | बोलते / बोलती | बोले / बोली |
| वे / ये (They) | बोलते / बोलती | बोले / बोली |

# 16. पढ़ना — *to read*
Used to indicate the act of reading.

| Person | Pres. | Past | Fut. | Imp. | Cond. |
|---|---|---|---|---|---|
| मैं (I) | पढ़ता हूँ / पढ़ती हूँ | पढ़ा / पढ़ी | पढ़ूँगा / पढ़ूँगी | - | पढ़ता / पढ़ती |
| तुम (You, infor-mal) | पढ़ते हो / पढ़ती हो | पढ़े / पढ़ीं | पढ़ोगे / पढ़ोगी | पढ़ो | पढ़ते / पढ़ती |
| आप (You, formal) | पढ़ते हैं / पढ़ती हैं | पढ़े / पढ़ीं | पढ़ेंगे / पढ़ेंगी | पढ़िए | पढ़ते / पढ़ती |
| वह / यह (He / She / It) | पढ़ता है / पढ़ती है | पढ़ा / पढ़ी | पढ़ेगा / पढ़ेगी | - | पढ़ता / पढ़ती |
| हम (We) | पढ़ते हैं / पढ़ती हैं | पढ़े / पढ़ीं | पढ़ेंगे / पढ़ेंगी | - | पढ़ते / पढ़ती |
| वे / ये (They) | पढ़ते हैं / पढ़ती हैं | पढ़े / पढ़ीं | पढ़ेंगे / पढ़ेंगी | - | पढ़ते / पढ़ती |

| Person | Pres. Part. | Past Part. |
|---|---|---|
| मैं (I) | पढ़ता / पढ़ती | पढ़ा हुआ / पढ़ी हुई |
| तुम (You, informal) | पढ़ते / पढ़ती | पढ़े हुए / पढ़ी हुई |
| आप (You, formal) | पढ़ते / पढ़ती | पढ़े हुए / पढ़ी हुई |

373

| वह / यह (He / She / It) | पढ़ता / पढ़ती | पढ़ा हुआ / पढ़ी हुई |
|---|---|---|
| हम (We) | पढ़ते / पढ़ती | पढ़े हुए / पढ़ी हुई |
| वे / ये (They) | पढ़ते / पढ़ती | पढ़े हुए / पढ़ी हुई |

# 17. लिखना — *to write*

Used to describe the act of writing.

| Person | Pres. | Past | Fut. | Imp. | Cond. |
|---|---|---|---|---|---|
| मैं (I) | लिखता हूँ / लिखती हूँ | लिखा था / लिखी थी | लिखूँगा / लिखूँगी | - | लिखता / लिखती |
| तुम (You, informal) | लिखते हो / लिखती हो | लिखे थे / लिखी थीं | लिखोगे / लिखोगी | लिखो | लिखते / लिखती |
| आप (You, formal) | लिखते हैं / लिखती हैं | लिखे थे / लिखी थीं | लिखेंगे / लिखेंगी | लिखिए | लिखते / लिखती |
| वह / यह (He / She / It) | लिखता है / लिखती है | लिखा था / लिखी थी | लिखेगा / लिखेगी | - | लिखता / लिखती |
| हम (We) | लिखते हैं / लिखती हैं | लिखे थे / लिखी थीं | लिखेंगे / लिखेंगी | - | लिखते / लिखती |
| वे / ये (They) | लिखते हैं / लिखती हैं | लिखे थे / लिखी थीं | लिखेंगे / लिखेंगी | - | लिखते / लिखती |

| Person | Pres. Part. | Past Part. |
|---|---|---|
| मैं (I) | लिखता / लिखती | लिखा / लिखी |
| तुम (You, informal) | लिखते / लिखती | लिखे / लिखी |
| आप (You, formal) | लिखते / लिखती | लिखे / लिखी |
| वह / यह (He / She / It) | लिखता / लिखती | लिखा / लिखी |
| हम (We) | लिखते / लिखती | लिखे / लिखी |
| वे / ये (They) | लिखते / लिखती | लिखे / लिखी |

# 18. खेलना — *to play*
Used to describe the act of playing.

| Person | Pres. | Past | Fut. | Imp. | Cond. |
|---|---|---|---|---|---|
| मैं (I) | खेलता हूँ / खेलती हूँ | खेला / खेली | खेलूँगा / खेलूँगी | - | खेलता / खेलती |
| तुम (You, informal) | खेलते हो | खेलते थे / खेलती थीं | खेलोगे / खेलोगी | खेलो | खेलते / खेलती |
| आप (You, formal) | खेलते हैं | खेलते थे / खेलती थीं | खेलेंगे / खेलेंगी | खेलिए | खेलते / खेलती |
| वह / यह (He / She / It) | खेलता है / खेलती है | खेला / खेली | खेलगा / खेलगी | - | खेलता / खेलती |
| हम (We) | खेलते हैं | खेलते थे / खेलती थीं | खेलेंगे / खेलेंगी | - | खेलते / खेलती |

| वे / ये (They) | खेलते हैं | खेलते थे / खेलती थीं | खेलेंगे / खेलेंगी | ़ | खेलते / खेलती |
|---|---|---|---|---|---|

| Person | Pres. Part. | Past Part. |
|---|---|---|
| मैं (I) | खेलता / खेलती | खेला / खेली |
| तुम (You, informal) | खेलते / खेलती | खेलते थे / खेलती थीं |
| आप (You, formal) | खेलते / खेलती | खेलते थे / खेलती थीं |
| वह / यह (He / She / It) | खेलता / खेलती | खेला / खेली |
| हम (We) | खेलते / खेलती | खेलते थे / खेलती थीं |
| वे / ये (They) | खेलते / खेलती | खेलते थे / खेलती थीं |

# 19. सोचना — *to think*

Used to express the act of thinking or considering.

| Person | Pres. | Past | Fut. | Imp. | Cond. |
|---|---|---|---|---|---|
| मैं (I) | सोचता हूँ / सोचती हूँ | सोचा / सोची | सोचूँगा / सोचूँगी | - | सोचता / सोचती |
| तुम (You, infor-mal) | सोचते हो / सोचती हो | सोचा / सोची | सोचोगे / सोचोगी | सोचो | सोचते / सोचती |
| आप (You, formal) | सोचते हैं / सोचती हैं | सोचा / सोची | सोचेंगे / सोचेंगी | सोचिए | सोचते / सोचती |

| | Pres. | Past | Fut. | Imp. | Cond. |
|---|---|---|---|---|---|
| वह / यह (He / She / It) | सोचता है / सोचती है | सोचा / सोची | सोचेगा / सोचेगी | - | सोचता / सोचती |
| हम (We) | सोचते हैं / सोचती हैं | सोचा / सोची | सोचेंगे / सोचेंगी | - | सोचते / सोचती |
| वे / ये (They) | सोचते हैं / सोचती हैं | सोचा / सोची | सोचेंगे / सोचेंगी | - | सोचते / सोचती |

| Person | Pres. Part. | Past Part. |
|---|---|---|
| मैं (I) | सोचता / सोचती | सोचा / सोची |
| तुम (You, informal) | सोचते / सोचती | सोचा / सोची |
| आप (You, formal) | सोचते / सोचती | सोचा / सोची |
| वह / यह (He / She / It) | सोचता / सोचती | सोचा / सोची |
| हम (We) | सोचते / सोचती | सोचा / सोची |
| वे / ये (They) | सोचते / सोचती | सोचा / सोची |

# 20. समझना — to understand

Used to express comprehension or grasping of a concept.

| Person | Pres. | Past | Fut. | Imp. | Cond. |
|---|---|---|---|---|---|
| मैं (I) | समझता हूँ / समझती हूँ | समझा / समझी | समझूँगा / समझूँगी | - | समझता / समझती |

| तुम (You, informal) | समझते हो / समझती हो | समझे / समझीं | समझोगे / समझोगी | समझो | समझते / समझती |
|---|---|---|---|---|---|
| आप (You, formal) | समझते हैं / समझती हैं | समझे / समझीं | समझेंगे / समझेंगी | समझिए | समझते / समझती |
| वह / यह (He / She / It) | समझता है / समझती है | समझा / समझी | समझेगा / समझेगी | - | समझता / समझती |
| हम (We) | समझते हैं / समझती हैं | समझे / समझीं | समझेंगे / समझेंगी | - | समझते / समझती |
| वे / ये (They) | समझते हैं / समझती हैं | समझे / समझीं | समझेंगे / समझेंगी | - | समझते / समझती |

| Person | Pres. Part. | Past Part. |
|---|---|---|
| मैं (I) | समझता / समझती | समझा / समझी |
| तुम (You, informal) | समझते / समझती | समझे / समझीं |
| आप (You, formal) | समझते / समझती | समझे / समझीं |
| वह / यह (He / She / It) | समझता / समझती | समझा / समझी |
| हम (We) | समझते / समझती | समझे / समझीं |
| वे / ये (They) | समझते / समझती | समझे / समझीं |

Made in United States
Troutdale, OR
09/03/2024

22575759R00213